second edition

# THE SPEAKER

## The Tradition and Practice of Public Speaking

Joseph M. Valenzano III

Stephen W. Braden

UNIVERSITY of

DAYTON

Kennesaw
State UNIVERSITY

FOUNTAINHEAD
PRESS

Our "green" initiatives include:

**Electronic Products**
We deliver products in non-paper form whenever possible. This includes PDF downloadables, flash drives, and CDs.

**Electronic Samples**
We use a new electronic sampling system, called Xample. Instructor samples are sent via a personalized web page that links to PDF downloads.

**FSC Certified Printers**
All of our printers are certified by the Forest Service Council which promotes environmentally and socially responsible management of the world's forests. This program allows consumer groups, individual consumers and businesses to work together to promote responsible use of the world's forests as a renewable and sustainable resource.

**Recycled Paper**
Most of our products are printed on a minimum of 30% post consumer waste recycled paper.

**Support of Green Causes**
When we do print, we donate a portion of our revenue to Green causes. Listed below are a few of the organizations that have received donations from Fountainhead Press. We welcome your feedback and suggestions for contributions, as we are always searching for worthy initiatives.
Rainforest 2 Reef
Environmental Working Group

Designer: Susan Moore
Editorial Consultant: Gina Huck Siegert, Imaginative Solutions, Inc.

Books may be purchased for educational purposes.

For information, please call or write:

1-800-586-0330

Fountainhead Press
Southlake, TX 76092

Web Site: www.fountainheadpress.com
E-mail: customerservice@fountainheadpress.com

Second Edition

ISBN: 978-1-59871-522-4

Printed in the United States of America

# PREFACE

Speech is both a skill and a field of study. Today, however, the rich tradition of speech communication studies is either reduced to a few quick mentions of Aristotle and Cicero or, at worst, lost altogether. Why have we forgotten where we come from and, more importantly, why are we not sharing those origins with our students? In this book we bring that extensive tradition to the forefront of public speaking instruction while also maintaining the skills aspect of public speaking pedagogy. In short, we help you understand the "why" behind the "how" in effective public speaking.

We have often lamented the fact that public speaking has become a skills course, almost devoid of any connection to the rich tradition that informs its instruction. It has a history that dates back to Classical Greece and Rome, but that history—and the advice on achieving eloquence those teachers provided—is given short shrift or worse, left out entirely in public speaking education today. Finally, we decided to stop complaining and do something about it. You are reading our updated effort at correcting what we feel is an egregious error in collegiate instruction today.

When we wrote the first edition of *The Speaker*, we designed it to bring public speaking back to the basics. Along with tips and practices to help students become better speakers, we provided explanations grounded in theory and the long tradition of rhetorical instruction. We introduced students to scholars—both classical and contemporary—whose thoughts and writings are the reasons why we teach what we do to students. In this improved second edition, we remain focused on that core mission of re-introducing the link between the rhetorical tradition and public speaking pedagogy, and time has allowed us to enhance the way in which we fulfill that mission. So, what has changed in this edition?

In addition to updating examples to keep them current, we made several substantive changes to *The Speaker*. The most noticeable difference between the first and second editions is the shift of the Outlining Appendix to full chapter status. We extended our discussion of outlining so as to better demonstrate the movement from principles (discussed in the first half of the book) to the preparation of presentations (covered in the second half). Specifically, we spend more time discussing general and specific purpose statements. In addition, we provide extensive treatment of connective statements and explain the difference between speaking and full-sentence outlines in greater detail.

We added coverage of content in other chapters as well. In Chapter 1 we now discuss different communication models and how they help explain the public speaking dynamic. In Chapter 2 we added more focused content on ethical public speaking, including coverage of demagoguery. In our treatment of plagiarism in Chapter 3 we provided new material regarding the concept of ghostwriting. In Chapter 6 we updated and extended the discussion of PowerPoint by explaining how animation can effectively be employed by a speaker. When covering public speaking situations, we now include explanations of digital formats for public presentations and how they can impact speech development and delivery. In Chapter 12 we extended coverage of ways to establish ethos and generate pathos. Finally, in Chapter 14 we now go into even more detail on problem-solution arrangement and provide more complete coverage of Monroe's Motivated Sequence.

We also enhanced our pedagogical tools within each chapter. We added more "Spotlighting Theorists" boxes throughout the textbook to highlight more of the contributions made by scholars over the years. We created a new sidebar called "Speaking of Civic Engagement" in every chapter that offers a cursory examination of a speech from history and shows how it demonstrates some of the concepts discussed in the chapter in which it appears. This rudimentary rhetorical criticism helps demonstrate both the civic-mindedness of speech, as well as illustrate to students how to examine discourse with a critical eye—tools essential for becoming productive citizens today. Finally, we added more activities at the end of each chapter that suggest ways to practice the principles and ideas included in each chapter.

We feel that these changes make this second edition even better than its first iteration and also help put speech back into public speaking instruction.

## Chapter Breakdown

Chapter 1 explicates the classical tradition and explains who some of the ancient philosophers were and what they contributed to our knowledge of public speaking. It also covers basic communication models relevant to public speaking today.

Chapter 2 discusses the one aspect of public speaking most prevalent for students today: speech anxiety. It also covers the importance of understanding the listening process, an important feature of any speaking situation. Finally, it discusses ethical speech-making and provides some guidelines for how to ensure you become a good person who speaks well.

Chapter 3 explains the research process and discusses different types of information and how they fit into different parts of your speech. It also explores some of the technological advances that enable searches for information in a far quicker manner than the Greeks and Romans ever would have imagined.

Chapters 4 through 8 focus on the speaking situation, with each chapter exploring different aspects in greater detail. Chapter 4 focuses on your verbal and physical delivery as a speaker and Chapter 5 explores presentation aids and how they can help enhance your speech when used properly. Chapter 6 covers different speaking environments in which you might find yourself, while Chapter 7 takes an in-depth look at ways to analyze your audience before, during, and after your speech. Chapter 8 focuses on language and covers some stylistic flourishes you can employ within your speech to make it more appealing to the audience.

Chapter 9 expands our coverage of various elements of the outlining process and also provides a clear distinction between speaking outlines and full-sentence outline formats. This chapter serves as a bridge between the principles and components of the speech development process covered in the first eight chapters and the practical applications of those concepts embedded within the remaining chapters, which focus on types of speeches.

The final chapters of the book focus on the applicability of public speaking in different scenarios. Chapter 10 spotlights the principles of informative speaking and is followed by a chapter that provides the tools for constructing an effective informative speech. Chapters 12 and 13 concentrate on the persuasive process and the importance of logic and reasoning in that process. These two chapters are followed by a chapter that explains how to construct and organize an effective persuasive speech. Finally, Chapters 15 and 16 discuss epideictic speaking and how to develop a good commemorative address.

We invite you to read the book and see for yourself how fully we have integrated the classical origins of speech with the skills aspect of public speaking pedagogy. So, turn the page and explore how much the Greeks and Romans contributed to public speaking and oratory.

Joseph Valenzano and Stephen Braden

# TEXTBOOK FEATURES

*Emphasis on Rhetorical Theory*—We connect the ideas of rhetoric with the practice of public speaking throughout the textbook. We begin with a chapter devoted to an introduction to classical rhetorical theory and then show students how those ideas actually play out in speech today throughout the rest of the textbook.

*Spotlighting Theorists*—In each chapter we introduce students to the life and ideas of particular theorists whose work contributes to how we teach public speaking today. These sidebars explore the stories behind the people whose ideas we discuss throughout the book, making it more interesting and personal for them as readers.

*Speaking of Civic Engagement*—New to the second edition, these additions help put the emphasis of public speaking back on speech by briefly introducing students to significant speeches from the past and present. These speeches tie in with the concepts of the chapters in which they appear and help to both model good speeches as well as show students some ways to notice unique aspects of finished presentations.

*Summary Graphs and Charts*—Since many of the ideas and theorists we discuss can get a bit complex, we created several charts and graphs throughout the book to help students more easily access and understand those concepts. This will help visual learners as well as students who retain information from the prose within the chapters.

*Review Questions*—At the end of each chapter we provide several review questions meant to get students to do more than recall and review material. These are designed to get students to question and think about the ideas presented in the chapter and how they can affect the way they construct speeches and consume messages.

*Activities for Action*—These new tools appear at the end of each chapter and provide the reader (or instructor) with ideas for how to learn the concepts from each chapter in a more active manner. They include suggestions for individual as well as group activities.

*Instructor Materials*—We have created a very extensive and practical set of materials to help instructors effectively deliver the textbook to their students. These include updated lecture notes, test questions, and PowerPoint slides for each chapter.

*Student Speech Videos*—There are now 15 video examples of student speeches. There is at least one student speech example for every type of speech we discuss in the book, and in most cases there are good and bad versions of each speech. Most of the speeches also come with outlines done in the format we teach students to use in the textbook. Additionally, most of the videos come with a set of discussion questions and talking points to help instructors and students identify what principles from the text are exemplified in each speech.

*"Going Green"*—We are proud to say that the book is not as long as one might think given the focus on connecting contemporary public speaking education to classical rhetoric. Additionally, it is printed on recycled paper at an FSC-certified printer. Finally, in yet another way to conserve paper and minimize the cost of the book, we are delivering all ancillary materials electronically. These efforts go a long way toward conservation and also help keep the book affordable for students.

## ACKNOWLEDGMENTS

There are many people we would like to thank for helping make this book a reality. To be quite honest, it would never have happened if not for a chance meeting with Tim French and the subsequent support of Scott Timian and Felix Frazier of Fountainhead Press. They took a chance in letting us write the book we wanted to write, and we are very grateful for their support and encouragement throughout the entire process.

Family also plays a crucial part in any endeavor as large as this, and ours are no exception. For their patience and support while we wrote at night and on the weekends we each want to thank our respective partners in life, Lauren and Elaine.

We would also like to thank our colleagues and friends in the field. They never disparaged the idea of writing a textbook and often provided candid observations and ideas. In particular, we want to thank Tom Burkholder, Bill Belk, Jason Edwards, John Sisco, and Keisha Hoerrner. We also wish to acknowledge our respective graduate advisors, Mary Stuckey and Andrew King.

We also want to acknowledge the graduate students in the Department of Communication Studies at UNLV for their help in creating the student speech videos. Specifically, we would like to thank Shannon Stevens, Amanda Pinney, Ian Beier, Grace Saez, Daniel Coyle, Justin Eckstein, William Saas, and Jenny Farrell. Their willingness to help, enthusiasm, and generous donation of time are greatly appreciated.

Last, but certainly not least, we wish to thank the reviewers: Kristine Bruss, University of Kansas; Michael Eidenmuller, University of Texas—Tyler; Jim Kuypers, Virginia Tech University; Ben Voth, Southern Methodist University; and Nancy Legge, Idaho State University, without whose careful readings, frank commentary, and helpful suggestions you would not be holding this text. Their efforts were instrumental in the development of this book and for their help we will always be grateful.

# ABOUT THE AUTHORS

## Joseph M. Valenzano III, Ph.D.

Dr. Valenzano received his Ph.D. in Public Communication from the Department of Communication at Georgia State University in 2006. Upon completion of his degree he became the Basic Course Director at the University of Nevada, Las Vegas, where he served for five years. In 2009 the basic course program that he directs received the *Basic Course Program of Excellence Award* from the Basic Course Division of the National Communication Association. Now, he is the Basic Course Director at the University of Dayton, in Dayton, Ohio. Additionally, Valenzano has authored and co-authored articles on presidential rhetoric, religious rhetoric, and media studies in the *Southern Communication Journal, Journal of Media and Religion,* and *Communication Quarterly*.

## Stephen W. Braden, Ph.D.

Dr. Braden received his Ph.D. in Rhetoric and Public Address from the Department of Speech Communication at Louisiana State University. Braden has taught public speaking for 21 years at four universities and was a Public Speaking Coordinator at Georgia State University. In 2004 he was awarded the *John I. Sisco Excellence in Teaching Award* from the Southern States Communication Association, the organization's top teaching award. Braden is currently Director of First-Year Seminars in the Department of First-Year Programs at Kennesaw State University in Kennesaw, Georgia.

For Lauren Valenzano, Elaine Braden, Joe and Patricia Valenzano,

and the late Roger and Betty Braden

# SPEAKING OF CIVIC ENGAGEMENT BOXES

# SPOTLIGHTING THEORISTS BOXES

# TABLE OF CONTENTS

# Public Speaking, A Long Tradition

## 1

# **Practically**SPEAKING

Imagine being tutored by one of the greatest minds ever to live. Imagine personal attention from a man responsible for some of the most important writings in history. Of course, such an opportunity is not really available today, but it was in the Classical World, and one person managed to receive such an education: Alexander the Great of Macedon. From his early teenage years Alexander was personally tutored by Aristotle, the man who wrote books that are still considered foundational texts for communication studies, philosophy, political science, and even the natural sciences. You might think that such an opportunity came about largely because of the wealth and power of Alexander's family, and in that you would be only partially correct.

In 343 B.C. Philip of Macedon, Alexander's father, approached Aristotle with an offer to tutor his son, then 13 years old. At the time, Aristotle had not written many of his works and only recently had finished 20 years of studies at Plato's Academy and had left Athens. In fact, he was little more than a roaming refugee in exile since Philip himself had ordered the complete annihilation of Aristotle's home city, Stagiros.[1] So, the fact Philip chose him is interesting. There was also a personal connection between Philip and Aristotle in that they knew each other from childhood when Aristotle's father, Nicomachus, was the personal physician to Philip's father. Perhaps the combination of the childhood connection, Aristotle's education under Plato, and Philip's possible desire to extend an olive branch to the remaining people of Stagiros led to the choice of Aristotle as personal tutor to Alexander.[2]

It did not take long for Aristotle to accept the offer and begin schooling Philip's son and a few other sons of nobles at Mieza, a spot of land west of the Macedonian capital of Pella.[3] While there Alexander learned about medicine, ethics, literature, Greek culture, and other subjects while sitting outdoors on stone benches. One can easily see the impact these lessons had on the young prince. When he became king and began his conquest of the known world at the time, Alexander would collect samples of flowers and animals and send them back to his former tutor for study.[4] He also carried a volume of Homer's *Iliad* with him that Aristotle had personally edited. Even more practical of an impact was the fact Alexander used his knowledge of medicine garnered from his time with Aristotle to personally treat wounded soldiers on the battlefield![5]

The education of Alexander by Aristotle provides us with an early example of what we now call a classroom and the broad outline of what we call a liberal arts education. Alexander was schooled in a wide array of subjects from ethics and philosophy, to rhetoric and politics, to medicine and physics, and today universities take a similar approach in designing a general education for students. The lasting impact of the way schools were structured and students taught in Classical Greece and Classical Rome can still be seen today.

In this chapter we will explore some of the great thinkers of Classical Greece and Rome and look at how their schools were structured. It is important to note that some of these great thinkers taught in schools, like Plato and Aristotle, but others were more like wandering tutors. All of these individuals and groups, however, understood the importance of education and the place of speech in it. To cover this much history in such a short space we will highlight aspects of classical education relevant to our focus on public speaking and introduce you to figures such as Aristotle, Cicero, and Quintilian, who we will revisit later in the book. We will conclude the chapter with a brief discussion of different contexts today where the lessons of these ancient Greeks and Romans are still relevant.

## EDUCATION THEN AND NOW

Right now, all across the country, students are sitting down, learning how to become an effective public speaker. They are taking a similar class to the one you are enrolled in right now; some courses are titled "Oral Communication," others may be "Introduction to Public Speaking," and others still perhaps refer to the class as "Speech Communication." The point is, you are not alone, and what you are doing is nothing new. In fact, public speaking instruction is rooted in a long tradition that we can trace back to at least Classical Greece (approximately 490–322 B.C.). There remain, however, two significant differences between your educational experience and that of the Greeks.

The first is in the nature of education. For our purposes, the Classical Period refers to Ancient Greece and the Roman Empire, and during that time education was not what it is today. Whereas today there is much government intervention and control over education (public schools, state-sponsored universities, etc.), in the Classical Period the state had very little influence over the nature of education. In fact, the two primary ways in which someone could receive an education were through hiring a teacher to essentially home-school a child, or, if the parents could afford it and the child showed enough promise, they could send their child to one of the few prominent schools. This model of education is nothing like what is available to students today.

The second major difference between education today and education in the Classical Period involves the curriculum. One of the fundamental tenets of an education in the Greek city-states or Roman Empire was rhetoric, which for them essentially meant the ability to speak well and persuade audiences. There were some who decried rhetoric in favor of philosophy, but there was no denying the importance placed on teaching people to speak well in the Classical Period. Today's education system, however, has moved away from this emphasis, and students are often only introduced to formal training in speech at the college level—and even there for only one semester. Education today does not emphasize the importance of speaking well, and one of our aims with this book is to show you how speaking well should be as important today as it was in the days of the Greeks and Romans.

To do that, we will first explore the different ideas several prominent Greek and Roman teachers had about rhetoric, as these concepts provide the foundation for how we still approach public speaking today. Then we will discuss ideas proposed by those who did not necessarily run schools in the Classical Period, but who still proposed ideas that have helped shape our understanding of the power of speech. Finally, we will explain why public speaking should be as important today as it was when the Greeks and Romans studied the craft.

## PUBLIC SPEAKING AND CLASSICAL EDUCATION

We probably will never know with any amount of certainty who was the first formal public speaking teacher, but we do know that the Classical Greeks were the first to put quite a bit of emphasis on developing oratorical skills. For instance, the Greek poet Homer's *Iliad* and *Odyssey* contained quite a few long speeches by major characters. In this section we will describe the three different modes of education available during the Classical Period. First, we will look at the itinerant teachers known as Sophists. Second, we will investigate the more formal schools Greeks attended for training. Finally, we will discuss one Roman school made possible through state-sponsored efforts to promote education.

### Sophists

The Greek democratic city-states often called for citizens to make speeches in order to discuss public policy and make cases for clients in the courts. Since no lawyers existed, people prevailed or failed in court and in the assembly purely on their ability to speak well, so some turned a profit from teaching others how to speak well.

**Sophists**
............
itinerant teachers who traveled from city-state to city-state in Classical Greece, training people in public speaking

These teachers, also known as *Sophists*, traveled from city-state to city-state selling their instruction to well-to-do Greeks. There was little to no consistency in the teachings of the Sophists as they all had a different degree of training. One might even say public speaking professors today are the modern day equivalent of Sophists—although they have more consistent training than the Sophists in Classical Greece!

One of the more notable Sophists was Gorgias (480–376 B.C.), who understood the relationship of speaker and audience as linear, whereby a speaker fills the audience with knowledge, or moves them to action. Gorgias was a foreigner in Athens who nevertheless developed a strong following. He believed audiences were passive and could be moved by elaborate and "magical" language that captured their attention. Language and words, according to Gorgias, accomplished things by encouraging human emotions, and so many of his teachings concentrated on different styles of language use. For Gorgias, the power of persuasion lay in style and the construction of creative linguistic phrases.[6] Gorgias's views on rhetoric and public speaking, however, differed from the views of other Sophists.

Protagoras (484–414 B.C.), another Sophist, taught a different understanding of rhetoric and public speaking to his students. For Protagoras, anything and everything could be argued. In fact, he taught his students to know both sides of an argument, because doing so was the only way to know which side they should believe. He asked his students to come with arguments for and against the same issue so they could better analyze which was stronger and, thus, more accurate. His critics, however, said that this approach merely instructed people to make the worse case look better in an effort to win the debate. The different views on rhetoric by Gorgias and Protagoras are contrasted in Table 1.1.

**Table 1.1**

| Views on Rhetoric | |
| --- | --- |
| Gorgias's Views on Rhetoric | Protagoras's Views on Rhetoric |
| • Audience and speaker relationship is linear<br>• Speaker fills the audience with knowledge/moves them to action<br>• Audiences are passive and can be moved by language<br>• Language can be used to stir emotions | • Anything and everything can be argued<br>• Important to know both sides of an issue<br>• Important to prepare argument for both sides of an argument to see which is best and more accurate |

The "for-hire" nature of the itinerant Sophists, however, represented only one way in which instruction in the art of public speaking took place in the Classical Period. Many famous Greeks also opened schools designed to instruct those who could earn and afford entry. In the next section we will discuss several of these schools and their "headmasters," who had very particular views on speech.

## The Formal Greek Schools

Classical Greece had several schools that many well-to-do citizens would send their students to for instruction. These schools often produced politicians and thinkers that defined the next generation. In some cases the schools competed with each other for students, but not to the degree universities and colleges do today. The first school we will discuss is generally regarded as the first school of rhetoric in Athens, and it was created by Isocrates. One of the first chief critics of Isocrates built another institution, which we know of as Plato's "Academy," and it is the second of the formal schools we will explore. Finally, we will discuss a school developed by a graduate of Plato's Academy, Aristotle, who was also employed as a tutor for one of the most successful conquerors in history.

Plato's Academy

### *The School of Isocrates*

Isocrates (438–335 B.C.) shared several of the views held by Sophists; however, unlike the Sophists, he was an Athenian citizen. He opened a school where rhetoric and speech were core components of the education his students received. He charged quite a bit in terms of tuition, and even had very rigorous entrance requirements, accepting only the best and brightest students Athens had to offer.

Isocrates taught his students that a person's capacity to know things was limited, and so to expect to know the right course of action in every situation and on every issue was impossible. For Isocrates, only a well-educated man could determine the best course of action through a well-informed, yet incomplete, opinion. He believed that "it is much better to form probable opinions about useful things, than to have exact knowledge of useless things."[7] Essentially, Isocrates felt that good speakers were well-learned on a variety of subjects.

Isocrates also believed that good speakers were morally sound individuals who could discern right from wrong. He felt that education on many subjects was the best way to ensure ethical goals for a speaker. He also believed that ornate language and lofty sentence construction within a speech about a worthy topic—which could only be identified by well-informed individuals—evidenced an ethical, moral speaker. This emphasis on style and content represents a sort of fusion of the approaches taken by Gorgias and Protagoras.

Isocrates emphasized an amplified rhetoric that used many different rhetorical strategies (which will be discussed later in the book) to keep audiences focused on points for long periods of time. He did not, however, offer a set of rules and characteristics of a well put together speech like some of his contemporaries we will discuss in a moment.

**kairos**
Greek term meaning timing and recognition of the needs of the occasion

The one constraint to good speeches Isocrates recognized was **kairos,** or timing and recognition of the needs of the occasion. He believed you could not teach this to people through a handbook, only through extensive repetition and exposure to civic life, which is where the speaking of his time took place. This almost constant involvement in social and political life was emblematic of the deep commitment to the strength of community felt by Isocrates. Despite his call for his students to immerse themselves in civic life, he himself never truly participated in the political arena.[8] That said, Isocrates influenced many great orators in his time and in the years that followed, especially those in the Roman rhetorical tradition.

## Plato's Academy

A contemporary of Isocrates, Plato held a less than favorable view of Sophists and Isocrates. Plato was a student of Socrates, whom he used as a character in several of his writings that serve as the foundation for his understanding of rhetoric, government, and education. As these documents indicate, students at the Academy received very different instruction than those trained by Isocrates.

Plato derided the Sophistic approach for a variety of reasons. First, he believed it was dangerous and not conducive to living what he termed "a good life," where

understanding justice and living a just life were the ultimate goal for an individual. Plato referred to rhetoric as "a knack" and felt that the Sophists trained people in how to achieve personal goals through the use of persuasion that used language to manipulate public opinion. He believed, instead, that education should focus on philosophy, or the search for truth, rather than persuasion, so that people could determine true knowledge. For Plato, rhetoric was a form of flattery, while philosophy was inquiry into the truth of things.

Additionally, Plato felt not everyone was capable of conducting the arduous task of seeking and knowing the truth. He believed that the only people capable of doing so, and thus the only people who could tell the difference between good and bad, were philosophers, and therefore they should lead the people. In his famous book *The Republic*, Plato argued that leaders of this kind might still need to employ the knack of rhetoric to deceive the public for its own good. Rhetoric in a just society, for Plato, was an advocacy tool for the philosopher, nothing more.

Plato and Aristotle in The School of Athens, by Italian Rafael

Several things can be said regarding Plato and his approach to education. The first is that he decried the Sophists and Isocrates for elevating rhetoric and devaluing philosophy. Second, he was skeptical at best regarding the use of rhetoric. He understood the way it was employed during his day as an evil, but when used properly in his vision of a just society, it became a utopian tool for philosophers. Regardless of the debate between which was better or more important (Rhetoric or Philosophy), Plato foreshadowed discussions about the power and purpose of speech that last to this day. He understood its power, and more importantly its relationship to shaping the world around us.[9]

One of Plato's brightest students, Aristotle, went on to tutor one of the world's greatest conquerors and eventually opened a school of his own. Aristotle, however, as we will see next, did not share his mentor's animus toward rhetoric and actually saw some redeeming value in the practice.

### Aristotle's Lyceum — Plato's student

As we discussed at the very beginning of this chapter, Aristotle (384–322 B.C.), the most prominent of Plato's students, was hired by Philip of Macedon to tutor his son, the child we now know as Alexander the Great. Aristotle, like Plato, was also a contemporary of Isocrates, and like his mentor he regarded the teachings of Isocrates and Sophists as inadequate. Later, after his services for Alexander were completed, Aristotle opened his own school, the Lyceum, where he taught students a different conception of knowledge, philosophy, and rhetoric than his teacher had taught him.

Aristotle differed from his teacher in many respects, growing up when Athens was at the pinnacle of its power. He did not share Plato's mistrust of rhetoric and understood it as serving several beneficial purposes in a free society. Whereas Plato believed rhetoric was merely persuasion and philosophy was the only way to search for the truth, Aristotle disagreed. Aristotle, as we will see now, was very much a pragmatist.

Aristotle proposed three ways in which someone could know something, as opposed to the one way Plato advocated. The first of the three types of knowledge Aristotle described we will call experiential knowledge, or *techne*, because it comes from a person's own encounters. This knowledge is of particular things based on our interactions with the world around us, and although it is somewhat unreliable it is Aristotle's preferred form because, as he explained, we are aware that we know something because we have experienced it. That said, the Greek philosopher acknowledged that our senses, at best, see things differently and, at worst, can be easily deceived. Look at the optical illusion in Figure 1.1.[10]

**techne**
············
experiential knowledge; knowledge of particular events in the world around us; the least reliable form of knowledge

**Figure 1.1**
**Optical Illusion**

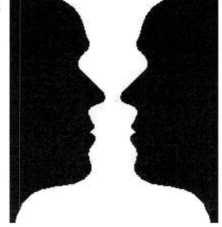

Is it a vase? A candlestick? Or two people about to kiss? Whatever your visual experience, we all see the same thing, but interpret it differently. Some of us see it as two faces, others see it as a vase or candelabra. So, we see the same thing, but can know it differently. Such is the unreliability of experiential knowledge.

The second form of knowledge taught by Aristotle is similar to the one true knowledge professed by Plato. *Episteme*, or universal knowledge, the understanding about the common characteristics of like materials, resembles Plato's idea of metaphysical forms, where he felt true knowledge existed. For Aristotle, knowing a particular thing comes from experience, and knowing universals comes from education and exploration. Public speaking allowed people to learn and search for universal characteristics by sharing knowledge of particulars with each other.

**episteme**
············
universal knowledge, or understanding about the common characteristics of like materials

Aristotle's final form of knowledge represents an intermediate form. For Aristotle, this type of knowledge primarily concerned ethics, where neither the practical nor the universal worked. His idea of *intermediate knowledge*, or knowing what does not reflect an excess or a defect but instead what is intuitively correct to the person, is exemplified in his Golden Mean, where he claimed too much, or too little, of anything is a bad thing. Taken together, these three ways of knowing the world around us represent a huge departure from his teacher, Plato, who advocated a truth only one type of person—the philosopher—could know. In this way, Aristotle was much more democratic than Plato, and thus he saw significant uses for speech in a civil society for educated people.

**intermediate knowledge**
············
knowing what does not reflect an excess or a defect but instead what is intuitively correct to the person

Aristotle fundamentally disagreed with Plato on the nature of rhetoric and speech. He saw rhetoric as a creative process of determining what should be said, whereas Plato equated rhetoric with persuasion. While both understood rhetoric as relating to persuasion, they disagreed on how rhetoric and persuasion intersected.

## SPOTLIGHTING THEORISTS: ARISTOTLE

### Aristotle (384–322 B.C.)

Born in the village of Stagiros, near what was then considered Macedonia, in Northern Greece, this Greek philosopher and teacher was responsible for many contributions to rhetoric and public speaking. During his life he accomplished a great many things, including mentoring Alexander the Great of Macedonia.

Due to Aristotle's close connection to the kingdom of Macedon, many Greeks, especially those in Athens, probably viewed him with a great bit of suspicion. In 367 B.C. Aristotle moved to Athens to study under Plato at the Academy. Despite his fondness for Plato, Aristotle was much more realistic and practical in his approach to philosophy than his teacher. Aristotle used his education and exposure to great thinkers of his time while at the Academy to guide his academic pursuits. He was the first to outline what we refer to as formal logic, and he crafted an ethical code grounded in living a happy life rather than adhering to religious codes. Further, he developed a political philosophy vastly different from Plato's, that found as its inspiration the democratic and constitutional governments of his time—approaches Plato clearly held in disdain.

In the 350s Aristotle taught rhetoric at the Academy, largely as an attempt to compete against the school opened by Isocrates. Aristotle's rhetoric courses focused on logic, in direct contrast to what Isocrates and his Sophistic plan of study offered. In 347, just around the time Plato died, Aristotle left Athens and went abroad where he studied other subjects, like biology. Around 343, however, he moved back to his roots at the request of King Philip of Macedon in order to educate the prince, Alexander.

Within eight years, but well after his tutelage under Aristotle ended, Alexander conquered Athens and Aristotle returned to the home of his mentor. In 335 Aristotle opened the Lyceum, his version of the Academy, and taught students there until the death of Alexander the Great in 323 B.C. When Alexander passed, Aristotle gave his school over to his most prominent student, Theophrastus, and died a year later on the island of Euboea.[11]

Aristotle wrote extensively on a variety of subjects and remains one of the most influential philosophers on oratory, philosophy, logic and politics in all of history. He serves as an excellent example of the importance of education. Even today he is one of the most recognized of all Classical Greek thinkers and figures.

Aristotle noted that rhetoric, as a means rather than an end, fulfilled four functions in an open society. First, rhetoric through the application of speech allowed for true and just ideas to prevail, because he noted all things in public debate are not equal and capable speakers need to advocate for them to win out. In addition to the preservation of truth and justice, Aristotle also believed rhetoric offered the ability to instruct people on how to connect their ideas with the experiences of their audiences; in short, it allows us to teach others.  Thirdly, Aristotle saw rhetoric as the means of analyzing both sides of a question—similar to the view taken by Protagoras as we saw earlier.  Finally, Aristotle understood rhetoric as a means to defend oneself, noting that speech and rational thought are abilities unique to human beings.[12]  He understood public speaking as one of the most important tools a person can possess for engaging in civic life.  Table 1.2 notes how these four functions of rhetoric can pragmatically be used today.

**Table 1.2**

| Aristotle's Four Functions of Rhetoric ||
| Function | Example |
| --- | --- |
| Upholding truth and justice | In a courtroom |
|  | In a legislative body |
|  | In a classroom |
| Teaching to an audience | Classroom |
|  | Encouraging civic engagement |
|  | Pulpit |
| Analyzing both sides of a question | Jury |
|  | Voting decision |
|  | Making a final decision |
| Defending oneself | Personal or public disagreement |
|  | On the witness stand |

Aristotle defined rhetoric not as a knack the way Plato did, but rather as the means of identifying probabilities inherent in an issue or interpretation. He focused on rhetoric as a persuasive process, and this is an approach still taken by scholars today.  Despite his more favorable view regarding rhetoric than his mentor, Aristotle understood the dangers inherent in a purely sophistic understanding of speech, so he conducted an exhaustive analysis of how persuasion works.  In this analysis he determined three sources of persuasion, two forms of proof for arguments, and stylistic virtues for speech.

**ethos**
. . . . . .
the credibility of the speaker

**logos**
. . . . . .
the logical dimension of the appeal

**pathos**
. . . . . . .
the emotional dimensions of the appeal that can influence an audience's disposition toward the topic, speaker, or occasion

Aristotle taught his students about the interconnection of three component parts of persuasion.  The first part he called *ethos*, or the credibility of the speaker.  He felt that the more believable, honest, and learned on the subject a speaker was, then the more persuasive the message.  In addition to ethos Aristotle proposed that *logos*, or the logical dimension of the appeal, contributed to a message's persuasive effect.  Aristotle believed that persuasive messages must follow a logical order; without this orderly argument then persuasion is much less likely to occur.  The third source of persuasion Aristotle called *pathos*, which referred to the emotional dimensions of the appeal that can influence an audience's disposition toward the topic, speaker, or occasion.  He said that language can be used by a speaker to emotionally connect an audience with a topic and thus move listeners to an ethical and correct action.  Ethos, pathos, and logos each focus on a different dimension of persuasion: the speaker, the audience, and the message, respectively. For a visual depiction of this, look at Figure 1.2.

Aristotle referred to ethos, pathos, and logos as **artistic proof**, or something created by the speaker for the presentation. The speaker's credibility is dependent on the occasion and topic, and the emotions of the audience are also directly related to the speech; thus both are crafted for the specific moment by the speaker. Likewise, you develop the logic in the speech that is meant to sway an audience. The other proof identified by Aristotle, **inartistic proof**, concerned all the evidence, data, and documents that exist outside of the speaker and the audience but nevertheless can aid in persuasion. Inartistic proofs are not manufactured by the speaker in the same way as artistic proofs.

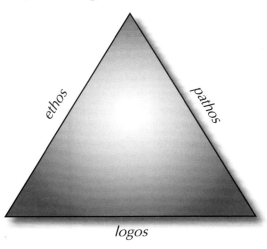

**Figure 1.2**
**Three Parts of Persuasion**

**artistic proof**
constructed by the speaker for the occasion; concerns ethos, pathos, and logos

**inartistic proof**
all the evidence, data, and documents that exist outside of the speaker and the audience, but nevertheless can aid in persuasion

Aristotle also understood that style played a part in the ultimate success or failure of persuasive appeals, and so he laid out three virtues of style by which **rhetors**, or speakers, should abide. The first stylistic virtue is **clarity**, or the ability of a speaker to clearly articulate what he or she wishes to say. Clarity manifests itself with simple, direct sentences, and we will discuss more about how to construct such messages in the chapter on language. Aristotle's second stylistic virtue, **correctness**, relates to the accuracy of information presented and the honest representation of the speaker. Quite obviously, this virtue is intimately tied to being an ethical speaker, which will be discussed further in Chapter 3. Finally, Aristotle emphasized the virtue of **propriety**, or good behavior and faithfulness to what one considers moral and just. Propriety, therefore, relates to the idea that you should be both ethical and clear in your content, but also in your delivery. It is an overarching virtue that essentially encompasses both clarity and correctness.

**rhetors**
speakers

**clarity**
the ability of speakers to clearly articulate what they wish to say

**correctness**
the accuracy of information presented and the honest representation of the speaker

**propriety**
good behavior and faithfulness to what one considers moral and just

As we previously noted, Aristotle differed from Plato in many ways, but perhaps most importantly, he viewed rhetoric and speech as a potentially important component of civil society. He felt that through the use of ethical and proper speech people could continue to search for truth. Further, societies would become more open and therefore a sense of justice and fairness would be encouraged. He trained his students to examine arguments, defend themselves, and ultimately be able to teach the next generation these important skills. It is safe to say that Aristotle saw good public speaking skills as the foundation of a lasting productive civil society.

Isocrates's school, Plato's Academy, and Aristotle's Lyceum represented three important Greek schools. The Greeks, however, were not alone in writing and thinking about speech, rhetoric, and persuasion.  Next we will examine two Romans, Cicero and Quintilian, who also had much to say on these subjects.

# Cicero and the Practice of Rhetoric

Although schools in the Classical Period were sources of a significant amount of writings and information regarding rhetoric and speech, some notable contributions were made by those who did not operate schools or seek to train students.  In this section we will discuss one individual whose major contributions to understanding speech and language came from his experience as a student and his implementation of those practices in his political life.

## Cicero (106–43 B.C.), Speech and Politics

Cicero

Marcus Tullius Cicero is one of the most influential figures in the history of rhetoric.  Born in 106 B.C. near Rome, Cicero received a strong education in Roman schools and began a career in the courts, later moving into the Senate.  Eventually he rose to the highest position in the Roman Republic, that of consul, and developed a reputation as a well-spoken champion of the people. Like Plato in Greece, Cicero lived during tumultuous times, watching the rise and fall of Julius Caesar and the subsequent establishment of the Roman Empire under Octavian.  Throughout his career, Cicero fought against the nobility and the threat of military dictators, and it ultimately earned him the same fate as Plato's mentor, Socrates.  Unlike Quintilian, Cicero lived and wrote during the waning days of the Roman Republic, not the Roman Empire, and thus he valued all uses of rhetoric.

While on one of his forced retirements from public life Cicero wrote *De re Publica* and *De Oratore*, two enormously influential books on speech and delivery, and these served as sequels to his earliest publication on speech, *De Inventione*. Whereas *De Inventione* was written when Cicero was in his late teens and is more of a compilation of educational approaches to teaching rhetoric at the time of his schooling, the two later works represent much more sophisticated and original thought on the subject.

**invention**
the first canon of rhetoric where you choose the best possible arguments for your case

In his works, Cicero did for the speech-making process what Aristotle did for persuasion: he broke speech down into its component parts, which he numbered at five (See Table 1.3).  These five canons of rhetoric are the foundation for developing a strong speech.  The first is *invention*, which is when you identify the best arguments for your case in a given situation.  This is the creative dimension of speech where you find the best possible way to convince someone to agree with you.  If you argued that Mickey Mantle was the best baseball player of all time, you would invent, or choose, certain facts that support your case.

The second of Cicero's five canons concerns organizing your arguments in the most effective manner. *Arrangement,* in which you determine the most effective way to organize your case for the topic and the audience, can be done in a variety of different ways. To arrange points in the best possible way requires that you understand your topic and your audience, because the most effective arguments on a given topic may not be the same for a different audience hearing a speech on the same topic. For example, political candidates make different arguments to different audiences when trying to get each group to vote for them. We will look at various arrangement options available to you when we look at how to craft the different types of speeches later in the book.

Cicero's third canon refers to how you design the specifics of your speech. *Style* involves your word choices, phrasing, and the level of formality in the language you use to present your case to the audience. All speakers have their own language style, and discovering yours will make this creative stage much easier and more enjoyable. Of course, style must also fit the situation and the audience. We cover the nuances of style in greater detail in Chapter 8.

Today, people tend to place the most emphasis on the fourth of Cicero's five canons. *Delivery*, or the manner in which you physically and vocally present the speech, has now become erroneously equated with good public speaking. For Cicero, delivery was part of the speech, but not the sole determining element of its effectiveness. In this way he recognized the power of good delivery, but also by connecting it to the content itself cautioned against the dangers of emphasizing physical and vocal delivery. We will cover more on delivery in Chapter 4.

The final canon of rhetoric proposed by Cicero is less important today than it was during his time but still remains a part of the speech process. *Memory*, according to Cicero, refers to one's ability both to use her or his memory to recall names and important information in the middle of a speech as well as to deliver a cogent speech without notes. The ability to speak without notes is less of a concern today thanks to things like PowerPoint and Teleprompters, but in Classical Rome performing speeches without notes was a sign of eloquence and intelligence. That said, the ability to recall information relevant to a speech and incorporate it into the presentation is still a valued speaking skill.

Cicero contributed much to public speaking, and he himself was a gifted orator, but eventually his speaking ability got him into trouble. During the Roman Civil War between Octavian and Marc Antony which followed the death of Julius Caesar, Cicero vocally fought against a dictatorship and found himself at odds with Marc Antony. Eventually, Antony had him killed and nailed his tongue and hands to the door of the Senate as a sign to all those who might have aligned themselves with Cicero against him. The hands and tongue were symbols of Cicero's ability to persuade others, and the nails a warning to those who followed in his footsteps. Such was the sad death of Cicero.

**arrangement**
the second canon of rhetoric where you determine the most effective way to organize your case for the topic and the audience

**style**
the third canon of rhetoric; involves word choice, phrasing and the level of formality in the language you use to present your case to the audience

**delivery**
the fourth canon of rhetoric; the manner in which you physically and vocally present the speech

**memory**
the fifth canon of rhetoric; refers to one's ability to recall names and important information in the middle of a speech as well as to deliver a cogent speech without notes

| Table 1.3 | Cicero's Canons of Rhetoric | |
|---|---|
| Invention | Identifying the best argument or topic on which to speak |
| Arrangement | Determining the most effective way of organizing your speech |
| Style | Choosing the best words and phrasing to get your point across |
| Delivery | Physically and vocally presenting the speech |
| Memory | Your ability to recall important information during the speech |

## Quintilian's Public School

Roman education valued rhetoric, especially during the years of the Republic when Cicero lived. Rhetoric was such a core component of Roman education that even with the advent of the Roman Empire, speech training remained; however, it focused less on political speech and more on epideictic address, which focuses upon praise and/or blame. During the time of the Emperor Vespasian, who reigned from 69–79 A.D., rhetoric and public speaking rose in emphasis. Vespasian awarded grants to artists and teachers throughout the empire to encourage education and civic engagement in Rome. One of those to receive a grant from the Emperor was Marcus Fabius Quintilianus, or Quintilian (ca. 35–100 A.D.). Quintilian used the money to help fund his school and wrote *De Instituine Oratoria* (*On the Education of the Orator*), a manual for becoming the perfect speaker. This 12-book work spent a significant amount of time on every aspect of speech and evolved from the writings of Cicero.

In his book, Quintilian prescribes a definition of rhetoric that he felt encompassed all the ideas of those who came before him. He succinctly said rhetoric was simply "the art of speaking well."[13] He further argued that the art of rhetoric was only useful insofar as people applied it to practical and public affairs. To that end, he believed there were only five principle duties for any speaker:

- Defend Truth
- Protect the Innocent
- Prevent Criminal Behavior
- Inspire the Military
- Inspire the Public

Quintilian's approach mirrors the intense focus that the Greeks placed on the relationship between speech, politics, and civic engagement, be it in government or the courtroom. In fact, his five duties are an outgrowth of the functions Aristotle proposed earlier. Whereas Cicero's commentaries on public speaking emanated from his experiences, Quintilian's writings were essentially instructional tools developed for his school which he ran during the Roman Empire.

| Early Scholars and Schools of Speech | | Table 1.4 |
|---|---|---|
| **Early Scholars and Schools** | **Ideas on Speech** | |
| Isocrates | • Believed good speakers were learned on a variety of topics<br>• Believed good speakers were morally sound<br>• Believed broad education helped ensure ethical speakers<br>• Advocated ornate language and sentence construction<br>• Emphasized an amplified rhetoric that used many different rhetorical strategies<br>• Recognized kairos was a constraint on good speaking | |
| Plato | • Believed that Sophists used persuasive language to manipulate people<br>• Felt that education should focus on philosophy and the search for truth<br>• Felt that rhetoric was only about persuasion | |
| Aristotle | • Thought that rhetoric had value to a society<br>• Believed rhetoric allowed true and just ideas to prevail<br>• Believed rhetoric was useful for instruction of ideas<br>• Believed rhetoric helped one see both sides of an argument<br>• Believed rhetoric was useful to verbally defend oneself<br>• Believed rhetoric was useful for finding probabilities<br>• Identified three forms of artistic proofs: ethos, pathos, and logos<br>• Argued that inartistic proofs were an additional form of persuasive evidence<br>• Felt style was important | |

| Quintilian | <ul><li>Saw rhetoric as the act of speaking well</li><li>Saw rhetoric as useful for practical and public affairs</li><li>Believed speakers had five principle duties:<br>　　Defend Truth<br>　　Protect the Innocent<br>　　Prevent Criminal Behavior<br>　　Inspire the Military<br>　　Inspire the Public</li><li>Saw rhetoric as useful in politics and civic engagement</li></ul> |
| --- | --- |

## Contemporary Scholars and the Speech Communication Process

Isocrates, Plato, Aristotle, Quintilian, and Cicero represent a small sampling of those who contributed to the rhetorical tradition, but they provided much of the foundation for the study and practice of speech. The ideas of four of these scholars are summarized in Table 1.4. Throughout this book we will introduce you to various other noteworthy figures and their contributions, some from the Classical Period and others from more contemporary times. The important thing to understand is that the practice of public speaking and our understanding of rhetoric, speech, and persuasion have evolved over time, but that evolution could not have taken place without these important individuals from Greece and Rome. That evolution has led us to understand and study the communication process from a variety of perspectives. In fact, contemporary scholars have developed various models that help explain the communication process that the Greeks and Romans taught. Let's take a look at these more modern models and explore the components of the speech communication process as we understand it today.

### The Linear Model of Communication

**sender**
the person who desires to deliver a message to another person or group of people

**encoding**
the process of attaching symbols to ideas and feelings so that others may understand them

**message**
the actual content you send to an audience, both intentional and unintentional

Amazingly, the first modern model of communication came not from a member of the communication discipline, but from a research mathematician named Claude E. Shannon. Shannon designed this model in an effort to explain and train people on communication over telephone lines. As such, it concentrated on one-way, or linear, communication. Warren Weaver later added a component to Shannon's model, and so this linear model of communication became known as the Shannon-Weaver model of communication.

The Shannon-Weaver model essentially describes communication as a process much like injecting someone with a drug. There are essentially seven components to this model of communication. First, there is a *sender*, or the person who desires to deliver a message to another person or group of people. That person uses a symbol system, normally language, to encode the subject matter he or she wishes to send. *Encoding* is the process of attaching symbols to ideas and feelings so that others may understand them. The subject matter that is encoded is the *message* or the actual content sent to an audience, and it can be both intentional and unintentional. That message is then sent through a *channel*, or the mode through which the message is conveyed to another party. The traditional mode for transmitting messages is the voice or the written word; however, in today's society we also send messages through electronic channels like the radio, television, or Internet.

As the message travels through its channel it competes with other forces that sometimes disrupt its transmission. These disruptive forces are broadly referred to as *noise.* This term constitutes anything that interferes with the encoding, transmission, and reception of a message, and it can take many forms. When you think about noise, don't simply assume it is auditory, or the result of some loud "bang" or "boom." Noise certainly can include sounds, but it also includes environmental distractions such as scenery and temperature, personal biases and predispositions, anxiety, and confusing word choice by the speaker. It is an umbrella term for elements outside the communication message that can hamper its transmission from one party to another.

The sixth and seventh components of the Shannon-Weaver linear model of communication involve the party opposite the sender of the message. The *receiver* is the person or persons who receive the encoded message sent by the sender. Receivers are not always those for whom the message is intended. Think about a toast at a wedding where the bride's father is celebrating the marriage of his daughter. You may think everyone in the room cares deeply for the bride and groom and is listening intently to the speech, but you would be wrong. The service staff who quietly shuffle through the room serving food to guests and the bartenders in the hall have no connection to either the bride or the groom, and the speech by the father is not meant for them—nevertheless, they receive the message! There are always unintended recipients to messages we send, which only underscores our duty to pay close attention to what we say.

Unintended receivers are only one of the potential issues that we need to be aware of when it comes to this part of the communication process. We also must understand that receivers decode messages using their own knowledge and experiences, and so they may not decode the same message you encoded for them. *Decoding* is the process of taking a message that has been sent and using one's own experiences and knowledge to give it meaning. Have you ever listened to a lecture in class and thought you heard the teacher say one thing, when she actually said something else? Sometimes this is due to words sounding alike, other times it is due to not paying close enough attention, and yet other times it happens when a speaker misspeaks or mispronounces something. Ultimately, though, we cannot control how an audience will decode the messages we send, but we can maximize our potential for them doing so accurately.

In summary, there are seven components to the basic *linear model of communication*: a sender encodes a message and sends it through a channel where it competes with distracting forces called noise while on its way to a receiver who then decodes the message[14] (see Figure 1.3). Now that we have laid out the model, let's briefly explore what it means for us in the context of public speaking and how this book will help illustrate that connection.

**channel**
the mode through which the message is conveyed to another party

**noise**
anything that interferes with the encoding, transmission, and reception of a message

**receiver**
the person or persons who receive the encoded message sent by the sender

**decoding**
the process of taking a message that has been sent and using one's own experiences and knowledge to give it meaning

**linear model of communication**
communication process that involves a sender who encodes a message and sends it through a channel where it competes with distracting forces called noise while on its way to a receiver who then decodes the message

**Figure 1.3**
**Linear Model of**
**Communication**

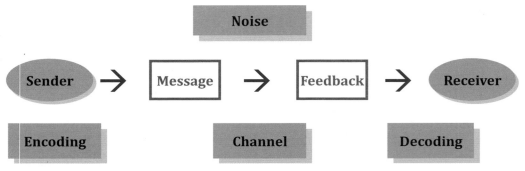

This model of communication is very speaker-centered, as it puts the onus of communication on the sender and places the receiver at the end of the process. Examples of communication situations where the linear model best explains what is happening include YouTube videos that broadcast a taped message or presentation. In this context, the speaker sends a message through two channels (voice and video) to you as a receiver and there is no further interaction. We will discuss mediated communication channels such as this when we cover the speaking environment later in the book, but it is important to know that the model for understanding presentations like these is the Shannon-Weaver, or linear, model of the communication process. This model also serves as the foundation for understanding the other models of communication developed by contemporary scholars.

### *The Transactional Model of Communication*

**transactional model of communication**
recognizes that we simultaneously send and receive messages; a cyclical model of the communication process

The linear model of communication, despite offering a clear explanation for the process of transmitting a message, does not adequately explain how all communication occurs—especially not even how most public speaking takes place. In fact, most public speaking does not occur in a one-way manner, but rather involves a constant exchange between the speaker and the audience. A more accurate model for public speaking as a process of communication, the ***transactional model of communication***, expands upon the Shannon-Weaver model of communication by recognizing and incorporating the notion that we serve as sender and receiver of messages simultaneously.[15] To do this, the transactional model adds an eighth component to the communication process.

**Figure 1.4**
**Transactional**
**Model of**
**Communication**

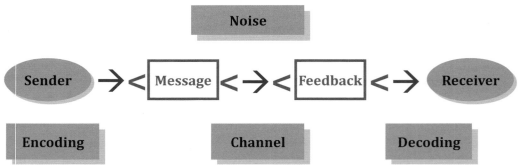

## SPOTLIGHTING THEORISTS: MARIE HOCHMUTH NICHOLS

### Marie Hochmuth Nichols (1908–1977)

Marie Hochmuth Nichols's influential career covered more than three decades. She was one of the more preeminent rhetorical scholars, teachers, and leaders in the communication discipline during the twentieth century. She was the first female president elected by the entire membership of the Speech Communication Association in 1969 and shepherded the discipline through a tumultuous period of transition.[16] Nichols also served as editor of the most prestigious periodical of rhetoric and public address, *The Quarterly Journal of Speech*. In 1976 she was awarded the Speech Communication Association's Distinguished Award.[17]

Nichols was a scholar of both theory and criticism in the neo-Aristotelian tradition. She also was heavily influenced by the work of Kenneth Burke and I. A. Richards.[18] Nichols published many essays; two of the most prominent were "Lincoln's First Inaugural Address" in 1954 and "The Criticism of Rhetoric" in 1955. In these and other essays she argued in defense of the discipline of communication and called on people to focus less on developing models and paradigms, and more on the ends and purposes of speech.

Specifically, she contended that the communication discipline is, and always will be, about understanding the uses and power of verbal symbols.

So highly regarded was Dr. Nichols that the National Communication Association (formerly the Speech Communication Association) named one of its most prestigious awards, The Marie Hochmuth Nichols Award, in her honor. It is awarded for published works in public address. In 1983 Kathleen Hall Jamieson issued the highest of praises for Nichols: "Some of us command an encyclical; some of us command a single rhetorical theorist; some of us command a rhetorical period. Marie Hochmuth Nichols commanded the tradition."[19]

This new component occurs after the receiver decodes a message, and is called feedback. *Feedback* consists of the responses and reactions to the messages transmitted by the sender and is itself a new message sent back to the original sender. The notion of feedback allows both parties in the message process to simultaneously serve as sender and receiver of messages (see Figure 1.4). Feedback can be verbal, nonverbal, or both, and it plays an important role in public speaking situations. Thus the transactional model of communication is a more appropriate explanation for communication in public speaking contexts.

**feedback**
the responses and reactions to the messages transmitted by the sender; is itself a new message sent back to the original sender

The feedback we provide in a communication situation can alter an unfolding interaction and can let senders know what our impressions are regarding the speaker and their message. Confused looks in an audience can tell a speaker to slow down and more thoroughly explain a concept, while head nods alert a speaker that an audience agrees with what he or she is saying. We will further explain audience feedback, what it means to you when delivering a speech, and how to adapt to it as a speaker when we cover audience analysis later.

There is one very important aspect to take away from the transactional communication model of communication as it relates to public speaking. We must always keep in mind that communication is an ongoing process, meaning that even as you give your speech the audience communicates with you just as much as you do with them. Paying attention to the dynamics of the communication process when delivering a speech will help you better adapt to the moment and increase your effectiveness at getting your messages across to an audience.

Both the linear and the transactional models of communication provide us with a logical way of understanding the communication process, but they cannot be understood as the "be all, end all" of the study of communication. In fact, several scholars have warned against emphasizing the development of models to the detriment of the more creative aspects of communication like language. Most notable among these contemporary thinkers is Marie Hochmuth Nichols, a former president of the Speech Communication Association (now the National Communication Association) who called on her colleagues to understand the power of the spoken word. Hochmuth Nichols can best be understood as someone who defended the roots of the discipline founded by Aristotle and the other classical figures we discussed earlier, but who also understood the potential of speech to change and affect the world around us. Her understanding of both the power of language and the models developed in the middle of the twentieth century provides important insight into how to craft and use speech today.

Thus far we have shown how essential rhetoric was in Classical Greek and Roman education. We explained that rhetoric resided at the heart of the curriculum, either as an element of the core (Isocrates and the Romans, for example), or as something to which the core responded (Plato's Academy, for instance). Today, training in speech is not as prominent a part of a student's education, and for many, their first exposure to rhetoric and speech education occurs in a dreaded required course in their first year of college. Speech training never used to be feared, but rather was welcomed as a means of participating in civic life. In the next section we will briefly explore a few moments in history where speech fundamentally altered civic life. These are key moments where the power of speech in the hands of those who knew how to wield it made an important and tangible impact on public life. After this discussion, we will then conclude by outlining the book and how it will help you get started in understanding how to become a better speaker.

## SPEECH AS A FORCE IN OUR LIVES

Despite their different beliefs regarding how to teach speech and the definition and utility of rhetoric, the classical thinkers and practitioners we discussed earlier would agree on the important role speech serves in public life. They all knew public speaking could move people to action, change their beliefs, and educate the masses, and history has proven their understanding accurate. At key moments in our history speech has helped move us to war, aided in shaping public attitudes and policies, and enabled us to express a definition of our identity with each other. There also have been important technological advances that have affected our ability to use speech to accomplish those tasks. In this section of the chapter we will briefly discuss the power of public speaking as a means of civic engagement and address how technology has influenced that power, especially in today's hypermediated world.

## Civic Engagement

The ability to use symbols to communicate with each other is what makes us human, and even neuroscientists recognize that speech, or put more formally, symbolic reasoning, is the one cognitive trait that separates humans from other animals.[20] Public speaking is also the way we negotiate and construct society's rules, values, and beliefs. The process by which we do this is called *civic engagement*, which can be defined as acting upon a sharp awareness of one's own sense of responsibility to his or her community. Unfortunately, our collective commitment to each other has seen a marked decline in recent years, despite enhancements in technology that make it easier than ever for us to communicate with each other.

**civic engagement**
acting upon a sharp awareness of one's own sense of responsibility to his or her community

For instance, Robert Putnam argued that our sense of community involvement and civic engagement has drastically decreased since the end of World War II as evidenced by low voter turnout, decreased membership in civic organizations like the Rotary Club and Knights of Columbus, and reduced subscription rates to newspapers.[21] These developments would shock the Greeks and Romans we discussed earlier who saw civic engagement, particularly through speech, as one of the most fundamental duties of a citizen.

Even though we may not experience it in the intense way the Greeks and Romans did, speech remains central to civic engagement. Have you ever wondered how to "have your voice heard" on a subject? Perhaps your state is thinking of raising tuition. How do you respond? Speech! Maybe your town wants to raise property taxes. How do you fight such an action? Speech! Or how do you let a congressman know that you don't like his behavior? Speech! Speech is central to understanding and participating in public life.

At a meeting of the G-20 in London, England, in March 2009, several thousand people rallied against the foreign leaders who gathered to talk about the world's economic troubles. How did they make their voices heard? They chanted, held posters, and gave speeches throughout the day in addition to marching. This is an example of civic engagement at its finest, and without speech all that would have happened was a bunch of people standing together in the middle of the street. Speech provided meaning for them, their purpose, and their protest. It allowed them to take an active role in the well being of their community.

Isocrates and Cicero, especially, recognized the relationship between speech and civic engagement. They understood that rhetoric and speech were central to a thriving democracy and that people needed to be taught how to deliver a speech, what to include in it, and how to ethically disseminate that information. Good people who spoke well could create a healthy and thriving nation. That belief still

## Speech to the NAACP Comparing Improving Childhood Obesity to the Civil Rights Movement
### by Michelle Obama

Delivered July 13, 2010, Kansas City, Missouri

First Ladies in the United States generally have a national agenda. Michelle Obama's cause is childhood obesity and she established a program entitled "Let's Move" to promote efforts to reduce childhood obesity.[23] She announced the program in early 2009 and it has remained a focus of her time as First Lady. She has delivered many speeches on the topic and in doing so she has kept a focus on the health of America's children. One of the reasons for her success is that she has what Aristotle would have termed strong ethos.

When Mrs. Obama spoke to the NAACP in Kansas City, Missouri, she had ethos, or credibility, not only due to the fact that she was the First Lady, but also because she was a working mother who had faced the task of feeding her children. She used this ethos effectively to reinforce her message.

Mrs. Obama noted some troubling statistics and spoke of the necessity to act immediately. She noted actions the government was taking but called on communities to get involved and individuals to exercise personal responsibility. Perhaps most importantly she told her audience that the battle could be won. In the speech conclusion Mrs. Obama called for action from the NAACP by linking the childhood obesity problem to the struggle for equal rights. Here is an excerpt from her address that shows how she did just that: "Surely the men and women of the NAACP haven't spent a century organizing and advocating and working day and night only to raise the first generation in history that might be on track to live shorter lives than their parents. And that's why I've made improving the quality of our children's health one of my top priorities."[24] Her speech in Kansas City is an example of ethos, but more importantly of how speech is central to civic engagement and can be a source of positive change in society.

holds true today, and many contemporary communication scholars continue to explore ways to speak well and encourage civic engagement.

Today, communication scholars and students explore speeches on a wide range of issues. Although many examine political figures and their comments, others analyze speeches by everyday folks because their words more than any others create the fabric of our society. For example, they look at how people discuss race, ethnicity, and even sports because these are the ties that bind us as a community. A good speaker in today's world, just like those in the days of Aristotle and Cicero, needs to be knowledgeable about the common characteristics of a community in order to effectively engage its members through speech.

Throughout this book you will encounter excerpts of speeches accompanied by a brief discussion of the issue being addressed by the speaker and how she or he approached it. The issues and speakers all vary, from the famous Dr. Martin

Luther King, Jr., to the contemporary and controversial Glenn Beck, to the classical Pericles of Athens. What they all have in common is a genuine appreciation of the power of speech to affect their community and the lives of their fellow citizens. Take a look at the *Speaking of Civic Engagement* box in this chapter that discusses a speech by First Lady Michelle Obama in which she seeks to motivate the NAACP to get behind her fight against childhood obesity.

As the Greeks and Romans taught, exposing yourself to a great many speeches is essential for learning how to become a better speaker yourself. These excerpts are designed to help you do that. Even though the importance of speech as a means of civic engagement has remained constant throughout history, there have been some developments that have changed the way we use it to enact change and send messages to audiences of which we need to be aware.

## The Mediated World

Unlike Classical Greece and Rome, today we find ourselves bombarded with messages through a variety of different media, not just speech. We see billboards and magazine advertisements designed to persuade us to buy something; we watch occasional speeches and see television commercials; we listen to music and read social commentaries on the Internet. One might say all of these things are modern, and speech and rhetoric have thus become less important, if not obsolete. Nothing could be further from the truth!

Most messages we hear, read, or see are designed to persuade us in one way or another, and if we do not understand how persuasion works, then how can we defend ourselves from being manipulated? Knowing the fundamental tenets of persuasion allows us to not only critically analyze those messages sent to us but also craft messages of our own. Understanding how speech works, from invention to delivery, and recognizing that it gains its power from a fusion of both content and delivery allows us to become more critical listeners and more productive participants in our daily lives.

Today, training in speech, rhetoric, and persuasion is not defunct, but rather more important than ever because today we don't just have speeches that might influence us—we have commercials, articles, and images that attempt to move us to believe something or act in a certain way. The best way to counteract these influences is to learn about them yourself and then to employ the principles of persuasion in a just, ethical, and proper way.

## SUMMARY

In this chapter we discussed how fundamental rhetoric and speech were to education in the Classical Period, and how scholars today define the communication process. We discussed the different ways in which rhetoric was taught and practiced by detailing five major contributors from Greece and Rome: Isocrates, Plato, Aristotle, Cicero, and Quintilian. We also explored several areas where rhetoric and speech education can help us in today's world; specifically, by making us more critical consumers of messages and allowing us to improve society through ethical and effective civic engagement.

| | |
|---|---|
| arrangement   13 | linear model of communication   17 |
| artistic proof   11 | logos   10 |
| channel   17 | memory   13 |
| civic engagement   21 | message   16 |
| clarity   11 | noise   17 |
| correctness   11 | pathos   10 |
| decoding   17 | propriety   11 |
| delivery   13 | receiver   17 |
| encoding   16 | rhetors   11 |
| episteme   8 | sender   16 |
| ethos   10 | Sophists   4 |
| feedback   19 | style   13 |
| inartistic proof   11 | techne   8 |
| intermediate knowledge   8 | transactional model of |
| invention   12 | communication   18 |
| kairos   6 | |

## REVIEW QUESTIONS

1. What would be considered the major contributions of the Sophists to our understanding of speech and persuasion?

2. What are the three elements of persuasion identified by Aristotle?

3. What are the five parts of a speech as proposed by Cicero?

4. What are the five responsibilities of a speaker according to Quintilian?

5. What are the two major ways in which a greater emphasis on rhetoric and speech in today's curriculum would improve our abilities?

## THINK ABOUT IT

1. How are rhetoric and literature different disciplines if they both study the use of language?

2. Should rhetoric and public speaking be taught to young students and continued throughout their education, like it was for Classical Greeks and Romans?

3. Do speakers today still adhere to the principles and practices of the Greeks and Romans in this chapter? If so, how?

1. As noted in the chapter, there is a clear connection between the power of speech and civic engagement, but as Robert Putnam noted, people are less and less likely to join clubs and social groups in the community. Take a moment and consider this by doing an informal poll of those around you. How many clubs are they a member of? How faithfully do they attend meetings? What are the goals and what is the mission of that organization? Then ask the same questions of someone older. See if you notice any difference and think about what this means for the nature of the relationship between communication and civic engagement.

2. The chapter notes that we are constantly exposed to messages in society today, and that training in the art of persuasion is essential for being a critical consumer of those messages on a day-to-day basis. We often think, however, that speech is not that pervasive in society—that visuals are what we are exposed to most often. For one day keep a journal of the various messages you encounter by providing a brief description of how the message fits either the linear or transactional model of communication. Then, at the end of the day, look back at your journal and see how often you actually are exposed to messages through speech.

## ENDNOTES

1. Peter Green, *Alexander of Macedon: A Historical Biography* (Berkeley, CA: University of California Press, 1991), 54-56.

2. Ibid.

3. Ibid., 54.

4. Paul Cartledge, *Alexander the Great: The Hunt for a New Past* (Woodstock, NY: Overlook Press, 2004), 84.

5. Philip Freeman, *Alexander the Great* (New York, NY: Simon & Schuster, 2011), 24.

6. James A. Herrick, *The History and Theory of Rhetoric* (4th Ed.) (Boston, MA: Pearson, 2009), 42-45.

7. Quoted in Thomas M. Conley, *Rhetoric in the European Tradition* (Chicago, IL: University of Chicago Press, 1990), 18.

8. Ibid., 20.

9. Herrick, 72.

10. http://www.123opticalillusions.com/pages/Facevase.php (accessed December 3, 2008).

11. All the information regarding Aristotle's life discussed here can be found in: George A. Kennedy (trans.), Introduction of *Aristotle: A Theory of Civic Discourse* (New York, NY: Oxford University Press, 1991), 5-7.

12. Herrick, 81-82.

13. Ibid., 39.

14. Claude E. Shannon and Warren Weaver, *The Mathematical Theory of Communication* (Urbana, IL: University of Illinois Press, 1949).

15. For example: Michael Dunne and Sik Hung Ng, "Simultaneous Speech in Small Group Conversation: All-Together-Now and One-at-a-Time?" *Journal of Language and Social Psychology* 13 (1994): 45-71.

16. Marie Hochmuth Nichols. http://www.natcom.org/Default. aspx?id=73&libID=94 (accessed June 11, 2011).

17. Marie Hochmuth Nichols, http://blog.umd.edu/ncapublicaddress/2011/03/09/ call-for-nominations-2011-nichols-award/ (accessed June 11, 2011).

18. Ibid.

19. K. H. Jamieson, (November 1983). In honor of Marie Hochmuth Nichols. Paper delivered at SCA Convention, Washington, D.C.; As cited in "Marie Hochmuth Nichols," by Jane Blankenship. Available: http://www.natcom.org/Default. aspx?id=73&libID=94 (accessed June 25, 2011).

20. John Medina, *Brain Rules: 12 Principles for Surviving and Thriving at Work, Home and School* (Seattle, WA: Pear Press, 2008), 32.

21. Robert Putnam, *Bowling Alone: The Collapse and Revival of American Community* (New York, NY: Simon & Schuster, 2000).

22. http://blogs.suntimes.com/sweet/2010/07/michelle_obama_in_naacp_speech. html (accessed May 7, 2011).

23. As reported by Sunlen Miller of ABC News on July 12, 2010. For article where quotation was found see: http://blogs.abcnews.com/politicalpunch/2010/07/ michelle-obama-to-the-naacp-now-is-not-the-time-to-rest-on-our-laurels.html.

# The Practice of Public Speaking

2

# Practically SPEAKING

Many people suffer from phobias of one sort or another. For example, those who suffer from arachnophobia fear spiders of all shapes and sizes. Then there are those who fear animals, and they suffer from zoophobia. Perhaps you know someone with aerophobia, or the fear of flying. Maybe one of your friends has nyctaphobia, or the fear of the dark. There are other more unique fears, like triskaidekaphobia (the fear of the number thirteen) or the fear of older people (gerontophobia). One of the most debilitating fears happens to be agoraphobia, or the fear of public spaces that comes from a feeling of inescapability. People who suffer from this fear cannot even go outside their own homes without risking severe anxiety. For a list of the top 10 phobias, see Table 2.1.

Fear is as human an emotion as love or happiness, and so it is not a bad thing to be afraid of something. In fact, it can make you function better. Take the example of Oscar-winning actor Sir Laurence Olivier. Olivier, named to the American Film Institute's list of Greatest Male Stars of All Time,[1] suffered from debilitating anxiety attacks before performances.

From the age of five or six, Olivier demonstrated a penchant for drama and acting, creating a makeshift stage in his parents' house from window curtains and a wooden chest to perform for his sister, visiting neighbors, or even extended family members. Olivier's formative years took place during World War I, a time when England's image of itself as Europe's dominant force came under fire. Despite his commitment to the lines of each of the plays and roles he would perform, Olivier still suffered stage-fright, or performance anxiety.

One of the more poignant insights he offered to this fear was "it comes in all sorts of forms; I suppose it's always there, but most of the time it hovers unseen."[2] Olivier also suffered from fear right before going on stage, describing it as "nothing like first-night nerves…the breathing becomes affected: the breath becomes shorter when you want it to become longer and deeper…you try to calm down but the sweat breaks out again. The voice in the head starts to ramble."[3] Do any of these feelings and emotions sound familiar when you prepare to deliver a speech? Well, fear not, because Olivier mastered his fear, made it work for him, and went on to become a world renowned performer.

In this chapter we will first define and discuss exactly what performance anxiety is, as it goes by many names. We will then talk about the causes of it and provide strategies for managing it so it can help rather than hurt your efforts. We then talk about one of the skills we can develop as a speaker and an audience member that can help diminish our fear when we speak, as well as the fear of others when they speak: listening. If we can practice becoming courteous and effective listeners then we can create a more comfortable environment for speakers, no matter how nervous they are.

# FEAR AND PUBLIC SPEAKING

Public speaking represents one of the most frightening experiences possible for a great many people and that fear is not abnormal. In this part of the chapter we will discuss the various ways in which the fear of public speaking is defined by the general public and academics. We will also explore the variety of factors that contribute to the anxiety associated with speech performances. Finally, we will provide several suggestions on ways to alleviate much of the trepidation associated with delivering a speech in front of an audience.

| Top Ten Phobias/Fears |
|---|
| 1. Arachnophobia: fear of spiders |
| 2. Social phobia: fear of being evaluated |
| 3. Aerophobia: fear of flying |
| 4. Agoraphobia: fear of not being able to escape |
| 5. Claustrophobia: fear of being trapped in a small space |
| 6. Acrophobia: fear of heights |
| 7. Emetophobia: fear of vomit |
| 8. Carcinophobia: fear of cancer |
| 9. Brontophobia: fear of thunderstorms |
| 10. Necrophobia: fear of death |
| http://www.phobia-fear-release.com/list-of-the-top-ten-phobias.html |

**Table 2.1**

## Defining the Fear of Public Speaking

The fear of public speaking, also called performance anxiety or stage-fright, is a specific manifestation of *sociophobia*, or the fear of people and/or social situations. The fear of public speaking is essentially a combination of any of the following fears: fear of rejection, fear of criticism, fear of judgment, and fear of failure. In this section we will illustrate the academic definition of the fear of public speaking and then discuss what students fear most when they speak in front of audiences.

**sociophobia**
the fear of social situations and/or people

Academics call the fear of public speaking **communication apprehension** and define it as "the fear or anxiety associated with real or anticipated communication with another or others."[4] Communication scholars apply this definition to more than public speaking situations, as it also helps to define shyness in interpersonal situations. Here you see why there are multiple ways of describing fear of public speaking. Fear and anxiety are synonymous, but one (anxiety) connotes a state that is easier to handle.

What is important to realize is that everyone has fear and everyone experiences anxiety in their lives. Perhaps things get really busy at work and you become easily agitated over things that normally do not bother you. This stress is a result of a heightened anxiety level. If you experience some level of anxiety before a speech, that is normal as it is a high stress situation. This level of anxiety is common.

There are some individuals who experience abnormal levels of anxiety, or who become anxious for no reason at all. These people have what psychologists call an **anxiety disorder**. A perfect example of someone with an anxiety disorder is the fictional character Adrian Monk, formerly of the USA Network's award-winning

Tony Shalhoub plays TV's *Monk*

drama *Monk*. Adrian suffers from multiple phobias as well as obsessive compulsive disorder, significantly hampering his ability to function in mainstream society. His anxiety prohibits him from functioning, whereas normal anxiety does not do that, although it does cause a level of discomfort.

In the case of public speaking, the differences between anxiety and having an anxiety disorder are easy to identify. First, normal anxiety may result in sweating, a knot in your stomach, slightly elevated blood pressure, or the general "willies" before a speech. People with an anxiety disorder, however, would not go to class on the day of their speech simply to avoid being judged. The Mayo Clinic provides a list of several other defining characteristics of a social anxiety disorder:

- An intense and persistent fear of social or performance situations
- Avoiding the situations you fear
- Fear of being embarrassed or humiliated
- Fear that others will see your physical manifestations of nervousness
- The anxiety limits how you can live your life
- You recognize the fear is excessive[5]

Additionally, the Social Phobia and Social Anxiety Association reports that those who suffer from social anxiety disorder recognize the irrational and illogical nature of their fear, but nevertheless the fear remains with them.[6] Anxiety that results in these feelings or behaviors should be treated by a professional, but the fact is most people can find ways to manage or even overcome their fears—especially those with public speaking. Later in this chapter we will discuss how.

So, why do students experience communication apprehension, or a seemingly high level of anxiety about delivering a speech? What is it that they are afraid of? Some fear speaking too quickly, or too quietly. Some are afraid of boring the audience, or sounding as if they do not know what they are talking about. Others fear mispronouncing words, or having something on their teeth or face at which people will stare. Many people are afraid of making eye contact with those in front of them for fear that they will forget what they were going to say. Others erroneously believe that their nerves will be visible to the entire audience.

Ultimately, there is just something about the speaking situation that makes people worry and become anxious. In fact, just as the tradition of public speaking is a long one, so too is the history of fearing to give a public presentation. Isocrates, the Greek teacher whom we discussed in the first chapter, suffered from a fear of public speaking so intense he himself tried never to speak publicly. That didn't stop him from training some of the best speakers of his time, though!

In the next section we will discuss three major causes of speech-fright: environmental, psychological, and physiological factors. Following that we will provide some helpful suggestions on how to manage your performance anxiety.

## Causes of Speech-fright

Speech-fright is often the result of a variety of factors, ranging from specific fears about the situation, aspects of a person's personality, or the physiological make-up of an individual. Environmental factors stem from the fact that speaking in public is different from speaking in a conversation with a friend or someone you know. We often see these differences and ignore the commonalities between the two situations, resulting in a fear of the one scenario and comfort with the other. Psychological factors that influence speech anxiety include your approach to everyday life and how you handle stress. Finally, different people have different physical reactions to stimuli, and sometimes these stimuli are present in a given speaking situation.

Three environmental factors influence a person's level of anxiety when delivering a speech, and each stems from fundamental differences in the nature of public speaking and conversation. The first two involve the audience. An audience for a speech is typically much larger than that of any conversation, and we often find this intimidating. That intimidation is only exacerbated by the fact that we are not as familiar with the people to whom we are speaking when we deliver a speech as we are with those we talk to over lunch. The third environmental influence is *spotlight syndrome*, or the perception encouraged by the room setup that all eyes are focused on you as the speaker.

**spotlight syndrome**
the belief encouraged by the room setup that all eyes are focused on you as the speaker

As those environmental characteristics illustrate, the public speaking environment is different from the atmosphere for most conversations. Public speaking uses more formal language, has a very structured format, and involves more than just a few people. Conversations are less structured, often employ slang, and typically involve only a few people. Differences aside, the two situations share certain characteristics as well, and understanding those common components can help reduce anxiety over speaking in public.

Conversations and public speaking share several elements that make them more similar than they are different (see Table 2.2). Both entail extensive nonverbal communication when delivering messages and receiving feedback. Both call on you to logically organize your thoughts. Public speaking and conversation also require you to adapt to audience feedback in order to tell a story in the most effective manner possible. Finally, in both situations you need to tailor your message to the audience. All told, conversations and public speaking have far more commonalities than differences! So, just think of public speaking as having multiple conversations at the same time and your anxiety will be dramatically reduced.

**Table** 2.2

| Differences and Similarities in Conversation and Public Speaking | |
|---|---|
| **Differences** | **Similarities** |
| • Public speaking has more formal language<br>• Format is more structured<br>• Involves more than a few people | • Use of nonverbal communication<br>• Logic is needed<br>• Must adapt to feedback<br>• Message is tailored to the audience |

The environment is only one set of influences on a person's anxiety; the mental approach also can contribute to heightened stress in advance of a speech. Many people believe that public speaking is a talent and not a skill, and thus they enter into a speaking situation under the false assumption that they lack the tools necessary to effectively deliver a speech. The fact is public speaking is a skill, something that can be learned, and not a talent, something people are born with. Through practice and experience you can become a very effective speaker—just look at the example of Laurence Olivier from the beginning of the chapter.

**self-fulfilling prophecy**
••••••••••
believing that something will happen before it actually does, and then when it does come true reinforcing the original expectation

Psychological elements can also contribute to a person's reluctance to stand up and deliver a speech. Many people, especially as their performance draws near, allow worrisome thoughts to creep into their mind, creating a *self-fulfilling prophecy*. If you convince yourself that a speech will not turn out well, you will invariably not practice well and your performance will be poor, resulting in the original expectation coming to fruition. This and other forms of worrisome thoughts can cloud a speaker's mind to the point where it increases anxiety and gets in the way of a successful performance.

Nerves are not simply psychological, they appear in physical ways as well. When we get nervous our heart rate increases, resulting in potential blushing, we sweat, and we may even shake. These are some of the ways our bodies respond to stress, and often we believe people see them and immediately attribute them to nerves. Neither of those beliefs, however, are true. Often, people do not see us sweat, or our blushing, or even see our hands shake. The truth is that we can hide the physiological manifestations of nerves without even trying; the audience sees a fraction of what we feel.

Now that we are aware of the environmental, psychological, and physiological factors that affect speech-fright we can address how to manage performance anxiety and eventually make it work for us. In the next section we discuss several strategies for handling and reducing the anxiety present before and during a speech.

## Managing Performance Anxiety

Fear is one of the most potent human emotions, and when you are afraid of something fear grips you and controls your thoughts and actions. It can be paralyzing, but it does not need to be so. One technique for overcoming a fear is to confront it head on and immerse yourself in the fear until you realize there is nothing to be fearful of. For example, if you were afraid of heights you could climb to the top of the tallest building and stare out over the edge of the roof until you got used to it. Although this immersion technique sounds logical, albeit a bit cruel, there is some truth to it.

Experience with that which is fearful ultimately will help you manage your fear. Unfortunately, this technique fails to address how you handle the fear while it is still there. Thankfully, overcoming performance anxiety entails both immersion and incremental management techniques. On the one hand, the more experience you get with delivering speeches, the less nervous you will become giving speeches in the future. On the other hand, there are several strategies for helping you manage the fear while delivering a speech, because you will not manage or master your fear overnight.

One of the ways you can combat worrisome thoughts and avoid creating a self-fulfilling prophecy is through visualizing success. Thinking positively about the speech and imagining yourself successfully delivering the speech will increase your belief in your ability to do so. Taking a positive approach and visualizing pulling off the presentation without any problems will also allow you to practice more comfortably.

Changing your mental approach also can minimize the influence of physiological factors on your anxiety levels. Understanding that people cannot see your nerves and acknowledging that there are a multitude of other reasons why you might sweat or blush alleviates the worry that people might "see that you are nervous" (see Table 2.3). You might be sweating because the room is hot, or blushing because of the same reason. Your shakes might be because you are sick, or the room is cold. Just because you know that you are anxious does not necessarily mean others know that too.

**Table 2.3**

| Manifestations of and Reasons for Stress | | |
|---|---|---|
| Physical Manifestations of Stress | Could Be Caused by... | But It Might Be Caused by... |
| Perspiring | Nervousness | Room temperature |
| Blushing | Anxiety of embarrassment | Illness or room temperature |
| Trembling | Apprehension | Room temperature or illness |
| Breathing heavy | Anxiety | Physical exertion |

Breathing can also help you combat nervousness and get more comfortable in front of an audience. You do not need to start your speech immediately upon getting behind the podium. If you are feeling tense, take a deep breath or two before you begin speaking. If you find your nervous state is still there, or that it returns during the delivery, do the same thing. Breathing increases your intake of oxygen and can reduce blushing and calm your nerves, so always remember that stopping and taking a breath is an option available to you when you get nervous during a presentation.

Finally, and perhaps most importantly, proper preparation and practice will undoubtedly make you more relaxed when you get to the point where you must deliver the speech. The easiest thing you can do to gain more confidence in your ability to speak is to practice, and practice often in advance of a speech. The more you practice, the more comfortable you get with the material, and the more comfortable you get with the material, the more you know it when you get in front of an audience. Practice and experience breed confidence, and confidence in your ability is the strongest tool you can develop to fight your fear. Realize that you do not have to present the speech using the exact same words each time. Focus on the content. As an example, a professor may deliver a lecture to one class, then leave and go deliver the lecture to a different section. He will not give the exact same lecture, as word choices may vary, but the content, or purpose, will be the same. See Table 2.4 for a summary of strategies for dealing with speech anxiety.

**Table 2.4**

| Strategies for Dealing with Speech Anxiety |
|---|
| • Directly confront it by presenting speeches<br>• Visualize success<br>• Realize the audience only sees a portion of what you feel<br>• Take deep breaths for calmness<br>• Adequately prepare and practice |

So far we have covered performance anxiety, discussed several causes of it, and suggested some ways to combat the tension associated with preparing and delivering presentations. One skill we can develop to help create a more comfortable speaking environment—as both a speaker and an audience member—

## SPOTLIGHTING THEORISTS: SOCRATES

### Socrates (469–399 B.C.)

Virtually all we know of Socrates comes to us by way of his student, Plato, and his contemporaries Xenophon and Aristophanes, because he himself did not write any philosophical texts. Socrates perfected the art of listening to criticize through what we now call the Socratic Method and Socratic Questioning. In Ancient Greece, Socrates would wander through the marketplace questioning the political and moral positions of people in Athens. He did so by carefully listening to them talk and then asking questions about their statements. His questions almost invariably illustrated significant problems with the philosophies of his contemporaries. This would not have been possible had Socrates not carefully listened to and critically analyzed the positions they took. He can rightly be considered the father of modern logical intellectual inquiry, but even more to the point, he demonstrated the power and purpose of listening carefully to the messages of others.

Socrates was an Athenian who devoted his life to teaching philosophy, although according to Plato he did not accept payment for his educational services. He went through life poor in terms of money, but was highly regarded by his students. In addition to his teaching efforts he also served in the military during three Athenian campaigns.

Socrates lived in Athens during a time of turmoil, when neighboring Sparta and its allies defeated Athens. After this defeat, Athenians seemed to have doubts about democracy, and from Plato we can see how Socrates may very well have shared those doubts. One of his greatest roles during this time was as moral and social critic of the city he loved, leading to eventual problems with those in power at the time. Greeks at the time held a "might makes right" philosophy toward justice and governance and Socrates vehemently disagreed with this position.

Plato called Socrates the "gadfly of the state" because he spurred Athens into action through his various encounters with leaders, philosophers, and politicians. The story goes that one of Socrates's friends asked the Oracle at Delphi who was wiser than Socrates, and the Oracle responded that no such person existed. Upon hearing what he believed to be an erroneous statement, Socrates set out to show that there were wiser people throughout Greece by entering into dialogues with politicians and philosophers.

He used a dialectic method of discussion in these conversations whereby he would solve what he saw as problems by breaking problems down into a series of questions that eventually produced the answers sought by those around them. These discussions almost always centered on moral and social dilemmas and the concepts of justice and goodness.

Socrates's questioning agitated the leaders of Athens, because he often made them look foolish. They eventually had him arrested. When convicted he was sentenced to death, and despite the opportunity to flee and escape prison, he decided to stay and face judgment. Socrates was forced to drink a cup of hemlock, a poison, and died in his cell. His philosophy, however, has survived 2,400 years to this day and greatly influenced Western Thought.

is listening. In the next part of this chapter we will define the different types of listening, discuss some of the obstacles to becoming a good listener and how to overcome them, and illustrate how becoming a better listener when speaking and serving as an audience member can help minimize some of the factors that increase speech anxiety for some people.

# LISTENING AND PUBLIC SPEAKING

People often confuse listening with hearing when, in fact, they are quite different. *Hearing* is the physiological process of capturing sound and it is conducted by one's ears and brain. *Listening* is the psychological process of making sense out of sounds and involves paying attention to the external world. Listening is an important skill for both speakers and audiences. For some rhetors, knowing that many people will be paying attention to them when they speak causes a high level of anxiety and contributes to their fear of public speaking. But like many things, once we understand what listening is and how people use it our level of discomfort will lessen. This part of the chapter will help you understand the complex nature of the different types of listening audiences employ, as well as discuss the importance of listening for the speaker as well.

## Listening for Speakers and Audiences

Both speakers and listeners engage in listening, and it is key to understand the importance it holds for both parties. Speakers use listening as a means of measuring how well an audience is receiving their message, and how to adapt if they determine people are not getting it. Audience members use listening to gather information and form judgments; however, listening properly is far more difficult for them than for speakers.

Listening should be thought of as more than simply making sense of sounds, as it encompasses paying attention to nonverbal messages and processing them as well. Speakers both listen to the audience's verbal responses to statements—which can be as simple as making grunts of agreement or disagreement, or shouts of praise—and their nonverbal actions, which can include leaving the presentation, staring off at something else, or even nodding off. All of these actions indicate to a speaker who listens that changes need to be made in the speech to return the audience's attention to the message.

One way in which listening skills are exceedingly helpful for speakers is during a question and answer session. In fact, the questions that an audience asks are much more indicative of what they have learned than any statement they may make. Questions can be quite revealing in terms of an audience's retention of the message. In Ancient Greece, Socrates knew this all too well, as he developed a method of inquiry that balanced speaking with listening. *Socratic questioning* is the process of asking questions of a speaker focused on the responses to previous questions; its ultimate goal is to uncover the truth.

Audience members have a more difficult time listening than speakers because it is the only thing they are asked to do for the majority of the speech. Compounding this singular duty, the average human attention span is not very long and ranges anywhere from a few seconds to about 10 minutes, depending on the subject to which they are paying attention. When audience members do not pay attention to a speaker and the speaker notices, it may heighten the speaker's level of anxiety; convinced they are boring, they may lose confidence in their speaking ability. It is, therefore, an audience's ethical obligation to maintain attention to the speaker and his or her message as much as possible.

## Types of Listening

One of the main reasons audience listening makes people nervous is because they are afraid the audience will catch them making a mistake or saying something inaccurate and call them on it. Although that is a remote possibility in some speeches, it is not common and only reflects one form of listening. There are, in fact, three listening purposes and two listening types audiences employ, and each engenders a response by the audience to the speaker and his or her message.

The first listening purpose is for appreciation. *Listening for appreciation* encompasses activities where you listen for enjoyment. Loading your favorite CD on your way to work or listening to the radio are examples of listening for appreciation. In these environments audiences are not waiting in the wings to pounce on an incorrect statement or to disagree with a speaker; they are listening to relax. Audiences do not employ high levels of cognitive commitment when they are listening for appreciation.

**listening for appreciation**
listening for enjoyment; not high in cognitive commitment

A second purpose of listening is *listening to comprehend*. When we try to understand a message or learn about something we do not know we listen to comprehend. This listening purpose involves a higher level of cognitive commitment than listening for appreciation because we pay attention to the message in order to gather and store information about a topic. Think of classroom lectures or news broadcasts as examples of listening to comprehend. We do not look for things to argue about in an instructor's lecture; rather, we take notes so we can learn about something with which we are unfamiliar. Like listening for appreciation, this type of listening by an audience is not combative.

**listening to comprehend**
listening to understand a concept or message

The final purpose of listening is the one we almost always ascribe to audiences, even when it is not what they are doing. *Listening to criticize* entails paying attention to the information and the argument presented by the speaker so that the audience can make a judgment about the message. Listening to a political candidate's speech is a prime example of listening to criticize. The word *criticize* holds such a negative connotation, however, that most people fear this type of listening. Unfortunately, that perception distorts the true benefits of this type of listening by audiences, such as encouraging debate and dialogue. Critical

**listening to criticize**
listening to make a judgment about a message; involves a high level of cognitive commitment on the part of the audience

listening is a fundamental part of any thriving democracy and is not something to fear. When we listen to criticize we are not looking to attack speakers or even make negative judgments about them. We are merely evaluating their message on its merits, and sometimes people simply must agree to disagree.

Both critical and comprehensive listening purposes require audience members to employ *active listening*. Active listening occurs when audiences have high cognitive involvement with the speaker's message and seek to understand the message. In other words, they are processing, storing, and potentially evaluating the message as it is being delivered. Active listening also involves some form of reaction by the listeners to demonstrate they are gathering the data being presented. This is not an easy process and takes much practice to develop, but it is an important skill to develop as both a speaker and an audience member.

**active listening**
listening to understand a message by processing, storing, and potentially evaluating a message. It also involves reactions by the listener in some form

**spare brain time**
the time available for your mind to wander due to your ability to process messages faster than it takes to construct them

**passive listening**
listening without reacting

There is also a difference between how you speak and how your brain functions. You speak at a rate of 150 words per minute, but your brain processes words at over 600 words per minute, resulting in lots of time for your mind to wander. This time is referred to as *spare brain time*, or the time available for your mind to wander due to your ability to process messages faster than it takes to construct them. Be aware that spare brain time makes it easy for your mind to wander to other things.

*Passive listening* is another type of listening. This is essentially listening without reacting, although the listener may well be receiving the information presented. Passive listeners do not raise hands or inquire during a presentation. This is the "sponge" approach to listening and can be risky if you do not understand something. This type of listening occurs more often when you are listening to comprehend, or listening for appreciation. When it takes place during the latter, then the sounds are often referred to as background noise.

Some noise, like background noise, does not affect a person's ability to concentrate or listen attentively; however, other noise can interfere with a person's ability to receive a speaker's message. These noises are distractions, and in the next section we will discuss several different types of distractions that can negatively impact someone's ability to listen and thus create a more uncomfortable atmosphere for a speaker.

## Overcoming Three Types of Distractions

Distractions can engender an uncomfortable atmosphere, increasing a speaker's discomfort when delivering a speech. Some of these distractions occur because of a person's fear reactions, while others are external to the speaker. Nevertheless, all of these can inhibit a person's ability to listen. See Table 2.5.

Biological reactions to the environment in both speakers and audience members can distract people from listening. Think about a classroom situation in which you were too cold, or perhaps too hot. How hard was it to pay attention to the lecture in that room? Pretty difficult to be sure. Or perhaps you were ill, had a headache, or were hungry—all biological responses that diminish your capacity to pay attention to a message. So, how do we overcome these distractions?

Unfortunately, there are few remedies other than concentration and focus. You could try and eat or drink before a speech if you are hungry, and in fact if you are the speaker you should go into the presentation with a satisfied stomach. If you are ill, you could take medication, but even then the best course would be to acknowledge the illness to the audience at the outset so they are aware of it and do not spend time during the speech distracted by your reactions to the affliction.

In addition to biological distractions, there may be environmental occurrences that draw attention away from the presentation. Airplanes flying overhead, cars driving by, people coughing or sneezing, and even the howling of the wind can cause both speakers and listeners to turn their attention somewhere other than the message. Again, the best answer to these distractions is focus and acknowledging them to the audience.

The final type of distraction we will cover is also the rarest of them: hecklers.
Hecklers are those individuals who seek to interrupt a presentation to inject their own viewpoint, either through insult, unsolicited questions, or unwarranted commentary. Heckling could quite possibly be the most unethical behavior an audience member can display. Hecklers have appeared at political speeches, guest lectures by faculty, and even during comedy shows. In fact, comedian Dane Cook called out a heckler during one of his live albums, explaining that the person was destroying the experience for everyone else.

Comedian Dane Cook

There are two ways speakers can deal with hecklers, and two ways audience members can help deal with hecklers as well. Speakers can choose to ignore hecklers in the hopes that they will eventually quiet down because they are not receiving attention. Rhetors also can acknowledge the hecklers and ask them to be quiet or face removal from the area. Audiences can help control hecklers by ignoring them, especially if this follows the lead of the speaker. They also can confront the heckler and express their displeasure with that person's behavior. Either way, hecklers can make both speakers and audiences uncomfortable for as long as they are making their unwanted contributions loud enough that people hear them. Choosing to be an attentive listener who allows speakers the opportunity to say their piece prevents this type of behavior from occurring and contributes to creating a more comfortable atmosphere for a presentation.

**Table 2.5**

| Dealing with Distractions | |
| --- | --- |
| **Type of Distraction** | **Coping with Distractions** |
| Biological | Be sure to get enough rest, food, and water, and if ill, let the audience know |
| Environmental | Maintain focus and acknowledge distractions to the audience |
| Hecklers | Ignore them<br>Directly address them<br>The audience may support the speaker |

## Types of Nonlistening

**nonlistening**
providing the appearance of listening without actually paying complete attention to the message

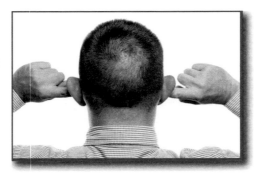

Oftentimes we think we listen, when in fact we do not. What we are doing is called *nonlistening*, or providing the appearance of listening without actually paying complete attention to the message. Nonlistening comes in a variety of forms, and in each instance we believe, or pretend that, we are listening, but in fact we are not.

The first, and perhaps most common, form of nonlistening is called *pseudolistening*. This occurs when listeners attempt to hide their inattention to the message by appearing as though they are listening attentively to the speaker. Think about phone conversations you may have had where you take the phone away from your ear only to come back in time to say something like "uh-huh" to make it sound as though you were listening to the person on the other end. Or perhaps you went to lunch with someone and had to ask "are you listening to me?" because he or she seemed not to understand what you said. Finally, perhaps you have spent time sitting in class, looking at the professor, perhaps occasionally nodding your head, just pretending to pay attention. These are all examples of pseudolistening.

**pseudolistening**
when someone attempts to hide their inattention to the speaker's message

**glazing over**
daydreaming instead of hearing the message

A second form of nonlistening is *glazing over*. At some point in all our lives we have looked out the window or stared at a wall during a lecture in school, only to realize later that we missed important information. This daydreaming is a form of nonlistening common to situations where the audience is not enthralled with the topic. Although it may appear somewhat benign, speakers may internalize this as their poor speaking skills creating boredom in their audience.

**ambushing**
selective listening where the audience ignores the strengths of a message and hears only the weaknesses

*Ambushing* is a third form of nonlistening audiences may engage in. This involves selecting only the weaknesses of a presentation and ignoring the strengths of the speaker's argument. It is a negative form of nonlistening that can encourage a hostile atmosphere that increases a speaker's anxiety toward delivering the speech. It is important to listen to a speech with an open mind and judge the entire presentation on all its merits, not selected points that are made. This is the listening version of the strawman fallacy in crafting a logical argument, which we will discuss later.

*Prejudging* is the last of the nonlistening forms we will explore. It is dangerous and a potentially negative form that stems from an audience member's inability to enter the presentation with an open mind. Audience members have an ethical obligation to enter into any presentation with an open mind and allow the speakers to make their case. If you have already formed an opinion on the topic prior to the event, then the speech is pointless. For example: Suppose your university has been raising student fees quite often. An SGA representative is coming to your organization and you know she supports yet another increase in mandatory student fees. Your passion and attitude about the topic make it easy for you to already have a decision made before she even begins her speech.

**prejudging**
entering into a presentation with a judgment already formed about the message being delivered

Most times a speaker can easily determine whether people have prejudged the speech and the speaker before a word is spoken and this is not fair to the audience or the speaker. Listen for the evidence and the argument and then make your judgment.

Listening is an important skill for speakers and audiences and it should be treated as such. When both sides are attuned to the message then they create a more comfortable speaking situation and help to reduce speech anxiety on the part of the presenter.

Listening is a key component to any public presentation, and it is a requirement for an ethical speaker and audience member. In the next section of this chapter we will discuss four types of ethical public speaking and one form that violates the principle of a "good person speaking well."

# ETHICAL CONSIDERATIONS IN SPEECH

Recall from our discussion in Chapter 1 that the Greeks and Romans noted the importance of ethics in public speaking, although they focused their attention on providing speakers, rather than audiences, with guidance for ethical message construction. They understood the immense power speech had over the actions of the public, and so in their schools they often took care to teach not just the skills of speech construction and delivery, but how to wield speech for the public good. For them, and for us today, why you say something is just as important as what and how you say it.

The ethical principles and duties laid out by Isocrates, Quintilian, and other Classical thinkers still apply today. Just as with citizens during the time of Isocrates and Quintilian, when we speak to the public—be it our fellow students, our church congregation, or a rally—we are asking them for their time, attention, and trust. Whenever we speak we want someone's attention, thus we ask them to place value in our message by committing time to listen to us. That value rests on the principle that what we are saying is the truth that we know to the best of our ability. It also means that we have the audience's best interests in mind and that our goal is to achieve some good on behalf of the group.

## The Struggle for Human Rights
## by Eleanor Roosevelt

Delivered September 28, 1948, Paris, France

Former First Lady of the United States, Eleanor Roosevelt, lived a privileged existence. Despite her well-off origins, however, she witnessed much hardship and human suffering during her life: the Great Depression and World War II. To her, human rights were a fundamental issue worth fighting for. After her time in the White House alongside her husband, Franklin Delano Roosevelt, she confronted her growing concern over the expansion of the Soviet Union and how its policies infringed on human rights.

Mrs. Roosevelt became an advocate for human rights and delivered many speeches on the subject. One of the more notable of these speeches was given at the Sorbonne in France, where she noted: "It was here the Declaration of the Rights of Man was proclaimed, and the great slogans of the French Revolution—liberty, equality, fraternity—fired the imagination of man."[7] Speaking at virtually the front door of the Soviet Union and its allies on these issues would have been a risky proposition for any speaker, but Mrs. Roosevelt found it important and necessary to do so.

Mrs. Roosevelt noted that the charter of the recently formed United Nations concerned human rights and that the Human Rights Commission was working on language concerning those rights. She also commented on the objections of the USSR and a few other countries and outlined differences between the United States and the Soviet country.

Mrs. Roosevelt recognized that achieving universal human rights would be difficult, but she concluded her speech with a prayerful message of hope for the future of human rights: "I pray Almighty God that we may win another victory here for the rights and freedoms of all men."[8]

One such moment we can use to illustrate a speaker addressing a group with the global community's best interests in mind came following World War II when Eleanor Roosevelt spoke about human rights to a group in France. The issue of basic human rights is something that affects all of us, and speaking on behalf of protecting those rights represents a good and ethical goal. If we have good goals, we should also share our intentions with the audience honestly and acknowledge any personal interests or biases we may have related to the topic.

As a more current example, consider charity work in your community. A "good" that you may seek to achieve could be convincing your class to donate money to breast cancer research. We can all agree that the elimination of breast cancer is a good thing and that raising money for research to achieve that end is a noble and good pursuit. Using a speech to encourage support of this charity work would fit the characteristic of an ethical speaker because you are seeking a good goal, and as Isocrates and Quintilian said, good speakers must have good goals.

But ethical speaking is not just about achieving goals or ends, it is also about the means we use to achieve those ends. Let's look again at the previous example about a speech in which you seek donations from your classmates for breast cancer research. This time, as a piece of evidence in your speech, you state that there is a 75% chance that each audience member's mother will develop breast cancer—except this data is not accurate and you do not even provide a source for the information. In fabricating the statistic you would be violating the principles of ethical public speaking because you would not be, in Quintilian's words, defending the truth. Despite the fact this story may help your case and move the audience to donate to a noble cause such as breast cancer research, the ends would be achieved through deception and manipulation, two things not characteristic of a good person. Additionally, this behavior would damage your ethos.

Fabricating statistics and other forms of evidence is not the only way we can be unethical public speakers—and it is probably not even the most common or insidious. In fact, today speakers in society tend to rely primarily on demagoguery when crafting appeals, rather than outright mistruths. **Demagoguery** refers to speech that attempts to win over an audience through appealing to their prejudices and emotions, particularly those of fear, anger, and frustration. Unfortunately, the practice of demagoguery has become even more common with the advent of mediated communication and 24-hour news channels.

**demagoguery**

speech that attempts to win over an audience through appealing to their prejudices and emotions, particularly those of fear, anger, and frustration

Demagogues originally referred to leaders of the common people in Classical Greece, but like today, the term carried a negative connotation that implied deceit, selfishness, and a desire to create mischief in the population. Demagogues typically seek to gain power for themselves by activating and exacerbating the darker side of human emotions. For example, Huey Long, governor of Louisiana in 1928, won election by demonizing the wealthy and corporate interests while promising a utopian community where "every man is a king, but no one wears a crown." He referred to the wealthy as "parasites" and used them as a target for the anger of the Louisiana public that had begun to feel the effects of an economic downturn.

Perhaps the most famous demagogue in American history was Senator Joe McCarthy who, in the 1950s, accused high ranking officials, Hollywood celebrities, and even newsman Edward R. Murrow of being either communists or communist sympathizers bent on destroying the fabric of American society. This period, now referred to as the Red Scare, saw many people lose jobs and suffer damaged reputations that could not be repaired, even when McCarthy's accusations were discovered to be baseless and unfounded. His speeches and accusations created a public frenzy by playing solely on the public's fear of communism.

Ethical speech also requires that you stand up for what you believe to be right, just, and good. This may present an uncomfortable situation, but if your motives are to benefit the audience and not serve a personal interest, and if your ideas are sound, just, and logical, then you owe it to your audience and yourself to speak up,

**Figure 2.1**
**The Ten Commandments of Ethical Public Speaking**

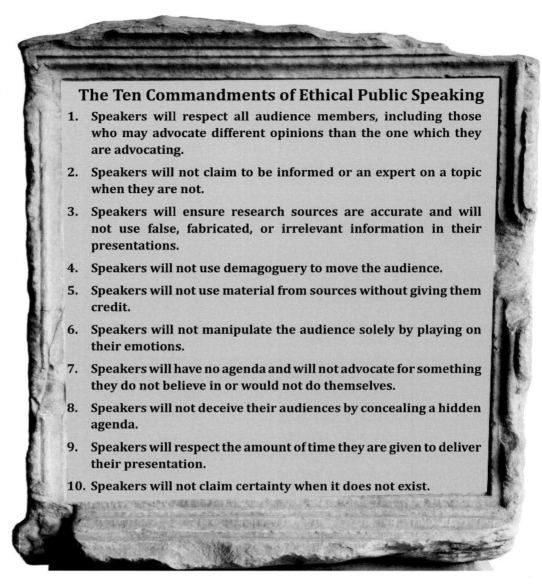

**The Ten Commandments of Ethical Public Speaking**

1. Speakers will respect all audience members, including those who may advocate different opinions than the one which they are advocating.

2. Speakers will not claim to be informed or an expert on a topic when they are not.

3. Speakers will ensure research sources are accurate and will not use false, fabricated, or irrelevant information in their presentations.

4. Speakers will not use demagoguery to move the audience.

5. Speakers will not use material from sources without giving them credit.

6. Speakers will not manipulate the audience solely by playing on their emotions.

7. Speakers will have no agenda and will not advocate for something they do not believe in or would not do themselves.

8. Speakers will not deceive their audiences by concealing a hidden agenda.

9. Speakers will respect the amount of time they are given to deliver their presentation.

10. Speakers will not claim certainty when it does not exist.

like Edward R. Murrow did with McCarthy and like Cicero did in Rome. Cicero's speeches denouncing Julius Caesar and then Marc Antony cost him his life, but his ideas and the principles he espoused live on. Today such penalties for speaking out are protected in a variety of contexts, but consider this: Perhaps we are afraid to speak up or raise our hands in class because we are aware of the power of speech. Making good ethical decisions on the small things you encounter in your everyday life will best prepare you for speaking up on the more complex ethical challenges when they confront you.

Emotions are an important part of effective message construction, but it is when speakers use emotions to further their own ends or fabricate evidence to create particular emotional reactions in the audience that their use becomes unethical. There are plenty of emotional appeals that are both ethically constructed and designed to achieve ethical ends, but as a speaker we must be cognizant of both the means we use to move an audience to action, and the action toward which we move them. Demagogues violate both of these principles by capitalizing on an audience's emotions to achieve personal, rather than communal, goals. See Figure 2.1 for a summary of the ten commandments of ethical public speaking.

## SUMMARY

Many people suffer from performance anxiety, or what we call fear of public speaking. It is only natural to be nervous in such a situation for a variety of reasons, ranging from environmental factors, to physiological reactions, to a person's psychological approach to the situation. Thankfully, there are a variety of ways to counter and manage this feeling so that it can work for you and make your speeches better in the long run. There are also ways in which audience members can contribute to making the atmosphere more comfortable, and one of the easiest ways is to be an ethical and effective listener. Avoiding nonlistening techniques and actively paying attention to the speaker's message will only serve to create a more open and relaxing environment for any speaker. Conversely, speakers have ethical responsibilities to their audiences to present the truth and be honest about their goals.

## KEY TERMS

| | |
|---|---|
| active listening   38 | listening to criticize   37 |
| ambushing   40 | nonlistening   40 |
| anxiety disorder   30 | passive listening   38 |
| communication apprehension   30 | prejudging   41 |
| demagoguery   43 | pseudolistening   40 |
| glazing over   40 | self-fulfilling prophecy   32 |
| hearing   36 | sociophobia   29 |
| listening   36 | Socratic questioning   36 |
| listening for appreciation   37 | spare brain time   38 |
| listening to comprehend   37 | spotlight syndrome   31 |

## REVIEW QUESTIONS

1. What is the difference between fear of public speaking and an anxiety disorder?

2. What are the three major factors that can cause speech-fright?

3. What are some strategies for combating speech anxiety?

4. What are the three listening purposes and two listening types?

5. What are the forms of nonlistening prevalent in an audience?

## THINK ABOUT IT

1. If someone is deaf, can they listen?

2. At what point does general speech anxiety become an anxiety disorder?

3. How can you actually tell if a speaker is nervous or anxious?

4. As an audience member how can you aid a nervous speaker?

## ACTIVITIES FOR ACTION

1. Take a moment and make a list of things that you fear. Now, take each one and write out an explanation of why you fear each of these things. Finally, look at the reasons and causes of your anxiety and write a plan that will help desensitize you to the fear.

2. Think of a song to which you like to listen. Write down the title, band, and what is appealing about the song. Now, find the lyrics to the song and write a description of what the song is about based upon the lyrics alone. Finally, think about what the speech is about and how you feel about the message within the song. Do you agree with the message? Why or why not? In doing this exercise you practice appreciative listening, listening for comprehension, and critical listening.

3. Find the lyrics to a song you like and deliver those lyrics as you would a speech. Do the same with a poem and page from a book. In practicing speaking with each of these texts you will become more comfortable in the speaking situation and reduce the anxiety public speaking can cause.

## ENDNOTES

1. American Film Institute, "AFI's 100 Years...100 Stars," http://www.afi.com/tvevents/100years/stars.aspx (accessed June 25, 2008).

2. Laurence Olivier, *On Acting* (Simon and Schuster: New York, NY, 1986), 181.

3. Ibid., 183.

4. James C. McCroskey, "Oral Communication Apprehension: A Review of Recent Research," *Human Communication Research* 4 (1977) 78-96.

5. "Social Anxiety, Social Anxiety Disorder/Social Phobia: Symptoms, Types, Causes, Treatment and Support," http://www.helpguide.org/mental/social_anxiety_support_symptom_causes_treatment.htm (accessed June 25, 2008).

6. Ibid.

7. http://www.americanrhetoric.com/speeches/eleanorroosevelt.htm (accessed May 9, 2011).

8. Ibid.

# Research and Preparation

# Practically SPEAKING

Students today typically react to the necessity of venturing to the library with a mixture of dread, loathing, and reluctance; however, that has not always been the case. In fact, there was a time when libraries held an exalted status and represented more than simply storage facilities for the printed word. In the ancient world, libraries were castles of learning and homes to schools, zoos, museums, and the brightest minds of the day. They were, in point of fact, the backbone of empires and kingdoms.

The most famous library in history was located in Alexandria, Egypt, and its history is a mixture of both fact and myth. King Ptolemy I (Soter) and his son King Ptolemy II (Philadelphus) commissioned the Great Library at Alexandria and modeled it after Aristotle's Lyceum in terms of mission, but the Alexandrian library dwarfed the Lyceum in terms of size, structure, and content. This model, however, occurred for good reason.[1]

Ptolemy I was one of Alexander the Great's generals, and after the death of his leader and subsequent partition of the empire, Ptolemy ruled Egypt. Alexander was a student of Aristotle's, and so he made sure his generals were schooled in the same vein. Additionally, through his conquests Alexander attempted to Hellenize the world by spreading the value of the *enkyklios paideia*, or rounded education, which tiered instruction into the *trivium* (grammar, rhetoric, and logic), and *quadrivium* (arithmetic, geometry, music, and astronomy).

The Ptolemys sought to create a universal library, one where knowledge of all things could be found, not just a localized culture-specific repository of knowledge. The Great Library also contained a Museum and together they represented one of the greatest achievements in all of antiquity.[2] The Great Library and Museum worked in tandem to store and develop the wisdom of the ages. Scholars from around the known world lived and worked tax-free at the Library copying scrolls secured by the government. On several occasions, Ptolemy and his successors even brought scrolls on loan from Greek city-states and copied them only to keep both the original and the copy! It was the epicenter of scholarship and innovation because many of those holdings were original Greek works and translations of non-Greek texts of religious, poetic, and political significance.[3]

Unfortunately, nothing much remains of the Great Library and Museum and the histories of it are the product of researching letters and writings that reference it. No one is sure how it was destroyed, but destroyed it was, and many writings contained there are now lost forever. Ironically, we know about the ancient world's research mecca only through research, as it no longer exists and its documents are long gone.

Nowadays we think of libraries simply as places where knowledge is stored, and the university as a whole fits the model set forth by the Great Library. Nevertheless, the Greeks and Romans recognized that libraries and research skills are central to the development of a critical mind, and we should learn from that example.

In this chapter we will explore the very nature of research and illustrate the importance of becoming information literate. We will discuss different types of sources and how you can find the ones most appropriate to your project. Finally, we will detail the importance of properly citing sources you use and provide two examples of how to do so. A successful speech is predicated on good research and helps you determine your topic.

# Topic Selection

In many situations speakers know their topic because someone provided it for them. There are, however, times when speakers need to pick topics on their own, such as in your public speaking class. Regardless of the speaking situation, determining one's own topic is the first step toward performing a successful act of public speaking. In this part of the chapter we will discuss ways to find a topic, develop a research question for that topic, and eventually refine the topic so it is clear for you and your audience.

## Finding a Topic

There are three primary ways to determine a topic for a speech. One is easy, and takes little effort from the speaker; unfortunately, it is not always available. The second involves a person's familiarity or expertise in an area, and the final method for picking a topic hinges on a speaker's curiosity.

As we mentioned earlier, many times speakers are provided not just the opportunity to speak, but the topic on which to speak. This makes things relatively easy as they know what to research and what to say. Take, for instance, a business situation when a budget director must report on sales and earnings for the company at a shareholder meeting. The budget director knows his topic well in advance, but how he chooses to deliver the message and the data he uses rest largely with him.

Other times the specific topic is not provided, but speakers are given a general guideline for their presentation. This often happens when professors are asked to deliver guest lectures. In fact, the non-fiction book, *The Last Lecture,* by Randy Pausch (with assistance from Jeffrey Zaslow), is about a

**enkyklios paideia**
rounded education spread under the reign of Alexander the Great

**trivium**
grammar, rhetoric, and logic

**quadrivium**
arithmetic, geometry, music, and astronomy

Randy Pausch
at Carnegie Mellon

professor who, while dying of cancer, prepares to deliver a talk at Carnegie Mellon University during its "Journeys" series. The only direction provided was that Pausch must speak about his career and how he ended up doing what he did. He gave a speech that creatively addressed achieving your childhood dreams.[4] Tragically, Pausch lost his fight with pancreatic cancer on July 25, 2008, at age 47. His speech, however, remains a perfect example of how speakers use their own creativity to determine a specific topic when provided with only general criteria for a speech.

There are times when even this type of minimal direction is not provided for you. One easy option for you then is to select a topic with which you are very familiar, or perhaps one in which you are an expert. Consider this fictional case involving Donald, a freshman in a public speaking class who needs to deliver an informative speech. Donald loves baseball, and so he chooses to inform the class about the rules of the game. He knows exactly where to go to find the proper sources, knows of several easy-to-find anecdotes to support his speech, and feels confident that he knows the material. Donald's prior knowledge and familiarity with the topic make it easy for him to pick this topic.

Perhaps you do not wish to speak on a topic with which you are familiar; such topics bore you and you want to actually learn about something new in the process of developing your speech. Let's look at Phyllis, who has always wanted to know more about the Dow Jones Industrial Average because she has invested so much money in it over the years. Unfamiliar with the topic, Phyllis's curiosity leads to her discovery of a wealth of knowledge about the Dow Jones Industrial Average she never would have known had she not chosen the topic. Choosing topics on which you know little but wish to know much can be a valuable tool in expanding your knowledge. It also exemplifies how rhetoric and public speaking cut across disciplines and require knowledge of many subjects, not just skill at delivery.

## Crafting a Research Question

**research question**
the question about your topic you seek to answer

Once you determine your topic, you need to focus your research around a question about that topic. This question is called your ***research question***, and it guides you through the rest of your preparation for your speech. Regardless of whether you are delivering an informative, persuasive, or epideictic address, a research question is essential for providing you with a focus for your presentation. There are three characteristics of every quality research question.

Bob Dylan

First, a research question is an open-ended question and cannot be answered with a simple "yes" or "no." The answer to the question is complex and requires a level of detail and description that are not necessary for a "yes" or "no" question. If your general topic is an informative speech about a famous musician, and your specific topic is Bob Dylan, then your research question might be, "What inspired Bob Dylan to write his song "Hurricane"?" Answering such a question calls for you to talk about who Bob Dylan was, discuss some history of the song, provide some background on its topic, and perhaps discuss some cultural issues at play during the time he wrote the song. Of course, you could craft a myriad of different research questions from the specific topic of Bob Dylan, and each would need different data and information to answer, but any question you seek to answer must be open-ended.

In addition to being open-ended, the research question must be tailored around the topic. In other words, it must be relevant to the general and specific topic of the speech in some way. Using the Bob Dylan example again, some other successful research questions might be, "What was Bob Dylan's childhood like?" "Why did Bob Dylan choose music as a career?" or even, "How has Bob Dylan influenced contemporary musicians?" What would not work in the framework of this general and specific topic would be persuasive questions like, "How can I convince people to listen to Bob Dylan?" or this informative example of a question unrelated to the topic: "Who else was a successful speaker at the time of Bob Dylan?" This question, though it mentions Dylan, is not about Dylan, thereby violating the requirement that the research question be tailored around the specific topic of the speech.

Finally, the answers to strong research questions will inevitably become the thesis statement or argument for your entire presentation. Look at the Dylan example from a few moments ago. Let's say that your research indicates that Dylan wrote his hit song "The Hurricane" because of a personal sense of social justice, the desire to right a wrong perpetrated on a minority, and to shed some light on the situation in which Rubin "Hurricane" Carter found himself. That presents a strong thesis for an informative speech about the song and how it reflected the plight of Carter, a former boxer who was accused, convicted, and later exonerated for the murder of three people at a bar in Paterson, New Jersey, in 1966. This topic is

Rubin "Hurricane" Carter

obviously complex and warrants further explanation, hence the need for a longer speech built on the foundation provided by the answer to your initial research question. See Table 3.1 for some examples of poorly and properly worded research questions.

**Table 3.1**

| Wording Research Questions | |
|---|---|
| **Poorly Worded Research Questions** | **Properly Worded Research Questions** |
| Who is Barack Obama? | What is the history of Barack Obama's political career? |
| Is it easy to pass Calculus 1? | What are some study strategies to successfully pass Calculus 1? |
| What is an easy way to break up with someone? | What is an ethical method to end a romantic relationship? |
| Why do service learning? | What benefits can students receive from engaging in service learning? |
| Are you a healthy eater? | What are the factors to consider for a healthy diet? |
| Why did Germany start WWII? | What were the historical, economic, and social events that led to Germany's military aggression leading to WWII? |
| Why play video games? | How can playing video games improve hand and eye coordination? |

## Refining Your Topic

As you search for the answer to your research question you also must adapt to the results of your research. To do this, you must be prepared to refine your specific topic and even your research question to better guide you on your quest for information. First and foremost, when you begin you must be prepared to discover that the focus of your speech when you finish researching may very well not be the focus you wanted or had in mind when you began. This is only natural and is the result of good research skills.

One of these skills is note-taking. Good researchers have a method of note-taking that works best for them. This may involve note cards, photocopying information to better write margin notes, keeping a research notebook, or even using post-it notes to label where you found information. Regardless of how you choose to take notes, you need to develop a categorizing system that makes sense to you so that when it comes time to organize the information into meaningful points for the speech you can easily do so. Taking good, organized notes while you research will help you refine your topic and focus your speech even more.

Good researchers seek information with an open mind and do not simply look for data that supports their original idea. It is important to allow contrary information to count as much as material that supports your ideas when conducting research. There are multiple interpretations of a variety of different data, from statistics to events to the lives of people, and good researchers find as many of these as possible to better balance their results. The more relevant information you collect, the stronger your speech will become. Let the information be your guide, rather than you guiding the research.

It is tempting for any student to simply go and locate the minimum amount of sources to complete the assignment, but that defeats the purpose of expanding your knowledge base and contributing to the research field. If you research properly, sometimes it can take you to places you never thought about. Many students have lost track of the time, reading through newspaper articles from long-ago, interesting times, only to realize they spent far more time in the library than they had planned! Remember, those who used the Library at Alexandria lived there, they did not just visit. Follow the information, don't simply collect it, and you might just find the experience enjoyable and enlightening.

One final tip for conducting research and developing your topic is to think big initially, then reduce your topic down to something more precise. There is a reason why we talked about a general topic, then a specific topic, and finally a research question. Each step gets progressively more specific and thus smaller than the previous one. As you gather more information you can fine-tune your focus and make it more specific, thus helping you determine what you need in your quest for information. When you know your topic, you then have a better idea of where to look for information; however, you also must be able to distinguish useful and reliable information from useless and unreliable material.

# INFORMATION LITERACY

Literacy refers to the ability to read, while information literacy is the ability to read information. Specifically, *information literacy* is the ability to figure out the type of information you need, find that information, evaluate it, and properly use it. There are five characteristics of an information literate person, and in this part of the chapter we will explain each of them, paying particular attention to the last: understanding the issues regarding the use of information. We will then differentiate between three different types of information researchers encounter and eventually use.

**information literacy**
the ability to figure out the type of information you need, find that information, evaluate it, and properly use it

## Characteristics of Information Literacy

Just as literate people can read properly, information literate people can successfully research material they need. There are five characteristics of information literate people. First, they are able to determine what they need information for. Second, they are able to go out and find that information. Third, they can evaluate the information for accuracy, bias, and relevance as it relates to their purpose. Next, they can use the information they find to create new knowledge for themselves and/or others. Finally, the information literate person understands the issues relevant to using information, such as plagiarism.

Once you have a topic and purpose you are ready to begin to research, but what will you look for? Good researchers take an intermediate step between determining the topic and researching material. They determine their information need. Are they seeking background information? A strong anecdote for an attention-getter? Or evidence for their claims? Knowing the type of information you need will determine where you look, because not all types of information can be found in the same place. Depending on your need, you will look at different sources to find the information that best suits your need.

In today's media-rich environment we tend to believe we can find anything we need on the Internet, but the Internet is not a cure-all to the difficulties of research. In fact, it presents some disadvantages along with all the advantages it provides for researchers. Because it is rife with biased and sometimes false information, the Internet should be considered only one of several options for researching materials. Libraries, specifically the ones on your campus, hold vast stores of potentially useful information that might not even be available on the Internet, such as articles from a remote British newspaper during the Nazi's London Blitz of World War II. Knowing where the information is, however, is only one part of finding the information you need. The second part is recognizing which tool will net you the best results in your quest. Is it the Internet? The library? A book? A journal?

**accuracy**
the truthfulness or correctness of a source

**bias**
presenting information in a way that unfairly influences someone's perception of something

As an information literate researcher, when you find information you think might help with your project you need to evaluate it for accuracy, bias, and relevance. *Accuracy* refers to the source's correctness or truthfulness. *Bias*, or the attempt to unfairly influence someone's perception of something, is also a concern. Accurate information can be presented in a manner that unfairly influences how one side is perceived by, among other things, excluding certain pieces of relevant material that might dispute a claim. Information also must be judged for relevance to your topic. Researchers able to evaluate material they find for accuracy, bias, and relevance will create stronger presentations and contribute more to the world around them.

The fourth characteristic of an information literate individual, using the material garnered through research to create new knowledge for others, is associated directly with the contributions produced by research. Information literate researchers use the information they discover to educate and enlighten themselves and those around them. They make connections from work by others and information they find that others did not see to create a new perspective on a topic or issue. They also may be providing valuable information about something to a group of people who were unaware of what they needed to know about it. Building new knowledge from old research and information is one of the chief

Nevada Congressman
Jim Gibbons

aims of research. Doing so without committing plagiarism is a chief component of the final characteristic of an information literate researcher.

## *Plagiarism and Accountability in Information Use*

In addition to the four characteristics we just discussed, information literate individuals understand the gravity of the issues involved with information use. The most important of these issues is giving credit where credit

## SPOTLIGHTING THEORISTS: MELVIL DEWEY

**Melvil Dewey (1831–1931)**

Although computers, and more specifically the Internet, have eased the difficulties inherent in research, there still remains no greater influence on the research process than the development of the Dewey Decimal Classification System. Although not a communication scholar per se, Melvil Dewey changed the way in which scholars of any discipline conducted research. His classification and indexing system changed the way libraries operated, making the Great Library at Alexandria seem more like a warehouse than a library.

Melvil Dewey was born in New York and attended Amherst College in Massachusetts. From 1874–1877 he worked as assistant librarian at that college's library. It was during his time at Amherst College that he developed the now famous cataloguing system that bears his name.

In 1883 he took the position of chief librarian at Columbia University in his native state only to go on and be named director of the New York State Library in 1888. While in New York he championed the development of state and local libraries and was the first to instruct young librarians. He also managed to convince the state that the library system should be supported through the same tax revenue used to support public education, as public libraries, he argued, were a logical extension of public education.

These contributions to the creation of a modern library system and public education system greatly influenced the development of contemporary scholarship. Dewey helped make access to books and research materials easier through his coding scheme and efforts to link libraries to state and local educational efforts.

---

is due. Not to give credit to people whose work you use in a report or speech is *plagiarism*, or presenting another person's work or ideas as your own. It is important to understand that intent is irrelevant with plagiarism (e.g., "I didn't mean to do it" carries no weight). It is best to overcite sources than not to cite them enough.

**plagiarism**
to present another person's work or ideas as your own

Plagiarism comes in three different forms, but all are equally wrong. The first is *incremental plagiarism*, or failing to give credit for parts of a speech borrowed from a source. Incremental plagiarism is the most common form of plagiarism, as many people fail to reference parts of a speech they have paraphrased or even lifted directly from a source. In 2005 Congressman Jim Gibbons (R-NV) ran for governor and delivered a speech that seemed to rail against liberals. In this speech he delivered 15 paragraphs that were taken directly from a speech delivered by Alabama Auditor Beth Chapman two years earlier.[5] This is a perfect example of incremental plagiarism.

**incremental plagiarism**
failure to give proper credit for parts of a speech that are borrowed from others

**patchwork plagiarism**
∙∙∙∙∙∙∙∙∙∙∙∙∙
stealing ideas from two or three sources without referencing them

Another form of plagiarism is called **patchwork plagiarism,** or stealing ideas from more than one source and pawning them off as your own. Patchwork plagiarism involves lifting whole sections of information from several sources and linking them together without referencing any of them. This may appear to be using various forms of information to build new knowledge, but it is not, as there is little to no integration of the sources to an argument. This type of plagiarism occurs most often when students list information within a speech without referencing where the data has come from.

**global plagiarism**
∙∙∙∙∙∙∙∙∙∙∙∙∙
taking an entire speech from a single source and pawning it off as your own

The final form of plagiarism, **global plagiarism**, is the one most people are familiar with. Global plagiarism involves stealing an entire speech or paper from a single source and calling it one's own. Global plagiarism takes many forms, from cutting and pasting, to having someone write a speech for you, to buying a paper off a website. None of these give proper credit to the source of the ideas and information that have become the speech and, as such, they represent plagiarism.

Perhaps the greatest problem with plagiarism, aside from the fact it is an ethical and moral affront, is the fact that it destroys the fruits of researching. No longer are you able to learn about something, build new ideas, or expose yourself to things you may never have explored if not through research. You lose the opportunity to expand your own knowledge and help others do the same. Plagiarism attacks the very heart of a university's mission and thus is typically punished harshly; it is the worst academic crime possible. An information literate researcher is aware of all of this and avoids plagiarism at all costs by properly citing information found through research. There is one exception to the rule when it comes to presenting someone else's ideas as your own—but it does not apply in the classroom. *Ghostwriting*, or to write for and in the name of another person, is a fairly common practice among politicians and business leaders. In fact, presidents employ an entire speechwriting staff to write their speeches because they simply do not have the time to do so. Business executives also employ staff members who research and write many of their presentations because of time constraints.

**ghostwriting**
∙∙∙∙∙∙∙∙∙∙∙∙∙
to write for and in the name of another person

The difference between ghostwriting and plagiarism is that ghostwriters are professionals who still abide by the rules of research and expectations for citations and allow the speaker to take credit and accountability for what is eventually said in the presentation. Most importantly, their participation in the speech's development is not hidden from the audience. In short, we all know the president uses speechwriters, but in the case we discussed earlier about Jim Gibbons of Nevada, there was no ghostwriter and the material was appropriated from a source without letting the audience know from whence it came.

Ghostwriting is also not a new phenomenon. In Classical Greece, citizens often hired professionals to help them write speeches. The Sophists whom we mentioned in Chapter 1 sometimes fulfilled this role and made a pretty penny doing so! Clients often sought out professionals to help them write speeches to use in assemblies or in court, in much the same way business leaders and politicians use ghostwriters today.

Ghostwriters are examples of people who are information literate. A little earlier in the chapter we mentioned that information literate people know their information needs. Specifically, they know what material they need to research. In the next section we discuss the three main forms of information used within a speech: background, "adding flavor," and evidence.

## Using Information

Information contributes to speeches in a variety of ways. Researchers sift through the data they find and determine if and how that material can be used. One way information can be used is to provide background for the speech topic. Another way it can help a speech is by "adding flavor" or color to the presentation. The third and final form of useful information is evidence, or information that supports main points within a speech.

*Background information* provides context for your topic. It covers things such as definitions of key concepts, dates of events, and the key players or moments related to the topic. This type of information helps you further narrow your speech topic and point you in the direction of evidentiary information for your topic. Despite the fact you will undoubtedly not use all of the background information you gather in early drafts of your speech, you should hold onto it until you deliver the speech as it may be useful later.

**background information**
material that provides context for a topic

A second form of useful information is information that may capture the audience's interest in your speech. This type of information may be only slightly related to your topic but, it is nevertheless interesting and can be used to draw an audience in as an attention-getter. It also includes tangential anecdotes that can be placed in the body of a speech to illustrate a point. The more popular forms of *tangential information* include startling statistics, famous quotations, and unique stories; all should be related to the speech in some way, but not necessarily directly linked to the topic. Each of these may not support main points within a speech, but they do help make the speech more enjoyable, creative, interesting, and effective by adding unique data to the presentation.

**tangential information**
evidence used to provide color and capture an audience's interest

The third most common and most important use of information is to support main points. *Evidentiary information* is information that supports main points within a speech and is directly related to the topic. It allows us to bring the voices of experts to bear through building on their research findings. Without evidentiary information there would be little support for any points in a speech. It is, essentially, the "meat and potatoes" of a speech. This information can take the form of personal accounts, newspaper stories, or statistics, but all of it has to be directly connected to the main point it is intended to support. One example of the effective use of evidentiary information in a speech can be seen in an address given by the Reverend Billy Graham to the Empire Club in Canada in 1995 (see the nearby box).

**evidentiary information**
information that supports main points within a speech and is directly related to the topic

So far we have discussed both how to determine a topic and what type of information to seek to support a topic. In the next part of this chapter we will cover how to find information, because knowing how to find information is an essential characteristic of an information literate researcher.

### Leadership in the Third Millennium by the Reverend Billy Graham

Delivered June 6, 1995

The Reverend Dr. Billy Graham presented an invited speech to the Empire Club in Toronto, Canada.[6] Reverend Graham is a well-known author and evangelical Christian minister who has promoted a message of redemption through Jesus Christ since the late 1940s. In this address Graham spoke of the importance of leadership in a world fraught with challenges. Graham utilized multiple different sources of information to support the main points in his speech—all of which emphasized what he saw as the five attributes needed for contemporary leaders: integrity, personal security, sense of priority, sacrifice, and commitment.

Graham quoted numerous people throughout the address, ranging from Alexander Solzhenitsyn and George Washington to Queen Elizabeth. He quoted the Bible several times, particularly passages in the New Testament. Additionally, he quoted writers and reporters, as well as data on suicide rates in Canada. All of these various forms of evidentiary information provided data in support of his claims.

Graham's conclusion included a quotation from Sir Edmund Hillary, the famous mountain climber, who during a London speech when he reflected on his latest attempt to climb Mount Everest stated: "'I tried to conquer you once and you beat me. I tried to conquer you the second time and you took the lives of two of my best friends. But Everest, you will not be victorious. I will be victorious because you can't get any bigger, but I can." This piece of information fit perfectly with Graham's message of what it takes to be a leader in the third millennium and serves as an example of how speakers can wield information in different ways to maximum effect within a speech.

## FINDING SOURCES

Finding information is no longer as difficult as it was during the days of the Great Library of Alexandria. Advances in technology and access now allow researchers to gather plenty of materials for projects without even leaving the comfort of their own office. In this section of the chapter we will discuss three places the contemporary researcher can explore when seeking information: libraries, personal correspondence, and the World Wide Web.

### Libraries

Even with the advent of the Internet, the library still represents the largest and most reliable source for research materials. Every college and university still maintains a library, and many towns and cities also have public libraries that are easy to access. Libraries store books according to the Dewey Decimal System, and many allow for searches according to that classification system or by identifying other search criteria. Libraries also typically hold subscriptions to many different research databases that can help researchers find the information they seek. Above all, however, the most practical and useful tool in a library for assisting in research is the staff of the library. Many libraries provide the service of library tours. Signing up for a tour can save a novice researcher many hours of frustration. It will help you when you research because you will become more familiar with where libraries store the information you seek.

Libraries catalog and store books, magazines, and journals using the *Dewey Decimal Classification System*. This system has been revised 22 times since it was developed by Melvil Dewey in 1876. It organizes information into 10 major classes, which are then divided into 10 divisions which each have 10 sections. Except for fictional books, information is categorized by subject, and then further labeled according to relationships to time and place. Fictional books are coded differently and are not listed with nonfiction books. This system allows researchers to find several sources relating to the same subject just by initially finding one. When the Dewey Decimal Classification System first appeared it was a physical card catalog and took time to search. Now, most libraries allow for electronic searches of their holdings according to subject, author, keyword, and even publisher in some cases, making researching even easier.

The same types of searches are also available for databases to which a library subscribes. These databases allow for specified searches of discipline- or source-specific material. For example, databases such as *JSTOR* allow a researcher to explore only academic journal articles related to politics. *Communication/Mass Media Complete* allows the same for journals and mainstream references related to communication and journalism. While those are examples of discipline-specific databases, *Lexis-Nexis* is a source-specific database available to many researchers. Lexis-Nexis allows people to sift through newspaper and magazine articles from publications around the world, thereby limiting its reach to newspaper and magazine sources. There are many, many more databases of which researchers can avail themselves, and the best way to find out which one best fits your needs is to make use of the most approachable tool in the library.

Even with the advances in organization and technology that have revolutionized the research process, it is important to remember that librarians remain one of the best resources for locating information. Librarians know where to go to find information on many different topics, and the chances are high they know how to help you as well. They also have that human knack for thinking on their feet and trying different tactics if initial lines of thought do not prove fruitful. It is important to talk to librarians when starting your project because they will be able to cut down on your research time and assist you in finding the most accurate, unbiased, and relevant information for your project. They also will counsel you on how to find information from more places than databases and the full-text information found there. They will open doors to print sources not uploaded on the web but just as relevant to your project, sometimes even more so.

**Dewey Decimal Classification System**
the coding system for books, magazines, and journals used in libraries

**JSTOR**
an electronic database for political journals

**Communication/ Mass Media Complete**
an electronic database for academic journals and popular sources related to communication and journalism

**Lexis-Nexis**
an electronic database for newspapers and magazines

# Personal Correspondence and Interviews

Libraries often carry special collections of materials previously owned by private citizens. Within these collections are personal correspondence such as letters and diaries. These materials, as well as more structured personal correspondence such as surveys, make up yet another potential resource for researchers. Additionally, less scientific, but equally useful, communications such as interviews and emails can be used for background or evidentiary information. They also can sometimes be used to provide a colorful anecdote or clever attention-getter.

**formal survey**
................
time-consuming way of gathering data on a population that employs randomized sampling to ensure reliability and validity

Researchers survey groups of people to find out the moods, feelings, or characteristics of them. These surveys can take two forms, the first being formal surveys. A *formal survey* employs scientific methods to ensure random sampling, reliability, and validity. These take time to administer, and oftentimes in preparing for a speech, a person will not conduct an original formal survey, but rather find the results of one conducted by someone else that provides insight into the topic on which they are speaking. The second form of surveying is an *informal survey*, whereby the person preparing a speech asks a handful of people their opinions on a topic to add context to a topic. These surveys are not reliable or valid, but can still yield useful information for a speech.

**informal survey**
................
polling a few people based on convenience

**interviewing**
................
a direct method of gathering information from a human source that allows for questions to adapt to responses

Informal surveys sometimes morph into another method of gathering information, especially when conversations become deeper than the planned survey questions. This method, *interviewing*, allows for more information from an individual than a survey, which aggregates group responses. Interviews follow a specific format that respects both the needs of the interviewer and the rights of the interviewee.

When conducting an interview it is important to first identify what you hope to learn from the interview. After developing these goals, then set out to find the person to interview who will best help you achieve those information-gathering goals. Once the person is contacted and agrees to the interview you develop the questions in advance for the interview. During the interview, you must allow for the possibility of asking questions you did not initially plan for based upon the responses provided by the interviewee. Following the interview it is important to take your notes from the conversation and translate them to source material as quickly as possible, because memory fades and becomes unreliable the longer you wait to record information from the interview.

**undercover interviewing**
................
when the interviewer disguises either himself or his purpose in an effort to trick someone into sharing more information than they may have if the interviewee knew to whom he or she was speaking

One ethical issue related to interviewing concerns undercover interviewing. *Undercover interviewing* is when an interviewer either disguises himself or his purpose in an effort to trick someone into sharing more information than they may have if the interviewee knew to whom he or she was speaking. Many reporters and researchers use this technique to gather information, but it raises ethical questions. Is it right to disguise your motives or identity to gather information? Are there other, more honest, options available to get the information you seek? Researchers must weigh these questions when thinking about hiding their identity and/or purpose during an interview.

Interviews are not limited to face-to-face interactions and can take place through email or letters; however, these interactions, especially emails, must be viewed carefully. Research indicates emails are often read with a negative bias, and that plays a role in how researchers may interpret information they receive through email. People also write emails in a more informal style than letters, where letters typically follow proper rules of grammar. Some emails also contain disclosure notices at the end that may prohibit researchers from using the information contained within the message. It is important when sifting through such messages that you take care to see if this is the case with an email you are considering using.

## Internet

Email occurs on the Internet, but websites are far more commonly used as sources by researchers than email correspondence. Unfortunately, for the many benefits the Internet affords researchers, there are still many pitfalls of which researchers must be aware. There are different types of websites, each providing information on various subjects with varying degrees of accuracy. Credibility, therefore, is a significant issue when it comes to using the Internet to find information on a topic. Researchers must take care when evaluating information found on websites.

All websites have a form designation at the end of their URL. For example, government-produced websites end with ".gov," for-profit companies end with ".com," educational institutions end with ".edu," organizations end with ".org," and sites affiliated with a network are labeled ".net." International websites use abbreviations to identify their country of origin, as with the

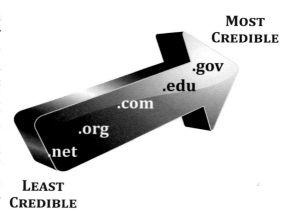

**MOST CREDIBLE**

.gov
.edu
.com
.org
.net

**LEAST CREDIBLE**

**Figure 3.1**
**Ranking URLs by Credibility**

United Kingdom, which is labeled ".uk," or Canada, which goes by ".ca." The domestic labels each carry different levels of accuracy, bias, and credibility. See Figure 3.1.

The most reliable websites are ".gov" because they are government produced and easily verified. A close second in reliability is ".edu" because educational institutions have lower levels of bias on a wider range of issues than any other website designation except ".gov." Typically placing third in terms of reliability are the ".coms," which represent the interests and biases of companies. Most financial, historical, and organizational information found about the company on these websites is usually accurate; however, other information may not be as reliable. ".Org" is the next on the list, and only slightly more reliable than ".nets" because both of these URL designations can be obtained by almost any group or individual, making it more likely their biases will bleed through onto their websites. This is not to say all of these URLs are untrustworthy, just that researchers should take care to check the authorship of the website before citing it and using information contained on its pages.

Researchers should also pay attention to the timeliness of the website. Sometimes websites never remove information, and if you are not careful you might use outdated statistics, quotes, or data by citing a website that has not cleaned out old material. This may not always be the way the timeliness problem manifests itself, however. Consider giving a speech on the election of 2000. Blogs and postings from 2000 would be very relevant. However, those from beyond that year would not be. It is important to pay close attention to when the material you find was produced.

Authorship of a website also matters. A few moments ago we discussed websites designated with ".org" and how they can be questionable sources. Most organizations pursue an agenda, and looking at the mission statement of the organization or the biography of the author that produces the website will give you greater insight as to the biases inherent in the information found on that site. The harder authorship is to determine, the less credibility the researcher should attribute to the information.

Two popular resources on the web are Wikipedia.com and About.com; however, entries on these websites can be unreliable. Anyone can post, edit, or delete information within entries on these websites, thus causing one to question the veracity of the material found there. A good researcher will not use these as references, rather as initial places to get an idea of potential research questions that direct them toward alternative sources of information. See Table 3.2 for tips on how to use these websites.

**Table 3.2**

| Using Wikipedia and Other Online Encyclopedias | |
|---|---|
| **Improper Uses** | **Proper Uses** |
| Citing in paper or speech | Background information that can direct you to other sources |
| Believing its accuracy is always reliable | Ideas for speech topics |

The web provides many benefits in terms of access to information, but it also makes determining the quality of that information ever more important. An information literate individual can both find the appropriate information and determine its quality, especially when it comes from the Internet.

# CITATION GUIDES

Referencing sources is a must for all researchers. When you deliver speeches it creates an added component to the process of identifying sources in that not only must you reference sources in the written outline, you must verbally attribute sources when you speak as well. This attribution is a matter of good ethical behavior because it lets the audience know what is your original work and what you have borrowed from someone else. Properly attributing sources adds to your ethos, or credibility, by demonstrating you give credit where credit is due. When you do not cite your sources or verbally attribute them in your speech, then you call yourself and your information into question and raise the possibility that you may appear to be manipulating your audience. So, to avoid such impressions, always reference your sources in your written and oral work.

Within the field of communication there are two preferred forms for references, each one slightly different from the other. Most who conduct rhetorical research follow the *Chicago Manual of Style (CMS)*, while those who utilize a social scientific approach to exploring communication follow the *American Psychological Association (APA)* manual. You may also encounter a third citation style, that of the *Modern Language Association (MLA)*, when you research in other fields within the liberal arts and humanities. In addition to formal written bibliographies and in-text citations, when speaking students must also verbally attribute their sources. In this part of the chapter we will provide a cursory guide for all three manuals when referencing some common resources, and then we will provide some useful tips for verbally attributing sources within a speech.

## The Chicago Manual of Style (CMS)

*The Chicago Manual of Style* requires the use of footnotes in addition to a bibliography at the end of a manuscript. The CMS publishes a manual that covers all the specifics of citations and bibliographical references, and it is available here: http://owl.english.purdue.edu/owl/resource/717/01/. Here are nine different types of sources and how they are to be cited using the CMS:

**Chicago Manual of Style (CMS)**
preferred reference manual for rhetorical studies

**American Psychological Association (APA)**
preferred reference manual for social scientific communication scholars

**Modern Language Association (MLA)**
a citation style used in disciplines within the liberal arts and humanities

### MAGAZINE/NEWSPAPER ARTICLE WITH SINGLE AUTHOR:

*Footnote*:

> 1. John A. Smith, "Proper Bibliographical Form," *U.S. News and World Report,* April 12, 2006, 30.

*Bibliography:*

> Smith, John A. "Proper Bibliographical Form." *U.S. News and World Report* vol. 189, issue 6 (12 April 2006): 30.

### MAGAZINE/NEWSPAPER ARTICLE WITH MULTIPLE AUTHORS:

*Footnote:*

> 2. John A. Smith and Joanne Doe, "Proper Bibliographical Form," *Financial Times of London*, June 1, 2000, 17.

*Bibliography:*

> Smith, John A. and Doe, Joanne. "Proper Bibliographical Form." *Financial Times of London* (1 June 2000): 17.

## MAGAZINE/NEWSPAPER ARTICLE WITH NO AUTHOR:

*Footnote:*

> 4. "Footnoting Correctly," *The Economist,* December 7, 1999, 19.

*Bibliography:*

> "Footnoting Correctly." *The Economist* (December 1999), 19-22.

## JOURNAL ARTICLE:

*Footnote:*

> 4. John Smith, "The Works Cited Page Is Awesome," *Geopolitics* 9, no. 4 (2002): 38.

*Bibliography:*

> Smith, John. "The Works Cited Page Is Awesome." *Geopolitics* 9, no. 4 (2002): 35-60.

## CHAPTER IN AN EDITED VOLUME:

*Footnote:*

> 5. John Smith, "Footnoting in Alphabetical Order," in *Proper Citations and Works Cited Pages,* edited by S. Clark, J. M. Thompson & P. L. Jones (Boulder, CO: Westview Press, 1987), 8-14.

*Bibliography:*

> Smith, John. "Footnoting in Alphabetical Order." In *Proper Citations and Works Cited Pages,* edited by S. Clark, J. M. Thompson & P. L. Jones. Boulder, CO: Westview Press, 1987. 8-14.

## BOOK:

*Footnote:*

> 6. John A. Smith, *The Value of Footnotes* (Wilmington, DE: Scholarly Resources, 1981), 212.

*Bibliography:*

> Smith, John A. *The Value of Footnotes.* Wilmington, DE: Scholarly Resources, 1981. 212

## WEBSITE:

*Footnote:*

> 7. "Health and Pregnancy," *WebMD,* http://www.webmd.com/baby/guide/amniocentesis.

*Bibliography:*

> "Health and Pregnancy." *WebMD.* http://www.webmd.com/baby/guide/amniocentesis.

## A LETTER TO THE EDITOR IN A NEWSPAPER:

*Bibliography:*

Smith, John. "Why I Love Citations." *Las Vegas Review-Journal* (14 August 2007): 12.

## GOVERNMENT REPORTS:

*Bibliography:*

U.S. Department of the Treasury. *Citations and Taxation, 2006.* Washington, DC: U.S. Government Printing Office, 2007.

> Note that there is a difference when citing a letter to the editor and any other article found in a newspaper. CMS also uses footnotes in the text, rather than parenthetical citations. These are identified by a number superscripted at the end of a sentence. Footnotes allow for the use of "ibid" which can be used in place of a full reference when the source is the same as the one in the previous citation. Additionally, if you have already used the full citation for a source in a previous footnote you need only list the author's last name and the page number on all subsequent references to that source. Of course this is just an abbreviated guide for CMS, but it should enable you to get started on citing material properly.

## American Psychological Association (APA)

Unlike the CMS, the APA uses in-text parenthetical citations instead of footnotes. These occur at the end of sentences or after an author's name that is referenced in the sentence. In the event the source does not have an identifiable author then it is referenced using a truncated form of the title and the year of publication. In this section we will offer some brief guidance for some common reference types using APA style. First, let's look at some examples of in-text citations using APA:

- One author, not directly quoted: (Smith, 1990)
- Multiple author, not directly quoted: (Smith, Jones & Thompson, 1998)
- With author, directly quoted: (Johnson, 1981, p. 242)
- Multiple author, not directly quoted: (Smith, Jones & Thompson, 1990, p. 461)

- Website with author, not directly quoted:  (Stevens, December 1, 2008)
- Website with no author, not directly quoted:  ("The sky is blue," April 2, 2003)
- Website with author, directly quoted: (Morris, June 1, 2001, para. 2)
- Website with no author, directly quoted: ("Great sea," February 2, 1991, para.1)

There are some idiosyncrasies to keep in mind as well.  For instance, if a work has more than six authors, you should use the last name of the first author and then the phrase "et al." to refer to the rest of the authors.  Additionally, if the authors name is written in the sentence then the parenthetical citation needs only to have the year or the year and page number if it is directly quoted from the source. Finally, when a works author is credited as "Anonymous" cite the word anonymous followed by the date in the parenthetical citation.

In addition to the in-text citations, APA calls for a "Reference List" page, which is conceptually the same as the Bibliography in the CMS.  Just as is the case with the CMS bibliography page, it is organized alphabetically and contains only the sources referenced within the project.  If there is no author, the title is treated as author when it comes to placing it in the proper alphabetical spot in the works cited list. Following are the APA forms of the same references used for the previous CMS examples:

### MAGAZINE/NEWSPAPER ARTICLE WITH SINGLE AUTHOR:

Smith, John. (2004 November 9).  Proper bibliographical form.  *The Toronto Star*, A8.

*Magazine articles only require the month, and not the specific date of publication, so they would appear (2004, November) in the above example.

### MAGAZINE/NEWSPAPER ARTICLE WITH MULTIPLE AUTHORS:

Smith, John, Johnson, Stephanie O. & Morris, Melvin.  (2000 January 21). Proper bibliographical form.  *Winnipeg Free Press*, A9.

### MAGAZINE/NEWSPAPER ARTICLE WITH NO AUTHOR:

The bibliography must be correct.  (1987 March 1).  *The New York Daily News*, A14.

### JOURNAL ARTICLE:

Smith, John. (1993).  Studies show bibliographies are easy to do. *European Journal of Communication, 19* (1), 89-114.

*Include the issue number only if the journal is paginated by issue.

**CHAPTER IN AN EDITED VOLUME:**

> Smith, John A. & Morris, Eugene. (2008). Bibliographies difficult to master. Tom Johnson, Cedric Phillips, and Maurice Jones (Eds.), In *Citing correctly,* pp. 101-121. New York, NY: Routledge.

**BOOK:**

> Jones, Bridget (2007). *The power of citing correctly.* Chicago, IL: University of Chicago Press.

**WEBSITE:**

> Simpson, Homer. (2007 April 1). A letter to John Smith. Retrieved on: January 12, 2008. http://www.xgtsfjmnouiyh.com/jstr/htm/070908

**A LETTER TO THE EDITOR FROM A NEWSPAPER:**

> Smith, John. (2008, June 1). Citations are important [Letter to the editor]. *Miami Herald,* p. A9.

**GOVERNMENT REPORTS:**

> S. Rep. No. 207-294, at 9 (2003).

Pay close attention to the capitalization and punctuation schemes in both APA and CMS as they can be tricky. Citations in either form allow readers and audience members to know where you found the information you used so they can verify it or even use it for their own work. It also is designed to give proper credit to the person whose ideas you are using. Personal interviews do not need to appear in either the CMS or APA reference pages, but must be cited in text by listing the initials and last name of the interviewee and as exact a date as possible for the interview.

## Modern Language Association (MLA)

The MLA is a third option for properly citing research within your outlines, manuscripts, or essays. It can be best described as a combination of both CMS and APA in many respects. For example, although footnotes and endnotes can be used to expound upon certain points in the text, the proper way to reference materials in the text is with parenthetical citations just like APA. Unlike APA, the MLA guidelines call for the page number in every parenthetical reference, not simply the ones where you attribute a direct quotation. Here are some examples of in-text citations using MLA guidelines:

- With author: (Smith 3)
- Multiple authors: (Smith, Jones and Thompson 15)
- Unknown author: ("Lakes and Mountains" 72)
- Website: (Stevens, "Lakes and Mountains")

In some ways MLA allows for a simpler method of citing sources within your outline or essay because it calls for the same information regardless of whether or not you used a direct quotation.

In addition to the in-text citations, MLA calls for a "Works Cited" page just like APA. It is organized alphabetically and contains only the sources referenced within the project, just like the bibliography in CMS and the "list of references" in APA. The "Works Cited" page for MLA, however, is closer to that of CMS's bibliography in terms of style. The following are the MLA forms of the same references used for the CMS and APA examples given above:

### MAGAZINE/NEWSPAPER ARTICLE WITH SINGLE AUTHOR:

Smith, John. "Proper bibliographical form." *The Toronto Star,* 9 Nov. 2004: A8. Print.

### MAGAZINE/NEWSPAPER ARTICLE WITH MULTIPLE AUTHORS:

Smith, John, Johnson, Stephanie O. & Morris, Melvin. "Proper bibliographical form." *Winnipeg Free Press,* 21 Jan. 2000: A9. Print.

### MAGAZINE/NEWSPAPER ARTICLE WITH NO AUTHOR:

"The bibliography must be correct." *The New York Daily News*, 1 March 1987: A14. Print.

### JOURNAL ARTICLE:

Smith, John. "Studies Show Bibliographies Are Easy to Do." *European Journal of Communication* 19.1 (1993): 89-114. Print.

### CHAPTER IN AN EDITED VOLUME:

Smith, John A. & Morris, Eugene. "Chapter 5." *Citing Correctly.* Eds. Tom Johnson, Cedric Phillips, and Maurice Jones. New York, NY: Routledge, 2008. 101-121. Print.

### BOOK:

Jones, Bridget. *The Power of Citing Correctly.* Chicago, IL: University of Chicago Press, 2007. Print.

### WEBSITE:

*Cool Stuff and Things.* East Western University, 2007. Web. 12 Jan. 2008.

### A LETTER TO THE EDITOR IN A NEWSPAPER:

Smith, John. "Citations are important." Letter. *Miami Herald.* 1 June 2008: A9. Print.

**GOVERNMENT REPORTS:**

United States. National Institute of Health. *Citations Are Good for You.*
DHHS Publication No. ADM 88-788867. Washington: GPO, 1998.
Print.

Notice that there are some aspects of the MLA works cited entries that make it unique. For instance, titles of articles are placed within quotation marks while names of journals, newspapers, books, and magazines are in italic. Also, with regard to journal entries, their volume and issue numbers are depicted using decimals rather than parentheses.

Each of these three citation styles have their place in academic work and under most circumstances you will be instructed as to which style to use. Your instructor may prefer one form, a journal or magazine may require another—but more often than not you will be informed as to which style to use. If you are not, then use the style you are most comfortable with, but be sure to use it consistently and accurately.

## *Verbal Attribution*

In a speech you not only need to cite sources within your manuscript or outline, but you must verbally do so as well. This is much easier than it sounds and helps you build credibility with your audience. Some common ways speakers verbally attribute sources is to preface the information being cited with "according to" or "so-and-so says," but here are a few more examples to use when constructing a speech that gives proper credit to source material:

- According to a recent Gallup Poll, Senator John McCain is seen as more knowledgeable on foreign policy than his opponent.

- In his book, *Perilous Times*, Dr. Geoffrey Stone argues that the First Amendment should not be suppressed during wartime.

- Some people, like Dr. Johann Strauss, argue the Motion Picture Association of America should think about the intentions of the moviemaker when rating films for public consumption.

- Many major league baseball players used steroids in the 1990s, according to the Mitchell Report produced by former Senator George Mitchell and his investigative team.

Each of these examples provides verbal attribution to the sources where the information was obtained. It is essential for a researcher to give credit like this when speaking because it helps the audience differentiate between the speaker's ideas and ideas that came from someone else.

## Summary

Selecting and narrowing your topic and research and preparation are the most important steps toward developing a successful speech. Proper research skills come from being an information literate person. Information literate people know what they need information for, where to go to find it, and how to use it properly, as well as the ethical implications of information use. It is important to make use of all the research tools at your disposal, from librarians to the Internet, when seeking different types of sources and information for your speech. It is equally important to use a consistent and accepted citation style when referencing material you have gathered from other places.

## Key Terms

accuracy   54

American Psychological Association (APA)   63

background information   57

bias   54

Chicago Manual of Style (CMS)   63

Communication/Mass Media Complete   59

Dewey Decimal Classification System   59

enkyklios paideia   48

evidentiary information   57

formal survey   60

ghostwriting   56

global plagiarism   56

incremental plagiarism   55

informal survey   60

information literacy   53

interviewing   60

JSTOR   59

Lexis-Nexis   59

Modern Language Association (MLA)   63

patchwork plagiarism   56

plagiarism   55

quadrivium   48

research question   50

tangential information   57

trivium   48

undercover interviewing   60

## Review Questions

1. What are the three ways you can find a topic?

2. What are the five characteristics of the information literate researcher?

3. What are the three primary forms of information?

4. What are the three main places to find source material?

5. What are the three major citation styles?

## Think About It

1. Is it ever ethical to employ undercover interviewing?

2. How do you determine whether you need to cite a piece of information?

3. Which reference style is better? Why?

1.  Sit down with a group of friends, classmates, or colleagues and brainstorm topics for speeches.  Each time a person introduces a statement about a topic they are interested in reframe it as a research question.  By the end of this discussion you should have a list of potential speech topics that are written as research questions rather than topic statements.

2.  Find a partner and go on a scavenger hunt for the following items:  a magazine article; a newspaper article; a government document; a peer reviewed journal article in communication studies; a documentary film; a news page from microfiche records; a survey result; a blog entry; and an interview transcript.  To complicate this activity, give yourself a topic that each item must relate to.  For instance, find one of each item related to the topic of the "Beatles musical invasion."

3.  Find a bibliography at the end of a journal article.  If it is in APA format, translate it into MLA and CMS style;  if it is in MLA style, change it to CMS and APA style; if it is in CMS style, reformat it into APA and MLA style.

## ENDNOTES

1.  Edward Alexander Parsons, *The Alexandrian Library* (Barking, Essex, England: Elsevier Publishing, 1952), 83-106.

2.  Ibid.

3.  Roy MacLeod, "Introduction: Alexandria in History and Myth," in *The Library of Alexandria: Centre of Learning in the Ancient World,* ed. Roy MacLeod (New York, NY: St. Martin's Press, 2000), 4-7.

4.  Randy Pausch with Jeffrey Zaslow, *The Last Lecture* (New York, NY: Hyperion Books, 2008).

5.  Erin Neff, "Gibbon's Speech Plagiarism: 15 Paragraphs Came from Copyrighted Talk by Alabama Woman," *Las Vegas Review Journal,* March 4, 2005.

6.  http://speeches.empireclub.org/61435/data?n=2  (accessed May 28, 2011).

# Delivery

- Discusses the elements of verbal delivery and ways to effectively use it when giving a speech
- Focuses on the various nuances of nonverbal styles and discusses the symbiotic relationship between nonverbal and verbal delivery
- Differentiates between the four main ways a speech is delivered

# **Practically**SPEAKING

In the 1986 movie, *Ferris Bueller's Day Off*, the economics teacher, played by Ben Stein, goes on a tirade about the economy when his students do not respond to questions. Using a lethargic delivery, Stein woefully makes his potentially vibrant points seem irrelevant, boring, and hard to focus upon. Stein uses the term "anyone?" 14 times during the entire scene.[1] While he is speaking the students in the class predictably fall asleep, put their heads down on desks, and stare off into the distance, daydreaming. Stein's portrayal of the dreadfully boring teacher emphasizes the importance of vocal and physical delivery when addressing an audience.

The combination of word repetition, vocal emphasis, and proper posture and gestures can add force and meaning to a speaker's words, but when delivered in a monotone voice with no energy, the rhetorical effect is minimal. In addition to no vocal variety, Stein's posture is lethargic, making him appear as bored as his students. He lacks presence, despite having content.

Verbal delivery works in tandem with nonverbal delivery. The verbal content of Stein's speech in this scene is clear, but the repeated begging for "anyone" to answer does nothing to get the audience's attention. His leaning posture and pleading facial expressions underscore his poor verbal delivery and only worsen matters. As illustrated by Stein, verbal and nonverbal delivery can display the speaker's attitude toward themselves and the audience.

Too much focus on delivery, however, can also produce problems. A powerful delivery can detract from content if the audience members focus more on delivery than content. Good delivery comes from practice and balances a desire to gain and maintain attention with the need to keep the audience focused on the message. Audiences do not notice good delivery, rather they remember the content conveyed without saying much about how the speaker conveyed it.

A speaker may have great ideas, a new way to do something, or a way to improve life on campus, but if the speaker mumbles, does not project his voice, fails to make eye contact, and does not present himself in a pleasing physical manner, the ideas will likely be lost upon the audience. All of us have seen, or delivered, a speech in an awkward manner. This makes not only the speaker feel uncomfortable, but can also cause anxiety and even mental pain in the audience, and that makes it doubtful that the audience will believe the information or take an action the speaker desires.

This chapter will cover the basics of good speech delivery, both verbal and nonverbal, and how the two work together. It will also provide some commonsense ways to improve delivery and discuss the four distinct ways a speaker can deliver a speech to an audience.

# VERBAL ELEMENTS OF DELIVERY

The most obvious aspect of public speaking is verbal delivery. Without a voice you cannot speak. That said, just because you have a voice does not mean verbal delivery is easy for you. In fact, mastering verbal delivery takes lots of practice even when you understand the fundamentals of verbal delivery. Those fundamentals include pronunciation and articulation. Both of those characteristics contribute to the development and use of different dialects and slang. In this part of the chapter we will cover each of those four aspects of verbal delivery and how they play a part in public speaking.

## Pronunciation and Articulation

Having a strong vocabulary depends upon two things: knowing the words, and being able to pronounce them. If you only know the words and cannot speak them properly then all you can do is listen to someone speak, inhibiting your ability to respond. If, on the other hand, you can also pronounce the words correctly, then you can become conversant in a particular language.

Proper word *pronunciation*, the accepted standard of how a word sounds, is very important to a speaker. It is one thing in casual conversation to mispronounce words, but quite another in a formal public speaking situation. Mispronouncing words sends a message of lack of preparation and creates the possible impression that the speaker is illiterate or not very bright. See Table 4.1 for a list of commonly mispronounced words.

**pronunciation**
the accepted standard of how a word sounds when spoken

We mispronounce words for a variety of reasons. Sometimes we learn how to say a word from hearing others say it first, except they may wrongly pronounce the word to begin with. Other times we try to speak too quickly, resulting in slips of the tongue on more complex words. Whatever the reason, speakers need to correctly pronounce words. Mispronunciation damages a speaker's credibility, the heart of a speaker's ethos. It might not be quite as big a deal in conversation or even in the classroom, but in the business world it can mean getting a job or making a sale—or not.

**Table 4.1**

| Most Commonly Mispronounced Words |
|---|
| The website yourdictionary.com lists 100 of the more commonly mispronounced words on its website.[2] Do you make any of these errors? The left column notes how these incorrectly pronounced words would be spelled. |

| Common Mispronunciation | Correct Pronunciation |
|---|---|
| anartic | Antarctic |
| aks | ask |
| calvary | cavalry |
| fedral | federal |
| hiarchy | hierarchy |
| irregardless | regardless |
| jewlry | jewelry |
| libel | liable |
| libary | library |
| nucular | nuclear |
| perogative | prerogative |

**articulation**
physically producing the sound needed to convey the word

Closely related to pronunciation is ***articulation***, or physically producing the sound needed to convey the word. In many cases we commit articulation errors by picking up bad habits from others through modeling; in other cases we are just plain lazy. Some of the more common articulation errors occur when speakers intermingle and blend two words together. For example, "I don't know" becomes "I dunno," "give me" is reduced to "gimme," or "would have" transforms into "woulda." There are more egregious articulation errors, such as running three words together like when "I bet you" becomes "Ibetcha." A speaker may get away with sloppy pronunciation and articulation in casual situations, but professional settings often demand correct speech.

## Dialects and Slang

People from different regions of the United States sound different when they speak, yet they speak the same language and communicate with general success. Anyone who travels to Boston will hear people articulate their "a's" as "ah's," and anyone who goes to states below the Mason-Dixon line will find people saying "y'all" rather than "you all." The latter of these two examples is often referred to as southern drawl due to the slower speech pattern.

**dialect**
aspects of articulation, grammar, vocabulary, and pronunciation that differ from Standard English

So, what are these differences and how do they occur? They are referred to as ***dialect***, or aspects of articulation, grammar, vocabulary, and pronunciation that differ from Standard English. The term "dialect" comes from the Ancient Greek term *dialektos,* meaning a tongue, or the language of a particular group of people that makes them distinct.

A dialect is a sort of subgroup of a language, and it can result in some miscommunication between a speaker and an audience when an audience is either unaware of or cannot decipher a speaker's dialect. As Sarah Trenholm notes: "Problems occur when one dialect is defined as the standard and given greater status than other dialects."[3] The important thing to remember is that dialects are regionally accepted errors of articulation and/or pronunciation, and one is not any better or more accurate than another.

Those who speak a particular dialect sometimes develop additions to the general standard vocabulary. In the case of Standard English, certain regions develop words and phrases that are understood by those who reside there, but not by those who do not. Over time these words are appropriated by the general population and become part of mainstream culture. When this happens the terms become *slang*, or words derived from dialects that most people understand but do not use in professional writing or speaking.

**slang**

words derived from dialects that most people understand but do not use in professional writing or speaking

Cultures usually develop their own forms of slang. Watch an old gangster movie and you will hear actors using terms such as "heater," "roscoe," "piece," or "rod" when referring to a weapon used to "bump off," "ice," or "whack" an enemy. If caught, the shooters might find themselves in "the big house." Each of these terms grew from a small part of society and infiltrated mainstream culture. The terms represented the language used by a subsection of Americans, and eventually they were immortalized in the movies and through other cultural experiences. At that point, the words no longer belonged to a particular group, but rather they became part of the general population.

Take the case of the word "ain't," which until recent versions of the Webster's Dictionary was not considered a word, but rather a slang pronunciation of the term "isn't." The use of the word "ain't" can even be seen in some landmark speeches in American history, such as the one delivered by Sojourner Truth at the Women's Convention in 1851 (see the nearby box).

Slang also is not cemented in society; that is to say, some terms may die over time. Think about the gangster example from the previous paragraph. Do you hear about people being sent to "the big house" for "bumping off someone" at the same level you might have 50 or 60 years ago? The answer is no, and the reason is that the usability of the terms as slang is dying out. Now you might hear that someone is "in the can" for "popping a cap" in someone. This phrasing, too, may leave common vernacular if it hasn't already!

Slang, although common, has no place in a professional setting or speech. For quite some time "that sucks" has been used to show displeasure, but carefully listen to how that sounds. Professionalism or intellect does not come to mind when we hear people use this phrase. The context surrounding a speech invites the use of Standard English, not slang.

# NONVERBAL ELEMENTS OF DELIVERY

In addition to verbal delivery, or the words you use, nonverbal delivery also aids in the transmission of messages to an audience and can, in fact, play a much larger role in the success of a speech. Nonverbal delivery can be broken down into two

### Ain't I a Woman?
### by Sojourner Truth

Delivered in 1851 at the Women's Convention in Akron, Ohio

Born Isabella Baumfree, Sojourner Truth was raised in slavery. She worked the fields as men did and suffered many physical abuses, including beatings at the hands of more than one slave master.[4] Truth eventually became a free woman and well-known minister. One memorable speech she delivered in this role was entitled "Ain't I a Woman."

The speech was short, especially by the standards of the day, clocking in at only 3,356 words, but nonetheless compelling. She made use of repetition in her address, specifically a phrase that included grammatical slang. The inclusion and repetition of that slang phrase enhanced the delivery of the speech. Take a look at the following excerpt:

"And ain't I a woman? Look at me! Look at my arm! I have ploughed and planted, and gathered into barns, and no man could head me! And ain't I a woman? I could work as much and eat as much as a man - when I could get it - and bear the lash as well! And ain't I a woman? I have borne thirteen children, and seen most all sold off to slavery, and when I cried out with my mother's grief, none but Jesus heard me! And ain't I a woman?"[5]

In this speech Truth brought issues such as race and gender to the forefront of her audience's minds. Given that it took place in 1851, these issues would remain important for the American public for years to come. When one considers the lack of rights that all women had at this time and then considers her race, Sojourner Truth's speech was certainly remarkable.

distinct areas: nonverbal elements related to voice, and nonverbal characteristics of the body. These aspects of your delivery serve several purposes when it comes to speaking, and a successful presentation incorporates good nonverbal delivery with strong verbal delivery. In this part of the chapter we will discuss the two types of nonverbal delivery and the functions of nonverbal delivery for public speakers.

## Vocalics

When people think of the nonverbal aspects of speech they focus on the body, but actually most nonverbal behaviors emanate from the voice. When we focus on how loud a person is, whether their voice is dull or nasally, and how fast or slow they speak, then we are looking at nonverbal actions. Think about it this way: are any of these things associated with pronunciation, articulation, or vocabulary? No, so therefore they are not categorized as elements of verbal delivery. We call these things a *vocalic*, or anything that contributes to the creation or maintenance of sound in a person's voice.

**vocalic**
•••••••
anything that contributes to the creation or maintenance of sound in a person's voice

One vocalic is the volume of a person's voice. Volume refers to how loud or soft a person's voice is when they speak, and controlling it is trickier than you may realize. Volume can be augmented or reduced based on environmental factors, such as the acoustics of a wall. The distance between the speaker and the audience and whether a microphone is available for use can also influence volume. If a voice is too loud then the audience may leave; if it is too soft they may not receive the speaker's message.

Each of us, at one time or another, has been an audience member when someone was speaking too softly and we had to strain to hear what the speaker was saying. At its best this is a distraction, but it may also be considered either lazy or rude. It can show shyness, anxiety, a lack of preparation, being unsure, or a speaker's lack of interest in being there. In all of these cases, if an audience cannot hear a speaker then the credibility of that speaker is damaged.

That does not mean that the speaker should shout at the audience. Rather, the speaker should use sufficient volume so that the person farthest from him can hear with ease. The size of the room can often influence your decision on how loud you must speak. If you are in a large room, especially one not having a microphone, it might be necessary to simply ask if everyone can comfortably hear you. If not, perhaps you speak louder or move closer to the audience to make sure everyone can hear you.

Volume alone does not constitute vocalics. Another element is *tone*, or the syllabic emphasis on a sound that expresses emotion or meaning. Think about our example from the beginning of the chapter. The tone of Ben Stein's character illustrates how speech that has no tonal inflection or variety can quickly lose an audience by conveying a lack of interest in the subject, audience, and occasion. Monotone deliveries can also quickly bore the audience and distract them from the purpose and goals of the speech itself. If you are excited about your speech, topic, and opportunity to speak to the audience it will be conveyed in your tone and make the speech all the more interesting to listen to for the audience.

**tone**
••••••
the syllabic emphasis on a sound that expresses emotion or meaning

Tone also expresses different emotions when you adjust it for specific words. Sarcasm is often conveyed through the use of a different tone of voice when making a statement that otherwise might mean something else. Think about the inflection in someone's voice when they respond to the question, "How are you doing today?" If they respond "fine" it could mean they are doing ok, but it can also intimate that they are not ok if the word is given a sharper, more cutting edge. This is when we might hear someone say that they "heard" some emotion in the person's voice. Tone is a nonverbal vocalic that expresses emotion.

Another aspect of vocalics is the rate at which you speak. The rate, or pace, of your speech can be the result of a variety of things. The average rate of speech in the United States is 150 words per minute.[6] This rate may vary by region. For example, people often observe that individuals from the Northeast speak much faster than those from the rest of the country, so culture can play a role in speech rate. It is also quite normal for a nervous speaker to speak more rapidly than someone who is comfortable.

Just as failing to speak loudly enough can communicate many negatives to the audience, speaking too rapidly can also communicate nervousness, a desire to just get the speech over with, and the perception that you are speaking directly off of notes. If you are worried about your rate of speech there are a few things you can do. You might want to audiotape yourself in a normal speaking situation or practicing your speech. If you have a concern that you might get caught up in the moment and begin to speak rapidly, you might want to put visual cues in your notes, such as a hand-drawn slow or stop sign on your speaking outline to remind you not to speak too fast.

One final element of vocalics is pausing. Pauses are normal, necessary, and, in many circumstances, useful tools. Professors use this tactic quite often to quell students talking among themselves in class. Pausing can be effectively used, as when you stop after making a point you want the audience to consider. They also can be effective for allowing the audience to catch up, and you yourself to catch a breath. They can even be used to recognize and subdue an unruly or rude audience. Consider this scenario: Some students are chatting among themselves during class, and the professor pauses and looks at the students until they stop. They stop because the students feel that the whole class's attention is on their conversation, resulting in them ending the rude behavior.

Pauses can be a powerful tool for any speaker, as they can help emphasize something of importance. After providing a compelling statistic, or story, a pause of a few seconds will alert the audience that something dramatic was just said, or is about to be stated. As with all other vocal qualities, the pause must seem natural and timing is crucial. Using pauses effectively is a skill you learn with practice, and they can be a distraction if you are not careful. Awkward pauses make the speaker look unprepared, unsure, or nervous.

Some speakers feel pressure to speak all the time, and thus they do not pause. Instead they fill the perceived void with a noise like "er," "um," "ah," and "uh" when they speak. These utterances have a variety of names, but generally they are called *vocalized pauses*. Even polished speakers can fall prey to this speaking irregularity. We have all seen speakers stammer and overuse these annoying pauses and inflections, and we realize how much they hurt the delivery of the speech. Kept at a bare minimum they may not be much of a problem, but as a speaker you should strive to limit their interfering with your speech's delivery.

## Kinesics

Your voice, although an important element, is not the only nonverbal aspect of your delivery. Your body also conveys information about credibility and emotions to the audience through facial expressions, gestures, posture, appearance, and eye contact, otherwise known as *kinesics*. These nonverbal behaviors are often the

**vocalized pauses**
utterances that are not words and have no place in a speech, but are done instead of pausing the delivery of the speech

**kinesics**
nonverbal behaviors related to movement

hardest to control, but when you learn to do so they can significantly impact your speech.

The face is often the first thing people notice about you in any situation, and speaking is no different. Your face expresses emotions and sends messages to the audience in a way that can either aid or damage your ability to get your message across to an audience. If you try to say something you do not believe in, your facial expressions will often give you away, but when you do believe what you are saying then it can illustrate your sincerity to the audience in a way no amount of evidence or list of credentials ever could. How you handle your facial expressions is important, but not nearly as challenging as determining what to do with other parts of your body.

One of the things speakers often struggle with when giving a presentation is what to do with their hands. Hands can be effective tools for a speaker, but they also can become unwanted distractions if not treated properly. Hands are the primary source of a *gesture*, or physical movements used to convey a message. Skilled speakers use their hands to complement their messages, pointing to people mentioned in a speech when possible, making forceful motions to emphasize a point, or even smiling when telling a joke.

**gesture**

a physical movement used to convey a message

**posture**

the position of your body

In addition to gestures, your posture is also important when trying to convey a message to an audience. *Posture* refers to the position of your body, and when it comes to public speaking it means more than simply facing the audience. If you lean over the podium or slouch behind it, your posture conveys a negative impression to the audience, just as it does when you stand rigidly and do not move. The key to good posture in delivery is being comfortable, yet confident. See the examples of good and bad posture in Figure 4.1.

**Figure 4.1**
**Examples of Bad Posture (top) and Good Posture (bottom)**

Having a comfortable and confident posture is related to the effective use of gestures. To maintain the ability to gesture effectively in a speech you should not keep your hands in your pockets, folded in front of you, or even held behind your back. These positions all negatively impact your posture by making you appear uncomfortable. Good posture is relaxed and allows you to make use of your hands when needed.

The next aspect of nonverbal communication we will discuss is appearance. Some professors require students to "dress up" when speaking, some do not. Even if you are not expected to wear more formal clothing you should always dress neatly, with your hair in place, and never wear a hat or cap. If you do not respect your own appearance your audience will not respect you and you will never be able to get your message across to them.

Appearance also can boost your self-confidence and help you feel successful even before you say a word. Consider how you feel when you have on your best clothes. We all feel more competent and confident in what we do. When you dress professionally for a presentation it often results in better actual and perceived performance. Appearance is especially important for speakers who address an audience that is unfamiliar with them, because the first impression the audience makes of the speaker is based on the speaker's appearance. See Table 4.2 for appearance tips.

**Table 4.2**

| Appearance Tips |
| --- |
| • Dress neatly |
| • Do not wear headgear |
| • Comb or brush your hair |
| • Overdress rather than underdress |

The last category of nonverbal action we will discuss is eye contact, perhaps the most feared nonverbal action undertaken by speakers. Novice speakers often get nervous when they realize they need to look at the audience during their presentation. This is understandable, but eye contact conveys confidence and interest in the audience, making it an indispensable aspect of any speech. One way to minimize the pressure created by eye contact is to look at a speech as a series of conversations. Instead of a speech consisting of you talking to a group of, for example, 25 people, view it as 25 individual one-on-one conversations. We typically are not afraid of individual conversations, and so we make eye contact with the other participant. Taking the same perspective on larger speaking engagements might help. In any event, eye contact, gestures, and posture all play a role in the delivery of a message to an audience.

## Functions of Nonverbal Communication in Speech

As individuals we send more nonverbal messages than verbal ones, and when we deliver speeches these nonverbal messages are under even greater scrutiny by an audience than they are in everyday interactions. As such, it is important for speakers to understand the various purposes their gestures, posture, and eye contact can serve with regard to their presentation. In this section we will look at the five positive ways nonverbal messages can influence perceptions of your speech, and the one negative role they could play in your delivery if you are not careful.

One way nonverbal actions can influence your message is by allowing you to reiterate your verbal message without saying it. When physical actions restate verbal messages in this manner, then nonverbal behaviors *repeat* their verbal counterparts. You can make use of this function by pointing to people in the audience as you reference them, or using your fingers to count along when listing certain items or points.

**repeat**
when physical actions restate verbal messages

Nonverbal messages can also amplify, or *accent,* your desired message. For example, when you wish to emphasize a point you can pound on the podium at the end of stating the point. When you get excited about something you are saying you can raise a fist in a mock sign of triumph. Not only do these behaviors support your message, but they increase its power and the likelihood the audience will understand your point.

**accent**
nonverbal behaviors that augment a verbal message

**complement**
when the action demonstrates the message contained in the verbal content

Nonverbal actions are most effective, however, when they *complement* the verbal message. This occurs when the nonverbal message is the same as the verbal message. A perfect model of this is when a speaker laughs at a joke he inserts into his speech. By laughing, he displays the action associated with the verbal content of the joke.

© Christopher Halloran/Shutterstock.com

Former President George W. Bush uses nonverbal communication to make a point during a speech

Facial expressions and body movement can also *substitute* for verbal content on occasion. A person who smiles after being introduced to speak does not necessarily need to state her enjoyment at being there as her smile conveys that message. When a speaker asks a question to which she (and no one else for that matter) knows the answer to, she may follow with a simple shrug of the shoulder instead of saying, "I don't know." These nonverbal actions substitute for verbal messages and can be effective ways to keep an audience's attention.

**substitute**
physical actions that take the place of verbal messages

One other positive function nonverbal messages perform is to *regulate* an interaction. During normal conversations nonverbal actions such as pauses and hand gestures can cue responses and comments from the other person. During speeches they serve much the same purpose, allowing an audience to know when they can ask questions, when they should clap, and when they should cheer. Speakers most often employ regulating nonverbal cues to indicate an end to the speech, or to help guide question and answer sessions.

**regulate**
nonverbal actions that help govern the course of a speech or interaction

On the downside, nonverbal cues that *conflict* can negatively influence your ability to get your message across. These occur when your message says one thing, but your body sends the opposite message. This underscores the importance for you as a student to select a topic you are interested in and care about when preparing a speech for class. If you choose a topic you do not care about, your body and vocal variety will betray you. It is extremely difficult to hide your true feelings about a topic or speech because of the prevalence of nonverbal communication in any speech.

**conflict**
nonverbal cues that convey a message that contradicts the verbal statements of the speaker

# MODES OF DELIVERY

Speech delivery encompasses more than verbal and nonverbal skills; it also refers to what style speakers use to deliver their messages to their audiences. Different contexts allow speakers the opportunity to bring different amounts of notes and preparation with them. There are four primary modes of speech delivery available, and in this part we will define and discuss each of them.

## Memorized Speeches

As you can recall from the chapter on classical Roman rhetoric at the beginning of the book, Cicero considered memory one of the five canons of rhetoric because during his time people considered memorizing a speech a characteristic of quality speech-making. Another famous Greek, Demosthenes, felt that the three most important parts of public speaking were "delivery, delivery, and delivery." Nowadays, a *memorized speech*, the likes of which Cicero and Demosthenes delivered, are rare thanks in large part to Teleprompters and the accepted practice of using notes during a speech. Nevertheless, students often believe instructors will force them to memorize their speeches before they deliver them, something that is often not the case.

**memorized speech**
when a speaker commits an entire speech to memory and delivers with no notes in front of him/her

Memorized speeches depend upon an intimate relationship between the speaker and the text. In addition to delivering the speech, the speakers must also author the speech well in advance. They must practice the speech, not just so they remember the exact phrasing, but also so they can pinpoint when to change their volume and tone and when to make gestures to help emphasize points.

Memorized speeches are typically only possible when there is significant advance notice for a presentation. The speakers then use that time to develop and practice the speech as much as possible so they can commit the words and timing of nonverbal actions to memory. These are, hands down, the most time-consuming speeches to deliver, and they also come with certain drawbacks.

One such pitfall of a memorized speech involves the speaker's inability to adjust her message to audience feedback. When delivering a memorized speech there is no margin for changing the wording based on a disinterested (or interested) audience. For example, if you deliver a memorized speech designed to persuade an audience to vote for a specific candidate and you notice at one point the audience expresses dissatisfaction with one of your arguments, as the speaker you cannot adjust or defend the point you made any further than what you memorized, thus inhibiting your ability to adapt to the occasion. Conversely, if the audience appears to really respond to one of your arguments, you also cannot adjust to capitalize on that excitement. In effect, with a memorized speech your speech is *it*.

A second, and potentially more dangerous, risk associated with memorized speeches relates to freezing up. You may extensively prepare and practice the speech beforehand, but when you get in front of the audience you might forget something, causing you to pause too long and lose your place. Such a mistake can cost you dearly as you have no notes to fall back on. The only way to salvage this

## SPOTLIGHTING THEORISTS: DEMOSTHENES

### Demosthenes (384–322 B.C.)

Considered one of the greatest of the Attic orators in Ancient Greece, Demosthenes reportedly gave his first speech in court arguing to receive what was left of his inheritance. He became a speechwriter and lawyer in Athens, and eventually became one of the leading voices in opposition to Philip II of Macedon and his son Alexander the Great. Demosthenes, like Socrates and Cicero, eventually died in the service of his principles. He took his own life rather than be arrested by Alexander's supporters. Many of his contemporaries lauded him and his contributions to oratory.

Praise for Demosthenes came from many corners of the classical world. Cicero, the father of the five canons of rhetoric, proclaimed Demosthenes the "perfect orator"[7] and Quintilian stated Demosthenes was "by far the most excellent"[8] of the Greek orators. Like Cicero, Demosthenes believed that speakers should be educated on what they talk about and therefore often declined to speak on subjects he had not studied before. Additionally, Demosthenes valued delivery (gestures) above rhetorical flourish and style, believing that these elements of a speech contributed more to its success.

To that end, stories tell of Demosthenes practicing his own speeches in unique fashion. One story tells that he practiced his speech in front of a roaring waterfall in order to work on projecting his voice. Another speaks of how he would practice his presentations with pebbles in his mouth to concentrate on improving his pronunciation and articulation of words. For Demosthenes, delivery truly represented the most important aspect of any speech.

type of brain freeze is to continue speaking at the next part of the speech you can recall. This will at least enable you to get back in some form of rhythm.

Thankfully, for beginning students memorized speeches are not typically expected as it takes extraordinary amounts of experience with public speaking to become comfortable with this type of delivery. On the opposite end of the spectrum, however, lie speeches most students want to deliver: ones where the entire speech is right in front of you when you present.

## Manuscript Speeches

Whereas most students fear the possibility of memorized speeches, they welcome the chance at delivering a *manuscript speech*. Manuscript speeches are commonplace today, although they may not seem to be so. Politicians frequently deliver them. When the president gives an address before Congress he speaks directly off of a Teleprompter; when he speaks from the Rose Garden he does so

**manuscript speech**
when a speaker has an entire speech written out word-for-word in front of him/her as s/he speaks

with the script right in front of him; and, when the president of your university or college speaks at a convocation or graduation he or she usually reads from a manuscript. Just because it is acceptable for a variety of occasions, however, does not mean it is the only, or even best, form of delivery.

Speaking off of a manuscript carries with it many positives for a speaker, particularly a newcomer to public address. You do not have to fear the freeze as you might with a memorized presentation. Your speech will come off as organized, or at least as organized as you made the manuscript. The opportunity to jump off the manuscript is possible, but it is constrained by the need to stay focused on your message. Finally, manuscript style speaking allows you to note where you need to make gestures and employ different nonverbal actions at moments during your speech. No wonder first-time speakers prefer the manuscript style!

Despite the enormous benefits afforded by manuscript style addresses, the form is not a panacea. Making adjustments to audience feedback, though possible, is extraordinarily difficult without experience. Additionally, there is a temptation to stare directly at the manuscript, reading to the audience, making you appear distant and disinterested in the audience—not to mention unable to gauge their reaction to what you say. Manuscript speeches invite speakers to focus on their script, and not the audience or their own gestures and reactions, making it hard to successfully incorporate effective and positive nonverbal communication into the presentation.

The main reason beginning speakers relish manuscript speaking is that it eliminates the freeze factor; however, it can also create a much less energetic speech and ultimately distance the speaker from the audience. There is a middle ground, however, between manuscript and memorized speeches and we will discuss that style next.

## Extemporaneous Speeches

**extemporaneous speech**

a speech delivered with notes but not the entire speech in front of the speaker

Since instructors do not normally expect memorized speeches, and yet typically do not allow students to deliver manuscript speeches, how then are most student speeches delivered? The answer is that most student speeches are an *extemporaneous speech*, or a speech delivered with notes but not the entire speech in front of the speaker. Extemporaneous speaking requires practice, much like memorized speeches, but also allows for speakers to have organized references in front of them in case they lose their place during the presentation. These speeches, much like the other two speeches discussed above, have positive and negative qualities of which every speaker needs to be aware.

The primary benefit of using notes instead of a full manuscript or memorized style of delivery is that you will have a more natural and fluid delivery. You can adapt to audience feedback and expound on or eliminate examples and points based upon the audience's reaction to what and how you are saying something. Your vocal inflections and physical gestures are not planned and therefore do not risk coming across as rigid and robotic, as in the other styles of delivery. When you stress an inflection of a word or syllable, or gesture in support of a particular statement, it comes from your emotions, not your guide, providing your audience with a perception of authenticity.

A secondary benefit of extemporaneous speaking is improved eye contact. This also helps improve natural delivery. With only notes in front of you it becomes possible to provide more eye contact to the audience, increasing your connection and identification with them, thus making you appear more believable. As we discussed earlier, eye contact is an essential part of any successful speech, and extemporaneous speaking allows you to make eye contact with the audience while also being able to check your notes if you lose your place.

As you can probably imagine, extemporaneous delivery depends upon two things: adequate practice and a strong organized set of notes. To deliver a believable address with only notes you must spend a significant amount of time practicing the speech. First, you practice with a full text draft, but over time you reduce it to a speaking outline where only direct quotations appear in full text form. This speaking outline comes from paring down a full sentence outline, and still retains the same structural format of the original, only with far fewer words and phrases. The process of drafting, practicing, and then constructing a speaking outline for use during the actual presentation takes a lot of time, but the payoff when you speak more than accounts for that investment.

The most significant obstacles to a successful extemporaneous speech involve creating an effective speaking outline and keeping your notes organized. Some people who deliver speeches off of notes use bullet lists or even note cards in their speech. Bullet lists are dangerous because they are not structured, and thus you can easily lose your place when staring back and forth at the list. Note cards can be problematic, especially if they are not numbered for their order of occurrence, because you might drop them or put them in an incorrect order, causing you to lose your place or get flustered when delivering the speech. These problems, however, can be minimized and even eliminated through extensive practice and preparation for the presentation. There are, however, some speeches that allow for little to no preparation.

## Impromptu Speeches

At one time or another in your life you will need to speak without any preparation, research, or notes. This unplanned, unprepared presentation is called an *impromptu speech*, and it can be as short as a minute or as long as 10, depending on the topic, speaker, and situation. This may also be the most nerve-racking type of speech. Even the most experienced orator will feel a bit jittery when called on to speak about something without any preparation.

**impromptu speech**
a presentation done with little or no preparation

When called upon to deliver impromptu remarks it is best to first collect your thoughts and quickly develop a mental outline of what you wish to say. Just because these speeches have no preparation time does not mean they should not be organized or logical. Two aspects are always handy when asked to deliver such remarks: the situation and the audience. Connecting your comments to both provides an easy way to focus your remarks.

Secretary of State Hillary Clinton delivers an impromptu speech at a press conference in Chappaqua, NY

©Marianne Campolongo/Shutterstock.com

One of the most common places where you may deliver impromptu remarks is during a celebratory event honoring someone or something. No one will warn you that you might speak, you will not have prepared for the moment, and you might be surprised at the opportunity, but remember to identify with the audience and the event. It may also behoove you to reference the fact that you had no idea you might be speaking, thus acknowledging to the audience the impromptu nature of the address. These are high stress speeches, but also often very short. Audiences also typically have lower expectations for impromptu speeches than they do for a planned presentation.

## SUMMARY

Delivery is a complicated and important element of any speech, and it is also the one part of public speaking that engenders the most fear in people. Delivery is divided into three parts, each with equal importance. The first is verbal delivery, which focuses on correctly speaking the language. The second part of delivery involves nonverbal actions, from vocal variety to physical gestures and posture. Finally, the style of presenting the material allows for memorizing a script, reading off a manuscript, blending the two to read off of notes, or delivering unplanned remarks. We must remember that presenting the speech is just as important (and complex) as planning it.

## KEY TERMS

accent   83

articulation   76

complement   83

conflict   83

dialect   76

extemporaneous speech   86

gesture   81

impromptu speech   87

kinesics   80

manuscript speech   85

memorized speech   84

posture   81

pronunciation   75

regulate   83

repeat   83

slang   77

substitute   83

tone   79

vocalic   79

vocalized pauses   80

## REVIEW QUESTIONS

1.   What are the two fundamentals of verbal delivery?

2.   What is the difference between dialects and slang?

3.   What are the two major nonverbal elements of delivery?

4.   What are the five functions of nonverbal communication in speech?

5.   What are the four types of speech delivery?

## THINK ABOUT IT

1.   How would you define great delivery?

2.   Which of the nonverbal characteristics of delivery is most important?

3.   How do you determine the proper relationship between nonverbal and verbal delivery?

## ACTIVITIES FOR ACTION

1.   Write down two sentences of average length about any particular topic; the content does not matter for this exercise.  Then, take a sheet of paper and cut it into six pieces.  On each sheet of paper write one of the following emotions:  angry, happy, sad, confused, excited, depressed.  Then, on the back of each sheet write a different emotion than the one on the front.  Ask a friend to pick a sheet of paper, then give them the sentences you wrote and ask them to say those sentences using the emotion on the top of the paper they selected.  Finally, ask them to convey the emotion on the other side of the paper without speaking.  See if you or others in the audience can accurately identify the emotions.

2.   Try saying the following tongue twisters as many times as you can in a row without any errors in pronunciation or articulation:  "Sally sells sea shells by the seashore;" "How can a clam cram in a clean cream can?" "The thirty three thieves thought that they thrilled the throne Thursday." "Picky people

pick Peter Pan peanut butter." And, if you really want a challenge: "Out in the pasture the nature watcher watches the catcher, while the catcher watches the pitcher who pitches the balls. Whether the temperature's up or whether the temperature's down, the nature watcher, the catcher, and the pitcher are always around. The pitcher pitches, the catcher catches, and the watcher watches. So whether the temperature rises or the temperature falls the nature watcher just watches the catcher who's watching the pitcher who's watching the balls."

3. We all know the challenge presented by vocalized pauses and the importance of limiting their occurrence. To practice speaking without using a vocalized pause have a friend time you speaking on any given topic as long as you can until you use a vocalized pause. The larger the audience the better for this exercise, as everyone starts listening for the vocalized pauses. The person who goes the longest wins.

# ENDNOTES

1. *Ferris Bueller's Day Off*, written and directed by John Hughes (Paramount Pictures, 1986).

2. http://www.yourdictionary.com/library/mispron.html (accessed June 10, 2008).

3. Sarah Trenholm, *Thinking Through Communication: An Introduction to the Study of Human Communication* (Boston, MA: Pearson Publishing, 2005).

4. http://www.lkwdpl.org/wihohio/trut-soj.htm.

5. http://www.feminist.com/resources/artspeech/genwom/sojour.htm.

6. http://www.ncvs.org/ncvs/tutorials/voiceprod/tutorial/quality.html (accessed June 9, 2008).

7. G. L. Hendrickson, trans., *Cicero: In Twenty Eight Volumes. Brutus, with an English Translation* (Harvard University Press, 1988), 41.

8. James J. Murphy, trans., *Quintilian: On the Teaching of Speaking and Writing* (Southern Illinois University Press, 1987), 136.

# Presentation Aids

In 1952 Adlai Stevenson won the Democratic Party's nomination for president only to run against Republican former General Dwight David Eisenhower, who had led the Allied Command in Europe in World War II. Eisenhower, immensely popular, won the election. Not one to give up easily, Stevenson again won his party's nomination in the 1956 Presidential election, but again lost to General Eisenhower. After the election, when asked if he had any wisdom to offer to other politicians, Stevenson replied: "Yes, never run against a war hero."[1]

Four years after his second defeat the public elected John F. Kennedy president, and the new chief executive appointed Stevenson ambassador to the United Nations. In the autumn of 1962 events of the Cold War between the United States and the Soviet Union put the two nations' already strained relationship in a tenuous position. In October 1962, American U2 spy planes flying over Cuba photographed the construction of Soviet missile silos capable of delivering nuclear warheads to U.S. soil. President Kennedy demanded that the USSR immediately cease construction and disassemble the structures. The Soviets denied their existence and continued to build the weapon sites. President Kennedy then ordered a naval quarantine of Cuba to prevent any more Soviet cargo reaching the island. He also ordered Ambassador Stevenson to confront Soviet Ambassador Valerian Zorin in front of the United Nations and present photographic proof of the offensive weapons.[2]

Ambassador Stevenson employed visual proof. Up until Stevenson's visit to the UN the United States and the Soviet Union were in a war of words. However, when Ambassador Stevenson provided visual the proof he added further evidence supporting the United States's claims, making them almost impossible to deny. Had these pictures not existed, what we now refer to as the Cuban Missile Crisis might have ended quite differently.

Presentation aids, also referred to as visual aids, can greatly assist speakers in getting their points across to audiences. Some speeches, depending upon the topic and/or speech purpose, naturally lend themselves to visual reinforcement, but not all speeches require presentation aids. As the speaker you need to carefully consider what your message is and what you want your audience to get from the speech. If presentation aids help you accomplish your goals, then use them; if not, leave them out.

In this chapter we will first discuss the various forms of presentation aids available for use in presentations. We will then explore the concept of visual communication in general and, specifically, how it applies to the construction of effective presentation aids. Finally, we will provide some suggestions for how to maximize the ability of presentation aids to enhance your speech.

# Presentation Aids

In this section we will cover traditional *presentation aids*, or visual devices used to assist a speaker in communicating ideas to the audience, such as models, graphs, charts, overheads, and objects. Next, we will discuss technological aids, such as videos and audio recordings, and Microsoft's PowerPoint. This section will end by discussing ways to combine both traditional and technological aids in a presentation.

**presentation aids**
visual devices used to assist a speaker in communicating ideas to the audience

## Traditional Aids

*Traditional aids*, or aids that do not apply electronic means to communicate ideas to the audience, have been employed by speakers for quite some time. They are usually basic but can still enhance a speaker's points and assist the audience in understanding and following a speech. For example, for decades teachers and college instructors have employed overhead projectors and transparencies to allow audiences to see diagrams, models, or even outlines of presentations. Doctors use life-sized skeletons to demonstrate parts of the human body to medical students and patients.

**traditional aids**
aids that do not apply electronic means to communicate ideas to the audience

Those skeletons are an example of a *model*, a to-scale device that depicts an actual object. To-scale models can be replicas of objects that are the same size as the original or proportionally larger or smaller than the original. Suppose a biology student, Michelle, is speaking on human cell structure. Michelle will obviously need a model thousands, if not millions, of times larger than an actual cell for her audience to realistically picture what she is talking about. On the other hand, Brittany, a pre-med major, is presenting a speech about the workings of the human heart. She may use a same-size model to illustrate how the heart works if the audience is small enough. Finally, suppose Seth, an aeronautics major, is planning to speak on how the physics process of lift allows an airplane to defy gravity. He will need to use a scaled down model of a plane to demonstrate how lift occurs because an actual plane would be too large to use.

**model**
a to-scale device that depicts an actual object

Models, though, are not the only types of presentation aids you might use in a speech. If you plan on using statistical data to support your points you might want to use a *graph*, a presentation device that indicates relationships found in numerical data. Audiences like statistics, since people value numbers and feel

**graph**
a presentation device that indicates relationships found in numerical data

that they can interpret numeric data easier than other forms of evidence. Think of how your academic life is explained by statistics; everything is numerically determined, from your GPA, to the number of course hours in a semester, to rising tuition and fees, to the cost of textbooks. You interpret and understand this data rather easily. Graphs make more complicated numeric data simpler to interpret by illustrating it to audiences in a visual manner.

Suppose Jodie, a Computer Science major, decides she wants to study how much time college students spend using various media. Jodie creates a self-report survey and distributes it to students in large lecture classes, asking them the percentage of time they spend using various media. Jodie's results are as follows: The students report spending 25% of their time watching TV/gaming; 20% on the Internet or using a computer; 30% on a cell phone talking/texting; and 25% on music. Jodie decides to make a bar graph for her research presentation (see Figure 5.1).

**Figure 5.1**
**Sample Bar Graph**

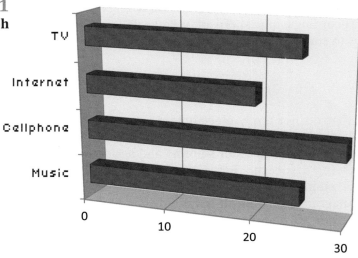

With this graph she can both verbally and visually explain to the audience how much time students spend with various media. In a speech, the graph, in addition to her verbal explanation, will make it easier for the audience to understand her point.

The bar graph used by Jodie is only one type of graph available to you. Another graph you could use to depict data is a pie graph. A pie graph works best when trying to illustrate how portions of a whole are allocated. For example, you attend a presentation by a retirement investment firm and a representative explains how you can diversify your investments in the firm's program. He shows you a graph like the one shown in Figure 5.2.

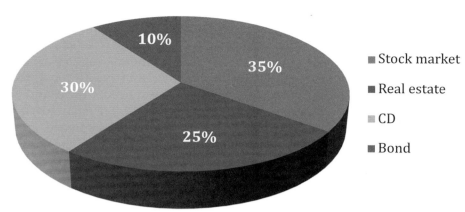

**Figure 5.2**
**Sample Pie Graph**

In this pie graph you can see that 35% of your investments are in the stock market, 25% in real estate, 30% in CDs, and 10% in bonds. The division of your money makes better sense when laid out in this visual manner.

Sometimes you need presentation aids to present lists of items to an audience. Under these circumstances the most effective presentation aid would be a *chart*, which is a visual device that helps you list and summarize blocks of information.

**chart**
a visual device that helps you summarize and/or list blocks of information

If you are delivering a speech about the relative economic strength of the United States to your economics class, you may wish to visually depict where the United States falls on the list of per capita wealth for nations around the world. To do this you could create a chart listing the richest countries, from highest to lowest (see Table 5.1).

**Table 5.1**

| Sample Chart | |
| --- | --- |
| Country | Per capita |
| 1.  Luxembourg | $55,100 |
| 2.  Norway | $37,800 |
| 3.  United States | $37,800 |
| 4.  San Marino | $34,600 |
| 5.  Switzerland | $32,700 |
| 6.  Denmark | $31,100 |
| 7.  Iceland | $30,900 |
| 8.  Austria | $30,000 |
| 9.  Canada | $29,800 |
| 10.  Ireland | $29,600[3] |

This chart makes it easy for you to explain where the United States fits in comparison to other countries in a way the audience can understand and is more likely to remember.

**transcencies**
..............
clear sheets containing
information illuminated
by a projector

Depending on the topic and what presentation equipment is available you may need to use overhead *transparencies*, which are clear sheets containing information illuminated by a projector. Some people consider this medium archaic. Though certainly not flashy, in some circumstances transparencies may be your only option. For example, even though classrooms around the country are being fitted with technology, there are still quite a few that do not have computers and digital projector equipment. In these rooms, using a transparency projector may be the best way to visually present material to the audience. Transparencies allow you to show, among other things, charts and graphs to your audience. Additionally, transparencies allow presenters to interact with material as they can draw and write on the transparency while speaking.

**object**
.......
a tangible item used
in conjunction with a
speech

Some speeches are made richer by the use of an *object*, which is a tangible item that supports and/or explains your speech topic. In a speech where you explain how to properly swing a golf club you can talk at length about the mechanics involved, but the best way to get your point across to an audience is to demonstrate the process to them. In this case you would need a golf club (and plenty of space!). You could stand in front of the audience and slowly go through each step using the golf club to illustrate certain aspects of the swing to the audience. Here, an object helps get your points across to the audience in a more effective way than simple description.

Pictures are yet another type of presentation aid that is available. Suppose you

are presenting a speech on the French Quarter in New Orleans. Pictures, if large enough to be seen, of locations such as St. Louis Cathedral, Bourbon Street, the French Market, and Cafe du Monde will help provide more concrete images for your audience of the places you are talking about. If your goal is to persuade the audience to donate time, money, or food to a homeless shelter, images of those who would be helped by those donations might increase the persuasive appeal of the speech. Pictures, as the saying goes, are sometimes worth a thousand words.

Photos of Bourbon Street (top) and the New Orleans skyline (bottom)

Traditional aids are not outdated; rather, they remain some of the most useful presentation aids available to you. Models, graphs, charts, transparencies, objects, and pictures all can assist you in your speech by simplifying complex information for your audience. Even with the advent of more advanced aids these traditional forms of assistance can still be effectively incorporated into your speech.

## Technological Aids

Technological advances have increased the number of available presentation aids for a speech. In this section we will discuss the distinctive qualities of these electronic presentation aids, beginning with video. In addition to video, audio recordings can also assist you when trying to get a point across to an audience. After covering video and audio we will discuss the program most people today erroneously believe is the only presentation aid available: PowerPoint. Finally, we will explore combining traditional and technological presentation aids in the same speech, an approach made possible thanks to technology.

Some speech topics are enhanced with the use of video. Videos can be movie clips, news stories, or cuts from homemade recordings. The key is that the clips are relevant to the speech topic and that they help explain or demonstrate a key point in the speech. Video also should be carefully planned and cued in advance so as not to take up too much of the speech's time or be overly distracting or possibly irrelevant. Earlier we talked about using a golf club as an object to assist you in demonstrating how to properly swing the club. Suppose you do not own a club or cannot demonstrate the swing due to an injury. You could find a film depiction of the most complicated step in the swing to visually illustrate the necessary movements to the audience. In this instance video becomes a very good aid for presenting complicated information to an audience. However, if you simply show a clip of a golfer from television and let it play for a long time with no explanation, then the video clip will do more harm than good to your speech.

If you just want the audience to hear something, an audio recording might be all you need. If you choose to speak to your audience about the hidden messages in old Beatles albums when played backward, you could find audio examples to play for the audience. Following the playing of those clips, you then could explain what was said and how the sounds got there. This exposure to the audio recording itself is far more effective than simply describing the curious messages. It also will enhance your ethos in much the same way the pictures did for Adlai Stevenson at the beginning of the chapter.

PowerPoint, Microsoft's presentation software, is a third technological aid that has become popular both for professors and students in the classroom. Professors can put their lecture outlines on the software and let it guide them and the class through the lecture. Some professors email or upload lecture notes and distribute them for their students in advance of class. PowerPoint, however, is most effective when it is used in conjunction with verbal messages.

To maximize the effectiveness of PowerPoint presentations you need to minimize a slide's ability to distract the audience. There should be just enough on each slide to enable the audience to keep up with the speaker, and rarely, if ever, should full sentences be crammed on a slide. When long sentences appear the audience tends to read the slide and ignore the speaker, defeating the purpose of presentation aids. Slides should be readable for everyone in the room listening to the speech, so fonts and colors must be adjusted accordingly. PowerPoint is one of the most effective programs for designing presentation aids that incorporate both traditional and technological aids. See the boxes that follow for an example of how to properly develop and use a PowerPoint presentation.

## DEVELOPING A POWERPOINT PRESENTATION

Earlier in this chapter we noted the popularity of Microsoft's PowerPoint in presentations. In this section we will demonstrate the visual theories and design principles in a practical application.

Suppose Hillary, an economics major, has decided to present an informative speech on the cost of college for students living on campus who use the school's dining plan. She does national research and then compares it to the results of a survey and interviews she has conducted. She finds students at her university have paid roughly the same amount as those in similar situations at other institutions.

She feels that since she has lists of items and statistics that the best way to present the info will be to carefully prepare a PowerPoint presentation. Hillary wants a slide that is a brief overview of her speech. She creates a slide for that purpose with a picture of a student union she found online. She picks a background color for her slides that matches her school's colors and chooses a font that is not distracting and is easy to read.

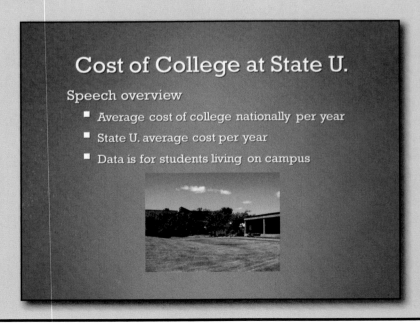

Hillary then creates a slide for information within the body of her speech. She wants it to be simple and easy to understand, so she places a chart on the slide. The chart depicts several expenses and their associated costs:

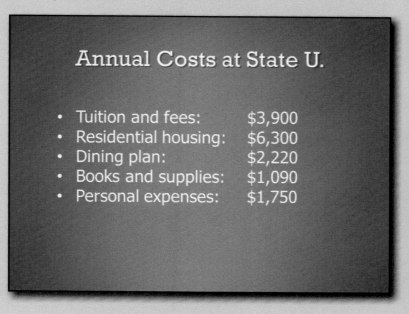

Hillary then creates a pie graph to reveal the percentage portions of each item on a chart.

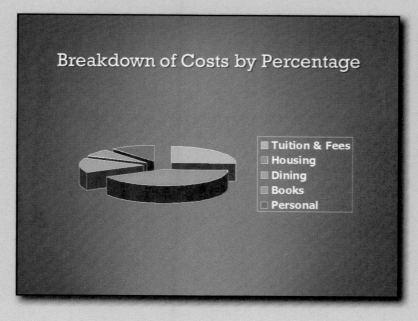

After creating that slide Hillary decides the form and depth are distracting and harder to understand than a more traditional approach, so she creates the following slide to explain the data:

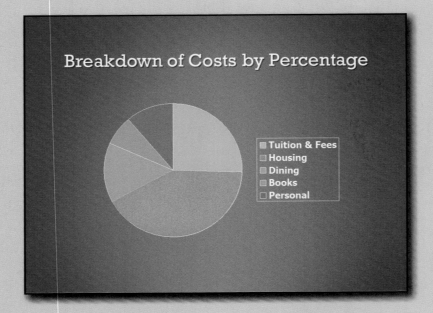

Hillary then goes on to create a final slide which summarizes her presentation. She feels comfortable that the four slides professionally and easily accomplish what she wants. In this example, Hillary has used proper form, depth, and color to create slides that provide enough information to make the message easier for the audience to understand, while not distracting from the speech's purpose.

PowerPoint is an extremely powerful tool; however, the software should be used with caution as the many capabilities it contains can be distracting. If you are taking a public speaking class then it is likely that your professor will give you some guidance on the use of presentation aids. Keep in mind that standards and expectations often differ among instructors. As such, any questions should be directed to the instructor teaching this course.

PowerPoint has custom templates, designs, fonts, and other features you can use to enhance your presentation. Unless otherwise instructed, use these features at a minimum. Using this software, you can choose to show the entire slide or sections of the slide either line by line or object by object. This may be advisable when making certain points. The software also allows you to use animation and to zoom, swivel on appearance, fly in, fade, and perform other actions (see Table 5.2). This can be a distraction, or even an annoyance, to audience members. Unless you are in a class that stresses creativity and artful display, approach these tools cautiously and, again, consult with your instructor.

When using PowerPoint, the use of a presentation clicker is advisable. Otherwise, this software can hinder your delivery by requiring you to stay by the computer's keyboard to transition between slides. A presentation clicker assists you with this and allows you to move around. In some locations, the computer may not be situated where you can center yourself before the audience, and the presentation clicker remedies this as well, as most clickers will accurately function several yards away. Plus, most clickers allow you to terminate the view if you so choose.

Finally, Microsoft's PowerPoint has an easy-to-use help function that can be accessed by pressing F1 on your keyboard. Typing in a topic typically leads to very usable information.

As technology has increasingly become a part of academics, students and professors now have the capability to deliver dynamic performances with a *multimedia presentation*, which combines and integrates video, audio, pictures, and notes into one medium. Not all topics are conducive to this presentation format, but when used effectively multimedia presentations can assist you in the delivery of difficult and complex material. Demonstrating knowledge of how to put together a multimedia presentation also enhances a speaker's ethos. You can use PowerPoint to craft multimedia presentation aids.

**multimedia presentation**

a presentation aid that combines and integrates video, audio, pictures, and notes into one medium

As noted above, you can use PowerPoint to incorporate animation into your slides. On the surface, this is a terrific new option when developing a presentation, but as with any presentation aid, you must be judicious in choosing when and what type of animation to use. Too much animation can distract the audience and make them pay attention to the slides and not you and your message. It is also important to be consistent in your use of animation. For example, if you wish to animate the title of each slide by making it "whoosh" onto the screen as you change slides, do so for *every* slide change, not just one. You can also use the animation function to illuminate a key part of a picture which can be very useful.

In the PowerPoint program there is a tab for animation options on each slide. There are 12 different options you can select from, each providing a unique movement for the text or image you place on the slide. See Table 5.2 for a description of each of the various animation options available in PowerPoint. Visual creativity through the use of animation can help make your presentation more dynamic if you implement it properly and practice with the animation tools you plan to use. Now, let's take a moment and discuss how you might actually use PowerPoint to get certain key concepts across to your audience in a dynamic fashion.

**Table 5.2**

| | PowerPoint Visual Effects |
|---|---|
| Appear | The text immediately appears |
| Fade | The text gradually appears in view |
| Fly in | The text quickly moves up into place from the bottom of the page |
| Float in | The text gradually moves into place |
| Split | The text begins to appear quickly from both sides of the word/phrase |
| Wipe | The text appears from the bottom of the word/phrase up to the top |
| Shape | The image appears to take form slowly on the slide |
| Wheel | The image appears slowly in a clockwise motion |
| Random bars | The image appears as if formed by the addition of various bars on top of each other |
| Grow and turn | The image moves from a distance to its place by turning on its side |
| Zoom | The image moves quickly from a distance into its place without turning |
| Swivel | The image turns three times before settling in its proper place |

Suppose you want to deliver a speech about the Center for Strategic International Studies (CSIS)[4] and its "Coming Seven Revolutions."[5] CSIS claims the seven coming revolutions are: population, resource management, technology, information flows, conflict, economic integration, and governance. You could use PowerPoint to integrate all the following: animated graphs that denote the rapid rise of the world population and grow accordingly while you speak; pictures to show pollution; video to show a clip from an interview with *The New York Times* columnist and author Thomas Friedman on economics; and a chart of the number of pirate attacks per year off the coast of Somalia. PowerPoint allows you to incorporate both traditional and technological presentation aids into the same presentation. To accomplish this type of presentation, however, requires quite a bit of familiarity with Microsoft's PowerPoint, so if you are new to the program be sure to give yourself plenty of time to develop your PowerPoint presentation and to practice your speech delivery.

In addition to familiarity with the software program, you also should be knowledgeable about the theories underpinning visual communication. In the next section we take some time to elaborate on the theories related to visual cues and design principles. These two concepts are of paramount importance when creating a presentation aid. Following that discussion, we provide some concrete suggestions and guidelines for effectively incorporating visual communication concepts into the development of successful presentation aids.

# VISUAL COMMUNICATION CONCEPTS

Thanks in part to television and the Internet, people increasingly are becoming visual creatures. We depend upon our eyes, oftentimes in deference to our other senses, to tell us about the world around us. Unfortunately, we all see things differently even if we seemingly see the same thing because we focus upon different stimuli. When we see something several things happen. First, we select a visual stimulus; next, we organize that stimulus in our brain so it makes sense to us, thus giving it meaning.[6] This process is how each of us develops our own *frame of reference,* or our own singular perspective of the world around us.[7]

**frame of reference**
our own singular perspective of the world around us

## Visual Theory and Practice

Due to the differences in our frames of reference you cannot assume that since you have presented visual evidence to an audience they will see it the same way you do. For that reason you must understand how to craft presentation aids in a way that takes the myriad perspectives in an audience into consideration. In this section of the chapter we will discuss the elements of visual depictions that can encourage particular meanings from audiences. We also will examine the principles of design associated with presentation aids to help you create effective images that will complement your speech.

### *Visual Cues*

Think about the things that often catch your eye. Colorful images are far more appealing than those that appear dull or even in black and white. An image's shape, or the shapes within a picture, also determine how attractive we consider something. Additionally, the details of the image might make us pay more attention. Finally, "active" images are more likely to gain our attention and maintain our interest. In this section we will discuss each of these visual cues, and how they might contribute to the development of an effective presentation aid.

**color pattern**
collection of hues in your presentation aids

The *color pattern,* or collection of hues in your presentation aids, should be pleasing to the audience and not distract them from your speech. There are six colors in the color spectrum: red, orange, yellow, green, blue, and indigo.[8] When you construct your aids, ensure that the colors you select for your visuals work together. For instance, when using PowerPoint do not use a yellow background with white lettering, as your audience will not be able to read your notes. But simply making out the words is not enough. When you use black lettering on a white background the audience will see what the words are, but such a color scheme does not illustrate creativity on your part. You also should test the colors you think work together, because sometimes they may appear effective on your monitor, but on a large projection screen they may bleed together and become hard for an audience to decipher.

**form**
how an item appears in terms of its representation, size, and texture

Colors are not the only visual cue you should consider when creating your presentation aids. If you plan to use models or objects consider their *form*, which is how they appear in terms of representation, size, and texture. Obviously, the item needs to be large enough, but it also has to resemble what it represents. For example, if you are discussing the plans for a new building in the center of town, you need to make sure the model you put together for a presentation aid is an accurate depiction of what the real building will look like. Grabbing any old model of a building will not do, as it will provide the audience with a visual that does not accurately depict your verbal explanation.

**depth**
the graphic nature of an item; involves both level of detail and the amount of background provided for the image

Your presentation aid also needs to take *depth*, or the graphic nature of an item, into consideration. Depth refers to both the level of detail you provide a visual image and the amount of background provided for the image. Take the model of the building we just talked about; you may want to be able to open and close the model to show the inside of the building and how it is designed. To do that you need to provide detail to each room in the model, giving it significant depth. Perhaps you also wish to show pictures of the proposed site of the building so the audience can get a clearer idea of how it might fit with its surroundings. Those pictures would provide greater background than a simple empty lot; they should be taken from a distance far enough away to show the buildings that would surround the new structure.

**movement**
appearance of or actual activity depicted with an image

One final visual cue to take into account is the level of action in the images you use. *Movement*, or the appearance of actual activity depicted with an image, can be effective if properly employed, but it can also be distracting if not crafted with care. Two ways in which movement can be distracting in PowerPoint presentations are through the use of the function that allows for words to "swim" on and off of slides and the creation of graphics such as exploding fireworks. Such movement may seem exciting, but in actuality it detracts from the overall message; audiences focus on the fireworks and moving words, instead of what you are saying. An example of a more effective use of movement is the use of pictures that illustrate people doing things instead of head shots or portraits.

Careful planning with visual cues can result in an effective presentation aid that successfully complements your speech. Color, form, depth, and movement are all important aspects of a presentation aid and, if you pay them proper attention, they can enhance your speech without being distracting. Visual cues represent only half the visual communication concepts relevant to developing effective presentation aids, however, as design principles must also be considered.

## Design Principles

Design principles generally, but not exclusively, concern media such as PowerPoint. These principles should guide you in developing a presentation aid that works together with your speech to effectively communicate your message. They concern where and when to implement the presentation aids, how to create aids that do not distract the audience from the speaker, and how to make sure all elements of the presentation aids complement each other and the speech.

# 5

When preparing presentation aids, you need to think about how the different elements of your presentation aid work together. To do this you must consider where to place items and how to arrange them so the audience sees something that makes sense and is appealing to the eye. This is often referred to as the design principle of *balance*, or the position of elements within the image. There are two types of balance. The first is *axial balance*, which is formal and strives for equal distribution of the elements of a visual so they do not appear tilted on one side of the image (see Figure 5.3). The second form of balance is *asymmetrical balance*, which emphasizes imbalance, thus creating an impression of stress, energy, and excitement (see Figure 5.4).[9] Oftentimes your topic dictates which type of balance you select for your presentation aid images.

**balance**
the positioning of elements within the image

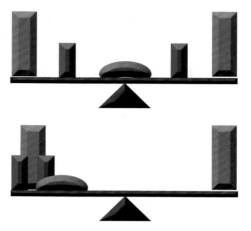

**Figure 5.3**
**Axial Balance**

**Figure 5.4**
**Asymmetrical Balance**

**axial balance**
formal balance that strives for equal distribution of the elements of a visual so they do not appear tilted on one side of the image

Suppose you wanted to deliver a speech on rap music. It is unlikely you would employ a strictly formal style because rap music feeds off of energy and excitement. Instead, you would create images using asymmetrical balance to create the impression of such energy for your audience. On the other hand, if you delivered a speech on how to change the oil in your car, the formal style would be more appropriate because chaos and excitement are not something you want to engender in your audience with such a topic.

**asymmetrical balance**
emphasizes imbalance thus creating an impression of stress, energy, and excitement

A second design principle to consider when developing presentation aids involves making images and wording work together effectively. You should integrate images and words so that what you want conveyed is in the foreground of the presentation aid, keeping the background simple. This idea is called *contrast*, or how objects and letters stick out from the background. You never want the audience to have to strain to interpret presentation aids; they should be easy to understand. As we mentioned above regarding color patterns, you should ensure that your colors go together well and do not clash or bleed as this will negatively impact the contrast. Additionally, if you are using a photograph or a video, make sure the background helps the image stand out by using a color like black to fill it in. This use of contrast helps direct the audience to focus on the video or photo, rather than the background.

**contrast**
how objects and letters stick out from the background

In addition to balance and contrast, presentation aids also need harmony. *Harmony* occurs when all parts and aspects of the presentation aid complement one another within the aid's framework. The color and image choices you select should work with and reflect the tone of the speech you deliver. For example, if you deliver a speech trying to persuade people to donate to breast cancer research, you may use pink wording on a blue or black background. Additionally, you might place a pink ribbon in the upper corner of each slide. These color and image schemes work in tandem with the message and augment the theme of your appeal. On the other hand, if you were to use black letters on a white background,

**harmony**
when all parts and aspects of the presentation aid complement one another within the aid's framework

## The iCloud Formal Announcement by Steve Jobs

Delivered June 6, 2011, at the Worldwide Development Conference, San Francisco, CA

Apple has been known for its technology for many years. From innovative desktop computers and easy-to-use laptops, to revolutionary developments like iPhones, iTunes, and iPads, the company is known for its technological wizardry. Steve Jobs, the well-known co-founder and chief executive officer of the corporation, was battling medical conditions when he appeared at the Worldwide Development Conference in June 2011 to announce Apple's latest product: the iCloud.

iCloud is an online storage device and a way to synchronize all Apple devices to enable the user to have common applications and programs on each device.[14] Such a complicated device required Jobs to use presentation aids to help his audience understand just what the iCloud could do. Appearing on a large stage, Jobs frequently moved around, talking as he walked, with a presentation clicker in his right hand. Behind him was a large dark blue wall with the images of Apple devices. As Jobs talked about the iCloud, he would change images, but the constant picture was of a cloud above each of the Apple devices he showed the audience.[15] Jobs showed the symbols for the three major features of electronic devices: mail, contacts, and calendars. He then used animation to switch between the symbols while showing data being synchronized automatically.[16]

The presentation was dynamic, informative, and made understandable through the use of creative presentation aids. It lasted only seven and a half minutes, but due to the presentation aids, the audience was fully informed of the power of Apple's newest technology.

or green on red, it would send a less forceful message and would not work with your appeal as well as the pink color scheme.

Proper choices for images also enhance the harmony of a visual aid. When the images represent the things you speak about it helps reinforce the message you send to the audience. For example, in June 2011 when Apple founder Steve Jobs announced the rollout of the iCloud, the company's latest product, he used images of a cloud covering all other Apple products to represent the iCloud itself, as well as the fact the product was meant to cover and integrate all of Apple's electronic platforms. Although it seems like an obvious choice, the use of a cloud image helped create harmony between the visual aid Jobs used, the topic of his speech, and the definition of what the product was meant to do.

Each of these three design principles can work to help you create artful and pleasing aids for your speech. After you decide which presentation aid fits your speech best, you can begin to construct it with a knowledge of how visual cues and design principles work. This will enable you to craft a creative and effective presentation aid that advances your speech. In the next part we will synthesize the chapter and provide some general guidelines for how to construct your presentation aids.

# DEVELOPING AND USING PRESENTATION AIDS

Theories drive application in a variety of fields, and visual communication and the development of presentation aids is no different. So far we have discussed the different types of presentation aids you can use during a speech and the theoretical ideas that should guide your creation of such presentation aids. In this part of the chapter we will first provide some tips and guidelines for constructing your presentation aids based on the relationship between aid types and visual communication concepts. We will then detail some tips and guidelines for how to effectively use your presentation aids during your speech.

## Guidelines for Presentation Aid Development

When putting your speech together it is advisable to think about and develop your aids as you prepare and structure the presentation. The power of presentation aids is that they can assist you in helping the audience to understand complicated and complex material. To maximize the effectiveness of your presentation aids, it is important to remember three rules when developing your aids in advance of your presentation: Parsimony, Practicality, and Practice.

First, presentation aids should make complex information simpler and easier to understand for the audience. To do this the presentation aid cannot be convoluted, extended, or extravagant; instead it should be parsimonious, or simple. A parsimonious image gets the point across to the audience without belaboring it or simply repeating the complexity of the concept in a different medium. As a rule of thumb, keep in mind *Occam's Razor*: "one should not increase, beyond what is necessary, the number of entities required to explain anything."[10] Put another way, all things being equal, the simplest explanation is the best explanation. Sir William of Occam was referring to verbal explanations, but the idea that the simplest is best applies to visual images just as well because when you use extraneous and unnecessary presentation aids you not only confuse your audience, but you also hurt your speaking credibility.

**Occam's Razor**
one should not increase, beyond what is necessary, the number of entities required to explain anything

You also should avoid creating distracting visuals. Complicated, extravagant presentation aids detract from the speech and cause the audience to focus on the aid and not the speech. As a general rule, paragraphs and full sentences are not advisable for placement on slides, as they keep the audience focused on something other than the speaker and the message. Pictures not directly related to the speech topic also keep audiences wondering about their purpose as a visual instead of keeping track of the speaker's argument.

**practicality**
the proper places within the speech (the where, when, and how) you can and should make use of presentation aids

Where parsimony calls for presentation aids to be simple, yet effective, and not distracting, *practicality* refers to the proper places within your speech—the where, when and how—you can and should make use of presentation aids. For instance, if you are speaking about the "Big Dig" transportation project that took place in Boston during the 1990s and early 21st century, then you might show pictures of the situation before the project began, then the blueprint of the plan the city enacted, and finally what the completion of the project looked like. These pictures could correspond with particular points of your speech and help the audience visualize what you are describing. As such, they would become practical. However, pictures of cars, buses, or even a large map of the area may not help you further your goals despite being tangentially relevant to the topic. When selecting your presentation aids, be practical about determining what the audience needs to see.

Finally, it is imperative that you practice your speech while using your presentation aids. This will enable you to become not only familiar but also comfortable with them. Work on making the references to presentation aids a seamless part of the speech until the motions and actions are natural to you. By seeming natural to you, they will also appear that way to your audience, and your presentation will be more effective.

In terms of practice, you should arrive at the speech location well in advance of the presentation if at all possible. This way you can make sure your presentation aids will work in the room in which you will speak. In many classrooms the computer and monitor are off to one side, not near the center of the room. Are you comfortable walking back and forth to change slides or pictures? If you are using PowerPoint or another computer assisted aid, be sure to have a backup plan in case something doesn't go as planned. If you saved your presentation to a disk, email it to yourself as well in case the computer cannot read the disk. Also, get to class early so you can save your presentation to the desktop before the class starts, thus making it easier to load it when it is time to give your speech.

Using presentation aids within a speech is more involved than simply creating an aid, showing up, and giving the speech. The presentation aid is a part of your speech, and so you should develop it in tandem with your speech. Keep the aids simple, choose the necessary moments in the speech to employ presentation aids, and practice using them with your speech. After you have practiced and feel comfortable with the whole speech, it is time to actually make the presentation.

## Using Presentation Aids During the Speech

Many times speakers incorrectly use presentation aids and damage their speech delivery. Some of this misuse stems from an individual not practicing his speech with the presentation aid in advance of the presentation. There are, however, other reasons for misuse. This section will provide you with some commonsense tips to help ensure you properly use your presentation aids during your presentation.

First, during your presentation you will need to reference your aids. For example, if you discuss statistics then you will likely use a table or graph of those statistics as a presentation aid. You will need to reference the trends it depicts so the audience sees the relationship. If you discuss the arrangement of the Gateway Arch in St.

## SPOTLIGHTING THEORISTS: WILLIAM OF OCCAM

**William of Occam (b. circa 1285–d. circa 1349)**

William of Occam was born around 1285 in the community of Ockham in Surrey, England. As a young man he joined the Franciscan Order of the Catholic Church and studied theology at Oxford University. During his course of study his theological views aggravated many of his instructors, preventing him from graduation. Pope John XXII eventually summoned him to the Papal Court in Avignon, France, in 1324 to discuss his controversial views on apostolic poverty.[11]

A former Oxford chancellor, Jogn Luterell, presented charges against William, but he was never condemned as he fled Avignon before the ruling could be announced. While living in a self-imposed exile in what we now call Germany, William of Occam wrote scathing criticisms against the papacy. He also wrote on the principle of parsimony, which became known as Occam's Razor. It stresses that we should keep things as simple as possible.[12]

William studied Aquinas and Aristotle and published many treatises on a wide range of subjects. His personal belief was that more is not necessarily better. In fact, he believed in using the least amount possible to achieve desired ends. He did not think that science needed multiple theories and hypotheses when one could explain what needed to be known. His ideas have continued to be valued by scientists, economists, and even politicians to this day. The best example of its recent application in political and popular culture is the popularity of the phrase "Keep it simple, stupid," or as James Carville famously opined in the 1992 presidential election, "It's the economy, stupid." William of Occam eventually died in exile around the year 1349.[13]

Louis you may need to point to particular features of the structure so the audience sees what you are talking about. Do not assume your audience will see things as you do and assume that presentation aids speak for themselves; they do not.

Many novice speakers also look at and talk to their presentation aid. Keep your eyes on the audience, not the aid, because when you look at the aid you lose your connection with the audience and you project your voice away from them, making it hard for them to hear you. Instead, refer to the aid and occasionally glance at it, but remember that the audience should be your primary focus. When referencing the aid you should also be clear about what is relevant in the aid itself; in other words, tell people what they should pay attention to. This can be done in several different ways:

- <u>This is a picture of</u> the site where engineers planned to build the Panama Canal.

- <u>Notice</u> the swamp-like area around the camps where the workers lived.

- <u>This is a bar graph representing</u> the number of students in each major; <u>the height of each bar</u> illustrates the number students in the major last year.
- <u>The legend indicates</u> that the area covered in yellow represents the land purchased in the Louisiana Purchase.

Another common mistake is the use of handouts as presentation aids. Handouts are not presentation aids and often work to distract an audience from the speaker. If you do use handouts, you will need enough copies for each audience member, and you should not distribute them until after you have finished speaking. Audience members are curious and if you provide them with a handout they will focus upon that and not upon you, thus leading them to miss the point of the presentation.

Finally, it is imperative that your listeners be able to clearly and easily see the presentation aid. Your presentation aid, whether it is a model or a PowerPoint slide, must be large enough for all to see. To ensure your entire audience can see the presentation aid you should go to the place where you will be speaking and see the size of the room. You also should try and get as much information on the estimated audience size as possible. That is easy in your class but when delivering an address at a business meeting, audience-size will be more difficult to measure. Finally, you should remember the principles of color and contrast to make sure the presentation aid is readable.

Presentation aids can be a great asset to you if used properly. For a summary of presentation aids "do's" and "don'ts", see Table 5.3.

**Table 5.3**

| Presentation Aids Checklist | |
|---|---|
| **Do** | **Don't** |
| Carefully prepare | Use if not needed |
| Practice | Talk to the aid |
| Make large enough for all to see | Focus on the aid |
| Make sure the technology works | Assume email will work |
| Have a backup plan | Assume technology is working |
| Make aids visually pleasing | Use slides as an outline |
| Keep it simple and relevant | Use as giant notecards |

## SUMMARY

Presentation aids can greatly enhance your speech. Keep in mind that there are many different kinds of aids, ranging from traditional to technological forms. Presentation aids must be pleasing, easy to understand, and relevant to your speech topic. You will need to practice them until you are fluid and comfortable with them as a part of your speech. Developing effective presentation aids takes time and effort, but the payoff can be immense when you deliver a presentation about something complicated to an audience and they walk away with an understanding of what you spoke about.

## REVIEW QUESTIONS

1. What are the two main types of presentation aids?

2. What are the six types of traditional presentation aids covered in the chapter?

3. What are the four types of visual cues?

4. What are the three design principles covered in the chapter?

5. What are the three rules to keep in mind when developing presentation aids?

## THINK ABOUT IT

1. When would a presentation aid possibly be a detriment to your speech?

2. How could you show emotion in a presentation aid?

3. How might a presentation aid be unethical?

## ACTIVITIES FOR ACTION

1. Take a look at some paintings and pictures and put them in two piles: those you like, and those you don't. Write a brief statement regarding why you either like or do not like the images. Then go through and determine if those you like and those you don't employ the same types of design principles.

2. Take a look at the text of a speech pre-1920 and make a list of ways in which the speech could have been improved using presentation aids. When the list is complete, choose one of the presentation ideas you came up with and create it. Then deliver the speech (without changing the text) using the visual aid. See if it actually does improve audience retention of the content of the speech.

# ENDNOTES

1.  "Stevenson, Adlai Ewing," http://etcweb.princeton.edu/CampusWWW/Companion/stevenson_adlai.html (accessed October 18, 2008).

2.  "Foreign Affairs, Cuban Missile Crisis, August 29-October 28, 1962," http://www.u-s-history.com/pages/h1736.html (accessed October 18, 2008).

3.  "Internet World Stat," http://www.internetworldstat.com/richest-countries-world.htm (accessed October 19, 2008).

4.  Center for Strategic International Studies, www.csis.org (accessed October 19, 2008).

5.  The Coming Seven Revolutions, www.7revs.org.

6.  David Moore and Francis Dwyer, *Visual Literacy: A Spectrum of Visual Learning* (Englewood Cliffs, NJ.: Education Technology Publications, 1994).

7.  Ibid., 35.

8.  Jeremy Vest, William Crowson, and Shannon Pocbran, *Web Design: An In-depth Guide to the Art and Techniques of Web Design* (Clifton Park, NY: Thomson, Delmar Learning, 2005).

9.  Asa Berger, *Seeing Is Believing: An Introduction to Visual Communication* (Mountain View, CA: Mayfield, Publishing Company), 56-57.

10. Principia Cybernetica Web, "Occam's Razor," http://pespmc1.vub.ac.be/occamraz.html (accessed October 25, 2008).

11. "Biography," http://wotug.ukc.ac.uk/parallel/www/occam/occam-bio.html (last accessed October 25, 2008).

12. Ibid (accessed October 25, 2008).

13. The Internet Encyclopedia of Philosophy, "William of Ockham, c.– 1280 – c. 1349," http://www.iep.utm.edu/o/ockham.htm (accessed October 25, 2008).

14. Steve Jobs at Worldwide Technology Conference: http://news.cnet.com/8301-13579_3-20068773-37/jobs-announces-apples-icloud-storage-service/ (accessed June 21, 2011).

15. Steve Jobs at Worldwide Technology Conference: http://news.cnet.com/1606-2_3-50105998.html (accessed June 21, 2011).

16. Ibid.

# The Speaking Environment

On March 19, 2003, President George W. Bush authorized the commencement of military operations against Iraq.[1] As one might expect when a superpower attacks a smaller nation, the war did not last very long. In fact, less than two months later, on May 1, 2003, Bush made a very public announcement that major combat operations against Iraq had concluded.[2] Bush did not just employ words when constructing this message, he also carefully choreographed and designed the setting where he gave the speech—right down to the outfit he wore.

President Bush arriving on the
USS Abraham Lincoln, May 2003

President Bush announced the end of major combat operations on May 1, 2003, aboard the USS Abraham Lincoln, a U.S. aircraft carrier at sea just off the coast of San Diego, California. The very name of the aircraft carrier from which he delivered the address elicits a specific impression regarding the mission. President Lincoln fought a war that freed African Americans from slavery, while Bush argued one of the primary reasons the United States invaded Iraq was to free an oppressed people from a vicious dictator. In fact, on the carrier he even stated, "We have fought for the cause of liberty."[3] Making that statement on a carrier named for arguably the greatest president in American history who fought for a similar goal cast Bush and the mission in a positive light. The stage, as it were, worked in tandem with the president's speech.

Another aspect of the setting of the speech is worth noting. In what is now an often-used punch-line, Bush arrived on the carrier by a military jet, an S-3B Viking, in a naval flight suit. Both of these elaborate elements of the scene attempted to portray Bush as a strong military leader. The jet arrival and flight suit both sought to create an image of Bush on the front lines with the personnel in Iraq, even though he was thousands of miles from them.[4]

The effects of Bush's declaration of an end to major combat operations in Iraq are not the concern of this chapter; rather his use of everything from apparel to the environment to his audience in an effort to enhance his speech are our focus. Speakers must marshal more than colorful language and strong physical delivery to give a successful speech. They also must pay attention to, manage, and, whenever possible, incorporate the context of their speech into their message to maximize success. This chapter sets out to explain the important relationship between scene and speech.

We begin by exploring the different types of speech environments you may encounter and discuss the opportunities and challenges inherent in each. We then move to a discussion of speech as spectacle, or the idea that speeches are carefully crafted moments, much like President Bush's address. Finally, we provide some tips for how to prepare and convey your speech in a way that integrates the scene into your message construction and delivery.

# The Speech Environment/Situational Speaking

There are four major elements of a speaking situation that speakers must be aware of when preparing and delivering their message. The first is the medium, or the setting through which a presentation is delivered. Each setting contains different opportunities and challenges for which speakers must prepare. The second involves the tools available for the presentation as these may influence parts of your physical delivery. Next, the layout of the dais is also essential for a speaker to know when delivering a presentation. Finally, dress code and apparel for the speaker and audience also can play a pivotal role in any presentation. This section of the chapter breaks down these four aspects of the speaking situation so you can better understand everything involved in delivering an effective public address.

## The Speech-Making Medium

Deciding how to disseminate a message plays a sizable part in the development and delivery of a speech. Traditionally, speakers take the physical setting of their speech into mind when preparing their presentations. Is it a small room, or a large auditorium? Will there be 10 people, or 200? Will the speech be outdoors, or indoors? Will it be a group presentation or will you be speaking as an individual? These are common questions when confronting speaking situations in a traditional format. The Ancient Greeks and students today all ask these seemingly basic questions about location. Today, however, we have more media through which we can deliver speeches. We can videotape presentations, upload speeches to YouTube, and even give face-to-face presentations through Skype. These more contemporary venues and the more traditional formats present their own sets of unique opportunities and obstacles. In this part of the chapter we will discuss the differences between these speaking environments.

## Traditional Speaking Situations

Traditional speaking situations are traditional because they have existed throughout history; as such, they are the most common type of speaking format. In Ancient Greece teachers like the Sophists often held "class" in parks or on the streets; Augustine of Hippo argued for the use of speech to help people find God through what we now recognize as sermons; and business leaders today give sales presentations, year-end reports, and five-year strategic plans at conferences. Traditional speaking situations contain two types of variables we will discuss in this part of the chapter. First, we will discuss the dynamics of a traditional group presentation, which is a second option for delivering a presentation as opposed to individual speeches. Group speeches can take place in the same locations as individual presentations, but they are done differently. We will briefly explain those variations, and then cover the different characteristics of the locations in which these speeches typically take place.

## Group Presentation Dynamics

Individual speeches are not the only type of presentation you may find yourself delivering. Often you may be called upon to work with a group to present a complicated topic to an audience. Businesses often employ this practice when giving a sales presentation, for example. This may seem complicated, but in actuality a group presentation follows the same general rules as an individual speech in terms of organization, structure, delivery, and source citation. In this section we will describe two general approaches to designing and delivering a group presentation that will help to ensure the talk follows those basic principles.

**moderator approach**
......
a way of delivering a group presentation whereby one person acts as the coordinator of the discussion flow and ensures a civil, organized, and complete delivery of information to the audience

The first approach is called a ***moderator approach***, whereby one person acts as the coordinator of the discussion flow and ensures a civil, organized, and complete delivery of information to the audience. This person previews the entire presentation by briefly explaining the topic and what each subsequent speaker will discuss. For example, Jamie is tasked with introducing her group's presentation on reality television shows to the class. Jamie begins by explaining that she will cover the origins of the phenomenon, followed by Sam, who will detail the most popular reality show of all time, *Survivor*. She then says that after Sam, Donna will describe the different types of shows on television today, and that she will be followed by Winston, who will offer an update and projection of where reality television is headed in the future. By previewing the entire speech, Jamie has effectively delivered the introduction to the entire presentation.

**bookend approach**
......
a version of the moderator approach whereby the first speaker in a group presentation is also the last speaker, providing both the introduction and conclusion for the group

The moderator approach is not the only effective way of designing and delivering a group speech, however, as there is also the ***bookend approach***. The bookend approach to group presentations involves the first speaker also being the last speaker of the presentation. So, in the case of Jamie and her group, Jamie would provide a summary of the group's presentation after Winston, providing a sense of closure to the talk. This puts more responsibility on the first speaker but can also be a more dynamic approach depending on each speaker's abilities and knowledge of the material.

There are other models for group presentations, and often the topic and the environment determine the approach you should take. It is important to remember, though, that regardless of how you structure the group presentation there are certain things to keep in mind. First, it is imperative to practice as a group and not as individuals. A group presentation is more than the sum of its parts, and if you do not practice together to develop a fluid presentation the audience will be able to tell. In addition to practicing the group should also ensure there is a clear and consistent way of transitioning between the speakers. These transitions should help link the topics of each speaker together and remind the audience of the common focus of the talk. Finally, much like in an individual speech, remember that maintaining a comfortable, clear, and dynamic delivery is also essential for a successful presentation.

Group presentations and individual speeches both take place in the same locations. In the next section we will describe these different possible locations and what you must take into account in each when preparing to speak to an audience about a topic.

## *Speech Locations*

The first location we will discuss is one you are most likely familiar with: a small room. Small rooms encompass everything from a boardroom to a conference room to a classroom. Smaller rooms usually have standard *acoustics* where your voice will echo off walls, thus increasing the perceived volume of your voice. These settings are also more intimate and allow for more opportunities for

**acoustics**
the way sound travels in a room

speakers to interact with their audience. In these situations audiences tend to be more receptive to speakers who move around the audience, sit down to deliver their speeches, or address specific people in the audience with comments or questions.

Because the dynamic created in small room atmospheres makes a speaker seem closer to the audience, there are also some potential challenges. In settings like this audiences typically expect speakers to be much more extemporaneous in their speaking styles than normal addresses. Speakers need to be very comfortable with their material to make the most out of this environment. This is not necessary, however, in much larger settings like ballrooms.

Larger rooms do not allow for the intimacy of smaller rooms because the speaker and audience are more often than not separated from each other by physical

barriers, and the sheer number of audience members precludes any substantive interaction between the two. This means that manuscript speeches are more the norm in this environment, but it also means there is more pressure on the speaker for a solid delivery. The intimacy in smaller rooms encourages more audience attention, but in larger rooms where the audience is bigger it is harder to keep attention. Speakers, therefore, must maintain a strong and consistent variety in the tone, pitch, and volume of their voice. The acoustics in large rooms vary more than in smaller classrooms, but they are not as unpredictable as in the case of outdoor speeches.

Outdoor speeches, like the one by President Bush at the beginning of the chapter, are very unique. They can occur in a variety of different formats like amphitheatres,

stadiums, or parks. Most students are not expected to deliver outdoor speeches in their classes, but they are nonetheless important to understand. When speaking outside, the number of distractions and the level of interference also tend to increase. Noises like airplanes overhead, wind, and passing cars are just a few examples of things that can interfere with an audience's ability to hear and focus on an outdoor speech.

Weather can also impact an outdoor speech. For example, William Henry Harrison was elected president in 1841 and delivered his inaugural address outside in a bitterly cold snowstorm. It also was the longest inaugural address in history, clocking in at one hour and forty-five minutes. It's no wonder he died in office less than one month after this address. Speakers need to recognize that there are a variety of environmental factors that can influence them, their audience, and their message when giving an outdoor presentation. On the other hand, outdoor speeches also allow for speakers to use environmental cues to reinforce their message, in much the same way President Bush tried to do with the aircraft carrier setting.

The issue of where and how speeches take place has been further complicated by developments in technology. These changes allow for speeches to reach a wider audience. They also create the opportunity to deliver a speech with no immediate audience present for the speaker. Next, we will explore aspects of several different contemporary mediated speaking situations.

## Mediated Speaking Situations

Until the early twentieth century, location considerations for delivering a speech remained restricted to a small room, a large room, or outdoors. However, this all began to change in the late nineteenth century when Alexander Graham Bell patented the telephone. This technological development led to other advances in communication, such as in 1906 when Canadian inventor Reginald Fessenden broadcast the first radio program.

American promoter Lee De Forest augmented the use and notoriety of those radio broadcasts when he transmitted a performance from the New York Metropolitan

## SPOTLIGHTING THEORISTS: MARSHALL MCLUHAN

**Marshall McLuhan (1911–1980)**
Media analyst and theorist Marshall McLuhan was born in Edmonton, Alberta, Canada, on July 11, 1911. He earned a B.A. and an M.A. at both the University of Manitoba and Cambridge University. He taught at, among other places, the University of Wisconsin-Madison and St. Louis University.[5]

In 1963 the president of the University of Toronto appointed McLuhan to develop a Center for Culture and Technology.[6] The center studied the relationship between technology, media, and human cognition. McLuhan had many other

appointments in business and government throughout his storied career. In addition to these jobs, McLuhan wrote *Understanding Media: The Extension of Man*, which challenged the assumptions many had of media and its uses and powers in a technologically advancing society.[7] He was also concerned with the consequences of media on society. McLuhan is perhaps best known and remembered for the statement "the medium is the message."[8] This phrase is used in various contexts in academe, including, but not limited to, media studies, rhetorical studies, film studies, and English.

---

Opera House several years later. Although not speeches, politicians quickly noticed the viability of radio as a format for delivering speeches to larger public audiences than they could muster on whistle-stop tours of the country. For over 2,000 years humans could deliver speeches only to an immediate audience; however, in the century since radio changed the scope and size of an audience technology has progressed exponentially and drastically impacted the situations in which speakers find themselves. For the purposes of speech and presentation, we will discuss two different forms of mediated speaking environments and how they combine elements of traditional situations with a more technologically advanced medium.

The first mediated speaking situation that you may encounter is over a *conference call*. Conference calls occur when more than two parties are on the same phone call. This approach grew directly out of Bell's telephone and has allowed businesses to sell products and exchange ideas with interested clients across great distances at low cost. Conference call presentations come with several considerations for speakers.

**conference call**
use of the telephone to connect more than two parties on the same phone call

First, a presenter can (and in most cases should) be introduced to those in the audience on the other end of the call by asking each to say hello. This makes personalizing your message easier by immediately identifying with people on the other end of the call. Second, speakers must pay attention to the structure of their presentation because, without visual aids or even nonverbal aspects of a message (outside of tone of voice), audiences will closely follow the content of the message and the logic behind its organization.

Finally, conference calls present unique types of interference that may disrupt the delivery of the presentation. People may try to speak over the presenters; audience members may try to interrupt the speakers; the call may have electronic feedback, making it hard to hear the speakers; or the call may be dropped entirely. Just think of the *Verizon Wireless* commercial where the technician constantly asks, "Can you hear me now?" If dropped calls were not a concern, this question and advertising campaign would make no sense!

The second mediated speaking situation we will discuss involves an extension of conference calling: ***video conferencing***. Video conferencing involves the live

**video conferencing**
live transmission of the video and audio of a presenter who is in one place to an audience in another place

transmission of video and audio of a presenter in one place to an audience in another place entirely. This is becoming more and more common, not just in business, but in our daily lives. A popular and free program that allows for video conferencing is Skype, a way of making video conference calls through the web. Businesses use other similar programs that utilize the same technology to give presentations to clients, just like you may use Skype to keep in touch with family and friends. There are obvious technological issues you may encounter when using video conference technology, such as losing the connection, poor image resolution, feedback from microphones, and, most problematic for presentations, lack of attention to the immediate environment in which the speech is being delivered.

Video conferencing is done through the use of a camera, which naturally restricts the line of vision for the audience. A presentation through this type of medium requires speakers to know what will be behind them, and what will be in front of them and to make sure the overall image of the environment they are in communicates exactly what they desire. One advantage to video conferencing is that often the speaker has a limited, or even nonexistent, immediate audience and this may reduce anxiety. That said, it is a live performance, and so the attention to detail and principles of preparation and practice must still be followed in order to have a successful speech.

Whereas video conferencing is live, modern technology also gives us the ability to record and upload presentations to the web. Speaking in this online environment combines elements of traditional speaking situations, conference calling, and video conferencing, but it also creates more things of which speakers should be aware. These uploaded speeches may have taken place in small rooms, large rooms, or even outdoors, and so the constraints of these locations still apply when taping a speech to upload to the web. There also may be interference issues with regard to the audio/video equipment that can make it more difficult to hear what is being said. Attention to detail is also important, in that the frame of the picture being taped should be controlled as best as possible. It would appear unprofessional and not be as effective, for example, if a taped speech were to take place in a dorm room where papers, books, and clothing were strewn all around the background!

Take care that the scene around you is what you want people to see when viewing the taped speech. This is especially important when uploading a speech because you never know who is taping and who will be watching later. A cautionary tale lies in the story of Phil Davison, a candidate in 2010 for Stark County Treasurer in Ohio. Someone taped Davison's speech delivered to the Stark County Republican Party seeking the nomination for County Treasurer, and his awkward performance quickly became a web sensation—much to his embarrassment! In fact, his video was noticed by comedian Daniel Tosh, who did a bit on his show *Tosh.0* where he offered Davison a chance to deliver the speech again, albeit with some comedic twists. The lessons here are twofold: first, make sure you practice your speech because you never know who may tape it; and second, anytime your speech is taped understand that if it is uploaded to the web it may never disappear!

Later in the chapter we will offer more specific advice for taking advantage of the scene and media when delivering a speech, but for now just remember that despite advances in technology, the instructions for good speeches taught 2,000 years ago have not changed much. In the next section we talk about the tools you have at your disposal as a speaker that contribute to the overall speaking environment, whether it is traditional or mediated.

## Speaking Tools

There are four elements of a speaking scene that can be considered tools. Much like a hammer, these tools can be very effective if used properly, but they can also destroy a speech if carelessly employed. The first, and most common, of these speaking tools is a microphone.

A microphone is most appropriate in either a large room or outdoor setting because it can help overcome the obstacles presented in those situations by augmenting the volume of your voice. Microphones are not always available, and when they are they often take different forms. Microphones can be attached to your lapel, be a wireless box latched to  your person, be set in to the podium or speaking stand, or even be a part of your computer when video conferencing. Some microphones allow mobility, but make sure you do not wander too far as you might pull the cord from the wall. Also, always assume the microphone is active and broadcasting. Just look at Donald Trump and his expletive-ridden tirade in early 2011 for the most recent example of a celebrity or politician caught saying something when they thought the microphone was off!

A second tool is the place from which you speak, and it is divided into two components. The first is the **podium**, which speakers can stand on to raise them above the audience. Podia are useful because they elevate speakers and help the entire audience see them. Where there is a podium there is usually a **lectern** or raised surface from which speakers read materials. Lecterns can also be used for emphasis in that pounding them can help the speaker exhibit emotion and make a strong point. They also provide a surface to store items you may be using as visual aids or examples. If you are taping a speech and speaking from a lectern or on a podium, make sure that the video focuses more on you than the lectern. In any event, podia and lecterns are useful elements of the speaking environment when utilized correctly.

**podium**
a platform used to raise the speaker higher

**lectern**
a reading desk affixed to a stand

Finally, there is lighting, an often overlooked element of the speaking environment. Lighting affects both outside and inside speeches, with the only difference being that you have more control over indoor lighting. Outdoors, be sure to pay attention to where shadows will creep in, whether the sun will be in your eyes as you speak, and even whether there will be sufficient light to give the speech if the presentation occurs at night. Indoors, lighting can be manipulated so visual aids are more easily seen. Lighting also can set a mood, but be careful because the dimmer the lights and the larger the audience, the higher the chance members of the audience will not pay attention. Darkness can encourage people to doze off. This is especially important when videotaping or video conferencing a presentation, because if the lighting is off then you and any visual aids you may be using become difficult to see. Always try to run through a short segment of the speech first and then view it so you can test the lighting in the background.

## Layout of the Dais

At most planned events speakers speak from a designated area. This area goes by many names, but in the end it is another part of the speech scene that can be used to boost the delivery of a message. Some call it a **rostrum**, while others call it a **dais**, but in the end it is simply the platform from which speakers address their audience. It is important to take note of the physical setting of the dais when delivering an address.

**rostrum**
the area a speaker speaks from

**dais**
the area a speaker speaks from

The dais usually is above the audience and the platform party typically needs to walk a short flight of steps to get to their seats on the platform. This height allows the speakers to speak to the audience in such a way that they are visible to everyone in attendance. On rare occasions the platform is not raised (like, for instance at a graduation ceremony), but the audience seating is such that they are above the platform. In either event, a dais is a useful tool for a speaker when attempting to make as much eye contact as possible with the audience.

# SPOTLIGHTING THEORISTS: LLOYD BITZER & RICHARD VATZ

The field of communication studies is dedicated to studying the construction of meaning. In 1968 scholar Lloyd Bitzer wrote an essay entitled "The Rhetorical Situation" proposing that situations dictate certain rhetorical responses by speakers. Five years later, Richard Vatz responded to this piece in another essay, "The Myth of the Rhetorical Situation." As you can tell by the title, he disagreed with the position Bitzer staked out, asserting that rhetoric determines, or creates, situations, not the other way around. In the over-forty years since this written debate emerged, rhetoricians have argued over which side represents the more accurate understanding of the construction of meaning. This "Spotlighting Theorists" capsule discusses who these two men are and explains the impact of their arguments on the relationship between situations and meaning.

## Lloyd Bitzer

Lloyd Bitzer, a longtime professor at the University of Wisconsin, published several important pieces of rhetorical scholarship, but none more controversial or widely read than his 1968 piece, "The Rhetorical Situation." This essay, originally published in *Philosophy and Rhetoric*, provided a specific definition of the relationship between scene and message. For Bitzer, situations hold inherent meaning that speakers identify through their responses. Situations essentially call rhetoric into being.

This position posits that rhetoric is a reaction to situations and that the power of meaning lies with context and not the speaker. Speeches are essentially predetermined responses to existing situations; they are descriptions of meaning and not meaningful in and of themselves. For example, he suggested that presidential inaugurations are situations that invite a specific form of speech from a president. The inauguration is why they speak and what they speak about.

Bitzer's essay has been widely cited and used as a foundation for rhetorical studies since its publication, but not everyone agrees with its propositions.

## Richard Vatz

In 1973 Richard Vatz, a professor at Towson State University in Maryland who primarily studies the intersection of rhetoric and psychiatry, published a response to Bitzer's essay entitled "The Myth of the Rhetorical Situation." The piece, which also appeared in *Philosophy and Rhetoric*, took on Bitzer's main argument. Vatz contended that situations do not invite rhetoric, but rather rhetoric creates situations.

For Vatz, meaning is created by speakers through their speech, not through the situation. Situations, therefore, lack meaning until they are defined by the speaker. Speakers, according to this position, hold the power to use rhetoric to define situations. Responses are the choice of the speaker, not the dictate of the situation.

To illustrate this, Vatz points to crises. He says that there is not a crisis until the situation is defined as such by a speaker. He also points to the fact political candidates often seek to "control the agenda," implying speakers define the campaign and not vice versa.

Scholars often cite Vatz's essay in an attempt to spur debate over the concept of the rhetorical situation.

To summarize the implications of Bitzer vs. Vatz: Bitzer takes a passive view of rhetoric, arguing that it describes situations. Vatz believes rhetoric has a more active role and is not simply derivative of situations. In fact, Vatz goes so far as to call the rhetorical situation "anti-rhetorical." The National Communication Association still convenes panels to discuss the debate between these two scholars, with the most recent at the 2008 annual meeting in San Diego.

Another component of the dais to take into account as a speaker is who you will be sharing it with. Many times there are several people sitting on the dais with the speaker, and they usually hold important status. On these occasions speakers should make some effort to recognize those people at the start of their speech. In some instances these people will sit behind the speaker, while in others they may be even with the podium and lectern from which a speaker makes his or her address. Both situations create unique speaking circumstances, with the former placing important members of the audience behind the speaker, and the latter placing them in a position where they must crane their necks to watch the presentation.

## The Speaker

The final, and arguably most important, element of the speaking scene is you, the speaker. Remember at the beginning of the chapter President Bush wore a flight suit to deliver his address. This is an example of how speakers can use their appearance to enhance the message they construct. Your clothing sends a message to both yourself and your audience, so take care to dress appropriately for your speech.

Consider this hypothetical example: Stanley presents a speech arguing for lower taxes in his home state of Idaho. He marshals his evidence properly, speaks clearly, and emphatically makes his points. For all intents and purposes, his speech goes off perfectly. The only problem is that his audience doesn't take him seriously because he is wearing a baseball cap, a pair of jeans ripped at the knees, sandals, and a Pearl Jam concert shirt. The way a speaker dresses influences his or her perceived credibility with the audience, and so for that reason you should always dress for the occasion and scene. This is not to say always dress professionally, because some instances, such as company picnics, do not warrant such attire. It does mean, however, to adapt your dress to your message and your location.

Example of a poorly dressed speaker (top) and a well-dressed speaker (bottom)

Your body also can be used to augment the argument you make. In Stanley's case, perhaps he could have worn a T-shirt stating "I favor lower taxes" or something like that. Presidential candidates always pick specific ties before appearing at campaign debates. Democrats typically wear blue ties to represent their party's color, while Republicans wear red ties for the same reason. Subtle changes to your person in the form of clothing can help you identify with an idea or even directly augment your argument.

You, the speaker, and the other three characteristics, are all components of the message you deliver with your speech—but they are not the entire speaking environment. They are part of the medium through which you communicate your message. The late Canadian communication scholar Marshall McLuhan once wrote that "the medium is the message," meaning that the manner in which you choose to deliver your message tells the audience just as much as the content of what you say. He was referring to technological media and primarily television; however, the principle still stands with public speaking. The environment you choose to speak through can send as powerful a message as the content of what you say.

For example, a technical representative for a company may choose to send a mechanical expert to a client to give a presentation or demonstration on how the product works, thus making it seem like a more important and personal investment; or, the rep may simply create a DVD of the presentation and send that to the client. The same message can be delivered both ways, but the manner in which it is packaged sends another message to the audience as well. McLuhan's words relate directly to the concepts discussed in this chapter. How you deliver a speech, whether it is live or mediated, and what the environment around you looks like are important dimensions of the speaking situation to which you must pay attention. Next, we will cover some theoretical ideas related to the speaking situation that serve as further evidence for why the scene and the speaking environment are important to understand when constructing a presentation.

# SPEECH AS SPECTACLE

Effectively incorporating location and environment into a speech can enhance the message you send. This symbiotic relationship between scene and message content has provoked plenty of research by rhetoricians, and this section introduces you to their debates and findings. First, we will explore the debate surrounding the concept of the rhetorical situation, a term coined by scholar Lloyd Bitzer in the 1960s. Then we will look at the notion of spectacle, a theory about the messages that inherently exist in a scene. Finally, we will provide some examples of how scene has risen in importance in the contemporary public speaking environment.

## The Rhetorical Situation

In 1968 Lloyd Bitzer published an essay that proposed a specific relationship between rhetoric and situations.[9] Specifically, he said that situations called rhetoric into being. Put another way, each moment in which you find yourself invites you to speak using a specific vocabulary. When you respond to a situation what you say alters the reality of the moment. By way of example he argued that when presidents are inaugurated they are confronted with a situation that invites them to speak. They do so, thereby changing the reality of the moment, redefining it for the audience and themselves.

Another aspect of the *rhetorical situation*, according to Bitzer, is that each rhetorical situation is different, and if a person does not respond to it, the moment is lost. Each moment presents a different *exigence* and thereby requires a different vocabulary for the speaker. Bitzer also stated that rhetorical situations require an audience, and that the audience, as we will learn in Chapter 8, requires speakers to use a specific vocabulary to craft their message. Finally, each rhetorical situation contains constraints that limit the ability of the speaker to respond only to the situation at hand. Not everyone, however, agreed with Bitzer when he published this argument.

Where Bitzer saw meaning as inherent in the situation and rhetoric as a way to define it, Richard Vatz argued that meaning exists only when rhetoric provides it.[10] That is to say, for example, a crisis is not a crisis until someone calls it a crisis. We do not find meaning, we create it through our speech. For Vatz, situations are defined by the speaker—the situations do not define the speech. This perspective essentially takes a position completely opposite that of Bitzer, but it also puts more of an emphasis on the power of public speaking to define and dictate events.

For example, the chairman of the Federal Reserve can move the markets simply by giving a speech. When the current chairman, Ben Bernanke, mentions that inflation is a concern, the markets dip, but when he declares the economy is in good shape, the markets improve. Why? Vatz would argue these effects were a result of Bernanke's rhetoric in that he defined the state of the economy. Others then perceived the same reality and ultimately the market brought itself in line with that perception. His rhetoric clearly influenced the situation.

Situations also can be influenced and defined by more than simply words. Sometimes, as we have already noted in this chapter, they can be choreographed to enhance a message. In the next section we will discuss the idea of spectacle, which explains how these instances work in tandem with message construction.

## The Rhetoric of Spectacle

In rhetoric, a *spectacle* is a symbolic event where the small pieces, or the details, send a deep message. In a spectacle, there is a deep connection between actor and scene.[11] The central characters, or actors, send a message simply through the environment in which they speak—what they wear, where they are, and who is around them. There are two different types of symbols involved in spectacle events. The first is a *referential symbol*, which is an element of an object or event that refers to specific messages or aspects of a message sent by a speaker. Essentially, a referential symbol stands for something specific.[12] A police badge is a good example of a referential symbol as it refers to a specific message about the speaker: the fact he is a police officer. The second type is a *condensation symbol*, which is designed to evoke an emotion by condensing the emotion into a symbolic event.[13] A cross, for example, condenses a variety of different emotions into one symbol and, depending on the circumstances of its use, can elicit emotional responses in the audience simply through its presence.

# 6

Travel may also be a form of spectacle. A ***travel spectacle*** is an event where the act of going somewhere sends a message to the audience, and often the act of travel is accompanied by a speech.[14] For example, following Hurricane Katrina former President George W. Bush toured the affected Gulf area and delivered a nationally televised address. The media covered his trip to the stricken region

**travel spectacle**
when the act of going somewhere sends a message

and showed images of him flying over flooded New Orleans wards in a helicopter. Later in the trip he spoke to the nation from historic Jackson Square in New Orleans and talked about the rescue, recovery, and reconstruction efforts. Other presidents have taken similar trips to places ravaged by tornadoes, earthquakes,

Former President Bush arrives in New Orleans after Hurricane Katrina

or floods. The trips themselves send a message that the government knows what has happened and is in the process of responding. Sometimes, as in the case with President Bush's trip to New Orleans, they arrive later than some believe they should and are roundly criticized for what is perceived as inaction and ignorance. So, location and timing both matter when it comes to crisis responses and messages delivered with the aid of spectacle.

Researchers argue that the importance of spectacle is on the rise due to structural changes in our society.[15] Society in general has become much more personalized thanks to developments in media technology. In fact, most events, from stock market movements to political elections to job searches for sports teams and major businesses, are treated as adventures and horse races. Such personal attention results in an individual's every action being scrutinized, thus increasing the importance of the relationship between action and speech.

Comedian Dennis Miller has joked about the short attention span of people in today's society thanks to the types of news reporting they are accustomed to hearing. He has poignantly kidded that, "once politicians spoke in sound bytes, now they think in them." At the heart of this joke is the idea that people do not want thought-out arguments, nor do prominent speakers wish to deliver them.

Comedian Dennis Miller

Instead, we send messages as quickly as we can, often through the use of well-designed visuals that may not send a verbal message at all. Making the proper and best use of your surroundings now translates into a higher chance of success for speeches.

Some scholars decry this seeming overemphasis on spectacle in contemporary affairs. They feel that the reduction of messages to short tidbits and slogans reduces the capacity of the audience to think critically. When we reduce complete thoughts and logic to visual items we overemphasize certain aspects of message construction and public speaking while underemphasizing things like logic. This often results in the misperception that appearances indicate action. For this reason, it is incumbent upon speakers to understand the relationship between speech and scene when crafting their messages. This is even more true when it comes to using media to transmit well-developed presentations, rather than simply images.

In the next section we will discuss a variety of different ways in which you can ethically and successfully integrate scene and spectacle into the rhetorical situations you confront. We will then look at how you can effectively employ media when delivering a video conference presentation or uploading a taped speech to the web.

# Making Proper Use of Scene

Speakers confront a variety of different situations, and regardless of whether you believe their rhetoric defines the situation or the situation dictates what rhetoric they employ, speakers need to be able to adapt. You need to confront each speaking situation quickly and take steps to adapt to the moment both before it occurs and during the speech itself. This part of the chapter will provide some tips on how to maximize your ability to integrate scene into your speech both before and during your presentation. It concludes by offering some advice on handling mediated presentations.

## Before Your Speech

In most instances you will have advance notice of your presentation and you should make every effort to go to the place where you will be speaking in advance of the speech. Do not go too early because the environment may very well change, especially if the speech will take place outside, where weather and sunlight frequently change. Still, getting a feel for the speaking environment will help you construct your speech, appropriately plan and practice your delivery style, and feel generally more comfortable when you actually give the speech. However, these pre-speech visits are not simply tourist trips.

The first thing a pre-speech visit does for you is give you a feel for how large the audience will be when you speak. This can tell you whether or not speaking tools such as microphones will be needed. If you feel they may be necessary then you have two options. First, contact the people who will prepare the space for you and ask if they can provide a microphone for you. Be specific as to the kind you want, such as a cordless microphone or one mounted into the lectern. The other option is to provide it yourself, in which case you need to check power sources available for the microphone in the speaking area. Although important, microphones are not the only speaking tool you need to look for in these advance visits.

If your presentation requires the use of visual projection devices, such as PowerPoint or video clips, you need to make sure these devices are both available and feasible. Again, checking with the people who prepare the space as to the availability of such items is the easiest way to find them. If you are using visual devices, an advance visit can also tell you how large the pictures and writing need to be to accommodate the audience size. It also can tell you if such devices are even advisable. For instance, if you plan on showing a video clip of an automobile accident during a speech about drunk driving and the space you are speaking in holds about 1,000 people, then a small television monitor simply will not cut it. If something larger is not available, then you may need to adjust the speech accordingly rather than make the vast majority of people futilely strain their eyes to see your clip.

Pre-speech visits can also enlighten you and influence the references you make in your speech. Let's say Juanita plans to give a presentation to her company's shareholders at their annual meeting. The presentation will be in a large ballroom at a major hotel in Houston, Texas, and on her pre-speech visit she notes that on the wall hangs a painting depicting the first oil wells in Texas. Juanita, wanting to be creative, incorporates a reference to that painting into a portion of her speech. When discussing the plans for the company in the upcoming year she states, "In addition to building on the past years' successful programs, we will—in the spirit of the first oil drillers here in Texas—explore new programs that could increase the company's profits in the future." In this example the reference to the scene helps add color to her speech, and it was made possible through her pre-speech visit to the ballroom.

Pre-speech visits may not always be available, thus limiting, but not eliminating, your ability to integrate scene into your speech. In the next section we provide a few suggestions for how to use scene effectively during your speech.

## During Your Speech

Using scene in the midst of your speech is another effective way of enhancing your presentation. Making proper use of the tools at your disposal, moving around the audience when possible, and referencing distractions are just a few ways to connect your speech to the environment in a strong and effective manner.

Whether you are using a microphone, lectern, or projector, you can enhance your speech by using the items appropriately. This means, of course, practicing with them, but also using them extemporaneously as well. For instance, when making a strong point several times in a row through repetition, you may want to gently, but noticeably, pound the lectern from which you are speaking. This dramatic movement increases the emphasis on those points for the audience. If no lectern is available, perhaps a desk, wall, or even the palm of your hand will suffice.

An underutilized, but nonetheless very effective way of using the environment to your advantage during a speech involves moving around the audience. Sometimes, as is the case at graduation ceremonies, this is not a viable option. During other less formal presentations, however, this can be a very good way of gaining and maintaining the attention of your audience. The human attention span is not very long, but by making people change their vantage point through your movement around the room you effectively "reset" their attention span, thus increasing your odds of holding an audience's attention. The larger the room, the harder this task, but movement around the podium can be used in the same manner. In addition to the attention aspect, this approach to speaking also increases the personal feel of your speech.

One caution when it comes to maneuvering through the audience during a speech is that you need to know your material. To do this effectively you cannot have memorized your speech or require a great many notes. Moving around the audience works best with extemporaneous speaking because movement is fluid, as is the delivery of an extemporaneous speech. Obviously, much more practice before the speech is necessary if you plan to walk around the room while making your presentation. See Table 6.1 for a summary of tips for making proper use of scene before and during your presentation.

**Table 6.1**

| Tips for Using the Scene |
|---|
| • Know the environment |
| • Ensure visual aids work and enhance your speech |
| • Can you refer to the scene itself? |
| • Be familiar with any sound systems |
| • Is the occasion conducive for you to move around? |

Regardless of the location and whether you move around through the audience or not, there will also always be some form of noise or potential distractions. These often are not obvious on a pre-speech walkthrough, but nevertheless you need to handle them during a speech. Simply letting these distractions frustrate you will not be helpful. One key point to keep in mind is that the noises do not just affect you, the audience also notices them. One of the best ways to handle such distractions is to reference them in your presentation. Noting that you hear or see the offending sound or object, just like the audience does, can inhibit its ability to divert your audience's attention.

Take the case of Jeremiah, who was giving his first speech of the semester in his Public Speaking class. After about two minutes, a loud noise started overshadowing his voice and he was forced to speak louder. After the noise passed, he made it a point to say, "Wow, this will be one fun semester with all those planes flying over the class when we speak." He then returned to his speech. Such references minimize the distraction of outside noises for the speaker and audience. Some distractions, though, are harder to handle and actually should not be referenced.

On rare occasions your speech may elicit exceptionally strong emotions or disagreement from members of your audience who lack a sense of ethics or decorum. These *hecklers* may attempt to distract you from your speech by

**heckler**
a self-aggrandizing member of the audience who tries to distract from the speech by confronting the speaker in the middle of a presentation

making comments directly to you. Although speeches share some similarities with conversations, they do not share this unstructured give-and-take aspect in the middle of the speech. One of the hardest, but most advisable, methods of handling hecklers is to ignore them. Doing so usually makes them become quiet very fast. When that does not work, calmly responding to their interruptions by indicating that they are disrupting the event for everyone else in attendance should be your next step. In the rarest of circumstances it might become necessary to involve security and have the person removed from the room.

Rest assured, hecklers are very rare and most speakers never encounter one. More common are environmental noises like traffic and airplanes. Effectively adapting to these challenges is an important step in becoming a successful public speaker.

## MEDIATED PRESENTATION CONSIDERATIONS

The challenge of hecklers is minimized, though not eliminated, when giving mediated presentations. This is primarily because audiences are typically smaller; however, when you deliver a traditional speech that happens to be taped hecklers may very well be a possibility and the same ways of handling them still apply. That said, there are some general guidelines that can help increase the effectiveness of a mediated presentation, some of which we have already touched upon.

First, it is important that the scene around you be as professional as possible. A messy area, a distracting wall-hanging, or an unexpected passerby will take the audience's focus off of you and onto something else. So, it is important to make sure that the area in which you choose to record the speech is quiet and innocuous.

A second and very important guideline for effective mediated presentations is to make sure that the equipment you are using is set up correctly and working properly. If you are using a conference call or video conferencing for the presentation it is important to test the phone lines or cameras you will use to connect with your audience. The last thing you want is to have the time of the presentation reduced, or its transmission interrupted, because the conference call could not be set up or you needed to spend time readjusting the camera. Such mistakes damage your ethos, even though they may have nothing to do with the speech topic.

In terms of yourself, pay attention to what you choose to wear. Color tones in particular are important, and you should try and keep to solid colors of blue or gray because they help bring out a healthy complexion for your skin tone. Conversely, you should avoid wearing bright colors such as orange, purple, or red because these colors can cause a hue that is very distracting to the audience. Additionally, try not to wear anything that matches your skin and hair tones because this will wash out your natural complexion and thus make you appear less confident and even unhealthy. Finally, highly decorative clothing, including striped shirts and suits, is not recommended for mediated presentations either.

Next, it is important to pay attention to noises that a phone or microphone can pick up. Tapping on a desk, rocking in a chair, typing on a computer, and whispering to someone else in the room all might be picked up and at a minimum be distracting to the audience. If you do move, try to do so when making a point, thus accentuating your verbal content with a nonverbal enhancement. Remember, the camera heightens the ability of people to see your gestures and movements and hear any sounds you make.

Eye contact is also an essential component to effective video conferences and taped speeches. Even though you may not be able to see your audience, they can see you and so eye contact is just as important in a digital presentation as it is in a traditional speaking environment. This is managed by looking straight at the camera when delivering your message. Looking away makes it appear as though you are distracted or disinterested.

SPEAKING of CIVICENGAGEMENT

### Television and the Public Interest
### by Newton Minow

Delivered May 9, 1961, to the National Association of Broadcasters

In 1961, newly elected President John F. Kennedy selected Newton Minow to be the Chairman of the Federal Communications Commission (FCC), the governmental agency responsible for governing television and radio.[16] Some were surprised at Kennedy's choice of Minow as he had been critical of television and lacked extensive experience with communication law or the media industry.

As FCC chairman, Minow challenged the content on television and asked for reform.[17]

In his speech Minow raised eyebrows, especially with this statement:

"But when television is bad, nothing is worse. I invite each of you to sit down in front of your television set when your station goes on the air and stay there, for a day, without a book, without a magazine, without a newspaper, without a profit and loss sheet or a rating book to distract you. Keep your eyes glued to that set until the station signs off. I can assure you that what you will observe is a vast wasteland."[18]

These words of Newton Minow became famous, or infamous depending on the audience. In fact, some felt his comments were elitist, and so they even named the S.S. Minnow of Gilligan's Island fame after him as an expression of criticism for his stance on the media industry.

Although Minow never achieved significant broadcast regulation, he did raise awareness of content and the impact of the "vast wasteland." After he retired from the FCC he became a partner in one of America's most powerful communication law firms.[19]

Finally, taping speeches presents many of us with what could be a huge positive for crafting successful speeches: the ability to stop and start over. This should not mean, however, that the first time you deliver the speech you tape it. In fact, you should practice it just as much, if not more, than if you had a live presentation. Do not use the re-recording capability as a crutch, but rather try to get it right the first time. If you quite often find yourself stopping and starting over, that can be frustrating, and that frustration will have a detrimental effect the more you stop and start over. The more you practice, the fewer attempts it will take to get the speech where you want it to be.

One important thing to remember, however, is that images are no substitute for content. You need to actually have a logical, well-developed argument and then use the scene to amplify that message. Television has often come under fire for lacking substance and using spectacular images and visual detail in lieu of a serious message. In fact, this is not even a new criticism, nor one of which the government is unaware. In 1961 then newly appointed chairman of the Federal Communications Commission, Newton Minow, gave a speech where he decried television as a "vast wasteland." Do not fall into the trap of sacrificing content at the expense of images and thus contribute to an expansion of that vast wasteland. You owe it to yourself and your audience to provide serious content in your speeches whether they are live or taped.

## Summary

Speakers confront a variety of different rhetorical situations, and each one presents different opportunities and challenges. In fact, rhetoricians debate the relationship between message and environment in much the same way sidewalk philosophers debate the "chicken and the egg" question. From large ballrooms to outdoor events, to the very classrooms in which you are sitting now, each space contains unique qualities that can be leveraged to enhance your presentation. Making the proper use of the tools at your disposal in each situation, paying attention to the layout of the speaking area, and even dressing for the occasion are all ways in which you can maximize the relationship between scene and speech.

## Key Terms

acoustics   117

bookend approach   116

condensation symbol   126

conference call   119

dais   122

exigence   126

heckler   130

lectern   122

moderator approach   116

podium   122

referential symbol   126

rhetorical situation   126

rostrum   122

spectacle   126

travel spectacle   127

video conferencing   120

## REVIEW QUESTIONS

1. What are the four major elements of a speaking situation?

2. What are the three fundamental characteristics of the rhetorical situation, according to Bitzer?

3. What are spectacles and travel spectacles?

4. If possible, what is the best way to adapt to a speaking situation before a speech?

5. How can a speaker use a lectern effectively as an element of scene during his or her speech?

## THINK ABOUT IT

1. Who, or what, constructs meaning?

2. Is rhetoric passive, as Bitzer suggests, or is it more active and creative, as Vatz proposes?

3. Why are speeches from disaster sites or famous places effective ways for politicians to send a message?

## ACTIVITIES FOR ACTION

1. When practicing your speech, try to do so in an atmosphere where there is some noise. This will help you project your voice and prepare for a noisy environment. This can be done by staying in your room, shutting the door, and turning up your radio or television while practicing your speech.

2. The next time you watch a political debate take note of the color of ties, dresses, and other items of clothing. Additionally, see how the dais is set up and in what order the candidates appear. Examine these characteristics to see if there is a correlation between party affiliation and color or perhaps order of finish in the latest polls in terms of where candidates are seated on the platform.

## ENDNOTES

1. For a transcript of this speech see: George W. Bush (March 19, 2003), "President Bush Addresses the Nation," http://www.whitehouse.gov/news/releases/2003/03/20030319-17.html (accessed June 13, 2008).

2. For a transcript of this speech see: George W. Bush (May 1, 2003), "President Bush announces Major Combat Operations in Iraq Have Ended," http://www.whitehouse.gov/news/releases/2003/05/20030501-15.html (accessed June 13, 2008).

3. Ibid.

4. In 2004 Bush's service in the National Guard came under scrutiny by Democratic presidential candidate John Kerry. For one article illustrating the debate over this issue see: "What Do You Make of the Bush National Guard Controversy?" (February 14, 2004), *Time Magazine Online*, http://www.time.com/time/question/20040212.html (accessed June 13, 2008).

5. http://marshallmcluhan.com/biography (accessed May 10, 2010).

6. Ibid.

7. James F. Golden, Goodwin F. Berquist, and William E. Colman, *The Rhetoric of Western Thought* (4th Ed.), (Dubuque, IA: Kendall-Hunt,1989), 235-236.

8. Lloyd F. Bitzer, "The Rhetorical Situation," *Philosophy and Rhetoric* 1 (1968): 1-14.

9. Richard Vatz, "The Myth of the Rhetorical Situation," *Philosophy and Rhetoric* 6 (1973): 154-161.

10. Bruce Miroff, "The Presidential Spectacle," in *The Presidency and the Political System*, ed. Michael Nelson (Washington, DC: CQ Press), Ch. 10.

11. Murray Edelman, *Constructing the Political Spectacle* (Chicago, IL: University of Chicago Press, 1988).

12. Ibid.

13. Keith V. Erickson, "Presidential Spectacles: Political Illusionism and the Rhetoric of Travel," *Communication Monographs* 65 (1998): 141-153.

14. Robert E. Denton, Jr., "Rhetorical Challenges to the Presidency," *Rhetoric and Public Affairs* 3, no. 3 (2000): 445-451.

15. Ibid., 235.

16. http://www.museum.tv/eotvsection.php?entrycode=minownewton (accessed June 1, 2011).

17. Ibid (accessed June 1, 2011).

18. http://www.americanrhetoric.com/speeches/newtonminow.htm (accessed June 1, 2011).

19. http://www.museum.tv/eotvsection.php?entrycode=minownewton (accessed June 1, 2011).

THE SPEAKER:  The Tradition and Practice of Public Speaking

# Analyzing Audience

## 7

### CHAPTER OVERVIEW

- Discusses how audiences can be broken down and analyzed before a speech
- Explains how audience analysis can be employed in developing points and using language within a speech
- Outlines how to effectively analyze a speech during its delivery

The 2008 presidential primaries represented the first time in over a half century when neither a president nor vice president sought their party's nomination for president. The campaigns for both the Democratic and Republican contenders were bitterly divisive, and each candidate needed to find a way to appeal to groups that normally would not support them. For instance, Republican Senator John McCain needed to quell criticism over what some party members saw as his questionable conservative record.[1]

In 2007 the Conservative Political Action Committee (CPAC) invited all the major candidates to speak at the conference and McCain was the only one not to attend.[2] As a result, he was crushed in the straw poll by his competitors and many conservatives refused to support him.[3] As the year progressed, McCain took further criticism from the right for his immigration policies, his refusal to vote for the Bush tax cuts a few years prior, and his maverick nature. The criticism became so severe for McCain in 2007 that his campaign almost went bankrupt.[4]

The Arizona senator's fortunes changed, however, in 2008 when voting began, and by the time he reached the podium at CPAC he was the likely Republican nominee for president. He had won significant election victories the previous week, and just a few hours before McCain's speech his chief rival, Mitt Romney, announced the suspension of his campaign. McCain could now attempt to unite the party behind him. Unfortunately for the senator, however, the audience still viewed him with skepticism at best, hostility at worst.

McCain needed to tailor his speech to the scene he faced. He knew he faced conservatives, but what kind? What was their age? Where did they come from? What was their economic status? Would race play a part in their perceptions of him? Were they ready to believe in his candidacy? What political principles did they espouse? The answers to these and other questions influenced the word choices within his speech and the evidence he chose to use to deflect their potential criticisms. But even knowing these things in advance, McCain still needed to be attuned to his audience while delivering the speech. All of these assessments are part of audience analysis, an essential skill for any speaker.

This chapter will discuss the various elements of audience analysis that can help you craft and deliver a successful speech tailored to your listeners. It begins with a discussion about the types of audience analysis available to you before you give a speech. It then discusses how that information, once collected, can be used to inform your decisions on phrasing and organization within the speech. Finally, it explains how audience analysis does not stop when the speech starts, but rather continues during the speech. Finally, it provides tips and suggestions on how to gauge the effectiveness of your message while delivering a speech.

# Methods of Audience Analysis

The old axiom, "Information is power" underscores the importance of audience analysis when speaking. Knowing about your audience allows you to make better choices regarding the examples, language, and organizational patterns you might use in a speech, thereby increasing your power as a speaker. Gathering information about your audience, however, is unlike gathering research materials for your speech, which you should remember reading about in Chapter 3. As a matter of fact, some of the audience characteristics you uncover may very well inform your decisions about where to research and what research to cite within your speech. This section explains three different ways of analyzing your audience, but all of them may not be available every time you speak. Like most other skills presented in this book, treat them like tools in a toolkit. When they are available and make sense to use, use them.

## Demographics

One of the most common ways of analyzing an audience involves collecting *demographic data*. Many of us recognize demographic data when we see it, and oftentimes we conduct rudimentary demographic analyses ourselves. Take, for example, the first day of class. You enter the room and look around at your fellow students, examining the makeup of the class. You note roughly how many women and men there are, and perhaps the number of minorities. You often subconsciously use this information when selecting your seat in the room.

**demographic data**
information on selected population characteristics used by the government, market researchers, and speech writers

We also encounter demographic data when we watch the news. Political election campaigns, like the one we discussed at the opening of this chapter, have developed into machines driven by demographics. Politicians seek to win the youth vote, the African American vote, the senior vote, or the middle class vote. Candidates often deliver speeches or use examples and statistics that appeal to that subsection of the population. Research groups and news organizations often report on polls that measure support for a candidate within a particular demographic group, especially immediately following an election. An *exit poll* helps politicians understand their appeal to different parts of the population so as to better refine their message for the next election.

**exit poll**
questions asked following an election that measure election results in terms of demographic categories

Market researchers also make use of demographic data when evaluating television shows. Different television programs appeal to different demographic groups, and that information allows studios to find specific advertisers for those shows that have products that appeal to the specific demographic groups that watch the show. For example, CBS debuted a show called *Jericho* in 2007 that received enthusiastic support from some fans but that did not translate into strong ratings with the coveted 18–49 demographic, resulting in its eventual cancelation. So angry were the fans that they mounted a campaign to save their show by mailing thousands of peanuts to CBS management. CBS finally gave in and restored the show for a short seven-episode season in 2008, but the ratings were not much better so the network canceled it again. *Jericho* is an example of a show that did not appeal to a demographic targeted by the network, and so the show lacked power to persuade advertisers to buy air time, leading to its cancelation. Just as with television shows, when speakers are unable to appeal to their audience they lose their *efficacy* and are less likely to be successful at sending their message to their listeners.

**efficacy**
. . . . . . . .
the ability to produce
a desired result

Demographic categories measure a variety of different aspects of a population. They detail observable and identifiable characteristics through survey techniques. Every time you place a checkmark next to your race or provide your age on a document you are contributing to demographic information databases. Think about your college applications: You checked these off and sent them back to the universities of your choice. The universities then used this information to examine the appeal of their college to certain targeted populations. Demographic information is powerful, and for that reason the use of it for anything other than description is prohibited by law.

In the United States most demographic categories are protected by law from discrimination. Race, age, sexual orientation, and religious affiliation represent specific groups shielded from discrimination. So, on the aforementioned college application, you could not be rejected from a school for checking the box next to, say, "African American." Demographic information, however, can be used to help construct appeals to select groups in a variety of ways.

One such way it can be used is through more complicated parceling of the population. Demographic questions and results can often be cross-sectioned to examine more than just one group, such as "Hispanics." That group can be categorized to explore responses from "Hispanics, ages 18–26," or even "Hispanic Catholics, ages 18–26 in Miami, Florida." Imagine the variety of uses for such information when designing messages to appeal to that group. The applications are nearly endless and the potential success of the message reaching the segment of the audience it is designed to reach increases as well.

A few moments ago we mentioned several different demographic categories. Most of us recognize these categories and can learn from a simple question. When examining demographic information on age, oftentimes the category is broken up into 8–10 year segments. For example, the young adult category is often broken down into those people who are 18–26, and middle age is usually seen as 40–50. The elderly are often typecast as the over-65 crowd. Appeals that work with one group might not work with another.

## SPOTLIGHTING THEORISTS: GEORGE GALLUP & JOHN ZOGBY

Anyone who even remotely follows politics and public opinion in the United States today has heard the names "Gallup" or "Zogby." The Gallup Organization and Zogby International are two of the most well-known polling corporations in the world.

### George Horace Gallup (1901–1984)

George Gallup grew up in a farming family in Iowa in the early 20th century and attended the University of Iowa, where he eventually received a Ph.D. in Political Science. Initially, Gallup pursued a career as a college teacher and researcher, but after stops at the University of Iowa, Drake University, and Northwestern, he left academia altogether for a position with the Young & Rubicam advertising agency. He spent 16 years with Y&R conducting public opinion surveys before leaving to found the American Institute of Public Opinion in 1935.

In 1936 his neophyte organization gained national attention by accurately predicting the presidential election with only 5,000 respondents. This was in contrast to a larger poll conducted by *Literary Digest* that got the results wrong. Gallup, however, was not always right himself as was famously the case in 1948.

In 1948 Gallup ended polling three weeks before the presidential election between incumbent Harry Truman and challenger Thomas Dewey. As a result, he forecast Dewey as the winner in a landslide. Early in the morning the day after America went to the polls Truman was announced the winner, casting a pall over Gallup's polling efforts. Never again did Gallup order polling to end before Election Day.

In 1958 Gallup consolidated all his polling operations into what we know today as The Gallup Organization. Despite his death from a heart attack in Switzerland in 1984, the organization has continued to be a success and is seen as one of the most reputable sources of public opinion data in the world.

### John Zogby (1948–)

John Zogby is the founder of Zogby International, a competitor to the Gallup Organization in the polling field. Zogby, a native New Yorker, was born in upstate New York and attended LeMoyne College and Syracuse University. He has taught history and political science at SUNY-Utica and the Arthur Levitt Public Affairs Center at Hamilton College. He received an honorary doctorate degree from both SUNY and the Graduate School of Union University. Zogby also serves as a Senior Advisor at the John F. Kennedy School of Government at Harvard University and is Senior Fellow at the Catholic University of America's Life Cycle Institute. In addition to his academic credentials, Zogby also is a member of the board of directors for the Advertising Research Foundation.

In 1984 he founded Zogby International, which conducts polls around the world. Although newer on the scene than Gallup, his group quickly gained notoriety in 1992 when he published a poll that showed popular former New York Governor Mario Cuomo would lose in a general election in New York to then President George H. W. Bush. This poll receives some credit for Cuomo's departure from that race. In 1996 his poll came within a tenth of a point of accurately predicting the real result of the presidential election. In 2000, he correctly predicted the cliffhanger presidential election when many had predicted an easy Bush victory.

Zogby has also been on the cutting edge of polling practices. He makes it standard practice to weight his political polls using party identification, something unheard of in the decades dominated by Gallup polls. He also has begun developing an interactive online polling device using a significantly larger representative sample than is typically available to pollsters.

Another category often used is race, although potential answers are often limited. A form usually has slots for white/Caucasian, African American, Hispanic, and Asian/Pacific Islander, with anything else relegated to the label of "other." Sometimes, depending on what the researcher analyzing these demographics is looking for, these categories are broken down a bit further. Regardless, this information can help when picking out examples for use in a speech that resonates with a particular racial group.

Take the case of Mary Church Terrell, a nineteenth century social activist who spoke out against gender and racial discrimination. Terrell often had to balance her speeches with examples that appealed to both women and African Americans at a time when the experiences of both had some commonalities, but also some

SPEAKING of CIVIC ENGAGEMENT

### What It Means to Be Colored in the Capital of the U.S.
### by Mary Church Terrell

Delivered October 10, 1906, to the United Women's Club, Washington, D.C.

In 1906 the United Women's Club invited African American advocate and teacher Mary Church Terrell to speak, and she delivered scathing commentary on racial equality in Washington, D.C.[5] Terrell noted in her opening that the nation's capital had been labeled the "colored Man's Paradise" but declared such a title must have been bestowed out of irony, because "it would be difficult to find a worse misnomer for Washington."[6] Terrell also argued that conditions for African Americans had worsened in the 15 years of her residence there, and that although many other minorities could find lodging, unless a black person had acquaintances they likely could not find a bed. She noted that if she resisted current standards that she would be "cast into jail and forced to pay a fine for violating the Virginia laws."[7] Such issues reflected the direct experiences of African Americans of her day, but her speech was not simply about race—after all it was delivered at the Women's Club!

Ms. Terrell vividly described the limitations on the possibility of education, specifically that black school children received a lower quality education than that of white children. Within her speech she also referenced many more examples of injustice and discrimination, all designed to connect the causes of women and African Americans, as the causes of these two groups were priorities in her life.

In the closing paragraph of her speech, Ms. Terrell made a statement of a stern tone: "It is impossible for any white person in the United States, no matter how sympathetic and broad, to realize what life would mean to him if his incentive to effort were suddenly snatched away."[8] Mary Church Terrell lived to see the successes of the women's suffrage movement and the significant victory of Brown v. Board of Education, dying shortly thereafter at the age of 90. In recognition of the power of her voice on civil rights issues, the United States Post Office honored her with a stamp in 2009.

significant differences. Terrell needed to pay attention to the racial demographic of her audiences each time she gave a speech to make sure she used the best possible examples.

Religion is also often used as a demographic category, and depending on what the purpose of the information is, it can be broken down in a variety of different ways. Religion is most commonly explored by denomination, or the specific religious faith a person practices. This refers to labels such as Catholic, Protestant, Muslim, Buddhist, Jewish, and the like. On the other hand, religion also can be explored by asking people how often they attend church services. Do they go once a week? Once a month? On holidays? Not at all? Just like racial demographics, this information can help you determine how strongly to make a point, as well as craft strategies for identifying with audience members through examples or quotations with which the audience might be familiar.

Education level and socioeconomic status are two other demographic categories that might be measured in advance of a speech. In the 2008 primary campaign we discussed at the beginning of the chapter, Senator John McCain, a Republican candidate for president, received a significant amount of support from those who felt that national security was a major issue. On the other hand, former Massachusetts Governor Mitt Romney was seen as pro-business and economically conservative and was supported by those who favored those topics. The demographic characteristics of these audiences played a part in the candidates' ability to construct messages that appealed to these groups.

Former Massachusetts Governor Mitt Romney

©Gage Skidmore/Creative Commons

Group membership also fits the description of a demographic category and can help a speaker when trying to tailor a message to a particular audience. Group membership refers to any affiliation not already discussed, like membership in the National Rifle Association, or Mothers Against Drunk Driving. Clearly these memberships contribute to a person's identity and the groups themselves obviously contain a large number of individuals with common characteristics. Group membership can tell speakers a lot about their audience, thus helping them make sound decisions about what to include in a speech.

| Possible Demographic Categories | |
| --- | --- |
| • Age | • Race |
| • Gender | • Sexual orientation |
| • Income level | • Religion |
| • Education | • Zip code |
| • Political party affiliation | • Vocation |

**Table 7.1**

One final demographic category worth noting is sexual orientation. Much like the other categories we have discussed, sexual orientation can also help speakers better understand their audience and construct messages more likely to appeal to them. Sexual orientation refers to whether a person is attracted to the same sex, the opposite sex, or both. Savvy speakers try to infer characteristics about their audience based upon this demographic category and tailor their speeches accordingly. It is an important demographic to measure in many cases; however, as is the case when referring to any of the demographic data mentioned above, it suffers from one major drawback: generalization.

Demographics are descriptive statistics, but in today's day and age they sometimes cause people to make erroneous generalizations about their audience based on the breakdown the statistics reveal about their audience. Often, people assume that a demographic category functions in unison, and that there are little differences among members within a category. For instance, suppose someone uses a demographic that says 54% of the students support eliminating the football program to say that "students support eliminating the football program." The statement used to describe the data is not entirely accurate because it makes a blanket statement about the student body that denies the fact that many students do not want to cut football from the athletic department. Care must be taken to accurately represent demographic results when citing them in a speech. Likewise, paying attention to the demographics of an audience before delivering a speech can help a speaker tailor his message to the audience.

Demographics also do not measure what motivates a person or population. Oftentimes, researchers make false assumptions about motives based on demographic data. As ethical and astute speakers, we must be careful not to make this mistake. For a list of several possible demographic categories, see Table 7.1.

## Psychographics

**psychographics**
data that measures attitudes, beliefs, behaviors, and motivations

*Psychographics* help provide information not available through demographic data. This type of data can tell a researcher about the beliefs, behaviors, and motivations of an individual, and one group of scholars at Stanford University even developed a program that breaks down this information even further. Psychographic information can provide even more useful information when constructing a speech because it gives a speaker insight into why a specific population acts the way they do. When you understand that, you can design your message even more specifically toward an audience, increasing the likelihood your speech will achieve the results you want it to.

One significant area measured by psychographics is beliefs. This is different than measuring, say, religion, which is a demographic category. Beliefs encompass more fluid categories of information than denominations of faith. They examine such things as attitudes toward issues or ideas. Beliefs are often as static a part of a person as their demographic characteristics, making them just as important to someone attempting to appeal to them. Measuring psychographic data is a more complicated process than determining the demographics of a group, and therefore it requires more advance time to gather and analyze.

A psychographic inquiry can be fueled by demographic data to make it more useful. For example, a speaker is about to give a speech on eliminating the death penalty to representatives for the United States Catholic Bishops Association and wants to know what they believe on issues related to that topic. The speaker designs a survey to gather that information, including questions like "Are you

**GOOD**                                                    **BAD**  **Figure 7.1**

**Example of a Likert Scale**

Extremely    Quite    Slightly    Neither    Slightly    Quite    Extremely

opposed to the death penalty?" and "How strongly do you believe in the sanctity of life?" The first of those questions is an affirmative/negative question with only two possible answers. The latter is a *Likert scale* question that may have several potential answers ranging from "not strongly at all," "very little," "no opinion," "somewhat strongly," or "very strongly." Averaging out the audience responses to these questions helps give the speaker a better idea as to how to structure and approach his speech on the death penalty. See Figure 7.1.

**Likert scale**
a way of measuring how strong a person's beliefs, attitudes, and values are. They usually consist of 3-7 possible answers

In addition to beliefs, psychographics also measure the motivations of an individual or group. What drives them to make the decisions they make, or act the way they do? Are they motivated by success? Fear? Money? Achievement? Psychographic questions can be designed to gather information on these characteristics. Oftentimes, the questions describe specific hypothetical scenarios and people are asked to answer based upon the answer given. They can be offered choices as well within these scenarios to better inform their decisions and better illustrate to the researcher why they made the choice that they did. Again, like beliefs, inquiries seeking to determine this type of data are more often than not driven by demographic data. Understanding what motivates your audience can assist you when developing the appeals you make within a speech. Properly motivating your audience will only improve the efficacy of your speech.

Beliefs and motivations both influence the behaviors of people and groups, and those behaviors are a third focus of psychographics. Behaviors are the actions an individual or group takes, often as a result of their beliefs and motivations. Behaviors can be idiosyncratic, or unique, or they can occur consistently, illustrating a trend of that population. Knowing the trends of a group or individual can help speakers predict the effect the words they use will have on an audience, making behaviors an important psychographic statistic when choosing what words to use within a speech.

We hope it is apparent that demographic and psychographic statistics have a tremendous amount of application in the marketing industry, in addition to their uses for speechwriters. In fact, one of the primary tools for categorizing individuals and groups according to psychographic information was developed for market researchers by the Stanford Research Institute. The *Values, Attitudes, and Lifestyles (VALS) framework* uses psychographic data to place people into one of eight categories, each indicating the beliefs and motivations of that class of people while predicting what type of market behaviors can be expected from

**Values, Attitudes, and Lifestyles (VALS) framework**
a tool used for categorizing individuals and groups according to their psychographic traits

**medium**
·········
the channel through which the message travels (Note: Medium is singular for the plural term media)

**innovators**
············
people involved in change, who have high self-esteem and plenty of personal resources

**thinkers**
··········
mature, responsible, well-educated professionals who are motivated by ideals

**believers**
···········
people motivated by ideals, but who do not have a significant amount of resources

**achievers**
············
people who are motivated by success, politically conservative, and work oriented; they value the familiar

**strivers**
··········
people who are low in resources, but motivated by achievement

them.[9]  This information is then used to target consumer messages.  VALS can also be adapted for use in the speech development process because the only thing that is different is the *medium* through which the message is communicated: for market strategists it is transmitted through commercials, but for public speakers it is transferred through a much longer speech.

*Innovators* are the first subgroup in the VALS framework.  These people are often involved in activities that stimulate change.  They have high self-esteem and a significant amount of personal resources.  They like the finer things in life, primarily because they can afford them and change easily from what they already have.  As you can guess, they are very concerned with image.  An audience that consists of innovators is therefore likely to be most receptive to messages that stress improving the quality of life and express good taste.

The second subgroup of the VALS framework consists of *thinkers.*  Like innovators, this group of people has lots of personal resources, but unlike the previous group, they are not primarily concerned with image.  They make rational decisions and are often well-informed on world events.  They are concerned with change, but not change to make themselves or their work appear better; rather, they value change that actually makes things better.  Speakers addressing thinkers should take care to structure their arguments carefully and logically, and be sure to demonstrate an appreciation for social improvement.

People who are motivated by ideals but do not have lots of resources are called *believers* in the VALS system.  These middle-class individuals are conservative consumers who prefer familiarity and consistency in their lives.  Believers' lives revolve around ideals that emanate from entrenched systems and organizations like churches, nations, and community groups.  That being the case, appeals that stress connections to these groups and the values they represent resonate with believers.

The VALS framework also includes *achievers*, who are similar in some ways to believers. Like believers, achievers are middle-class economically, but instead of being motivated by ideals, achievers are motivated by success.  That motivation comes from their focus on work, and they value things that let others know they have succeeded.  Achievers are also conservative and respect the rules and status quo, just as believers do.  Achievers want to be pushed, and speakers should be attuned to that characteristic if they know this is the audience to which they are appealing.

A fifth category of people in the VALS framework are called *strivers*.  Strivers are essentially achievers without the financial resources.  They are motivated by achievement, and are even more "about the bling" than their achiever counterparts. This group goes so far as to try and emulate those they admire in as many ways as their resources permit them to.  They are, for all intents and purposes, striving to be something they are not.  Due to the similarities they share with achievers, it makes sense that appeals to this group mostly mirror those directed toward achievers.

*Experiencers*, the sixth group in the VALS framework, are motivated by image and have the capability to express and improve it. They are a high-resource group and are typically younger than the other groups. They tend to stay physically active and spend a great amount of time on social activities, illustrating their image-conscious nature. They also make many purchases, especially on new products and services, so they can maintain their appearance as trendy and popular individuals. New, creative ideas appeal to them, and they are also the most susceptible of all the groups to the logical fallacy, bandwagon, which we will discuss later in Chapter 13.

**experiencers**

people motivated by image who have the capability to express and improve it

More economically challenged individuals who value self-sufficiency are referred to as *makers* in the VALS matrix. Makers have few resources and focus on familiar things like family, work, and physical activities. They have little time to spend on staying up to speed on current events so they do not care much for the broader world. Due to their emphasis on being self-sufficient, makers value things that are practical and functional. They are a fairly logical group who are more apt to listen to something if it can be demonstrated as purposeful and applicable in their daily lives.

**makers**

a low resource group that values self-sufficiency and the familiar

The eighth and final VALS framework category is *survivors*. Survivors have neither the resources nor the desire to improve their own image or be motivated by ideals. They are motivated more by need. Survivors try and do just that: survive. They are the least likely of any VALS group to be persuaded by anything other than the practical benefit something might have in their lives.

**survivors**

the lowest income bracket and the oldest median age of any VALS category

**Table 7.2**

| VALS Descriptor | Characteristics | Behavior or Appeal |
|---|---|---|
| | **VALS Framework** | |
| Innovators | High self-esteem, image conscious | Wine-tasting events High fashion |
| Thinkers | Personal resources, logical, not about image, change that improves things | Work to improve blighted neighborhoods |
| Believers | Conservative, like familiarity, consistency | Active in church and/or respected civic groups |
| Achievers | Success-driven with resources | Status symbols as proof of success |
| Strivers | Success-driven, few resources | Desire status of Achievers |
| Experiencers | Many resources, stress on image | Trendy clothes and technology, health clubs, active night spots |
| Makers | Self-sufficient, practical | Not trendy, not into image or status |
| Survivors | Few resources, motivated by need, thrifty | Spend money on essentials, not trendy |

As you can see, the VALS framework illustrates both the complexity and usefulness of psychographic information about an audience. Try to think of the context in which you might encounter members of each group, but just like demographics, try to avoid believing that all these different categories function as one monolithic whole. Use this information strategically to get your points across and increase your ability to identify with an audience, but remember this knowledge does not automatically result in success. For a summary of the VALS framework, see Table 7.2.

## Other Ways to Gather Audience Information

**open-ended questions**
................
items on a survey that allow room for the person taking the survey to answer in his/her own words

**fixed-response questions**
................
items on a survey that allow only for prescribed answers

Thus far we have explored two significant forms of data, demographics and psychographics, which can be ascertained through the use of survey instruments. Surveys can contain *open-ended questions* or *fixed-response questions*. Surveys are quite useful if you have the time, but a lot goes into their creation, distribution, collection, and analysis. Not only must you provide time for yourself to create the proper questions, but you also must allow your audience time to answer. Following that, you must again allow for time to analyze the results you find and then use that information to inform your speech. Because of their time-consuming and somewhat cumbersome nature, surveys are often difficult to employ before giving a speech. Instead, we try to find out desired information through a variety of other methods.

If we cannot conduct a survey ourselves, the first place to look to find the demographic statistics we need is on the web. If an organization is hosting the speaking event you often can find information on its membership through either its homepage or simply by calling it directly and asking for the statistics. The older the organization, the more likely you will find more detailed information on its membership.

Another technique for discovering information about your potential audience is through interviewing. If potential members of the audience are available and willing to speak with you in advance of the presentation, arrange appointments with them to gather specific information you need to help you develop your speech. Interviews primarily consist of open-ended questions because demographic questions are simply not suited for conversation, and the answers to some of them (like race and gender) are readily identifiable without asking the person. An added advantage to the interviewing strategy is that throughout the course of the interview you will develop a relationship with one of your audience members, thus increasing your comfort level when you actually deliver the address. Interviews are much more personal than a survey and, if used correctly and creatively, they can be very beneficial to the speaker.

If there is no organization to poll and if individuals who might attend your talk are not easily found and approached in advance of the speech, then the next step to gathering audience information is through on-site analysis. It is possible to conduct interviews at the site of the speech. However, that information can only help with small brief changes to the wording and structure of your speech. "Working the room," as some refer to it, does, however, increase your identification with the audience by letting them see you walk among them before the presentation. Many people try to work the room when at dinner parties or other social events, but speakers also can employ this technique before their speech to get a feel for the audience's disposition toward them and the occasion.

So far we have discussed methods of gathering specific types of audience information, but discovering the information is only half the battle to successfully appealing to your audience or even just capturing their attention. In the next part of this chapter we explore how you can wield this information when developing your speech, and we discuss various tips for doing so with regard to verbal and organizational strategies.

# AUDIENCE ANALYSIS AND SPEECH DEVELOPMENT

When you know the makeup of your audience it becomes much easier to construct appeals to them. Speaking in terms the audience knows, using examples designed to resonate with them, and referencing statistics they are more likely to care about becomes easier when you know who they are, what they care about, what they believe in, and what motivates them. After all, why use a BMW as an example of a car to buy when talking to an audience of low-income people? It makes no sense. Understanding your audience can help you create a more effective speech.

This section talks about two ways to make use of audience analysis information. The first is through verbal appeals, or the specific construction of what to say so you can better identify with your audience. The second strategy is through how to say it, or the organizational structure of your speech. Both the content and structure of any speech can be modified and magnified based upon information from an audience analysis.

## Content Strategies

There are three main ways of making use of your knowledge about an audience to augment your ability to successfully appeal to them. The first involves using the data as part of a strategy for identifying with the audience, or making you seem as though you are one of them. Secondly, audience analysis information allows you to incorporate knowledge of the audience into your speech. Finally, it allows you to choose more appropriate examples, statistics, or testimonials for the speech. Each of these builds upon the other to help you establish a strong rapport with your audience.

Identifying with your audience is possibly the most important result of conducting audience analyses. The information you find can help you understand who your audience is, and when you know that, you can find things you have in common with them. Once you determine what you have in common you can immediately stress those common bonds in your introduction, thus making yourself appear similar to the audience. Such an approach enhances your ethos, or credibility, with the audience and strengthens your ability to appeal to them.

For example, Anya is a 21-year-old college senior at New York University with a major in criminal justice. She plans to go to law school so she can eventually work in the district attorney's office in Los Angeles, where she grew up. When she was younger she observed the Rodney King riots of 1992 and watched as increasing gang activity tore apart her community, so she decided to pursue a career that would enable her to prevent those things from happening again. Now, as valedictorian of her senior class, she is addressing commencement on her campus.

She is at a ceremony celebrating graduating from school on the other side of the country from her native home, so how can she identify with her audience immediately? There are several ways.

First, like her audience, she is graduating and thus roughly the same age as many of them. Second, she knows that many of those in the audience live in New York City which, like Los Angeles, has also suffered from gang activity and occasional social unrest in the past two decades. This information can help her develop a speech that both celebrates the joy of graduation while also calling on her audience to help improve society. This can be done quickly in the speech by telling an abbreviated version of her story and linking it to New York. She could, perhaps, cite examples from the class's days at the school where fellow students may have been victims of crimes, or just mention they have all watched the news about crime in the city for the last four years. By making such references in her speech, Anya becomes more credible to the audience when calling on them to be more socially conscious. Audience analysis helps you find ways to connect with your audience in a very real way.

Think of the information you glean from audience analysis as contributing to the relationship between you and your audience. Picture a triangle where you are one corner of the triangle, the audience is another corner, and the message is the third corner (see Figure 7.2). You need to find a way to connect with the audience, and the best way to do that is through the message. The audience also wants to find a way to connect with you, and that also occurs through the message. The stronger your message appeals to the commonalities

**Figure 7.2**
**Connecting with the Audience**

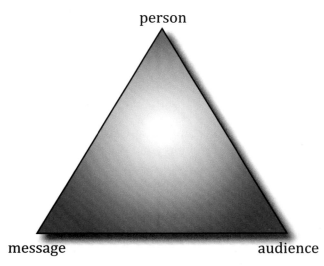

between you and your audience, the stronger your connection will be with the audience.

There is another way to identify with your audience through the use of words, but it can only happen after you establish common ground with your listeners. "We" language allows you to speak as if you are a member of the audience's group, and once you establish a connection between yourself and your listeners, this type of language should be used often. Instead of saying "I," say "we." Instead of saying "me," say "us." This approach enhances your connection to the audience, but if you use it too early, without creating common ground, it will actually diminish your credibility. People need to know *how* you are one of them before you declare that you are one of them.

A second way to use audience analysis information to enhance your connection with the audience is through incorporating what you know about your listeners into the speech. Obviously, this takes a bit of preparation and only the most advanced public speakers can successfully do this in an impromptu manner, but it is nonetheless another tool for you. University and college presidents often identify and reference outstanding graduates and alumni in their commencement speeches. They use these graduate references to help show that they are familiar

©Dean Evangelista / Shutterstock.com

Former Secretary of State Colin Powell gives a commencement speech

with their entire student body and also to identify with the students to whom they are speaking. In addition to citing specific students as representatives for the whole class, they may provide demographic data on the graduating class as well, such as the average age, the oldest and youngest graduates, the percentage of graduating students from particular ethnic and racial groups, and other such information. These types of references enhance the image that the president of a university is connected to, and familiar with, his or her students.

Another way to incorporate information about your audience into the speech is through descriptive statements. At many graduation ceremonies the college president will describe the demographic characteristics of the graduating class. This illustrates knowledge about the group to whom they are speaking and demonstrates that they cared enough about the group to "do their homework." Citing statistics alone probably will not do much, but creatively incorporating this information into a speech can go a long way to establishing a bond with your audience.

The third and final strategy for using audience analysis information to enhance the content of your speech involves the selection of stories, statistics, and examples that will resonate with your audience. When you know who your audience is it becomes easier to reference things that are familiar to them. The more you appear to know about them, the more you appear to be one of them. For example, if you are giving a speech in support of a presidential candidate and you know 80% of your audience is over the age of 65, then perhaps you could open your speech with a story about your own grandparents and what they feel is important about the upcoming election. The reference to your grandparents creates a common bond between you and the majority of your audience, potentially making them more receptive to your message. If you plan on speaking about the dangers of drunk driving or drug use to your class, then citing statistics about that age group and those activities increases the power of your message. Even Aristotle would recommend you select the appropriate inartistic proofs to enhance your ability to connect with the audience.

Information about your audience helps you make informed choices about the content of your speech. It ultimately helps you find ways to identify with your audience members through incorporating that information into your speech through the use of specific examples, statistics, and stories that are more likely to appeal to your listeners. Content, however, is not the only area where this information can help improve your speech.

## Organizational Strategies

Knowledge of the audience can influence the way you organize your speech, specifically how you arrange your main points and when (or even if) you reference members of the audience. The organization of points in a speech is one of the most important parts of the developmental process, and information about your audience can help you choose the best arrangement for your information. Traditionally, there are two ways to organize points in a speech, but knowledge about your audience can help you determine which one will work best for your speech.

One way to arrange main points for maximum effect involves placing your strongest point first. Each point that follows then builds off the foundation of the first main item. This allows you to draw your audience in immediately with a strong start and then build your case from there. In some ways this method serves as a "backup" attention-getter. This organizational pattern typically works best when an audience is not already prone to believing or agreeing with you or the topic of your speech. A strong first point then helps draw them in and realize that you have a valid argument that is worth listening to. So, when you determine there is initial dissonance between you, your audience, and/or your topic through audience analysis before the speech, consider arranging the points so that the strongest comes first.

Quintilian expounded on this approach to arrangement even more. He taught his students to make their strongest point first and to treat the strongest points of the speech individually and in depth. In other words, spend time on the strongest arguments and connect with the audience, while taking the weaker elements of your speech and lumping them together so as to appear stronger. In fact, he advised students to ditch the weakest parts of the argument if they need not be used—something you can determine both before and during a speech. For instance, if you notice your strongest cases are having a large impact on the audience, you may decide adding in the weaker cases might not be needed. This approach to crafting and delivering points makes as much sense today as it did when Quintilian lived.

The other traditional way of organizing a speech places the strongest point at the end of the body of the speech. This pattern puts less powerful points at the beginning and builds toward the most important main point in a *crescendo* pattern. Such an organizational approach could enhance the pathos of an appeal by building excitement, interest, and emotional attachment to the argument made by the speaker. This approach typically works best when you know the audience already agrees with, or is prone to agree with, the subject of the speech. It is even better when the speaker can create a strong sense of identification with the audience.

**crescendo**
.............
an organizational pattern where the strongest point is placed at the end and is built up to by smaller main points

One other organizational strategy that benefits from knowledge about the audience is knowing who, how, and when to reference members of the audience within your speech. Carefully planned references, and even the occasional impromptu nod from the speaker, can promote the appeal of your speech. If certain points within a speech will be magnified by relating them directly to the audience, or to a characteristic of the audience, then it makes sense to do so. Only when you are aware of those characteristics through survey information, or know members of the audience by working the room and interviewing, can you make proper use of this technique.

Creating your speech is not simply the process of putting words on paper; it also involves using audience analysis to choose the proper words. When time allows, analyzing the audience before a speech is an invaluable tool for any speaker. There is one approach to audience analysis, however, that does not involve extensive advance preparation and is, in fact, available to every speaker.

# ANALYZING THE AUDIENCE DURING THE SPEECH

Every speaker can watch, learn from, and adapt to an audience during a speech. There are also several tactics speakers can employ to maximize their ability to connect with and influence an audience based upon that constant feedback. This section details two ways a speaker can analyze the audience while speaking and offers some suggestions as to how to adapt during a speech based upon that information.

## Observing the Audience

Speakers play the role of both message deliverer and message receiver during a presentation, and so in some ways they are also an audience. The vast majority of the time speakers do not act as an audience to verbal cues from those to whom they are speaking, but rather they receive nonverbal messages from the audience while they speak. They can then use that nonverbal feedback to change certain things about their delivery and measure whether or not those changes are effective.

One key nonverbal activity speakers should be attuned to is eye contact. Not only should speakers themselves make significant eye contact with their audience, they also should monitor the amount of eye contact they receive from the audience. If the audience is looking away, at a wall, or reading, then chances are they are not paying attention and adjustments to the presentation need to be considered to recapture the audience's focus.

Audience members may also shift in their seats or move around during a speech. Sometimes this may be due to the discomfort of the chairs they are sitting in, but other times it may indicate boredom. If you are delivering a long presentation then such shifting is to be expected from time to time, but if your speech is short and they move around a lot it might indicate restlessness.

Two physical behaviors an audience may exhibit also might tell a speaker something about the reception of his or her message and whether adjustments should be considered. The first is if audience members continually check their watches or a clock in the room. This more often than not tells a speaker she has been talking a little too long and has lost the audience's attention. The other behavior audiences may exhibit is note-taking. If the audience is taking notes then they are most likely paying attention to your message and no adjustments may be necessary. But, take note of whether they can keep up with your pace and allow them time to write by pausing or at times slowing down the delivery.

## Polling the Audience

Another useful way to gain information about an audience during a speech is through impromptu polling. When you poll an audience during your speech the results are neither scientific nor generalizable, but they do provide immediate information for you and your audience. The most common occurrence of audience polling during a speech is during the introduction, when many people start with a question for the audience. Speakers ask the audience to raise their hands if they agree/disagree with a statement, or if they ever did or experienced something relevant to the speech.

Polling in this manner also can help you learn about whether or not the audience comprehends the information which you provide them. Oftentimes, stopping the speech to ask the audience if they understand or if they need something repeated can be a useful tool. It allows the audience to consider the information they have been given, determine if they need clarification, and play an active part in the speech. In short, it encourages cognitive activity and participation on the part of the audience. However, be wary of engaging your audience in a conversation as you do not want to lose control of the situation.

**classroom response systems**
devices that allow students to answer questions posed during a lecture and provide tabulated results of the poll for everyone in the room in a timely manner

Polling during a speech does not need to be public; that is, it can be done anonymously. If you plan to conduct an anonymous poll during the speech and use the results at a later time, be prepared to do so. This will require either a paper ballot or, if the room is equipped with technology, electronic devices to calculate responses for you. Many classrooms are moving in this direction, and yours may be one of them. These **classroom response systems**, or clickers, are two-part devices. The first part is a clicker that audience members (students in this case) use to answer questions posed through PowerPoint presentations. The second component is the software that allows for tabulation of the poll results so the presenter can gather immediate feedback on audience comprehension, agreement, or even enjoyment regarding the speech or portions of the speech.

As you can see, audience analysis can and should be conducted during a speech as well as before. Just as preparatory audience analysis allows you to design speeches for maximum impact, audience analyses during a speech also allow you to make adjustments in an effort to maintain audience attention and even increase your ability to identify as one of them. We now turn our attention to methods of adapting to audience feedback during a presentation.

Example of a handheld classroom response keypad

## Strategies for Adapting to Feedback During Delivery

Audience analysis during your speech can help you determine how to proceed when giving the speech. Those adaptations can occur immediately or later during the speech, but it is important to be aware of what you can do to increase the impact of your speech based on the audience's reaction to it. There are also two things you can do from the very beginning to increase the likelihood that the audience will pay attention and not get distracted or bored during your speech.

The first thing you can do in reaction to the audience's behavior at the beginning of the speech is make sure you effectively use the space you are speaking in. If there are many more chairs than audience members, and if those members are sparsely populating the room, ask them to move to the front in the same general area near you. This does two things for you. First, it decreases their ability to not pay attention because they are so close to the speaker. Second, and more importantly, it creates a more intimate setting where the speaker appears closer to the audience in proximity and personality.

The second action a speaker can employ either at the outset of the speech or at some point during the address involves eliminating a barrier between speaker and audience. Podiums are very useful items, but sometimes they act as an obstacle between a speaker and an audience. To increase the intimacy of the speaking environment, and to demonstrate your comfort among the audience (thus increasing your ability to appear as one of them), either move out from behind the podium and walk amongst the audience, or remove the podium entirely. These actions can make an audience feel more at ease with the speaker, thus making them more receptive to the message.

Other adaptation strategies work better during the speech. If, for instance, you notice that people look confused or seem to be lost, stop and ask them if they understand, or if they need something repeated and/or clarified. Revisit points through the use of impromptu internal summaries of the information if the audience appears not to understand a connection you make within the speech.

Sometimes people can seem bored or disinterested in a speech, and in this case it becomes important to vary your actions as the speaker. Remember, people's attention spans are not very long and so you need to change things up every once in awhile to "restart" their attention span. This can involve changes in the rate or tone of your speech, a noticeable change in the volume of your voice, going off on a short but interesting tangent, or moving from behind the podium. These surprising changes in your presentation behaviors will work to counteract negative audience behaviors you may notice. Adapting to the audience based on how they react to you as speaker is an important element of a successful speech.

## SUMMARY

This chapter explained the importance of audience analysis before and during a speech. We also discussed the different types of information you can and should try to find about your audience and provided several methods of gathering that data. We then detailed some suggestions about how to make the best use of audience analysis information when developing your speech. Finally, we learned about what to look for in your audience during a speech and how to adapt to their reactions. Remember, there can be no speech without an audience and no effective speech without understanding who the audience is, where they come from, and what they care about.

## KEY TERMS

achievers   146

believers   146

classroom response systems   154

crescendo   153

demographic data   139

efficacy   140

exit poll   139

experiencers   147

fixed-response questions   148

innovators   146

Likert scale   145

makers   147

medium   146

open-ended questions   148

psychographics   144

strivers   146

survivors   147

thinkers   146

Values, Attitudes, and Lifestyles
(VALS) framework   145

## REVIEW QUESTIONS

1. What do demographic data consist of?

2. What do psychographic questions measure?

3. The VALS program categorizes people according to what two significant characteristics?

4. What are some useful methods for researching demographic and psychographic data?

5. What audience characteristics would lead you to consider placing the most important main point first? Last?

6. What are some ways of measuring audience responses during a speech?

7. What adjustments can you make at the outset of a speech to help you identify with an audience and increase their attention?

8. What were some of the challenges Mary Church Terrell faced when speaking?

## THINK ABOUT IT

1. Is there a difference between audience analysis and stereotyping? If so, what is it?

2. Are there any ethical considerations for audience analysis?

3. Do we rely on survey information too much when developing speeches in today's society?

4. How could an unethical speaker use audience analysis to his advantage?

5. Is it possible for a speaker to overuse audience analysis?

## ACTIVITIES FOR ACTION

1. Once you have a speech topic in mind and you know where you will deliver your speech, devise a list of questions regarding demographic and behavioral/attitudinal beliefs. Format these into a survey for your audience to take in advance. Use a Likert scale for attitudinal questions, and phrase them as statements rather than questions.

2. Go to a website for a popular dating service, such as www.match.com or www.eharmony.com, and look at a handful of profiles. Take a look at the questions they ask and the options from which people can select their answers. Determine if these are demographic or attitudinal questions.

3. Watch a few films where characters deliver speeches, such as *The Contender, City Hall, Remember the Titans,* or *Mr. Smith Goes to Washington.* Listen to the speeches in these films and identify how these speeches are designed to reach the audiences in the film. Do they employ inclusive language such as "we" or "us"? Do they use a crescendo pattern to conclude the speech? What is done to make the speeches effective? This also can be done with contemporary speeches, but films are fun and effective to look at in this manner.

# ENDNOTES

1. Michael Grunwald, James Carney, and Michael Scherer, "A Right Fight," *Time* (February 18, 2008), 37.

2. June Kronholz, "Will McCain Make Nice to the Right?" *The Wall Street Journal* (February 6, 2008), eastern edition, sec. A.

3. Ivy J. Sellers, "CPAC 2007 Hosts Record Crowd of Enthusiastic Conservatives," *Human Events*, March 19, 2007, http://findarticles.com/p/articles/mi_qa3827/is_200703/ai_n18755647 (accessed May 23, 2008).

4. Robert Novak, "Fred Thompson's Progress," *Human Events.com,* July 21, 2007, http://www.humanevents.com/article.php?id=21616 (accessed May 23, 2008).

5. Mary Church Terrell, "What It Means to Be Colored in the Capital of the U. S.," www.americanrhetoric.com. http://www.biography.com/articles/Mary-Church-Terrell-9504299 (accessed June 11, 2011).

6. Ibid.

7. Ibid.

8. Ibid.

9. SRI Consulting Business Intelligence, http://www.sric-bi.com/VALS/types.shtml (accessed May 23, 2008). For the transcript of this speech, see: http://www.whitehouse.gov/news/releases/2001/09/20010920-8.html (accessed May 23, 2008).

# Language

In the United States, as in many democracies, there is a fundamental right to free speech for every citizen, but even that right is not absolute. For instance, we cannot yell "fire!" in a crowded theatre because that speech may result in the creation of a harmful situation. For the longest time, curse words could not be uttered on prime time television, although now that is hardly the case. Language is controversial because it is powerful. It can move people to action, convey a sense of identity for the speaker, or conjure one for the audience. Because language is powerful, even the right to free speech is curtailed. One famous legal case that underscores the power of language and illustrates society's desire to control it in some way involved the late comedian George Carlin.

Around 2:00 p.m. on a Tuesday afternoon in 1973, WBAI (FM), a radio station in New York City, aired a 12-minute segment from a monologue delivered by Carlin. The monologue, entitled "Filthy Words," was initially recorded before a live audience in California and concerned the words a person could not say on public airwaves. Carlin listed the seven words that fit that category and then discussed them in detail. Right before the station broadcast the words, it warned its audience that the monologue included language that might offend some listeners. Unfortunately for the radio station, not everyone heard the warning. One man complained to the Federal Communications Commission (FCC), and that government agency quickly responded.[1]

The FCC ruled that Carlin's satirical presentation was indecent because it depicted sexual acts and bodily functions, calling his presentation "obnoxious" and stating it reduced humanity to its "bodily functions." It further pointed out that the radio station was at fault because it aired the satire at a time when children would hear it.[2] The case eventually found its way to the U.S. Supreme Court. It ruled that the FCC did not censor the station because it did not edit it in advance or prohibit the broadcast from airing. For the Court, reviewing content after airing is not an issue of censorship.[3]

The Supreme Court's opinion, written by Justice John Paul Stevens, discussed why Carlin's monologue was not subject to the protection of the First Amendment. He wrote that Carlin's monologue was offensive and lacked literary, political, or scientific value and was not related to the marketplace of ideas. Additionally, Stevens claimed that time of day, content of communication, and the medium used are all important considerations when defining obscene and indecent language.[4]

In the case of Pacifica and Carlin, language proved to be inappropriate for some audiences. The words, in effect, endangered the standards and practices of society. Carlin attempted to point out what he saw as the silliness of language choices, but in so doing illustrated the reverence and power we accord language. In this chapter we will explain how you may tap into that power and enhance your speech. First we will discuss the basic building blocks of meaning to illustrate the source of language's power. We will then examine several different types of language strategies that can help you enhance the appeal and effectiveness of your message. Finally, we will offer some concrete guidelines for choosing these words when putting together a speech.

# MEANING AND SYMBOLS

Meaning, as we have pointed out in earlier chapters, can be expressed both verbally and nonverbally. In both instances we exchange meaning through symbols, and in that respect symbols are the building blocks of how we understand the world. Language is a common way in which we communicate meaning to others, and the symbolic base of language is letters. Letters are, for all intents and purposes, symbols that when connected to form words mean something. Words also are symbols that represent objects, thoughts, values, feelings, and ideas, and they are the foundation of communication. When we share an understanding of what symbols mean we are able to connect with each other in meaningful ways about the world around us. In this section of the chapter we will explore the four characteristics of any language.

## Language Characteristics

All languages share three characteristics, regardless of their cultural, ethnic, or regional origins. The first characteristic of a language is that it is ***arbitrary***, or that the symbols used to represent things are not intrinsically connected to those things. Since meaning is arbitrary it can change over time as different groups ascribe different definitions and purposes for words. The word "hot," for instance, formerly only meant raised temperature but now also refers to the attractiveness of something ("she/he is so hot") or the success of an action ("he's a hot hitter right now"). We also develop new words every year to the point where the English language has expanded exponentially over the past few hundred years. Words and phrases like "affirmative action," "mother board," and "airline" did not exist until the last century. The arbitrary nature of language illustrates its flexibility, as language changes according to our need to explain the world around us.

**arbitrary**
symbols used to represent things that are not intrinsically connected to those things

Because language can change and is dependent upon constant use to sustain itself, some languages can disappear. When a language is no longer used by a group we call it a dead language, but this does not mean we do not know how to use it or that we cannot read it. For example, Aramaic is considered to be a dead language and yet there are still people who know how to use it and read it—it just isn't a language you will overhear while waiting in line at the DMV! Some scholars focus their efforts on preserving and understanding language and how it reflects a particular culture. One of the more renowned researchers in this area was Mary

Haas, who worked on American Indian languages and did important work on the Thai language before World War II. In essence, Haas and other scholars like her focus on trying to understand the arbitrary qualities of language.

The fact that language is arbitrary also can be a bit shocking. Why do we call a cat a "cat"? It could very well have been labeled "schmoog," but it was not. There was no reason behind the selection of the symbol "cat" to represent that furry little creature. It just happened and people implicitly agreed to that meaning for the symbol "cat." It was a completely arbitrary creation of a symbol to represent something in our world so we could communicate about it.

**ambiguous**
language that does not have precise, concrete meanings

Another component of language is that it is *ambiguous*, or that it does not have precise, concrete meanings. Cultures imbue words with a variety of meanings, but even within that culture each word has an agreed upon range of potential interpretations. For instance, the term "cool" can refer to temperature or the appeal of someone or something. Even holidays like Thanksgiving vary in meaning from country to country based upon the specific circumstances surrounding that holiday. As a speaker it is always important for you to understand the potential interpretations words can have and use them in the proper context with your audience so that your message is as clear as possible. It is through the ambiguous nature of language that many misunderstandings develop, unless the meaning of the word is made clear.

Movie poster from
*Donnie Brasco*

Take, for example, the phrase "friend of mine." For many people this phrase defines a level of association between you and another person; however, different people have different definitions of exactly what a friend is. In the movie *Donnie Brasco*,[5] Al Pacino's character introduces someone he recently met, played by Johnny Depp, to the mobsters for whom he works. On the way over to the introduction he clearly spells out that when he introduces him to his bosses as "friend of mine" it means he is connected but not officially a part of the organization. He further explains that if he said "friend of ours" then Depp's character would have been accorded more respect because it would mean he was a full member of the mob. This example illustrates how ambiguous language can be, and how important it is to make sure the audience knows the meaning of the words and phrases you use.

**abstract**
words are not concrete or tangible items; they are only representations

The third component of language is that it is *abstract*. Abstract means that words are not concrete or tangible items; you cannot touch them or feel them as they simply represent something else. Language is removed from the actual objective phenomena it represents, thus making it an abstract construct. Words can vary in their abstractness, according to the degree to which they accurately represent the real thing. The tool for identifying and measuring the degree to which our language is abstract is called the ladder of abstraction, a concept developed by Alfred Korzybski and S. I. Hayakawa in the 1960s.[6]

## SPOTLIGHTING THEORISTS: MARY HAAS

**Mary Haas (1910–1996)**

During the 1930s the most renowned linguist of the era, Edward Sapir of Yale, trained a small number of graduate students. One of those students, Mary Haas, went on to become a renowned linguistic researcher and teacher in her own right.[7] Her dissertation concerned the Tunica Indians, a tribe once located in present day Louisiana, and she earned her Ph.D. in 1935. She also did linguistic work on several other Southeastern American Native American languages, including the Choctaw, Alabama, and Creek.

Prior to World War II she worked with the Thai language assisting in the preparation of training materials to be used by the Armed Services. In 1942–1943 she taught Thai at the University of Michigan. In 1943 Haas began teaching Thai in the Army Specialized Training Program at Berkeley. After the war she became a permanent member of the Berkeley faculty.[8]

Haas was a faculty member at that university until 1977 and during that time she directed the Survey of California Indian Languages. She is credited with leading students in doing valuable work on languages that have nearly become extinct.[9] Mary Haas died in 1996 at the age of 86.[10] The scholarly journal *Anthropological Linguistics* published a memorial in its 1997 Winter issue.[11]

---

The ladder of abstraction depicts the most abstract term at the top of the ladder, and the closest to the objective phenomenon at the bottom. So, in Figure 8.1, at the top of the ladder you see "animal." On the level below that, representing a term slightly less removed from the object, is the term "human being." Since there are several billion human beings on the planet we move to the next level and see "musician." Again, even though this term narrows our original term significantly, it is still abstract. The next rung uses the term "rock musician," improving the connection between the term and described object. Finally, on the bottom rung of the ladder of abstraction we see "Bruce Springsteen," a very specific use of language that is as close to representing the object as possible through words.

**Figure 8.1**
**Ladder of Abstraction**

The ladder of abstraction also is illustrative of the fourth quality of any language. Scholar Kenneth Burke first noted that language, like human beings, is *hierarchical* in nature. That is, it places values of more and less on everything. Think about how we talk about advancing in the workplace. We move up from the mailroom. We don't make lateral moves. When we go to a hotel we want to stay

**hierarchical**
·············
language that is structured according to more or less, higher or lower

in the penthouse on the top floor. Language, much like our social lives, reflects a hierarchy where one thing is more important, or valued more, than another.

Language is arbitrary, ambiguous, abstract, and hierarchical but it is also very useful. Language uses symbols to represent the world around us and serves as the foundation for our ability to connect with each other. Whereas in this section of the chapter we explained the characteristics of language, in the next section we will discuss general forms of language we use in everyday encounters. Understanding what language does for us and how it does so is essential for determining which terms and phrases we should incorporate into our speeches in order to maximize their effectiveness.

## FORMS AND USES OF LANGUAGE

Language can be used in many different ways to send a message to an audience. Sometimes single-word strategies are the best way to convey meaning to an audience. In other instances clusters of words form a coherent impression of something for people as well. In the United States and many other places around the globe, we are free to employ either, both, or neither of these approaches thanks to freedom of speech. In this part of the chapter we will first discuss some single-word strategies you may find useful in developing your speech. We then detail a few word-cluster strategies that also might be beneficial in constructing your speech. Third, we will explain a few creative ways to structure language within a speech. Finally, we cover the ethical issues related to word choice and freedom of speech.

### Single-Word Approaches

In this part of the chapter we will cover three types of single-word approaches to making language meaningful in a speech: metaphor, simile, and ideograph. A **single-word approach** does not necessarily mean that only one word is required for meaning to be transferred, but rather that meaning is derived from specific individual words used in a strategic way. We are all probably quite familiar in some way with the first two of these strategies and also probably can recognize words that fit into the third category although we may not recognize the name of that type.

**single-word approach**
meaning is derived from individual words used in a strategic way

The first single-word approach is a broad category that contains a variety of distinct subsets. **Metaphor** is the broad term used to define comparisons that show how two things are alike in an important way, despite being quite different in most ways. We often use metaphors to add color, flavor, and vividness to our everyday experiences. Take the following phrase as an example: "I will now shed some light on the issue." Obviously, there is no actual light, but a lack of understanding is compared to darkness, and the speaker's intention to provide knowledge is compared to illuminating that darkness through providing light. Another example is describing a person who is adept at gardening as having a "green thumb." Again, the person's thumb is not actually green, but the color reminds people of grass and plants, thus making the connection and comparison between the activity and the person who enjoys it. There are a variety of different

**metaphor**
comparisons that show how two things are alike in an important way, despite being quite different in most ways

forms and types of metaphors, but rather than go into any great detail explaining the forms and types we have provided you with the list shown in Table 8.1.

**Table 8.1**

| Types of Metaphors | | |
|---|---|---|
| **Type** | **Description** | **Example** |
| Dead metaphor | Meaning lost in time | "Son of a gun" |
| Submerged metaphor | One part is implied | "He legged out a base hit" |
| Mixed metaphor | No logical connection between the metaphors | "His machine gun mouth was going like a house afire" |
| Synecdoche | One element represents the whole | "She drives some really cool wheels" |
| Metonym | A word that says something but refers to a related matter | "I want to buy this. Do you take plastic?" |
| Extended metaphor | One main subject which applies to other metaphors | "I think that the world is one large main stage and politicians and military leaders are actors" |
| Absolute metaphor | There is no connection between the topic and the metaphor | "Light up another smoke and put a nail in your coffin" |
| Complex metaphor | When a metaphor is the root to another metaphor | "We need some light on the subject" |

A second single-word approach is often confused with metaphor but, in fact, holds one major distinction that separates it in theory and practice. A *simile*, like a metaphor, is a comparison between two objects, but whereas metaphors make both objects appear as if they are equal, similes allow each object in the comparison to retain their unique differences. When you use the word "like" or "as" in comparing two objects you are using a simile because the two objects in the comparison are similar but not equal. Here is an example of a simile: "The quarterback threaded that pass like a needle." The needle and the trajectory of the pass keep their distinctive qualities, but the comparison gives the object a reference to which some aspect, such as difficulty, can be ascribed. Another example: "She is strong as an ox." In this example the two objects in the comparison retain their distinctiveness while sharing a specific characteristic.

**simile**
a comparison between two objects that allows each object in the comparison to retain its unique differences

Similes sometimes need further explanation so their intended meaning can be properly conveyed. Consider this statement: "Her face was like an autumn sunrise." The intention is to convey a comparison regarding beauty; however, more detail of this simile provides greater and more specific meaning for the object. Just like metaphors, similes are very useful tools for enhancing the vivid nature of a speech and allowing an audience to visualize a concept or object within your speech.

A third single-word approach to conveying meaning was identified by scholar Michael Calvin McGee in 1980. An **ideograph** is essentially an ill-defined, politically powerful term or phrase that can push people to action. As shown in Table 8.2, examples of ideographs include terms such as "freedom," "terror," "rule of law," "equality," and "liberty," just to name a few.[12] Each of these has significant cultural resonance in the United States and has served as a justification for a variety of different arguments. As recently as 2001 and 2003 President George W. Bush used the terms "freedom" and "terror" to call for military action against Afghanistan and Iraq, respectively. They also have been used to justify actions such as warrantless wiretapping and indefinite imprisonment at Guantanamo Bay. "Equality" was used during the civil rights era to push for desegregation and has recently appeared again to justify changes in the tax code. Ideographs are very powerful because the meaning of the term or phrase is culturally provided. You can use such terms within your speech to augment the emotional dimensions of an appeal for action.

**ideograph**
an ill-defined, politically powerful term or phrase that can push people to action

**Table 8.2**

| Examples of Ideographs | |
|---|---|
| • Freedom | • Terror |
| • Rule of law | • Equality |
| • Liberty | • Justice |

Each single-word approach to conveying meaning discussed in this section holds specific power thanks to the arbitrary, ambiguous, and abstract nature of language. You can use them to effectively enhance your speeches by creating a more vivid and concrete presentation. The more vivid the descriptions you use and the more concrete the detail you provide, the more the speech will appeal to an audience. Single-word approaches, however, are not the only strategy available to you when making language choices within your speech.

## Word-Cluster Approaches

**word-cluster approach**
meaning is conveyed through more complex structures such as stories

Meaning is not simply found to be potent in simple words and phrases. In many instances meaning is transmitted through more complex approaches that use language to construct meaning for an event, person, or culture. For the sake of simplicity we will call this a **word-cluster approach** because, unlike the single-word approach, meaning is not contained in individual words used in a strategic way; rather, meaning is conveyed through more complex structures such as stories. In this section we will explore two different word-cluster approaches to conveying meaning: rhetorical history and myth. Either of these tools can be used by you to present information or make an argument in a vivid, creative, and interesting manner.

The first word-cluster approach we will examine involves how we understand and communicate about our past. Think about your past, the country's past, and even world history. Everything you know about these things is only part of their story, but these parts of our past are often used to justify actions in the present. These **arguments from the past** appropriate parts of history to justify present or future actions. Arguments from the past employ stories and explanations to convey meaning. Those stories are interpretations of events and provide the power for arguments from the past.

**arguments from the past**
appropriating historical events, facts, or people to justify present or future actions or explain events in the here-and-now

Take the events of September 11, 2001, for example, when terrorists attacked the World Trade Center and Pentagon. Immediately following these events people compared the attack to the Japanese sneak attack on Pearl Harbor that precipitated World War II. That comparison imbued 9/11 with certain qualities inherent in Pearl Harbor, thus allowing 9/11 to also become a justification for war against the Taliban in Afghanistan in the same way Pearl Harbor allowed war to be declared against Japan. In this case a past event is used to provide significance to a present situation so future policy can be enacted.

Language, as we have noted, is imprecise and only somewhat represents an objective reality. History is always incomplete because we were not there and our understanding is based on the reflections and documents that have survived the past. These provide an imprecise understanding of the past because they are incomplete and because they rely on words—which are ambiguous themselves—to tell the story.

A second word-cluster approach is even more abstract than incomplete stories about our past because it does not need to rely on even some actual facts. A **myth** is a rhetorical construction that tries to explain natural events or cultural phenomena and is used to identify with a group and justify actions or beliefs. Myths also carry similar power to arguments from the past. Speakers often use myths to identify with an audience that shares the values the myth contains, but myths also can be used as justification to preserve a seemingly sacred event, object, or institution, as well.

**myth**
a rhetorical construction that tries to explain natural events or cultural phenomena and is used to identify with a group and justify actions or beliefs

One of the central myths of any culture is the founding, or origin, myth. Early Mesopotamians portrayed their founding in the story Gilgamesh, while the Romans looked to the story we now call the Aeneid for the myth of their inception. The Aenied allowed Romans to connect their past to the legends of Troy and also served to glorify and legitimize Roman values and practices. Founding myths are useful because when a speaker tells a version of the myth it allows him to connect with an audience by identifying with their past and the values expressed within the story. The meaning of myths is not inherent in one word or phrase; rather, myths represent a more elaborate and complex use of language.

Myths and arguments from the past are both stories, and as such they need to follow some semblance of a sequence. Psychologist Walter Fisher proposed a reason that explains why such stories are effective at making arguments and explaining the world around us. His **narrative paradigm** argues that humans are storytelling beings by nature and evaluate all stories according to two

**narrative paradigm**
humans are storytelling beings by nature

**narrative coherence**

the degree to which a story makes sense in the world in which we live

**narrative fidelity**

the degree to which a story matches our own beliefs and experiences

elements. First is that the story has **narrative coherence**, or that it makes sense in the world. Myths and appropriations of past events need to make sense in our world for us to believe them when they are told to us. Second, stories must have **narrative fidelity** for us to find them acceptable. This means the story must not only make sense, but it must match our own beliefs and experiences. Stories such as arguments from the past and myths must, in essence, be believable and relate to our own worldview in order for them to be effective within a speech.

Simply knowing the characteristics of language and some of the ways in which it can be used to creatively and artfully convey meaning is not enough; in fact, it borders on the dangerous. It is also important that you understand the ethical dimensions of using language to convey meaning. In the next part of this chapter we will discuss some of the ethical issues that are only relevant in a society where you have freedom of speech.

## SPEAKING of CIVIC ENGAGEMENT

### "I Have a Dream" Speech
### by Dr. Martin Luther King, Jr.

Delivered August 28, 1963, at the Lincoln Memorial in Washington, D.C.

"I Have a Dream" is one of the most, if not the most, referenced and used speech in public speaking classes and other liberal arts classes. It is worthy of such recognition not only because of its historical significance, but also due to its beautiful tone, structure, and use of metaphor, parallelism, and other language devices.

Dr. King used many metaphors in the speech. One in particular stands out.

"In a sense we've come to our nation's capital to cash a check."[13] This statement infers that a check needs to be cashed to fulfill an obligation. Dr. King extends the metaphor further to make his point: "It is obvious today that America has defaulted on this promissory note, insofar as her citizens of color are concerned. Instead of honoring this sacred obligation, America has given the Negro people a bad check, a check which has come back marked 'insufficient funds.'"

This masterful orator also used a form of repetition to emphasize his points:

"Now is the time to rise from the dark and desolate valley of segregation to the sunlit path of racial justice. Now is the time to lift our nation from the quicksands of racial injustice to the solid rock of brotherhood. Now is the time to make justice a reality for all of God's children."[14]

This speech will go down in the annals of great speeches for centuries to come. Reading the speech is one thing, but actually hearing it and even viewing it brings forth the full power of the day and the man who later lost his life due to his course to improve the lives of millions of people.

## Structuring Language

The way you structure language within a speech can also help enhance both your ability to deliver meaning and the audience's ability to retain the meaning of your speech once it is over. In this section we will cover four specific strategies for creatively structuring language within your speeches (see Table 8.3). Strategic use of these structural patterns will greatly enhance your speech, but overuse or inappropriate use will damage your speech, so be judicious in choosing when to use any of these.

The simplest structural strategy can often be the most effective at helping audiences follow your speech as well as retain the main points from it. *Repetition* occurs in two forms, but both involve repeating the same words or phrases. The first form occurs by using the same pattern of words whenever you introduce a new point. The pattern is not immediately repeated because there is data and evidence between the repeated phrase, but audiences quickly determine the pattern, thus making it easier for them to identify when you introduce a new main point. The other version of repetition takes place when you want a specific claim, point, or piece of information to resonate with an audience. Here you simply repeat what you just said. For example: "American Idol was number one in the ratings last fall. Number one." The number is repeated, emphasizing to the audience that the number was important to know and remember.

**repetition**
repeating either the same phrasing pattern for main points, or a phrase you just stated, in order to maximize the audience's ability to receive the information

A second structural strategy also involves repeating something, but not words or phrases. *Alliteration* repeats the same consonant or vowel sound in subsequent words and audiences notice this form of speech because it is unique. Phrases like "peace, progress, and prosperity" or "direct, deliberate, and decisive" repeat the same consonant sound at the beginning of three words that follow each other, making it more pleasing to the ear. Additionally, the words build on and relate to one another, thus underscoring your description of an object.

**alliteration**
repeating the same consonant or vowel sound at the beginning of subsequent words

Repeating patterns of sounds or words is not the only structural way to enhance a speech. We can also use *parallelism*, similarly structuring related words, phrases, or clauses. By structuring different phrases and words in a similar fashion you can emphasize importance and create memorable wording that the audience is more likely to remember. One of the more famous examples of parallelism can be found in a speech by Martin Luther King. In fact, his use of parallelism is probably why you remember it. The "I Have a Dream Speech," as it is often referred to, is an example of this linguistic device because he uses the title phrase eight times in the speech in the same grammatical structure.

**parallelism**
similarly structuring related words, phrases, or clauses

The fourth and final structural strategy we will cover involves inverting language. *Antithesis* calls for you to take two ideas that sharply contrast with each other and juxtapose them in a parallel grammatical structure. A famous example of antithesis comes from John F. Kennedy's inaugural address: "Ask not what your country can do for you—ask what you can do for your country." On the one hand he decries socialism, and on the other he inspires individual effort. These are two ideas that compete with one another but work together to make a point in this statement. This is one of the more difficult structural strategies to employ, but the reward for the effort within the speech is high.

**antithesis**
two ideas that sharply contrast with each other and are juxtaposed in a parallel grammatical structure

**Table 8.3**

| Speech Structure Strategies | |
|---|---|
| **Type** | **Example** |
| Repetition | "The TV show *The Simpsons* has been running since 1989. 1989!" |
| Alliteration | "I want this report clear, concise, and concrete." |
| Parallelism | "My hobbies are hiking, boating, and fishing." |
| Antithesis | "To err is human, to forgive divine." |

## Ethics and Language

As we have discussed, language is a powerful tool that can help you accomplish the goals of any presentation. As the adage goes, though, with great power comes great responsibility, so you must be careful not to abuse language when constructing and delivering your speech. In this part of the chapter we will discuss two examples of language that cross the line from helpful to abusive.

**profanity**
.........
coarse and irreverent language

The first way in which language can be used unethically should come as no surprise to anyone as we hear examples of it everyday. *Profanity*, or coarse and irreverent language, is all around us—in movies, on the street, within songs, and in many other places. Oftentimes we use this language because we let our emotions get the best of us, but that does not make it right. There was a reason that the words George Carlin labeled "the seven dirty words" were considered outside the norm and inappropriate. Those seven words are common, but in some areas and within some cultures other words that you may not believe to be profane may be considered profane, so it is important to know your audience when making language choices.

Many novice speakers believe that saying something profane at the beginning of a speech is a great way to get the audience's attention, but that is not an advisable course of action. Many audience members may see it as unethical, unprofessional, and damaging to your credibility. This runs the risk of aggravating and alienating your audience from the very beginning. Some topics may call upon you to use profane language, such as an informative speech about George Carlin's monologue, and in those instances it is important to let the audience know that some language you will use is necessary, but that they might find it offensive. When you issue advance warnings of this form of language it makes you appear much more considerate of the audience and shows your understanding of the appropriate use of language in a professional setting.

**hate speech**
.........
rude and crude speech that attacks or demeans a particular social or ethnic group, many times with the intent of inciting action against that group

The second form of language that is considered unethical has become the source of legislation in some states. *Hate speech* is rude and crude speech that attacks or demeans a particular social or ethnic group, many times with the intent of inciting action against that group. Hate speech uses offensive and emotional language to incite hate in the audience and neither the language used nor the goal it is used to achieve are ethical. In the 1930s and 1940s Adolf Hitler used such language to move his country to war. He blamed the ills Germans faced on the Jewish community and began a program of systematic elimination of that group that we now refer to as the Holocaust. Kenneth Burke, the noted philosopher we mentioned earlier, published an essay in 1939 that pointed out the power rooted in Hitler's unethical language.[15]

Burke's analysis of Hitler's rhetoric provided the foundation for quite a bit of scholarship on similar language. Burke noted that Hitler's hate speech followed a particular structure whereby a social ill is found, a cause is identified, a defense of the good qualities of society is presented, and then action must be taken to rid society, or purify it, of the ill. One quality of this rhetoric is the ***dehumanization*** of a particular social group. In Hitler's speech, Jews were portrayed as less than human, thereby making it easier to purge them from society. In other instances enemies are compared to rats, insects, or even diseases to make the audience appear better than the hated group. Scholar Robert L. Ivie later took Burke's work and expanded it to illustrate that dehumanizing enemies in a battle makes it easier to motivate people to fight wars. Hate speech dehumanizes a particular group of people to make it easier for an audience to agree to action against them. For this reason it is often much more dangerous than profanity.

**dehumanization**

making people seem less than human in order to more easily motivate action against them

## GUIDELINES FOR USING LANGUAGE

So far we have covered the characteristics of language, some language strategies that can help you achieve your goals, and two very dangerous pitfalls of language use to avoid. We will conclude the chapter by providing five specific guidelines to help you determine the best possible language constructions to use within your speech.

1.  **Use Language You Know and Are Comfortable with:** One of the common pressures speakers feel is the misplaced idea that they need to sound smart. Understand that you sound smart by presenting evidence in a logical, cogent fashion and making a clear argument, not by filling your speech with big words. In fact, if used too often, complex words can lose an audience and also hinder your efforts to identify with them. You need to sound conversational and natural, not formal and forced.

2.  **Eliminate Wordiness:** Be economical in your choice of words. Just like every speech has a purpose, so too does every word. Be concise and clear rather than overly intricate and elaborate in your descriptions. Avoid using words that are unnecessary in helping you make your point. Excess words take attention away from the points within your speech and can confuse the audience.

3.  **Know When to Use a Thesaurus and When Not to:** An essential tool for any speaker also becomes a threat to a speech's success if used improperly. A thesaurus can help you find synonyms for words you may find yourself using quite a bit in a speech. However, when using a thesaurus you must be sure that you know the synonym, are comfortable using it, and use it in the proper context. Varying how you say something is a great way to

**Online Help**

www.merriam-webster.com
www.dictionary.com

### Kenneth Burke (1897–1993)

Born in Pittsburgh near the turn of the twentieth century, Kenneth Burke remains one of the most influential American philosophers of all time. Unlike many other twentieth century scholars, Burke never received a college degree. In fact, he dropped out of not one, but two, universities. He preferred to write on his own, rather than pursue a doctorate and career as a professor. He wrote multiple books and essays that influenced a variety of different disciplines.

Burke graduated from high school in Pittsburgh and then enrolled at The Ohio State University. Soon after attending he dropped out and chose to enroll at Columbia University. That experience also ended in his withdrawal from school. His lack of a college degree or formal higher education did not deter him from entrenching himself in academic life, however.

In 1939 he examined speeches by Adolf Hitler, then the chancellor of Germany. In this essay he eerily predicted the problems Hitler would cause in Germany simply by looking at how he managed to use speech to seize power. The essay entitled, "The Rhetoric of Hitler's Battle," proposed a process by which Hitler's speech explained away the troubles of the German people by scapegoating people of Jewish descent and purifying what it meant to be Aryan. This work helped future scholars work to identify the ways in which leaders talk about enemies and war, and even apologize for wrongdoings.

Burke also wrote original poetry, fiction, and a plethora of literary critiques that are still essential reading for students in many different fields. His early interests in music and poetry led to his later exploration of language and symbols as explanations of the structure of human action. He eventually theorized that all human action is drama.

Burke's dramatic pentad is still one of the most fascinating ways to understand the relationship between thought, speech, and action. He divided drama, or speech/action, into five component parts: the act, the agent, the agency, the scene, and the purpose.

A message always contains either an explicit or implicit subject performing an action. This subject is the agent, and what the speaker states the subject is doing is the act. For example, when your mother says "take out the garbage" you are the implied agent and taking out the garbage is the act. Agency is how the act is performed by the agent, and the scene is the context within which the act takes place. Looking at the example again, the agency is through manual labor and the scene is a dirty house. The purpose within the message is why the act is to be performed, and in the above example, the reason is to clean the dirty house.

## APPLICATION OF KENNETH BURKE'S PENTAD

The following is an excerpt of a speech delivered by Oprah Winfrey on June 15, 2008, to the graduating class of Stanford University:

"The world has so many lessons to teach you. I consider the world, this Earth, to be like a school and our life the classrooms. And sometimes here in this Planet Earth school the lessons often come dressed up as detours or roadblocks, and sometimes as full-blown crises. And the secret I've learned to getting ahead is being open to the lessons, lessons from the grandest universe of all, that is, the universe itself. It's being able to walk through life eager and open to self-improvement and that which is going to best help you evolve, 'cause that's really why we're here, to evolve as human beings.  To grow into being more of ourselves, always moving to the next level of understanding, the next level of compassion and growth."[16]

| PENTADIC ELEMENT | APPLYING THE PENTAD |
|---|---|
| Agent | Graduates |
| Agency | Openness |
| Act | Learning |
| Scene | Life on earth |
| Purpose | To evolve into better people |

According to Burke, all five components of the pentad work together within a message according to a ratio.  The ratio helps an analyst understand which parts of the drama are most dominant and important to the message's success.  In our "take out the garbage" example, the most important ratio is the scene/purpose ratio.  This pentadic approach is emblematic of how complicated Burke understood language to be, and how he believed language related to thought and action.

Although he was influenced somewhat by Marxism, throughout his life Burke never strictly adhered to any ideology or dogma.

He also never held a permanent academic post anywhere, preferring to stay as fluid in his career as he did in his works.  He passed away in 1993, having left an indelible mark on communication, philosophy, education, and literature.

So influential was Burke that many master's theses and doctoral dissertations employ and/or analyze Burke's criticism and theories. There also is a scholarly organization called the Kenneth Burke Society, and many different English, Philosophy, and Communication Academic Organizations have a Kenneth Burke Division dedicated to exploring or employing his work.

enhance the appeal of your speech and make it easier for the audience to pay attention, but using words just because they are different is a bad idea. Remember the first guideline: Use language you know and are comfortable with.

4. **Use Active, Rather than Passive, Voice Whenever Possible:** A simple way to inject excitement into your speech is to use active verbs. Active verbs depict movement. Passive voice, on the other hand, is boring and easily identified. Read through a draft of your speech and look for forms of the verb "to be," such as the following: "was," "being," "were," "is," and "are." These all indicate the passive voice. When you correct these constructions, look to craft sentences where there is a subject followed by the action it performs, followed by the object upon which it takes the action. Think about the following statements:

> Passive Voice: *"Harold and Kumar were driving to White Castle so they could buy a snack."*

> Active Voice: *"Harold and Kumar drove to White Castle to buy a snack."*

Which of these sounds more appealing? Which avoids the passive voice? As the example also illustrates, taking care to use active voice sentence constructions also eliminates wordiness.

5. **Use "I, Me, We" Language:** This guideline essentially asks that you take ownership of your ideas and statements. Be clear what is your language and what is attributed to someone else. Words like "we" and "our" also help you connect with your audience by making it appear as though you speak as a member of a collective group that includes the audience. This type of language helps you differentiate between your claims and the data that supports the claims, speak more forcefully without being rude, and enhance your relationship with the audience in a subtle but effective manner.

## SUMMARY

Without language we would not be able to understand the world around us, let alone communicate with each other. It also is controversial, as we saw with the case of George Carlin and his monologue. Without language, life would be quite dull indeed. In this chapter we discovered that every language, from Cyrillic to Greek to English, has four common characteristics. We also explored some word strategies that creatively and effectively help convey messages. Finally, we provided some general guidelines for you when constructing and delivering your speech to an audience. The creative and efficient use of words can vastly improve any speech you might deliver.

## KEY TERMS

## REVIEW QUESTIONS

1. What are the four characteristics of language?

2. What are the three single-word strategies for enhancing a speech discussed in this chapter?

3. What are the two word-cluster approaches for enhancing a speech discussed in this chapter?

4. What are the four structural strategies for using words to enhance your speech?

5. What are the three unethical uses of language discussed in this chapter?

6. What language tools did Dr. King use in his "I Have a Dream" speech?

## THINK ABOUT IT

1. Where did language originate?

2. Are there any other common characteristics of language in addition to the four mentioned in this chapter?

3. Are speech and language different? If so, where is the line between speech and action?

4. How do you see language evolving in the future?

## ACTIVITIES FOR ACTION

1. Print out the text of Dr. Martin Luther King, Jr.'s "I Have a Dream Speech" discussed in this chapter. Go through and highlight as many metaphors as you can find, and then see if you can determine their type. Think about whether or not those specific word choices and metaphor types he employed made the speech as powerful as it was.

2. Sit down and watch (or read) the famous vaudeville skit, "Who's on First?" by Abbott and Costello. What characteristics of language discussed in this chapter contribute to the humor of this classic comedy sketch?

3. Print out a famous speech—it does not matter by whom—and count how many versions of the verb form "to be" appear in the text of the speech. The chances are, it will be quite a small number. These forms include "have," "has," "was," "were," "be," and "being," to name just a few of the more common forms it takes.

4. Take a look at the Bugs Bunny cartoons from World War II. Watch a few of them, and then look at the posters the government produced during that era as well. What animals are depicted and who do they represent? Are they metaphors? If so, which type? In terms of ethics, do they dehumanize the subject? If so, how?

## ENDNOTES

1. Kent R. Middleton, William E. Lee, and Bill F. Chamberlin, *The Law of Public Communication* (Boston, MA: Allyn & Bacon, 2005), 405; T. Barton Carter, Marc A. Franklin, and Jay B. Wright, *The First Amendment and the Fourth Estate: The Law of Mass Media* (9th Ed.), (New York, NY: Foundation Press, 2005), 817.

2. Pacifica Foundation Station WBAI(FM), 56 F.C.C.2d 94, 32 P&F Rad. Reg. 2d 1331 (1975).

3. *Federal Communications Commission v. Pacifica Foundation*, 438 U.S. 726, 98 S. Ct. 3026, 57 L.Ed.2d 1073, 43 R.R.2d 493, 3 Med.L.Rptr. 2553.

4. Ibid.

5. *Donnie Brasco*, directed by Mike Newell (Culver City, CA: Tristar Pictures, 1997).

6. S. I. Hayakawa, *Language in Thought and Action*, 3rd Ed., (New York, NY: Harcourt, 1972).

7. Mary Haas: http://www.sealang.net/thai/haas-uc.htm (last accessed June 9, 2011).

8. Ibid.

9. www.britannica.com: http://www.britannica.com/EBchecked/topic/250703/Mary-R-Haas (accessed June 9, 2011).

10. Mary Haas: http://www.glottopedia.de/index.php/Mary_R._Haas (accessed June 9, 2011).

11. http://www.indiana.edu/~anthling/v39-4.html (accessed June 9, 2011).

12. Michael C. McGee, "The Ideograph: A Link Between Rhetoric and Ideology," *The Quarterly Journal of Speech* 66 (1980), 1-16.

13. "I Have a Dream," by Dr. Martin Luther King, Jr. www.americanrhetoric.com. http://www.americanrhetoric.com/speeches/mlkihaveadream.htm (accessed June 24, 2011).

14. "I Have a Dream," by Dr. Martin Luther King, Jr. www.americanrhetoric.com. http://www.americanrhetoric.com/speeches/mlkihaveadream.htm (accessed June 24, 2011).

15. Kenneth Burke, "The Rhetoric of Hitler's Battle," *The Philosophy of Literary Form*, 3rd Ed. (1941; Berkeley, CA: University of California Press, 1973), 191-220.

16. Oprah Winfrey, "Commencement Address at Stanford University," June, 15, 2008: http://www.americanrhetoric.com/speeches/oprahwinfreystanfordcommencement.htm (accessed November 24, 2009).

THE SPEAKER:  The Tradition and Practice of Public Speaking

Purpose: To inform my audience about a concept

Purpose: To inform my audience about the concept of libertarianism

atement: Libertarianism is based upon the principles of individualism and
overnment power.

ion

Attention Getter: Ask yourself what the role of government in a perfect world
rould be.

. Thesis Statement/Introduce Topic: The political philosophy known as
bertarianism believes that individuals should be responsible for a lot of their own
eeds, while the government should have a limited role.

I. Credibility Statement: I am a registered libertarian, and have always been
scinated with the role of government in our daily lives, so I went and spent the
st few weeks researching this political philosophy.

/. Preview : Today, I would like to share with you what the central tenets of
bertarianism are.

   A. Libertarians believe that each individual should be able to do as he or

# Outlining

## CHAPTER OVERVIEW

- **Explains the principles and guiding philosophy behind the practice of outlining**
- **Details the components of a full-sentence preparation outline**
- **Explains how to create a speaking outline from a full-sentence outline**

# **Practically**SPEAKING

One of the signature events in the history of the dreadful disease HIV/AIDS occurred, oddly enough, at the Republican National Convention in Houston, Texas, on August 20, 1992. HIV/AIDS had spread at an exponential rate from the late 1970s until this time, but the reaction from governments—in particular the Reagan and Bush administrations in the United States—was tepid at best. It is no coincidence that these presidents were Republican and therefore needed the support of members of the so-called religious right to receive their party's nomination. In order to do so, they could not be seen fighting on behalf of a disease that was, at the time, largely perceived as an affliction that affected drug users and homosexuals. This all changed thanks to a well-prepared, well-delivered, and poignant speech given by Mary Fisher, a heterosexual, blonde-haired, blue eyed daughter of a major Republican Party donor who had contracted the disease from her first husband, but before the birth of her children.

Fisher knew she was walking into a very difficult situation, but she used every contact she and her family had to speak at the convention. In fact, President George H. W. Bush supported her appearance at the convention, which ultimately paved the way for the speech to take place. The first three days of the convention were characterized by a conservative religious tone, where another speaker, Patrick Buchanan, specifically attacked homosexuals and other groups as destroyers of American culture. Other speakers also took a very anti-gay tone in their addresses at the convention. Fisher herself worried that the organizers of the convention would turn off her Teleprompter or even boo her off the stage.[1] It was such a nasty environment for someone like Fisher to try and speak that she took extra precautions when preparing and delivering the speech.

Fisher spent a great deal of time constructing her speech, incorporating vivid and beautiful language into her earnest appeal for a more humane approach to treating HIV/AIDS victims. She called the climate encouraged by people like Buchanan a "shroud of silence" for a disease that afflicted people from all walks of life, including herself. Most interestingly for this chapter's focus, however, Fisher carried a complete transcript of her speech with her in the event the rumors were true and the Teleprompter was turned off. Ultimately, this did not happen, but the amount of practice and the need to prepare materials to speak from should not be forgotten.

Fisher may have used a transcript, as many speakers do when they have access to a Teleprompter, but in order to get to that point the speech must first be organized and ordered through an outline. As acclaimed author Pearl S. Buck once noted, "order is the shape upon which beauty depends,"[2] and the beauty and power of Fisher's speech would not have been possible without a clear structure for the presentation. All speech contains an idea, a premise, but in order to convey the idea the points relating to it must be coherently organized. Outlining provides us with a mechanism for doing just that.

In this chapter we will explain both the theoretical and practical aspects of outlining. We will discuss the principles behind this organizational process and also the development of a full-sentence preparation outline. We then will explain how to turn a full-sentence outline into a shorter speaking outline that is far more effective at producing an extemporaneous speech. Finally, we will provide practical direction for how to craft a good outline.

# 9

# OUTLINING PRINCIPLES

Outlines are one of the most crucial components of a properly organized speech, and they are not simple things. In fact, most speeches and situations you will encounter call for two outlines. First, you should develop a full-sentence preparation outline which essentially works as your speech draft. Then, after practicing with this outline until you are comfortable with it, you will reduce it to a much shorter speaking outline. This chapter first provides the principles that guide the creation of an effective outline. It then gives you directions and models for how to format a full-sentence outline. Finally, it explains why outlines are much more useful than drafts and illustrates how to change full-sentence outlines into speaking outlines so you are not reading off your materials during your speech. Keep in mind, though, no matter how good your outline, if you do not practice with it, your speech will not be as successful as it could have been.

Much like the other aspects of public speaking, the process of outlining is grounded in theory. Many people believe that simply establishing bullet points or jotting down some notes is enough to call something an outline, but that is not the case. Outlines, in fact, are formal structures that organize content, but it is important to remember that the elements of an outline are not a part of the content of a speech. There are three tenets of outlining theory that are important to keep in mind when crafting an outline for a speech. In this section we will discuss each of the three principles relevant to developing outlines for speeches, but first we will detail the symbolization technique, which is the foundation of an effective outline.

Outlines are formal constructs that help organize the elements of a speech through the use of consistent symbolization. The symbols refer to things like main points and subpoints within the three main parts of the speech. As such, those three parts—the introduction, body, and conclusion—are not indicated by symbols. The first level within each part of the speech consists of main points, and these main points are indicated by Roman numerals. The second level, consisting of those subpoints related to the main points on the first level, are indicated by capital letters. A third level might also become necessary if you have a sub-subpoint, or an item that relates to the subpoint designated by a capital letter. Items on this level are indicated by Arabic numerals. Here is a sketch of how the symbol system for an outline works:

**Body** (denotes the part of the speech)

   I. Main point

      A. Subpoint (related to main point above)

         1. Sub-subpoint (related to subpoint A above)

         2. Sub-subpoint (related to subpoint A above)

      B. Subpoint (related to main point above)

         1. Sub-subpoint (related to subpoint B above)

         2. Sub-subpoint (related to subpoint B above)

   II. Main point

In this sketch you can see how each symbol designates something else but is related to the level above it. The basics of symbolization also illustrate one of the principles of effective outlining.

**subordination**
the organization of a hierarchy of ideas where the most general appear first, followed by subsequently more specific ideas

The idea that what appears on one level is more general than the information appearing in levels under it is called subordination. *Subordination* is essentially the organization of a hierarchy of ideas where the most general appear first, followed by subsequently more specific ideas. In the example above you can clearly see how each of the subpoints relate to the main point and how each of the sub-subpoints are subordinate to specific subpoints. The subordination of ideas allows for a more clear articulation of logic, as well as a more thorough articulation of the relationship between statements. Subordination is also indicated by the fact that each time you move from main point to main point, or between parts of the speech, the symbols reset. For example, in the example above, the sub-subpoints for each different subpoint begin with the number (1), and are not numbered consecutively, which would indicate they were all related. The use of ranked symbols allows subordination to occur within an outline, and it also allows you to put into practice another principle of effective outlining coordination.

**coordination**
all information on the same level has the same significance

Using symbols to rank items in an outline allows for the coordination of ideas and concepts. *Coordination* refers to the notion that all information on the same level should have the same significance. So, looking at the outline above, all Roman numerals indicate main points, while all capital letters are subpoints. Even though these items will be different in content, their meaning and significance is the same as indicated by their appearance on the same level of an outline. Subordination and coordination are the first two principles of effective outlining, and now we will cover the final principle.

**division**
in order to divide a point you need to end up with two or more items

Consider that each time you provide subpoints related to a main point, or even main points to a specific purpose of a speech, you are dividing the information into its component parts. This is important because when you divide something you must have more than one piece after the division occurs. If you divide a dollar between two or three people, all three do not end up with one dollar, right? *Division* is the third principle of outlining, and it states that in order to divide a point you need to end up with two or more items. So, in terms of symbols within an outline, there can never be a Roman numeral "I" without there being at least a Roman numeral "II"; there can never be an "A" without at least a "B"; and there can never be a "1" without at least a "2."

Now that we have covered the three basic principles of outlining and detailed the symbolization system used within an outline, we can discuss more specifically the components of a full-sentence preparation outline and a shorter speaking outline.

# PREPARATION OUTLINE COMPONENTS

After you have conducted research on your topic, identified the types of information you have found, and formulated your specific purpose and thesis statement (or argument), you are ready to begin constructing your speech. The natural temptation for anyone is to sit down and write a draft in essay format first; however, this is a dangerous proposition. Instead you should outline your speech structure using traditional formatting. The outline you create after gathering and organizing information for your speech is called a preparation outline. *Preparation outlines*, also commonly referred to as full-sentence outlines, are essentially detailed outlines that use full sentences next to symbols in an effort to help you organize the speech. They identify all the main components of an outline discussed in this textbook. They clearly separate the main parts of the speech, including the general purpose, specific purpose, thesis statement, introduction, body, and conclusion.

**preparation outlines**
.........
detailed outlines that use full sentences next to symbols in an effort to help you organize the speech

In this section of the chapter we will discuss and illustrate how outlines work to organize the components of your speech. This information will be more specifically adapted to the different genres of speeches and discussed in more detail in the chapters dedicated to each type of speech later in the book.

## General Purpose Statements

Before beginning the outline proper, you must first identify what you are trying to do with the speech. The *general purpose statement* is a brief statement representing what you intend to accomplish in the speech. There are three different types of general purpose statements: to inform, to persuade, and to celebrate.

**general purpose statement**
.........
a brief statement representing what you aim to do with the speech; there are three types

The first general purpose is "to inform." When the chief aim of your speech is to provide an audience with information or, as we will discuss in greater detail later in the book, deliver an informative speech, then your general purpose is to inform. This general purpose serves as the chief goal of your speech. There are instances where you will be called upon to provide information and that information may result in a persuasive effect on the audience. The effect in this case, however, was not the chief aim of the speech; the goal of your speech was to inform.

A good example of this may be when a sales leader is asked by the company to give a report on sales revenue for a particular territory. If that information is provided and the company's leadership feels the territory has underperformed, they may then use it as a reason to hire a different sales representative in the hopes of increasing productivity. Such an effect was not the general purpose of the speech, however. The general purpose of the sales leader's speech was to inform, not persuade.

The second possible general purpose for a speech is "to persuade." When your goal is to move the audience to do something, believe something, or act in a particular way, then your general purpose is to persuade. Just as when your general purpose is to inform and you may have the side-effect of persuading the audience, when your general purpose is to persuade you will in all likelihood provide the audience with information. All good persuasion, as we will learn later, contains solid evidence and information. Your chief aim, however, is to move the audience to action, not provide them with data; providing information is the means to an end rather than the end itself when your goal is to persuade.

The final possible general purpose we will discuss is "to celebrate." This is typically the purpose of epideictic speeches, and we will discuss them later in the book in greater detail. That said, when you seek to celebrate a person or occasion with an audience then your main goal is to praise. In these situations you primarily seek to enhance or create an emotional connection between the audience and the subject of your speech, not inform them about the topic in question or move them to perform some sort of action. Think about the case of your grandparents' 50th wedding anniversary. In giving a toast at this momentous occasion you seek to praise the love between your grandparents and their dedication to each other. You may provide some stories or information in doing so, and as a byproduct of the speech the audience may be persuaded to love your grandparents even more, but the goal was neither of those things—it was simply to praise them.

Identifying the general purpose of your speech is essential to its success. The general purpose is the broad foundation of your speech and knowing the purpose of your speech can help you stay focused on your goals as a speaker when constructing the remainder of your presentation. That said, as broad as a general purpose is it naturally lacks specificity. In the next part of this chapter we will detail how to craft the specific purpose of your presentation, a task that is much easier to accomplish when you know your general purpose.

## Specific Purpose Statements

**specific purpose statement**
• • • • • • • • • •
a narrower version of the general purpose statement that identifies what you will talk about, what you will say about it, and what you hope the audience will take away from the speech

After you determine your general purpose for the speech, you next need to determine the specific purpose statement. The *specific purpose statement* is a narrower version of the general purpose statement that identifies what you will talk about, what you will say about it, and what you hope the audience will gain from the speech. In this part of the chapter we will briefly discuss each of these three components of a strong specific purpose statement.

It is essential to understand that the specific purpose statement is not a "general purpose plus." Specific purpose statements should begin with the phrase "After my speech, the audience will," or "My specific purpose is to inform (or persuade) the audience," or something similar. This helps make the specific purpose statement a declarative sentence that identifies the specific goal you seek to accomplish through the speech. Rather than something you would directly say to your audience, the specific purpose statement is a guiding principle for organizing your speech. Everything you do in the speech should help fulfill the goal of the specific purpose.

Immediately following the aforementioned beginning phrases of a specific purpose statement, you need to insert a verb that best captures your intent with the speech. If you are delivering an informative speech, for example, you want your audience to "learn," "understand," or "be familiar with." If you are preparing a persuasive speech, however, you want your audience to "believe," "feel," or "do." Finally, if you are designing an epideictic speech you may want your audience to "remember," "recall," or "celebrate." These verbs help you focus on achieving a particular goal with the audience related to the type of speech you deliver. See Table 9.1.

**Table 9.1**

| Action Verbs for Specific Purpose Statements | |
| --- | --- |
| Informative speech | "to learn," "to understand," "to make aware of" |
| Persuasive speech | "to believe," "to convince," "to agree with" |
| Epideictic speech | "to remember," "to commemorate," "to recall" |

Once you insert the verb that best captures what you seek to achieve with the specific purpose, you need to identify both the speech topic and what you will say about it. This is where you include the specific topic on which you will be addressing the audience and mention the main points that will compose the body of the speech. Here is an example of a strong specific purpose statement for an informative speech:

> **Informative**: My specific purpose is to tell the audience what breast cancer is, what causes breast cancer, and what treatments are available for breast cancer.

Notice that after the opening clause of the specific purpose statement the verb "tell" appears, identifying what the speaker hopes the audience will do as a result of the speech. It is not persuasive, but rather informative and indicates simply that the audience will learn something they did not know before. Following the verb, the specific purpose statement also identifies what the topic is (breast cancer) and establishes exactly what information about the topic will be addressed in the speech. Thus, it narrows down the general purpose to a specific subject. Now, let's look at an example of a specific purpose statement for a persuasive speech:

> **Persuasive:** After my speech, the audience will know what Jimmy Choo shoes are, where they can be purchased, and why they should purchase them.

The specific purpose statement for the persuasive speech is quite similar to the one for the informative speech. In fact, the biggest difference—other than the topic—is found in the change of verbs. The declaration in this sentence is that the speaker desires the audience to feel like purchasing Jimmy Choo shoes after the speech. This is a specific action on the part of the audience sought by the speaker, thus making the specific purpose statement indicative of a persuasive speech. Finally, let's examine a specific purpose statement for an epideictic speech:

> **Epideictic:** After my speech, the audience will know that today is Labor Day, what Labor Day represents, and why it is important for us to celebrate.

Like the persuasive specific purpose statement and the informative specific purpose statement, the epideictic version also is distinguished by the verbs it uses. In addition to the verb "celebrate," note the use of the term "us" in the above statement. As we will discuss later in the book, one of the central tenets of epideictic speeches is their focus on shared communal values, hence the key term "us." Additionally, this statement makes the goal of the speech (to celebrate) quite obvious, thus placing it in the epideictic genre.

Developing a strong specific purpose statement provides you with a solid anchor as you develop your speech outline. It tells you what your goal is, what your topic is, and how you plan to address that topic. As you can see, the key difference between specific purpose statements for different types of speeches lies in the language choices. More importantly, however, specific purpose statements provide you with a rubric for the next component of your outline: the thesis statement.

## Thesis Statements

**thesis statement**
the verbalized foundation of your entire speech in a single sentence which presents your topic, main points, and goal to the audience in an explicit and understandable way

Just as the specific purpose statement builds upon the general purpose statement, so too does the thesis statement flow from the specific purpose statement. Generally speaking, the *thesis statement* reformulates the specific purpose statement for an audience's ears. It is the verbalized foundation of your entire speech and presents your topic, main points, and goal to the audience in an explicit and understandable way.

It should be clear that no speech would contain a statement to the audience that begins with, "After my speech the audience will," and so the specific purpose needs to be changed into something more suitable for public consumption. Let's revisit each of the above examples of specific purpose statements and demonstrate how they can be reconfigured to serve as verbalized thesis statements. Let's look first at the informative specific purpose statement:

> **Informative Specific Purpose Statement:** My specific purpose is to tell the audience what breast cancer is, what causes breast cancer, and what treatments are available for breast cancer.

How can we turn this into something that sounds more like something you would say to a group of your classmates? Let's try the following:

> **Informative Thesis Statement:** Today, I will talk to you about what breast cancer is, what causes it, and what treatments are available.

Small changes to the language help make this something you would be more comfortable saying to the audience and also help you maintain your focus when developing your outline. How about the persuasive specific purpose statement?

> **Persuasive Specific Purpose Statement:** After my speech, the audience will know what Jimmy Choo shoes are, where they can be purchased, and why they should purchase them.

> **Persuasive Thesis Statement/Argument:** Today I want to argue that you should purchase Jimmy Choo shoes because of their unique qualities, cost, and availability.

Again, notice how the small language changes help to focus the speech for the audience in a way that seems like something you would say, rather than read or write. Finally, let's examine the epideictic specific purpose statement and how we might consider changing it into a thesis statement:

> **Epideictic Specific Purpose Statement:** After my speech, the audience will know that today is Labor Day, what Labor Day represents, and why it is important for us to celebrate.

> **Epideictic Thesis Statement:** Today is Labor Day, originally established by President Grover Cleveland to recognize the importance of the American labor force, but now an important holiday because it gives us all a reason to celebrate the end of summer!

This thesis statement is a bit more detailed than the specific purpose statement but is crafted in a way that sounds more likely to be spoken than written. It fits well within the beginning of a speech and clearly establishes the goal of the speech, the topic, and how that topic will be covered within the speech.

Now that we have detailed the foundational elements of an outline—the general purpose, specific purpose, and thesis statements—we can turn to the organization of the outline itself. Each speech today contains three basic elements: the introduction, body, and conclusion. As we will learn in future chapters, this format is slightly different from that taught by the Greeks and Romans; however, the core elements are the same. Keep in mind, we will return to these concepts later in the book when we discuss constructing specific types of speeches.

## Introduction

Your introduction needs to accomplish five main goals, and your outline will help ensure that it does just that. First, your introduction needs to get the attention of the audience. Next, it needs to state your thesis or argument, which simultaneously introduces the topic of your speech and makes it relevant to your audience. Third, the introduction needs to establish your credibility on the topic. Then the introduction needs to preview the main body of the speech. Finally, the introduction needs to provide a transition to the body of your speech. Let's look at how an outline organizes information and helps you accomplish these goals.

**Introduction**

    I. Attention-getter

    II. Thesis statement [introduces topic]

    III. Credibility statement

    IV. Preview statement

        A. Preview continued

        B. Preview continued

[Transition to body]

It is important to note that if it takes more than one sentence to accomplish the attention getter, thesis statement, or credibility statement, then according to the outlining principles we discussed earlier, you will need to drop down and use capital letters to continue that segment of your speech. Doing so will allow you to subordinate your ideas and more clearly demonstrate an organized and logical speech.

**transition**
............
connective statements that signal you are finished with one point and moving on to another

When moving from the speech introduction to the body, you need to use a transition. *Transitions* are connective statements that signal you are finished with one point and are moving on to another. When moving from the introduction to the first main point in the body, transitions should connect the introduction to the first point in the body. In Table 9.2 you will see some examples of phrasing options for transitions from the introduction to the body of the speech:

**Table 9.2**

| Example Transition from the Introduction to the Body |
|---|
| "With these ideas in mind, let's look at my first main point" |
| "Now that you know what I am going to cover, let's get started" |
| "Since I have told you what I am going to, I am going to dive right into the topic" |

In an outline you will notice that the transition does not receive a symbol designation. This is because the outline must follow the principle of coordination, whereby each symbol designates items of the same level of significance. Transitions are not main points of an introduction or any part of the speech, for that matter. They also are not subpoints or subordinate ideas to other elements of the section of the speech. For that reason they are "set aside" in their own place in an outline. Next, we will discuss the speech body.

## Body

The body of a speech follows the same principles that the introduction does, but it contains different elements. The body, for instance, does not contain attention-getters and credibility statements; rather, it includes main points and subpoints. That said, strong evidence within the body of your speech can enhance your ethos during the speech. Like introductions, the body does make use of transitions between main points. Additionally, the body of a speech makes use of internal previews and internal summaries. These are similar to the preview at the end of the introduction, but tend to be more condensed and work to keep the audience connected with the speech's thesis or argument. Let's look at how the body of a speech is structured within an outline.

**Body**

 I. Main point #1

 [Internal preview]

  A. Subpoint

  B. Subpoint

   1. Sub-subpoint

   2. Sub-subpoint

  C. Subpoint

[Transition]

 II. Main point #2

  A. Subpoint

   1. Sub-subpoint

   2. Sub-subpoint

  B. Subpoint

 [Internal summary]

[Transition]

 III. Main point #3

  A. Subpoint

   1. Sub-subpoint

   2. Sub-subpoint

  B. Subpoint

  C. Subpoint

[Transition]

There are several things to notice in this example. First, you see where internal previews and internal summaries are typically inserted. Internal previews fit at the start of a main point as a way to orient listeners to what they should listen for in the immediate future. Speakers do not need to insert an internal preview for every point, but rather should use them judiciously. The most effective time to provide the audience with an internal preview is when the upcoming topic includes terminology or topics that may be unfamiliar to the audience.

In the example above, also notice the internal summary placed in the outline. Recall that internal summaries are statements that recap the points just made. Internal summaries work best following an important or complicated point within your speech. You should add internal summaries to highlight the central components of the point you just made to the audience. Like internal previews, internal summaries are not necessary following every main point in your speech; rather, they should be employed when they are necessary in your speech. It is also important to note that internal previews and internal summaries are placed in

SPEAKING of CIVIC ENGAGEMENT

## Three Lies
## by J.C. Watts

### Delivered to Students at Numerous Times and Places

Julius Caesar (J. C.) Watts was born in Oklahoma in 1957. Known as a football star at the University of Oklahoma, he went on to win MVP honors in the Canadian Football League's championship game, the Grey Cup.[3] Upon retirement from football Watts ran for office and was elected to Congress as a Republican in 1994, where he served four terms. Watts became known for his stance on family values and personal responsibility while in Congress.

Congressman Watts developed a speech about personal responsibility that he delivered to numerous audiences, but in particular student groups, around the country. His message was simple and contained three clear points. Additionally, Congressman Watts skillfully helped the audience understand the basic outline of his speech by verbally numbering his three points.

In the second line of the speech he clearly stated his first main point: "The first lie is this: 'I am entitled to one mistake.'"[4] He then told the story of the tragic death of NCAA basketball star, Len Bias, who died of a drug overdose soon after being the number one draft pick in the NBA draft. After completing the story Watts identified his second main point for the audience: "The second lie is 'It will never happen to me.'"[5] He then detailed Magic Johnson's confession of being HIV positive and that star's erroneous belief that it would never happen to him. Finally he identified his third point: "The third lie is this, and be careful that you understand this one: 'I've got plenty of time.'"[6] Here he told the students how lucky they were to have teachers and cautioned his audience regarding getting sidetracked from what is important.

In his conclusion, Watts again summarized his main points for the audience. Thanks to this type of structure Watts's speech was very effective and easy to follow.

brackets the same way transitions are and for the same reason: they are not main points, subpoints, or sub-subpoints.

Finally, in constructing the body of a speech, outlines can help with determining the number of main points. Most speeches that you will encounter will include 2-4 main points within the body. This is due to two factors: time and focus. The shorter the speech, the fewer main points you can include because they take time to develop and explain. Also, the more main points you include the harder it will be for you and your audience to focus on what is important. Speaking of focusing on what is important, once the body is complete, you have one last chance to reinforce your speech purpose and topic to the audience: the conclusion.

## Conclusion

Conclusions are essential when it comes to making sure your audience understands the important concepts within your speech, and outlines are helpful here as well. Just like the main components of an introduction, the central tenets of a conclusion can be laid out properly in an outline. Conclusions contain three main elements. First, you need a signpost to indicate you are beginning to wrap up the speech. Typically, we place the signpost at the end of the body, with the transition from the final main point, but in some cases instructors place it within the conclusion. The important thing to remember is that it indicates the end of the speech is about to begin. Additionally, you should be aware that many instructors have a pet peeve about hearing "in conclusion," so it is best to avoid using that phrase as your signpost. After signaling the end of the speech, conclusions need to restate the thesis and summarize the main points of the speech. Finally, conclusions need to contain a clincher. Let's look at how conclusions are structured within an outline:

[Signpost/transition]

**Conclusion**

    I. Summary [restate thesis]

        A. Restate main point

        B. Restate main point

        C. Restate main point

    II. Clincher

In this example you move to the conclusion through the use of the signpost, which in the above outline is placed before the conclusion and at the end of your final main point. Then, the summary begins with a brief restatement of the thesis or argument and continues with restating the main points. This illustrates the principles of subordination and division in that restating the main points relates to the summary and thesis statement. It also shows there is more than one main point that needs to be restated. Finally, the clincher statement finishes the conclusion.

This structure is a very effective way of providing the audience the "take-away" elements of your speech one last time. It may sound very pedantic and boring, but it works, and for this reason, politicians often use this technique for constructing conclusions to their speeches. Take the example of former Republican Congressman and football star, J. C. Watts of Oklahoma, who on several occasions delivered a speech entitled, "The Three Lies," (see the nearby box). The speech is easy to follow because it follows a very clear outline and concludes with all of the elements of a conclusion mentioned in this chapter.

To recap, outlines are formal structures that allow you to organize the content of your speech in a logical fashion. The structure of an outline allows you to ensure that you have incorporated all the elements of an effective speech in an appropriate and logical way. In the next section we will move from the form of outlines to a brief discussion of their linguistic content and why outlines are more useful than drafts.

## LANGUAGE AND OUTLINES

There are two reasons why you should avoid writing a draft and instead outline your speech. The first is that drafts tend to be free-flowing and less structured, allowing for the distinct possibility that you will lose your focus and go off on tangents in the middle of the speech. Drafts should be constructed only if the speech you plan to give is a manuscript speech, and even then only after you have outlined the address. The second reason drafts are a poor choice for a first step is that we write and speak differently.

When we write an essay for class we use different grammar, sentence structure, and vocabulary than when we speak, so if we write and deliver a draft, then we essentially read to the audience, as opposed to speaking to them. Writing calls for proper sentence construction where there is a subject, verb, and predicate, but oftentimes in speaking the best way to make a point to the audience and evoke emotion in them is not through this type of sentence construction. For example, when writing a letter to a subordinate, a boss may write, "Do not ask me for a raise, as your performance has not warranted it." When speaking, it might be delivered with more force this way: "Hello, Matthew. We will not discuss your pay. Do. Not. Ask. Me." This latter example does not contain properly constructed sentences, yet when spoken it makes sense and contains more emotional force than the written form.

When we write drafts we also try to vary the language, sometimes by consulting a thesaurus so the verbiage we use appears more formal and intelligent. In written communication finding synonyms and using them properly is perfectly acceptable and even encouraged, but in speech if you are using words that are not part of your normal spoken repertoire it may come across as awkward and unnatural. Look at these two examples. Which one seems more appropriate for written communication and which seems more natural in a speech?

> **Example 1:** *"There is a voluminous history of athletic accomplishment in the sport of soccer."*

**Or:** *"Soccer has produced its fair share of amazing achievements."*

**Example 2:** *"The daunting challenges presented will test the mettle and steadfastness of our citizenry."*

**Or:** *"Look folks, we have some tough times ahead and we need to stand strong."*

Both of the first statements get the same point across, but the first examples use more complex language than the second ones do, and therefore, are more suited for an essay than a speech. Speech uses terms and language we are comfortable using, and writing a draft encourages us to use the more formal written language than the more colloquial language we typically use when we speak. So, in addition to preventing tangents and keeping your speech focused, outlining also helps limit the use of formal language.

Despite the reduced emphasis on formal language, preparation outlines should use full sentences for each symbol. In fact, they should use one sentence per symbol to better illustrate the logic behind the placement of each sentence. If a sentence does not flow from the previous statement you should either move it somewhere else in the speech or eliminate it altogether. The only exception to this "one sentence per symbol" rule is when you are using a direct quotation. Then, and only then, should you include the whole excerpt next to the same symbol. Also, make sure to put quotation marks around the excerpt and properly document its source.

The preparation outline, however, is not the last step before your actual speech, although you will spend the bulk of your time before your actual presentation practicing from it, adjusting statements, moving points, and enhancing your language choices. When you are comfortable with the preparation outline it is then time to develop your speaking outline.

## SPEAKING OUTLINE

After practicing with your full-sentence outline you will become more conversational in your delivery and will not need to look at your outline as much. Additionally, you will begin to remember the information in the full-sentence outline rather than needing to read it. So, to help you deliver your speech in a more natural and conversational style, you will want to use a *speaking outline*, or a truncated form of your full-sentence preparation outline that does not include complete sentences unless you are using direct quotations from another source. Speaking outlines are easy to develop from a completed full-sentence outline.

**speaking outline**
a truncated form of your full-sentence preparation outline that does not include complete sentences

The same format you used to create your full-sentence preparation outline applies to a speaking outline. When you create your speaking outline you still retain all the formatting elements of the full-sentence preparation outline in terms of Roman numerals, capital letters, and numbers, and you still follow the principles of outlining we discussed earlier. The only elements that do not appear on a speaking outline that appear in a full-sentence preparation outline are in-text citations, your stated general purpose, and your stated specific purpose.

Below is a sample outline for an informative speech.
Notice how it follows all the requirements for a strong preparation outline.

# Informative Speech (Object)

**General Purpose:** To inform about an object.

**Specific Purpose:** To inform my audience about George Washington, the first president of the United States of America.

**Central Idea:** George Washington's ability to handle difficult circumstances in war and government grew out of experiences in his early life and his dedication to detail.

## I. Introduction

    A. *Attention-Getter:* Despite what your teachers may have told you, George Washington never chopped down a cherry tree and he did tell quite a few lies when shaping the founding of this nation, but who wouldn't when faced with the series of events he confronted throughout his life?

    B. *Central Idea:* In fact, George Washington's ability to handle difficult circumstances in government grew out of experiences in his life and his dedication to detail, not some mythic promise to always tell the truth.

    C. *Preview #1:* As a young adult in the British colony of Virginia, Washington sought the respect and pride that accompanied an aristocrat, but that desire almost led him to bankruptcy and forced him to pay closer attention to the economic environment around him in future business dealings.

    D. *Preview #2:* Later, when fighting the Revolution he understood how important seemingly simple tasks were to having any hope for success in fighting the British.

    E. *Preview #3:* Finally, during the war, Washington began to recognize the talents of others, and so he delegated authority and cultivated strong allies within his command to help him accomplish what needed to be done.

    F. *Transition:* Throughout his life Washington exhibited that vision all leaders must have, and it eventually served him well when he became our first president.

## II. Body #1

    A. *Topic Sentence:* Washington almost never became president, or even fought in the Revolution, because as a young aspiring Virginia gentleman he almost bankrupted himself.

    B. *Supporting Sentence #1:* Washington inherited most of his land from his family and friends, and the bulk of it was farmland in Virginia.

C. *Supporting Sentence #2:* Like many upper-class aristocratic farmers in his day, Washington farmed mostly tobacco and had it sold in England, but the profits were not large.

D. *Supporting Sentence #3:* Even in the face of limited profits Washington paid a lot of money for dozens of dessert glasses, a hogskin hunting saddle, a custom made mahogany case with 16 decanters, engraved stationery, and many other expensive items he barely could afford.[1]

E. *Supporting Sentence #4:* The costs got so high that in 1763 Washington almost ran out of money and was notified by his broker that he was short 1,800 pounds and interest would begin to accrue immediately.[2]

F. *Supporting Sentence #5:* Quickly Washington realized he would never be able to pull himself out of debt because of the system, and he blamed the British Empire for his problems.

G. *Supporting Sentence #6:* One of the saving graces for Washington was his getting out of tobacco as his main crop, and this move saved him from ruin because tobacco taxes became one of the major contributors to economic problems in the colonies.

H. *Transition:* The experience of almost losing his money contributed to his fiscal discipline later while president, and the vision that saved his money in this episode was also evident in other areas of his life.

## III. Body #2

A. *Topic Sentence:* Washington lost more battles than he won, but because of his attention to detail and ability to figure out the right risks to take he ended up winning the war.

B. *Supporting Sentence #1:* Perhaps the most important battle Washington fought was, according to historian Richard Brookhiser, "the battle for sanitation."

   1. **Detail #1:** In Washington's time troops did not always build latrines, and often took to relieving themselves in the ditches at the foundation of the fort.[3]
   2. **Detail #2:** Only when a German soldier who helped train the Americans arrived at Valley Forge was the practice of building latrines institutionalized in the *Regulations for the Order and Discipline of the Troops of the United States.*[4]

C. *Supporting Sentence #2:* In addition to the latrine issue, Valley Forge also represented another serious problem for Washington: Enlistments for most of his men ended in December.

---

1      Joseph J. Ellis, *His Excellency: George Washington* (Random House, NY: NY), 49.
2      Ibid., 50.
3      Richard Brookhiser, *George Washington on Leadership* (Basic Books, NY: NY), 14.
4      Ibid., 14-15.

1.  **Detail #1:** Wars during Washington's time took winter breaks, much like colleges do, to take a break from bad weather and regroup, and the winter of 1776 was no different.
2.  **Detail #2:** In need of a dramatic victory to keep his troops from leaving when enlistments ran out, Washington staged a successful surprise winter attack on a mercenary camp in Trenton on Christmas that year.[5]

D.  *Transition:* Almost losing his money made Washington financially responsible, almost losing his army made him a more efficient strategist, and, as I will discuss next, recognizing the talent of others made him a stronger leader.

## IV. Body #3

A.  *Topic Sentence:* The forces Washington commanded during the Revolution did not contain a lot of seasoned fighters, so the General was forced to look for skill sets in the unlikeliest of places in order to fight the war.

B.  *Supporting Sentence #1:* One of those Washington identified early on as having the necessary skills and drive to make things happen was Henry Knox.

1.  **Detail #1:** Knox was a bookseller from Boston whose only qualification was that he was well read on engineering.[6]
2.  **Detail #2:** Knox used that knowledge to become the chief artillery officer in Washington's army and a future confidant during his administration as president.

C.  *Supporting Sentence #2:* In addition to a bookworm, Washington also found a close ally and dependable lieutenant from the ranks of the pacifist Quakers.

1.  **Detail #1:** Nathaniel Greene of Rhode Island was a Quaker, but he supported the war against the British and quickly rose in favor with Washington.[7]
2.  **Detail #2:** Washington thought so much of Greene that he named Greene his successor if the General should fall in battle.[8]

D.  *Transition:* Washington had a knack for knowing when to change crops, how to strike the enemy, and who could be entrusted with difficult tasks, all skills he needed to be successful when he later became president.

---

5       Kathryn Moore, *The American Presidents: A Complete History* (Fall River Press, NY: NY), 10.
6       Ellis, 81.
7       Ibid., 81-82.
8       Ibid.

**V. Conclusion**

    A.  *Signpost*: In conclusion, George Washington's early years and time conducting the Revolution gave him the experiences he needed to be successful as president.

    B.  *Summary #1*: When he ran up debt trying to become a Virginia gentleman, he demonstrated vision by diversifying his crops and learned the fiscal discipline necessary to lead.

    C.  *Summary #2:* During the war, his ability to seize the right moment at Trenton illustrated his knack for understanding the importance of timing.

    D.  *Summary #3*: Finally, as a general with few competent soldiers in his army, he showed an ability to identify talented people who could accomplish the tasks the army needed done.

    E.  *Restate Thesis*: All in all, Washington's time early in life and as a general gave him the necessary experiences to develop important skills he needed when he was elected president.

    F.  *Clincher*: Now, the next time you see his face on a quarter or a dollar bill, you know that George Washington's life is more than myth or folklore; it is the story of a man with judgment and vision learned through hard experiences.

The core fundamental difference between the two outlines is that a speaking outline does not include full sentences unless you use a direct quotation, in which case getting the quote correct is of paramount importance. A speaking outline then includes a shorthand version of the full sentences within the preparation outline. Shorthand notes for speeches are not a new phenomenon. In fact, the speeches of Cicero were recorded using a shorthand system developed by one of his slaves who was later freed, Marcus Tullius Tiro. Tiro used what are now called Tironian notes, a shorthand system consisting of abbreviations for Latin words. Unfortunately, with the fall of the Roman Empire the system he devised fell out of use, but many copies of ancient texts transcribed through the use of Tironian notes were discovered in monasteries during the Protestant Reformation. Tiro and his shorthand note system allowed for many of the speeches of Cicero to survive the perils of history, thus making them available today. The idea of using shorthand to transcribe speeches is one of the fundamental precepts used in creating speaking outlines today.

**shorthand**
the process of shortening words or eliminating word clutter in the transcription process

*Shorthand* is the process of shortening words or eliminating word clutter in the transcription process. It allows for a document to contain the essence of what was said without taking it down word for word. As you can imagine, there are many words in every written sentence that you do not need to see in order to remember to say them. Let's look at this brief full-sentence example and see if we can identify unnecessary words:

**Introduction**

    I. *Attention-getter:* Imagine yourself stranded, along with about 50 other people, on a desert island after a plane crash.

        A. Well, that is the premise of the critically acclaimed television show *Lost.*

When looking to cut, look specifically at the full sentences. Obviously, the terms "with," "on," "that," "is," "the," "of," and "a" do not need to appear on a speaking outline because you could easily insert them when speaking without a prompt. But what else could you eliminate? What about the entire subpoint? It would make sense to delete the subpoint because it should flow naturally after the attention-getter. In fact, you might be able to deliver this attention-getter from a mere handful of words, such as this:

**Introduction**

    I. Imagine/stranded/50 people/island /plane crash. *Lost*

This is what a speaking outline contains: words and phrases from the original prose in the full-sentence outline separated by backslashes.

Speaking outlines can also contain delivery cues and directions for what to do during a speech. When practicing with the speaking outline you may notice certain points where you think a physical motion would help add emphasis. You also may want to remind yourself to pause or use a visual aid. If you are using PowerPoint, for example, you can put in a notation to change slides at specific points in the speech. The following example shows how you can effectively incorporate delivery cues into a speaking outline in a way that can enhance the delivery of your speech:

**Introduction**

    I. Imagine/stranded/50 people/island /plane crash. *Lost*

    II. Success/science fiction/ratings/critic reviews (change PowerPoint slide)

In this example the cue for the speaker to change the PowerPoint slide is embedded in the speaking outline. This serves as a reminder for a task many speakers often forget. One of the last things you want to have happen is to forget to change slides or pull out a visual aid during the speech, only to remember later and have to speed through slides for concepts you have already covered. This makes it seem like you did not practice and prepare, thus damaging your ethos with the audience. It also increases the likelihood you will become more cognizant of your nervous reaction to the mistake. Refer to Table 9.3 for some useful tips for creating an effective speaking outline.

## SPOTLIGHTING THEORISTS: CICERO

**Cicero (106–43 B.C.)**

Cicero is perhaps the second most important rhetorical figure in the age of classical rhetoric.[7]

Cicero was a brilliant lawyer and many of his judicial orations are available in a variety of contexts. He was a powerful force in politics and his speeches were known to rouse emotion and influence audience members. Cicero was also known for his writing on rhetorical theory. His most famous rhetorical work was *De Oratore,* or *On the Orator.* This book was more than simply a treatise on how to speak, but was also meant as an explanation of the power of persuasion. He used the book to make the point that the power of speech in the hands of men with no morals was one of the greatest threats to the community.

As an active politician, as well as writer, Cicero was quite outspoken in his support of the Roman Republic. As noted elsewhere, that outspoken support led to his death as the Republic gave way to the Roman Empire. He was killed by forces loyal to Marc Antony in a most gruesome way. He was decapitated, and his tongue and hands were cut off and nailed to the doors of the Senate in Rome as a warning to those who dared to criticize—through speech or the written word—the new leaders of the Empire. One of the most gifted rhetorical theorists and practitioners in history lost his life due to his insistence on standing up for and speaking his mind on political matters.

**Table 9.3**

| Tips for Creating the Speaking Outline |
| --- |
| Bold key terms |
| Write out quotes for accuracy |
| Do not have cluttered or congested text |
| Make main points easily recognizable |
| If using notecards, number them |

It is important to remember that you should move from practicing with your preparation outline to practicing with your speaking outline. In some cases, instructors may ask that you use notecards instead of a speaking outline. In this case it makes it all the more important to have a speaking outline done already. It provides the structure, emphasis, and cues you will want to transcribe to the notecards. Essentially, notecards can be more succinct, or even shorthand, versions of your speaking outline. It is essential though, that you practice a few times with the notecards. It is also important not to use the move to notecards as a reason to change the format from an outline to bullet points—a tempting but troubling idea. Doing so just runs the risk of damaging the format and delivery of what you have been practicing all along.

Even though we believe we have made a case for the use of outlines in this manner, some may still argue in favor of the use of bullet points instead of outlines. Bullet points do not visually display the logical hierarchy behind the speech and also create the danger of going off on tangents and not making your case to the audience as clear as possible. Bullet points are, for all intents and purposes, a list of items with no clear connection. Outlines provide that connection for the speaker and, consequently, the audience.

Others might agree with the use of an outline but object to the practice of indenting the tiers of information appropriately, arguing that it wastes space and the outline would make as much sense if the information were to appear on one side of the page. This, although better than bullet points, still does not clearly differentiate each level of information and its connection to the rest of the material in the speech for either the speaker or the audience. In short, it fails to properly employ the principle of subordination. So, the proper indentation of each level is essential for the speaker and the audience.

Outlining your speech begins early in the speaking process and continues until you deliver the presentation. It allows you to organize your thoughts and information into a coherent order. It provides you with something to practice from and thereby develop your speaking voice and rhythm, something altogether different from your written voice and rhythm. Most importantly, outlining is the manner by which a speaker arranges his speech from beginning to end.

## Outline Template

Below is an example of what an informative or persuasive speech preparation outline should look like and where specific pieces we have discussed in this chapter should appear. Understand that certain parts of the template may change slightly due to the organizational pattern you use, but this should provide you with a strong head start in developing your speech's outline.

*General purpose:* This is a simple statement and contains few words. It usually is "to persuade," "to inform," or "to celebrate."

*Specific purpose:* This statement is narrower than the general purpose statement. It begins with the phrase, "After my speech, the audience will," or "My purpose is to inform (or persuade, or commemorate)," and it ends with the specific topic of the speech and how it will be addressed.

*Thesis statement (or argument):* This is a single statement that encapsulates the overall argument and main points of the speech.

It takes the specific purpose statement and recalibrates it to more specifically address the speech topic and main points in a manner that is suitable for speaking.

**Introduction**

I. *Attention-getter*: A brief story, quotation, or example that draws the audience into the speech. It captures their attention.

II. *Thesis statement (or argument)*: Encapsulates the entire argument or main point of your speech. This is where you make your introduction or insinuation clear. It introduces the topic and main points of the speech to the audience.

III. *Credibility statement*: Details your expertise on the topic of the speech.

IV. *Preview*: A statement that broadly mentions the main point of your speech. It should begin with something like, "Today, I will discuss...."

    A. *Preview statement #1:* This sentence introduces the first specific main point you plan to address in your presentation, and it should begin with something like, "First, I will cover...."

    B. *Preview statement #2:* This sentence represents the second point you plan to cover in your speech. It should say something like, "Next, I will discuss..."

    C. *Preview statement #3:* This sentence represents the third point you plan to cover in your speech. It should say something like, "Finally, I will discuss...."

[*Transition:* This alerts the audience that the introduction is over and that you will now begin making your case by addressing the topic you mentioned in preview statement #1.]

**Body**

I. *First main point*: This statement declares the first main point you will discuss in depth. It is the same topic previewed in preview statement #1 in the introduction.

    A. *Subpoint #1:* This is the first piece of evidence regarding the first main point.

    B. *Subpoint #2:* A new piece of evidence regarding the topic of this section.

        1. *Sub-subpoint #1:* A further discussion of subpoint #2.

        2. *Sub-subpoint #2:* A further discussion of subpoint #2.

C. *Subpoint #3:* Another piece of evidence that relates to the topic of this section.

D. *Subpoint #4:* This may be another piece of evidence or a statement that illustrates to the audience how the main point you just covered relates to the overall thesis of your speech.

[*Transition:* Alert the audience that you are finished with the first main point and are now moving to a new main point.]

II. *Second main point*: This statement declares the second main point you will discuss in depth. It is the same topic previewed in preview statement #2 in the introduction.

[*Internal preview:* You may consider placing an internal preview at the beginning of a new main point to help orient audience members as to what is coming next in the speech.]

A. *Subpoint #1:* This is the first piece of evidence regarding the second main point.

B. *Subpoint #2:* A new piece of evidence regarding the second main point.

1. *Sub-subpoint #1:* A further discussion of subpoint #2.

2. *Sub-subpoint #2:* A further discussion of subpoint #2.

C. *Subpoint #3:* Another piece of evidence that relates to the second main point.

D. *Subpoint #4:* This may be another piece of evidence or a statement that illustrates to the audience how the main point you just covered relates to the overall thesis of your speech.

[*Transition:* Alert the audience that you are finished with the second main point and are now moving to a new main point.]

III. *Third main point*: This statement declares the third main point you will discuss in depth. It is the same topic previewed in preview statement #3 in the introduction.

A. *Subpoint #1:* This is the first piece of evidence regarding the third main point.

1. *Sub-subpoint #1:* A further discussion of subpoint #1.

2. *Sub-subpoint #2:* A further discussion of subpoint #1.

B. *Subpoint #2:* A new piece of evidence regarding the third main point.

C.   *Subpoint #3:*  Another piece of evidence that relates to the third main point.

D.   *Subpoint #4:*  This may be another piece of evidence or a statement that illustrates to the audience how the main point you just covered relates to the overall thesis of your speech.

[*Internal summary:*  You may wish to consider an internal summary to remind audience members what you have already covered.]

[*Transition:*  Alert the audience that you are finished with the third main point and are now moving to a new main point.]

[*Signpost:*  This statement lets the audience know you are entering the conclusion.  It usually begins with a phrase like, "Finally," or "To sum up." ]

## Conclusion

I.   *Summary statement*:  This statement summarizes your overall argument or thesis once again for the audience so they know what it was, generally, you spoke about.

A.   *Summary statement #1:*  This is a one-sentence summary of the first main point you covered.

B.   *Summary statement #2:*  This is a one-sentence summary of the second main point you covered.

C.   *Summary statement #3:*  This is a one-sentence summary of the third main point you covered.

II.   *Clincher*:   Here is where you again connect the speech to the audience. Sometimes, if your attention-getter was a hypothetical question, you answer it here.  If the attention-getter was a story without an ending, you end the story here.  It should be a statement designed to leave the audience with an emotional attachment to your speech.

## SUMMARY

In this chapter we explained the concept of outlining and how its structure can help you organize the information you research into a speech that makes sense to both you and your audience. We discussed the philosophy behind outlining and the six major components of an outline: general purpose statement, specific purpose statement, thesis statement, introduction, body, and conclusion. We also explained the importance of and how to create a full-sentence preparation outline and then, after practicing with it, how to collapse it into an effective speaking outline replete with delivery cues.

## KEY TERMS

coordination   182

division   182

general purpose statement   183

preparation outline   183

shorthand   197

specific purpose statement   184

speaking outline   193

subordination   182

thesis statement   186

transitions   188

## REVIEW QUESTIONS

1. What are the components of an outline?

2. What is subordination and why is it important?

3. What is the difference between the two types of outlines?

4. Why do some students think outlines are a waste of time?

5. Can an outline save you time in preparing your speech?

## THINK ABOUT IT

1. Can you prepare a good speech without an outline?

2. Can you devise another method to replace outlining?

3. Do you think that professional speechwriters use outlines? Why or why not?

## ACTIVITIES FOR ACTION

1. Locate the text of any presidential State of the Union address. Comb through the transcripts and ascertain what the central idea and subsequent main points are for the different parts of the speech. Then, reconstruct the speech using the outline format provided in this chapter. You will hopefully see that many speeches are not as well structured as the ones you will deliver and hear in your public speaking class and that they would benefit from outlining.

2. Take a speech outline you developed and switch around the order of your main points. Does this change the meaning of the speech? Does it make it weaker or stronger? Why?

3. Find an outline of a speech either by creating it yourself, using one from the materials that accompany this book, or using one that a classmate or colleague developed. Cut it apart so that one sentence is on each slip of paper. Now, evenly distribute the slips of paper within the group with which you are working. Take a minute to learn your slips of paper, and then try to engage the rest of the group to try and put the speech back in order. Did you find a better way of organizing the speech? Did you accurately recreate the speech?

4. Go to http://www.fountainheadpress.com/speaker.html and look in the right hand column under "Sample Student Videos." Select the "George Washington" video and watch it with the sample outline from the chapter (page 194) in front of you. Track the speech to see where there are deviations and where the speaker holds true to the form of the outline. This will help illustrate the connections between a preparation outline and the speech for which it is developed.

5. Take the sample outline on "George Washington" (page 194) and try to condense it to a speaking outline. What would you remove? What would you keep? Is there anything you would add, like notes for delivery? Why did you make those choices?

## ENDNOTES

1. Jennifer J. McGee, "A Pilgrim's Progress: Metaphor in the Rhetoric of Mary Fisher, AIDS Activist," *Women's Studies in Communication* 26, 2003.

2. Quotation found on: http://www.famousquotessite.com/famous-quotes-614-pearl-buck.html (last accessed May 31, 2011).

3. Julius Caesar Watts, Jr., Biography: http://www.bookrags.com/biography/julius-caesar-watts-jr/ (accessed June 21, 2011).

4. www.americanrhetoric.com. J.C. Watts, "Three Lies," http://www.americanrhetoric.com/speeches/jcwattsthreelies.htm (accessed June 21, 2011).

5. Ibid.

6. Ibid.

7. Patricia Bizzell and Bruce Herzberg, *The Rhetorical Tradition: Readings from Classical Times to the Present* (Boston, MA: Bedford Books of St. Martin's Press, 1990), 31-33.

# Informative Speaking

## CHAPTER OVERVIEW

- Differentiates between the different types of informative speaking
- Covers the goals and strategies for each form of informative speech
- Discusses various situations where informative speaking is most likely to occur

# Practically SPEAKING

In 2008 the U.S. economy slowed and then went into reverse, resulting in the significant loss of value in retirement accounts as well as the failure of numerous brokerage houses and banks. In March 2008 one of the oldest investment firms on Wall Street, Bear Stearns, collapsed and the Federal Reserve had to intervene and engineer a takeover by rival bank JP Morgan to ensure that people's assets would not completely vanish. In September another Wall Street firm, Lehman Brothers, also collapsed but the government did not intervene to save it. In the same month the government did, however, work to help Bank of America buy out Merrill Lynch. The result of all of these investment bank failures was an almost complete collapse of confidence in Wall Street. In fact, by October 9, 2008, the Dow Jones Index lost over one-third of its value from the beginning of the year.[1] That translated into huge losses for average Americans who invested in the stock market for their retirement.

Beginning with the Bear Stearns collapse, and accelerating with the events of September and October 2008, many Americans turned to CNN and other major news outlets for an explanation of what happened, how it happened, and how it would affect them. On CNN, chief business correspondent Ali Velshi became the network's de facto spokesperson for these explanations. He appeared almost daily on CNN to explain the complex world of global finance so people could better understand what happened. Oftentimes he employed graphs and charts to help him explain things. What he did the majority of the time was inform the American public on the state of the economy and how the economy functions. His aim was not persuasion, but rather he sought to provide people with information.

Despite Velshi's goal, words are inherently persuasive, even though persuasion may not be the general purpose of a speech. Some speakers like Velshi seek to inform an audience about something, but that information still may change the way the audience views the topic in question. Similarly, audiences may listen to a speech intended to persuade them only to gather information about a topic. This reality makes it nearly impossible to construct and categorize a speech as purely "informative." The purpose may be to inform, but even pure information has some level of influence over an audience. In Velshi's case, his explanation of the crash may have influenced people's decisions to keep money in the market or take it out, even though that was not his goal.

# INFORMATIVE SPEAKING OVERVIEW

We need to think of informative and persuasive speaking as lying on a continuum, rather than as two mutually exclusive boxes. On the one end of this spectrum lies the persuasive speech, where the purpose of the speaker is to persuade and the audience's purpose is to create an opinion based upon what is offered. On the other end of the continuum exists the theoretical informative speech. See Figure 10.1.

Informative speech                                                        Persuasive speech

**Figure 10.1**
**Informative vs. Persuasive Speech**

Continuum

We say theoretical because, as we have pointed out, information does not exist in a vacuum and will influence people, even in a small way.

Even though information always persuades on some level, there are those speeches that come close to the theoretical *informative speech*, and they provide information in as neutral an environment as possible, where both the speaker and the audience typically seek to teach and learn. Informative speeches are also structured differently than persuasive speeches and employ different vocabularies. For these reasons, it is important to define the purpose of your speech and know as much about the audience as possible when constructing your presentation.

**informative speech**
provides information in as neutral an environment as possible, where the speaker and the audience typically seek to teach and learn

An example of what we mean by this differentiation can be found on campuses throughout the country. Schools often bring in researchers to talk about their work with students in a variety of forums. These lectures provide information to the students and faculty in attendance, but they also may inspire new interest in topics for those audience members. A lecture by noted historian Doris Kearns Goodwin on her research on President Abraham Lincoln's cabinet primarily provides information to the audience. It also may very well influence the audience to study that aspect of history in even more detail or spark

Historian
Doris Kearns Goodwin

an interest in history for some students. So, as you can see, it is not a purely informative speech, but neither is it a truly persuasive type of speech.

One other difference between informative and persuasive speaking is the ability of an informative speech to occasionally use language very specific to a certain field. Persuasive speeches, because they seek to move entire audiences to action, necessarily use less field-specific language so more people can understand and follow the speaker. When informative speeches are geared toward people in a very specific field and use disciplinary-specific language, we refer to them as technical speeches. This chapter, however, focuses on informative speeches rather than the more advanced version of technical speeches.

In this chapter we will help you better identify a speech with an informative purpose. We begin by explaining the four different types of informative speeches and then move to a discussion about the goals and strategies that best achieve the purpose of informative presentations. We conclude with a brief chat about different situations where you might find yourself asked to deliver an informative speech. Regardless of the situation, it is always important to keep your purpose at the forefront of your mind and remember that all information influences audiences, even when you do not intend for it to do so.

## TYPES OF INFORMATIVE SPEECHES

There are four different types of informative speeches, each designed to convey a unique set of information to an audience. Each one lends itself to different topics and organizational strategies. In this section of the chapter we will discuss the four different informative speeches: speeches about objects, speeches about processes, speeches about events, and finally, perhaps the most difficult to construct as a speaker, speeches about concepts.

### Speeches about Objects

**speech of self-presentation**
a speech where the speaker's topic is introducing himself or herself to the audience

Speeches about objects are the simplest form of informative speeches. One of the most common informative speeches about an object is a ***speech of self-presentation***, where a speaker's topic is the introduction of herself or himself to the audience. Often these types of speeches are the first that a student delivers in an introductory speaking course. They are typically not long and touch upon the highlights of the speaker's life. They often include important events, individuals, and achievements by the speaker. Sometimes speeches of self-presentation cover elements of the person's philosophy and belief systems, but each speech is unique and what the speaker chooses to present tells you as much about the person as what they choose to leave out. After all, these are personal narratives constructed by the speakers, and whether or not they mean it, the story is always biased and incomplete, making these speeches fascinating in their own right.

Objects can also include people other than the speaker. Take the example of Doris Kearns Goodwin mentioned at the start of this chapter. Goodwin spoke about people in President Lincoln's cabinet, clearly not making herself the topic of the speech. These speeches differ from self-presentation speeches in that Goodwin

## SPOTLIGHTING THEORISTS: G. THOMAS GOODNIGHT

### G. Thomas Goodnight

G. Thomas Goodnight is currently a full professor and director of doctoral studies at the prestigious Annenberg School for Communication at the University of Southern California. Before joining USC he taught in the doctoral program at Northwestern University. The American Forensic Association recently named Goodnight one of the top five scholars in argumentation over the past 50 years for his contributions to the field. He has developed and taught courses on the Rhetoric of War, Science Advocacy, Risk Communication, Contemporary Rhetorical Theory, Rhetorical Criticism, and the Public Sphere. Additionally, his research has appeared in a variety of well-respected journals in the field of communication studies.

One of Goodnight's contributions is his work on the relationship between the technical and public spheres of argument. He pointed out that in the hard sciences (biology, physics, etc.) argument has different goals, aims, and even structure than it does in rhetoric, the humanities, and the social sciences (psychology, counseling, sociology, English, etc.). His work also has shed light on why public speaking courses typically separate speech types into the categories of informative, persuasive, and epideictic/special occasion when all ultimately have a persuasive effect.

The transmission of information is seen as a neutral effort in the hard sciences, while the social sciences see it as persuasive regardless of the intent of the speaker. But due to the disciplinary differences between the hard sciences and social sciences, speeches are typically separated into the categories we have today. Technical, rather than informative, however, is the better way to label those speeches that typically take place in the hard science fields.

Goodnight still conducts research in rhetoric and argumentation. Currently he explores issues related to deliberation in postwar society, science communication, argument and aesthetics, public discourse, and reason in controversy.[2]

does need to mention herself and her research to establish her credibility on the topic, but then her focus returns to the other individuals. In speeches about other people as objects, the topics the speaker chooses to cover are of the same variety as those in the self-presentation speech with the exception that they apply to others.

Another informative speech about an object involves places. These types of speeches are presented on tours. When visiting Boston, Massachusetts, on vacation you may decide to take a Duck Boat Tour of the city, during which the

A Duck tour boat

guide will speak about the history of the city, making special note of important historical locations along the route. Although this speech provides information, people on the tour may want to then learn more about places the tour guide has mentioned, prompting them to make another trip after the tour ends, again demonstrating that there is differentiation between informative and persuasive speaking.

The final type of informative speech about objects involves things. These can include something as meaningful as a memento or heirloom, or something as simple as a television or movie. Informative speeches about objects that are things encompass tangible objects that do not fall in the previously discussed categories. For examples of the three types of informative speeches about objects, see Table 10.1.

**Table 10.1**

| Thesis Examples about Objects | |
|---|---|
| **Speech Topic** | **Thesis Statement Example** |
| Michael Jackson | "The three main periods of Michael Jackson's life are his youth, his reign as the King of Pop, and the tragedies late in his life." |
| New Orleans | "The three primary areas of interest in New Orleans are the French Quarter, the Garden District, and the industrial area." |
| Buying a used car | "When purchasing a used car you should consider factors such as age, quality, and price." |

## Speeches about Processes

Another common type of informative speech is a speech about a process. Process speeches are delivered using a chronological organizational pattern because that is what allows the topic to make the most sense to the audience. Process speeches traditionally are reserved for delivering information about tasks an audience may need to complete. They are, for all intents and purposes, "how to" speeches.

Consider the following hypothetical example. Elaine is a mechanic and has been asked by her local church to deliver a speech to the Women's Club on simple ways to save money on car maintenance. She chooses what she believes to be the simplest but most effective way for her audience to save money: How to change the oil in their cars. In order to adequately explain how to accomplish this task Elaine needs to proceed in sequential order and detail what needs to be done in language everyday people who are not mechanics can understand. Other process topics vary from the sequence of building a house, to describing the process of how wine is made, and even, as in Ali Velshi's case earlier, explaining how the economy works.

The final type of process speech we will cover involves neither a job-specific task like changing oil, nor an everyday activity such as cooking; rather, these speech topics relate to social processes. Common to this category are political, economic, religious, or cultural procedures. Such speeches might cover "how to get elected," "how to celebrate a Catholic Mass," or "how interest rates work." These are more complicated and deal with social processes rather than task procedures, but they are still informative speeches about processes. Because of their complexity, these types of speeches often are the most interesting process speeches to hear. If you want to write such a speech just think of some type of social process and research how it operates.

Informative speeches about processes are excellent examples of the blurred line between informative and persuasive speaking. People hearing these speeches might be more inclined to do exactly what the speaker has described now that they know how. That influence could be branded persuasive rather than informative, but if the speech is presented simply as a "how to" speech it becomes much more of an informative address than a persuasive appeal. See Table 10.2 for examples of the different types of informative speeches about processes.

**Table 10.2**

| Thesis Examples about Processes | |
|---|---|
| **Speech Topic** | **Thesis Statement Example** |
| Brewing beer | "To brew beer you must have an initial fermentation, then a secondary fermentation, and finally, bottle it." |
| Health plan | "To live a healthy life requires a balance of nutrition, exercise, mental stability, and good lifestyle choices." |
| Applying for Communication graduate school | "To successfully apply for graduate school one must have at least a 3.0 GPA, an appropriate undergraduate degree, an official GRE report, official transcripts, and letters of recommendation." |

## Speeches about Events

The third form of informative speeches, those that cover events, combines elements of both speeches about objects and speeches about processes. Events can include objects, in particular people, but they are more complex than simply detailing a singular item. They can also include a process, or the unfolding of the event, but the focus is not on explaining the process; rather it is on detailing the importance of the event itself. Your goal is to provide information to an audience; what they do with it is up to them. This illustrates yet again the subtle difference between informative and persuasive speaking.

Artist: Francis Bicknell Carpenter

First Reading of the Emancipation Proclamation of President Lincoln

Think back to the example of the hypothetical lecture by Doris Kearns Goodwin on President Lincoln's staff during the Civil War. We illustrated how this could be an informative speech about an object, the individuals in the staff, but it also could be a speech about an event. Change the topic ever-so-slightly to "The President and the Civil War" and the speech becomes more about the event and the individuals become secondary.

Informative speeches about events can cover things that have happened in the past, are happening now, or may happen in the future. Like the Civil War example, an informative speech about an event can cover something from the past. These speeches can also cover events occurring in the moment, such as a public address by a public official during a hurricane or natural disaster. Event speeches can also discuss things that will happen, such as a speech opening a business convention that lays out the schedule, topics, and important organizational members for the ensuing meetings.

Informative speeches about events can employ several organizational patterns. Often the primary organizational pattern is chronological, but there are cases when event speeches can utilize topical and even spatial patterns. For example, the above speech about the Civil War could be set up as a chronological history of battles leading to the surrender at Appomattox. It also could focus on the leaders of the Civil War on both sides, making the primary organizational pattern topical. A third option for organization involves a discussion of the states and their participation in the war, thus encouraging the use of a spatial organizational pattern. See Table 10.3 for examples of the different types of informative speeches about events.

**Table 10.3**

| Thesis Examples about Events | |
|---|---|
| **Speech Topic** | **Thesis Statement Example** |
| 1942 WWII Pacific naval campaigns | "Three major naval operations in 1942 were the raids into the Indian Ocean, the Battle of Coral Sea, and the Battle of Midway." |
| Weddings | "The major events of a wedding ceremony are the exchange of vows, the wedding toasts, the cutting of the cake, and the first dance." |
| 9/11 | "The September 11, 2001, terrorist attacks on the United States included two airplanes hitting the Twin Towers, the attack on the Pentagon, and the crash of United Flight 93 in Pennsylvania." |

Informative speeches about events can be used to inform audiences about occurrences in the past, present, or future. They are organized in a variety of different ways, but they also contain elements common to both informative speeches about objects and informative speeches about processes. The fourth and final type of informative speech, however, is unique.

## Speeches about Concepts

Informative speeches about concepts focus on informing an audience about beliefs, values, or theories. These speeches do not seek to convert an audience to a particular point of view, but instead seek simply to explain a given philosophy. Informative speeches about concepts also almost exclusively employ the same organizational pattern, regardless of what concept they explicate.

One potential informative speech about a concept covers belief systems, such as a particular religion. Religions are not tangible objects, sequential processes, or fixed events, despite the fact elements of each may play a part in the belief system. For example, in Judaism, the Star of David is a prominent object, weekly service follows a specific regimen, and the conclusion of the annual reading of the Torah is a celebratory event. Each of these would make terrific topics for informative speeches about an object, process, or event, but none of them cover the beliefs of Judaism. An informative speech about a concept that conveys information about the beliefs of Judaism would cover its notion of the afterlife, its understanding of God, or its approach to keeping kosher.

Religion is only one example of a concept, and it is grounded in a specific worldview. A different way to approach beliefs would be to cover more abstract ideas such as love, hate, affection, or depression. The definitions for these concepts vary from culture to culture. An informative speech about a concept would attempt to convey an understanding of any one of those emotions, but in doing so the speaker would have to acknowledge the various ways different places define those feelings.

A third type of concept covered by this type of informative speech addresses theories. Take, for example, Dina, who wants to give a speech to her science class that defines the theory of evolution. She can cover who developed the theory and mention the controversy surrounding it, but the focus of her speech is to explain how evolution works. She can provide examples of how the theory proposes that large hairy mammals evolved into human beings, but again her focus is on explaining the concept to the audience. Examples essentially become data and evidence, where the main points are the theoretical propositions themselves.

One final category of concepts covered in an informative speech of this type are political or economic concepts. Like religious beliefs, political and economic belief systems may have important people, defined processes, or singular events that have contributed to their development, but the focus of the speech is to describe the core facets of the system. A speech of this type on communism, for example, might mention Karl Marx and Friedrich Engels as the pioneers of the philosophy, their expulsion from Germany as an event contributing to the creation of their worldview, and the explanation of the five epochs of history as a process that will eventually lead to the world adopting communism, but the focus is on explaining the tenets of a communist society. How is workload handled in a communist society? What is the role of money? How are leaders selected? These and other questions get at the central concept of communism and thus qualify the presentation as an informative speech about a concept. Table 10.4 provides examples of informative speeches about concepts.

**Table 10.4**

| Thesis Examples about Concepts | |
| --- | --- |
| **Speech Topic** | **Thesis Statement Example** |
| Pillars of Islam | "The five pillars of Islam are the profession of faith, prayers, giving of alms, fasting during Ramadan, and pilgrimage to Mecca." |
| Ethics | "The two major categories of ethical principles are teleological and deontological ethics." |
| Psychological Egoism | "The theory of psychological egoism states that altruism is a myth and that all acts are self-serving." |
| Free Market Economy | "A free market economic theory is based upon competition and no government intervention." |

Like each of the other types of informative speeches, speeches about concepts also provide information that may influence an audience. What qualifies them as informative rather than persuasive speeches is the speaker's goal of providing information in a neutral fashion to an audience that wishes to learn that information. Movement to action and changes in the audience as a result of this information are inevitable, but they are not the goal. As you can surely imagine, constructing an informative speech without calling people to action or asking them to change their beliefs and values can be difficult. In the next section we will provide some helpful tips on how to craft informative speeches about objects, processes, events, and concepts.

# GOALS AND STRATEGIES FOR INFORMATIVE SPEAKING

As we have emphasized throughout the chapter so far, informative speeches seek to convey information in as neutral a fashion as possible, despite the fact people may be influenced by that information. Yet another distinction can be seen in the nature of the audience. Audiences for informative speeches are relatively passive and seek to receive information. In contrast, those who listen to persuasive speeches are more active audiences, cognitively processing the information to formulate opinions and make decisions regarding calls to action. In this way audiences for informative speeches often employ comprehensive listening, which, you may recall from Chapter 2, involves listening to understand a message.

The speakers who deliver informative speeches also need to have strong initial and derived credibility. This makes sense because if an audience seeks to understand something from a speaker then they must believe that the person to whom they are listening knows about the topic. As they deliver information, speakers must continue to demonstrate their expertise and knowledge about the topic.

It is also important for speakers delivering information to behave ethically. Because they know more about the topic than the audience, they must not abuse the trust the audience has placed in them by skewing the information in favor of one interpretation. To do so would be to present a persuasive appeal under the pretense of an informative speech.

## Strategies for Informative Speeches about Objects

One of the reasons you would deliver an informative speech about an object is that the object is complex and hard for the audience to understand. This fundamental appreciation of the speech purpose is the basis for three strategies for effectively presenting speeches about objects.

First and foremost you must spend a significant amount of time detailing the object and explaining its purpose. These details should cover subjects relevant to the audience's understanding of the object. Such topics might include the history of the object, its purpose, and various ways in which it can be used (if indeed, it can be). Take, for instance, an object as simple as a baseball. While explaining the object you might want to explain how it is constructed, what role it plays in a baseball game, and how many different ways it can be thrown.

When detailing the object for the audience it is also essential for the speaker to use language the audience will understand. Oftentimes, when we are experts on a subject we talk about it as if everyone around knows the *jargon*, or terminology that relates to a specific activity, associated with the topic. When conveying information to an audience seeking to learn something we need to avoid using jargon without explaining the terms and phrases to the audience so they can follow along. Verbal explanations, however, are sometimes not enough to adequately explain a topic to the audience.

**jargon**
terminology that relates to a specific activity

Sometimes topics about an object require visual as well as verbal representation for the audience to understand. Visual aids are often effective tools when delivering informative speeches about objects, especially when the objects are large and complex. If the object you are discussing is a person, her life may be complex and therefore a timeline may be a useful visual aid for the audience; however, a bust of the person's head would not be. Recall two of the rules of using visual aids: do not create a distracting visual aid, and do not create visual aids for tangential aspects of the speech. A bust, or picture of the individual, violates both of those rules and does not help the audience better understand the topic of the speech. The timeline, on the other hand, does. Variations of timelines also might be helpful as a visual aid with our next subject: informative speeches about processes.

## Strategies for Informative Speeches about Processes

As we mentioned earlier, informative speeches about processes typically follow a chronological organizational pattern, and as such the sequence is important. In order to create an effective speech about a process you need to adequately explain not just each sequential step in detail, but how each step leads to the next one.

Especially important in that description are the starting and finishing points in the process. Another important aspect of informative speeches about processes is that they need to detail the practical applications of the process being described; in other words, what can it be used for?

Each step in a speech should build upon the previous one. Beginning with the first step you should explain what is needed to complete the process and then the order in which the steps should be executed to successfully complete the task at hand. For example, a speech about how to fish should begin by explaining what tools are needed to go fishing. Simply listing the fishing pole, lure, and line, though, should be avoided as it engenders boredom in the audience. Describe not just what is needed, but how to determine its quality and where it can be located so the audience does not have to guess.

## Comments Before the Credentials Committee
## by Fannie Lou Hamer

Delivered August 22, 1964, at the Democratic National Committee, Atlantic City, New Jersey

Fannie Lou Hamer, the granddaughter of slaves, was born in 1917 in Mississippi. She became a sharecropper on a plantation, and in 1962 when members of the Student Nonviolent Coordinating Committee (SNCC) came to town to hold a voter registration meeting, Hamer didn't even know that she had a constitutional right to vote. Once she knew she could, she volunteered to help register others to vote and was later jailed, beaten, and driven from the farm where she was a sharecropper as result.[3]

Hamer went on to become secretary of the SNCC and traveled to various places registering people to vote, spoke about voting rights, and co-founded the Mississippi Freedom Democratic Party (MFDP). The Credentials Committee of the 1964 Democratic Convention asked her to speak about racial injustice.[4]

Hamer told the committee of the treatment she had received from the police, how the plantation owner had pressured her to withdraw her registration request, and that when she refused he told her to leave his property. She also recounted the resistance at registration drives and how she and others with her were not allowed to eat in some restaurants or use restrooms.[5] She told of black prisoners ordered to beat her with blackjacks and of the terrible names the police called her. Here is an excerpt from her informative and emotional testimony:

"I was carried out of that cell into another cell where they had two Negro prisoners. The State Highway Patrolmen ordered the first Negro to take the blackjack. The first Negro prisoner ordered me, by orders from the State Highway Patrolman, for me to lay down on a bunk bed on my face. As I laid on my face, the first Negro began to beat me. And I was beat by the first Negro until he was exhausted."[6]

After describing what is needed in terms of materials, you should proceed to describe each step in the process. Using our fishing example, you should tell them that the next step is determining where to fish, renting a boat, and then setting a time for the trip. Be descriptive and tell the audience how to decide on each of these issues and describe what you would recommend doing for maximum success. Remember from our discussion of language earlier in the book that vivid language is a very effective way of maintaining audience interest and attention.

When you are finished describing all the steps in detail for the audience it is also important to let them know about the practical applications of the process so they will know when to use it. For the fishing example, you might suggest trying this activity on a vacation. Process speeches have a much greater effect when audiences believe they apply to their own lives. Otherwise, process speeches become simple instructions instead of a creative and eloquent way to invite an audience to learn something.

## Strategies for Informative Speeches about Events

Delivering an address informing an audience about an event requires different elements than a speech about objects or processes. For one, you need to set the parameters of the event to focus the speech for the audience. You must explain who the key players are and clearly establish the background on the event so the audience can identify the topic. To be effective you also need to make a conscious effort to deliver the speech in an active voice with vivid description.

Setting the parameters of the event you are talking about means providing the audience with the proper context. **Context**, or the conditions surrounding the event, includes who the prominent figures are, when the event occurred, and other relevant circumstances. It is important when talking about an event that you place it in the proper context by establishing a clear beginning and ending. Clearly, events do not exist in a vacuum and there are a multitude of factors that influence them, but as a speaker you must make decisions about which are pertinent to the event in question, and which elements are not essential for understanding the event.

**context**
the conditions surrounding the event

Take the case of Fannie Lou Hamer, a former sharecropper who helped register African Americans to vote during the Civil Rights movement in the 1960s. In 1964 the Democratic National Convention asked her to provide personal testimony on racial injustice in the South. To do so, she needed to provide the context for her experience in vivid detail so that the legislators and leaders at the meeting would not only understand what happened, but actually be able to visualize how it took place. Hamer did just that. See the nearby box.

When making such decisions you should remember your ethical responsibility to provide balanced and neutral information to the audience and not shape the speech so as to promote one particular interpretation. This may seem difficult, and sometimes even impossible, but so long as you keep ethical considerations in the front of your mind when constructing the speech, you will be doing your duty to the subject and the audience.

One of the more difficult tasks in any informative speech remains ensuring it is interesting. To accomplish this feat you should try to always speak about the event in an active voice and use vivid language. A good example of this can be found in the address given by former Senator Fred Thompson at the 2008 Republican National Convention. In his speech he discussed nominee Senator John McCain's time as a POW, stating:

> After days of neglect, covered in grime, lying in his own waste in a filthy room, a doctor attempted to set John's right arm without success... and without anesthesia.
>
> His other broken bones and injuries were not treated. John developed a high fever, dysentery. He weighed barely a hundred pounds.
>
> Expecting him to die, his captors placed him in a cell with two other POWs who also expected him to die.
>
> But with their help, John McCain fought on.
>
> He persevered.
>
> So then they put him in solitary confinement... for over two years.
>
> Isolation... incredible heat beating on a tin roof. A light bulb in his cell burning 24 hours a day.
>
> Boarded-up cell windows blocking any breath of fresh air.
>
> The oppressive heat causing boils the size of baseballs under his arms.
>
> The outside world limited to what he could see through a crack in a door.[7]

Former Senator
Fred Thompson

In this passage Thompson describes the event with language that encourages a specific picture in the mind of the audience. Notice that, despite the fact that the event has already occurred, not once does Thompson use passive voice through the terms "was," "would," "has," "is," or "have." Doing so provides the speech with an engaging feel while still conveying information about an event to the audience in an ethical manner. This skill is equally important, if not even harder to employ, within informative speeches about concepts.

# Strategies for Informative Speeches about Concepts

Concepts may be the most difficult thing to inform an audience about because they are so abstract. Objects, processes, and events are often very easy for a speaker to concretize for the audience, but concepts are not so simple for a speaker to describe. Concepts also are sometimes difficult for an audience to relate to, so finding a way to connect the audience to the speaker and the topic is essential when delivering an informative speech about a concept. One of the simpler components of constructing these speeches, however, is that you can effectively organize them only one way.

As a speaker trying to convey a concept to an audience you need to give the concept as concrete a foundation as possible. Employing examples of the concept in practice helps to provide that foundation. Take the topic of gravity which, as a law of physics, fits the definition of a concept. Merely describing what gravity is and how it operates keeps the speech on the abstract level, but by introducing examples of objects performing according to the law of gravity, the speech becomes more concrete and the concept becomes easier for the audience to visualize.

In addition to providing imagery illustrating the concept, you must also make the idea you are speaking about relevant to the audience. This can be done in several different ways. You can show how they might need to understand the concept to perform some of their daily activities. In the case of gravity, you can explain that when things fall it is because of this concept. This connects the concept to a person's daily life because people can fall, or objects around the house can fall and hurt them, thus making understanding gravity more important and relevant to the audience. You can also call upon the inherent curiosity of the audience regarding subjects and theories, thereby asking them to learn the idea you are speaking about because of their curious nature.

Regardless of how you hook the audience, any informative speech about a concept is likely to be organized in a topical fashion. Concepts do not follow an order, otherwise they would be a process. They also are not tangible and therefore cannot be organized according to space. They are abstract, and because they are abstract it is difficult to determine the logic by which they should be organized within a speech. It is most instructive then to proceed with constructing the speech in a topical fashion, covering the various topics of the theory, idea, or belief.

For example, consider an informative speech about Hinduism. The religion itself is a concept and invites the possibility of structuring a speech in a variety of different ways. For instance, you could start with the various gods in the religion, then move to sacred symbols, and conclude with its belief regarding life and death. You also could pick entirely different topics relevant to the concept of Hinduism and structure the speech around them. It is, by and large, entirely up to you as the person constructing and delivering the address. In the next section of this chapter we will briefly discuss various situations in which all four types of informative speeches might occur.

# Situations for Informative Speaking

Informative speaking occurs in a variety of different situations, but there are three that are the most prevalent. The first, and perhaps most common situation in the professional world, is the internal business setting. As students, though, you encounter informative speaking all the time as it is the primary mode of delivery in education as well. Finally, any time you attend an orientation program you will hear informative speeches. In this part of the chapter we will briefly discuss these three rhetorical situations and discuss which informative speeches are most likely to occur in each.

## Informative Speaking in the Business World

Professionals in the business world deliver two types of speeches, but they are each audience-specific. When the speech is internal, that is, given to employees and shareholders of the company, the majority of the time it is an informative address. When the speech is to an external audience of potential clients and investors then the speeches are more overtly persuasive in nature. Internal informative business speeches often occur at board meetings, planning sessions, and company conventions.

Board meetings often contain a report to the board on the state of the company. These speeches contain facts and figures regarding revenue, profit, company costs, and the performance of divisions within a company. These speeches often employ visual aids to deliver statistics regarding the success or failure of parts of the company in order to paint an overall picture of the current state of the corporation. These informative speeches also detail future plans of action for the company and the strategies going forward.

Planning sessions also contain informative speeches and occur in the business world as well. Planning sessions are far more common than board meetings and can occur within divisions of the company, not simply at the top of the administrative ladder. In these planning sessions the state of the department is usually described, followed by an account of available resources and concluding with the goals of the planning session. The idea is for everyone in the room to start off on the same page in terms of the available information and to then generate as many ideas as possible for how to achieve the goals of the division or company.

Most companies also have yearly conventions where the company's leadership delivers a state of the company address, or something similar. This address and others during the conference focus on the goals and plans for the next year. They address what succeeded and what failed during the previous year and lay out what still needs to be done. Of the three addresses we have discussed with regard to business settings, these speeches occur in front of the largest audience and are potentially the longest as well.

Informative internal business speeches often use visual aids and follow a topical organizational pattern, but by no means do all of them follow these two maxims. The context largely determines the topics covered in the speeches for businesspeople, but again the organizational pattern focuses on topics more often than it doesn't. Some exceptions might include planning meetings where a chronological path might need to be laid out for the group, or during conventions if the focus is on how the company developed over the past year. These are, however, exceptions.

## Informative Speeches in Education

A professor's lecture in a classroom is a perfect example of an informative speech, and depending upon the course content, it can take the form of any one of the four types of informative speeches. A lecture is not persuasive and instructors design them to deliver information to students using a variety of different methods. Courses also sometimes require students to issue reports to the class on research they conducted; again, these types of speeches are not persuasive but are meant to transmit information to an audience. In any event, you can hardly find performances that lean more toward the informative side of the continuum than a lecture.

Instructors talk about objects, processes, events, and concepts quite often. Every time they step in front of a class they attempt to help students learn about famous people, items of interest, important events, biological processes, philosophical ideas, and much more without advocating a specific position for students. In fact, *critical thinking*, or the ability for students to evaluate on their own the material they learn, is often stated as a course goal of many instructors. To facilitate critical thinking the lectures must not advocate or persuade, but rather provide data for students so they can make their own evaluations.

**critical thinking**
the ability for students to evaluate on their own the material they learn

Students also present reports to classes, thereby granting them the role of instructor-for-a-day. They are often evaluated on these reports based on the information they deliver and how well they deliver it. As with instructors delivering a lecture, students also often use PowerPoint to assist them in delivering the material. These reports range in length but almost always cover the same elements of any speech: introduction, body, and conclusion.

Informative speeches are common to academia, regardless of whether you are a student or an instructor. The speeches spell out information for an audience seeking to learn, and do so without any persuasive goals.

## Informative Speeches in Orientation Programs

The final common realm where you might encounter informative speeches is during an orientation or training program. Although one of the aims of these programs is to get you to perhaps do something a specific way, they are designed to provide information on how to do it. They do not advocate a belief, attitude, action, or value; rather they seek to describe a process or concept.

Orientation programs, such as a Sexual Harassment Orientation program required by many companies and organizations, often describe concepts through a systematic process. They go step by step ensuring audiences receive specific information when they are supposed to. People often consider such programs dull because speakers rarely incorporate context into their delivery of material.

Training programs are slightly different because sometimes the context is readily recognizable. For instance, if you attend a training program for how to use Microsoft Excel, you will most likely be placed in front of a computer and walked through the steps of how to use the program. Orientations cover concepts, whereas training programs cover processes, like learning a computer program.

## SUMMARY

There is no such thing as a purely informative speech; rather, there are speeches that focus on providing information which audiences can then do with as they wish. Informative speeches exist in four different forms: those about objects, those about processes, those about events, and those about concepts. Each requires different strategies and organizational patterns, but all simply attempt to convey information. These types of speeches occur most frequently in internal business settings, the classroom, and within training and orientation programs. The key to remember is that persuasion is not the goal of informative speeches.

## KEY TERMS

context   219

critical thinking   223

informative speech   209

jargon   217

speech of self-presentation   210

## REVIEW QUESTIONS

1. What is the difference between an informative speech and a persuasive speech?

2. What are the four types of informative speeches?

3. What are the three common situations where informative speeches occur?

4. What are the best ways to organize each type of informative speech?

5. Which speaking situation calls for all four informative speeches, depending on the topic?

## THINK ABOUT IT

1. Can information be truly objective and neutral?

2. Does even the choice of evidence make a speech persuasive?

3. Why do we separate informative speeches from persuasive speeches if they all influence people?

4. Do you think commemorative speeches are mainly informative or persuasive?

## ACTIVITIES FOR ACTION

1. Identify a commercial that tries to convince an audience to change its attitude about something or purchase a product. After examining the content of the advertisement, turn that persuasive appeal into an informative speech using the same evidence.

2. Find a famous person with whom you either strongly disagree or who you dislike. Create a list of information about that person that is corroborated with documented evidence. Be sure the information you use is factual and not colored by your own opinions.

## ENDNOTES

1. Prieur_du_Plessis, "Stock Market Crash 2008 Market Round Up," *The Market Oracle,* available: http://www.marketoracle.co.uk/Article6728.html (last accessed April 5, 2009).

2. Information contained in this segment was obtained through G. Thomas Goodnight's faculty web page at the Annenberg School for Communication at: http://annenberg. usc.edu/Faculty/Communication/GoodnightG.aspx (accessed September 6, 2008).

3. Fannie Lou Hamer of the NCCC, http://www.ibiblio.org/sncc/hamer.html (accessed June 13, 2011).

4. Ibid.

5. Fannie Lou Hamer testimony before the Credentials Committee, http://americanradioworks.publicradio.org/features/sayitplain/flhamer.html (accessed June 13, 2011).

6. Ibid.

7. Fred Thompson, "Fred Thompson's Address to the RNC," September 2, 2008, available: http://www.realclearpolitics.com/articles/2008/09/fred_thompsons_address_to_the.html (accessed September 3, 2008).

# Crafting an Informative Speech

## 11

On March 20, 2003, the United States and a coalition of over 40 countries invaded Iraq in an effort to oust dictator Saddam Hussein. The war itself was brief, but the occupation that followed went on for years. The ensuing presence of U.S. forces and the inability of Iraq's new government to quickly establish control across the country infuriated elements of the population and drew al Qaeda to what has become the primary front of the War on Terror.

With casualties mounting for both U.S. and Iraqi forces, many in the United States started to call for a change in tactics. In fact, several prominent members of Congress referred to the effort in Iraq as "lost." Facing mounting pressure to address the Iraq issue on January 10, 2007, President George W. Bush announced a new military policy for Iraq. He temporarily increased the number of troops in Iraq by 20,000 to assist the Iraqis with securing neighborhoods, protecting the local population, and training the Iraqi security forces to handle these duties moving forward. The policy was largely well received, especially given the fact it was the brainchild of General David Petraeus, commander of the multinational forces in Iraq and a counterterrorism expert.

In September 2007, Petraeus appeared before Congress to provide a report on the security situation and the effect of the surge in Iraq since its implementation. Petraeus informed Congress that the situation was vastly improved and that civilian and military deaths had been dramatically reduced as evidenced by the 70% drop in Baghdad civilian deaths from their peak the previous year.[1] He also noted that local tribes and neighborhoods had begun to reject al Qaeda and work with the U.S.-led coalition to secure Iraq.

The purpose and structure of Petraeus's speech are worth noting. The report to the House of Representatives committee was aimed at providing them with information, not persuading them one way or another on a particular policy. He began his testimony with a summary of the situation before and after the surge. He then reviewed the nature of the conflict in Iraq because it was different than any conflict the United States had been involved in over the last 200 years. His speech concluded with a report on his recommendations for moving ahead in the coming months. He approached the speech in a topical fashion, as you might surmise from your readings in the last chapter.

In this chapter we will discuss how to formulate a speech like the one given by General Petraeus in 2007, though you are likely to have a much different topic. We will first begin by discussing the elements of an introduction for an informative speech. Next, we will cover the different ways you can construct the body of an informative speech. Finally, we will explain the way in which you conclude an informative speech. You will then be ready to apply these elements using the outlining information in Chapter 9.

# Informative Speech Introductions

Introductions are, as the saying goes, your last opportunity to make a first impression on the audience. Many people believe that informative speeches are necessarily boring because they are not calling on an audience to do anything, but they need not be dull. What they do need to be, however, is clear and complete. As stated in Chapter 9, in order to create a strong introduction, you must first identify two things. The first is the general purpose of the speech. In the case of an informative speech, your general purpose is simply "to inform." The second is your specific purpose, which is a narrower version of the general purpose in that it identifies specifically what you are speaking about. For instance, a specific purpose for an informative speech about greenhouse gases would be: "To inform my audience about greenhouse gas emissions."

Once you identify the general and specific purposes of the speech you can start to work on the speech itself. In this section we will discuss the five main components of an introduction in an informative speech and illustrate how you can enhance an audience's interest in your speech using creativity.

## Attention-Getter

The first element of an introduction for an informative speech is the *attention-getter*, or a device that immediately attracts the audience's interest to the subject that the speaker plans to discuss. You can choose from a variety of different attention-getters when creating the introduction, but keep in mind that regardless of which type you use, your goal is to attract the audience's attention to the subject. In this part of the chapter we will outline four common attention-getters that you might employ.

**attention-getter**
a device that immediately attracts the audience's interest to the subject that the speaker plans to discuss

The first, and perhaps the easiest, attention-getter technique is the *rhetorical question*, or asking the audience a question related to the subject that does not require an answer from them. For example, if you plan to give a speech informing the audience about the history of the Philippine Islands you might begin the speech with the hypothetical question: "Did you know that the United States once occupied the Philippine Islands?" If your speech was designed to teach the audience how to play the game of tennis you might begin by saying: "Have you ever watched a tennis match and thought, 'How can I do that?'" These questions

**rhetorical question**
asking the audience a question related to the subject that does not require an answer from them

draw the audience in by orienting them toward a question which will likely be answered within the body of the speech.

A second popular form of attention-getter is the use of a *famous quotation* to begin the speech. Famous quotations are actual statements closely related to the topic of the speech made by individuals the audience will easily recognize. For instance, if you gave a speech to inform an audience about America's history with slavery, you might want to begin by saying: "Frederick Douglass once observed, 'I didn't know I was a slave until I found out I couldn't do the things I wanted.'" Or, if your purpose was to inform the audience about the landing on the moon, you might begin with, "'That's one small step for man, one giant leap for mankind.' Those were the words Neil Armstrong uttered when he first landed on the moon." In both of these examples you would pique the audience's interest in your topic by associating it with famous individuals who others recognize.

The third form of attention-getter we will describe is the use of startling statistics. People value statistics, and if you find some numeric data that might shock the audience into listening to your speech it might serve as an appropriate attention-getter. Think about a speech about how to change the oil in your car. The average oil change costs $25, and car owners need to have about four oil changes a year and about 40 if they keep their car for 10 years. So, to start a speech on this subject you might attract an audience's attention by beginning this way: "I am going to tell you how you can save $100 a year for 10 years, or $1,000." If your topic is informing an audience about a historical battle, you might want to provide them with the casualty count upfront in the attention-getter. Statistics are very good ways to get an audience's attention.

The fourth type of attention-getter is a short story or narrative that helps introduce your topic. The narrative cannot be too long because you risk beginning with a tangent and losing the audience's ability to focus on your speech topic. Suppose a student wanted to give an informative speech about the famous cycling race, the Tour de France. A short narrative about Lance Armstrong would be a good way to introduce the topic and would help garner the interest of the audience. See Table 11.1 for a summary of these four types of attention-getters.

You might recall our discussion of tangential information in Chapter 3 when thinking about these particular attention-getter strategies. Tangential information is often a very good source of attention-getters for a speech, so be sure to hold onto that type of data throughout the research process. However, despite the fact that attention-getters are important, and the first thing an audience hears, they are not the most crucial element of an introduction.

| Getting the Audience's Attention | | |
|---|---|---|
| **Topic** | **Introduction Function** | **Example** |
| Shooting a bow and arrow | Getting attention by asking a question | "Do you know what the primary weapons for hunting and war were before the advent of gunpowder?" |
| Community service | Getting attention by using a quote | "President John F. Kennedy once stated, 'Ask not what your country can do for you, ask what you can do for your country,' and today I plan to tell you the same thing." |
| College dropout rates | Getting attention with statistics | "Look around you; research shows that 50% of you will never graduate from college." |
| Safety on campus | Getting attention with a short narrative | "I want you to imagine a young woman who wakes up in her campus living quarters and notices a shadowy figure standing above her." |

**Table 11.1**

## Thesis Statement

Once you have your audience's attention with a creative attention-getter, you need to tell them exactly what you plan to discuss. This is done through the delivery of the thesis statement, or a single sentence that articulates the significance and relevance of the information you present in the speech. The thesis statement is the anchor for the rest of the speech because it is what all the main points and evidence presented throughout the body support or explain.

Proper thesis statements flow from the purpose of the speech and the information that you will present. As we mentioned in the previous chapter, the general purpose of an informative speech is to inform, and the specific purpose explains the specific topic you will inform the audience about. Although some speakers can get away with delivering thesis statements without the word "I," we suggest that as beginners you do not try that strategy.

Take the case of Carrie, whose specific purpose is "to inform the audience about the history of Christmas." Carrie used a creative attention-getter by using a hypothetical question. She asked the audience if they were aware Christmas has pagan roots. She then delivered her thesis statement: "Today, I will explain how Christianity co-opted pagan rituals and called it Christmas to attract more converts." This one sentence establishes the significance of the topic by linking Christianity to paganism, and it implicitly lets the audience know all the information that follows will unpack that statement in greater detail. For examples of possible thesis statements, see Table 11.2.

Whereas attention-getters attract the audience's interest, thesis statements begin the process of grounding the audience's focus on a more particular topic—your topic. But getting attention and focusing the topic are not the only goals of an introduction. In the next section we will elaborate on the next part of an introduction—establishing your credibility as a speaker on the topic.

**Table 11.2**

| Developing the Thesis Statement | |
| --- | --- |
| **Speech Topic** | **Thesis Statement** |
| Framing a house | "Today I will explain that to build a house you need to pour the foundation, create the subfloor, frame the building itself, and then finally form the roof." |
| Appealing a grade | "The grade appeal procedure starts with the professor, then the department chair, then the dean, and finally, if not resolved at one of these levels, the university provost." |
| Wine | "Wine can come in four different types: red, white, blush, and champagne." |

## Establishing Credibility

Even though you have gotten the audience's attention and told them the main point of your speech, they still need a reason to believe you. In an introduction for any type of speech—and especially in an informative speech—it is important to establish your credibility on the topic about which you are speaking. This will help enhance your ethos and will also aid in maintaining the attention of the audience. Everyone enters their speech with some level of credibility, and this is called your *initial credibility*. This can come from past work with which the audience is familiar, degrees you may have earned, or experiences you have had that the audience knows about.

**initial credibility**
the level of believability a speaker has before beginning his or her speech

Audiences see you as more or less credible entering a speech based upon a variety of factors. First, if you are an expert on the topic on which you are presenting and the audience knows this, then you will have high initial credibility. For instance, a designer for General Motors would have high credibility when discussing how to build a car engine. Perhaps, however, you are not a General Motors mechanic but have worked on cars before. Such experience heightens your credibility, regardless of the fact you do not have an official pedigree. Maybe you have delivered several addresses on the topic but have never actually built a car; if your audience is aware of these speeches then you may also enter the occasion with a relatively high amount of initial credibility.

You can also establish your credibility by referring to your research early in the introduction. Let's say Marcus is addressing his classmates for the first time and his goal is to persuade them to buy a home security system. Marcus is neither an expert in home security systems, nor does he own one at the time of his speech. In order to convince his audience that they should hear and believe what he has to say, Marcus could make a direct reference to his research into home security systems early in his introduction. This reference can take the form of something like: "I have spent the last few weeks examining various ways of protecting a home from burglars…." This statement immediately cites a reason why Marcus should be trusted speaking on this topic, thereby providing him with credibility on the topic.

Perhaps you have some experience with your topic that should be mentioned. By telling the audience that you have had this experience first-hand you become a more credible speaker. Think about the scene in the movie *My Cousin Vinny* where Marissa Tomei's character is interviewed by her fiancé about her automotive knowledge. After saying she is a hairdresser (not providing any credibility on the topic) she then goes on about her experience with her family—all of whom were mechanics. This experience makes her a more credible speaker on the stand.

One final way you can influence your credibility is through your appearance. Well-dressed speakers tend to be more confident, and as we have mentioned, confident speakers appear more believable to audiences. When you do not dress the part, the audience focuses on your appearance instead of your message, and this damages your credibility and your ability to get your message across to your audience. Poor dress, however, is not in itself a death knell for your credibility. That said, it is important to know what can influence your believability before you begin your presentation and establish your credibility in your introduction. For some examples of how speakers establish credibility, see Table 11.3. Once your credibility has been established, you can preview how you plan to explain your topic to the audience.

**Table 11.3**

| Establishing Speaker Credibility | |
| --- | --- |
| **Speech Topic** | **Credibility Example** |
| Writing a software program | "I know about designing software as I am a computer science major, and I have a part-time job writing software programs." |
| Genetically modified food | "I have thoroughly researched genetic food in our library and online." |

## Previewing the Body

At this point, you have the audience's attention, you have them focused on the topic of your speech, and you have given them a good reason to listen to what you have to say on the subject. The next thing to do is to let them know what points you plan to discuss and the order in which you will cover them. Introductions need to provide audiences with a roadmap for the remainder of the speech, and a good preview does this by explicitly identifying the main points to come and the order in which you plan to cover them. Previews also alert the audience as to how you have chosen to organize the speech, making it easier for them to follow you throughout the presentation.

A preview can be either one sentence or a series of sentences that touch upon what will be the main points of the speech. Previews do not give out any specific information, but rather focus on introducing topics. For a good example of a one-sentence preview, let's look at the speech General Petraeus delivered to Congress on Iraq. At the close of his introduction he issued the following one-sentence preview of the rest of his speech: "I would like to review the nature of the conflict in Iraq, recall the situation before the surge, describe the current situation, and explain the recommendations I have provided to my chain of command for the way ahead in Iraq."[2]

In this excerpt Petraeus clearly outlines the points he will cover and the order in which they will be delivered. First, he plans to review the form and type of fighting going on in Iraq. Second, he will discuss the situation on the ground in Iraq in terms of how it was before the surge, and then how the surge affected it. Finally, he plans to inform Congress on the recommendations he made to his staff for moving forward. This preview lets his audience know what he plans to address and when they can expect to hear it. This excerpt serves as an example of a one-sentence preview, but it could have easily been a multisentence preview. This could be done by simply breaking the component elements into separate sentences—much like we did in our explanation of the quote in this paragraph.

Previews are an essential part of any informative speech introduction, but there is one more aspect of a good informative speech introduction we have yet to cover: the transition to the body of the speech.

## Transitions to the Body

We have referred to introductions as the roadmap for the speech, but without a starting point any map is useless. The last part of an effective introduction is a transition, which is a statement that connects the introduction to the first main point of the speech. As noted in Chapter 9, transitions are one form of connective statement. There are several others which we will discuss later, but a transition is the only type of connective statement that works at the end of an introduction. A *transition* signals that you are done with one point, in this case the introduction, and that you are moving on to another.

**transition**
a connective statement that signals you are finished with one point and moving on to another

## When to Write the Introduction

As you can see, introductions are an essential part of any speech. They include various elements that capture an audience's interest, focus their attention, and preview the rest of the speech. One thing we have yet to mention about introductions, however, bears particular attention: Introductions are not the first part of the speech you construct. The introduction is not first because the "meat and potatoes of a speech," the body, might change form repeatedly during the development of the speech, depending upon what information you find and how you decide to present it to an audience. Obviously, the roadmap will change along with the body, so why keep changing the introduction? Instead, create one introduction when you are happy with the finished body of the speech. In the next part of this chapter we will discuss various ways to organize the body of your informative speech.

# INFORMATIVE SPEECH BODY

As you may have surmised from the last chapter, there are several different ways you might decide to organize the main points in the body of an informative speech. To a great extent, your particular topic and specific purpose will point you toward the best organizational pattern to employ in your speech. The information you collect through research needs to be organized in the manner best fitting your speech purpose and audience.

In this section we will discuss five different ways in which you can organize your main points in an informative speech. We will also cover some options for connecting those main points through the use of a variety of connective statements, like the transitions we just covered.

## Chronological Organization of Main Points

The first possible organizational pattern for informative speeches we will discuss is chronological. ***Chronological order*** involves arranging points in the order in which they occur, or occurred, from start to finish. When your specific purpose is to inform the class about an event or a process, then the vast majority of the time you will arrange your points in chronological order. This only makes sense because these two topics lend themselves to speaking about them in time order.

**chronological order**
......
arranging points in the order in which they occur, or occurred, from start to finish

Informative speeches about events often cover what happened at a particular moment in history, or what will happen at a specific time in the future. Take the case of Kylie, whose specific purpose is to inform her audience about the Battle of Thermopylae, where 300 Spartan warriors fought against hordes of invading Persians. This topic encourages a chronological organizational pattern. It would make sense for her to structure her main points like this:

> Body
> I.   Main point: How the Battle of Thermopylae Started
> II.  Main point: Repelling the Persian Army
> III. Main point: The Defeat of the Greeks

his sequence follows the order in which the events occurred and makes it easy for Kylie to achieve her specific purpose and the audience to learn about the Battle of Thermopylae.

Some lectures also are organized chronologically. For example, media mogul Rupert Murdoch was invited to speak about the state of the newspaper industry during the Boyer Lecture Series, an event sponsored by the Australian Broadcasting Commission. Murdoch addressed the industry by providing a chronological history of newspapers and his own experiences with them. It was more than just a sequential list of events, as he engaged the audience with both facts and personal testimonies that made the address quite engaging. Events, however, are not the only speech topics that invite chronological sequencing.

### The Future of Newspapers
### by Rupert Murdoch

Delivered November 14, 2008, at the Boyer Lecture Series

Australian media mogul Rupert Murdoch has spent much of his life in the media business. Murdoch knows about the media both past and present, so with many concerned by the shrinking of newspaper subscriptions, he addressed the future of the industry by discussing its origins.

Murdoch used a chronological organizational pattern to address several different topics in his rather complicated but informative address. When discussing his own history with media, he signified a chronological pattern with phrases such as: "When I was growing up...," "Over many decades," and "I became an editor and owner."[3] He also began one particular main point within his speech with, "When I took over the *News*..."[4]

Murdoch also spoke about implications for the industry from resources to technology changes, its challenges and opportunities, and the importance of brands. Murdoch completed his speech by reemphasizing the chronological development of his speech with this statement:

> "But I don't think I will be proven wrong on one point. The newspaper, or a very close electronic cousin, will always be around. It may not be thrown on your front doorstep the way it is today. But the thud it makes as it lands will continue to echo around society and the world."[5]

Informative speeches about processes also engender constructing main points in chronological order. For instance, Trevor's specific purpose is to inform his audience about how to apply for student financial aid. To accomplish the task of applying for financial assistance it is important to do things in order, and so his organizational pattern is chronological and looks something like this:

Body
I.   Main point: Determining your Eligibility
II.  Main point: Obtaining the Correct Forms
III. Main point: Submitting Materials

Like Kylie, Trevor needs to lay out the task at hand in the best way for people to understand it, and since it is an informative speech and he is trying to teach them about something, the best way for them to learn is through receiving the main points in a time sequence so they know what to do and when to do it.

## Cause and Effect Organizational Pattern

Chronological patterns for organizing main points are not the only method of ordering ideas in an informative speech. A second method is *cause and effect arrangement*, which orders your points first by discussing the cause of something that occurred, and then moving to an explanation of the impact of its occurrence. Although there are similarities with the chronological pattern in that the cause must necessarily precede the effect in the speech, this is a much more specific structural pattern as it pertains only to causes and their subsequent effects. Cause and effect arrangements are typically used in informative speeches about events, as both causes and effects are events.

An informative speech structured according to cause and effect typically will have two main points: the cause, followed by the effects. If there are multiple causes and/or multiple effects, however, it is possible for there to be more than two main points. As a means of an example, let's look at Wanda's informative speech in which the specific purpose is to inform the audience about the Great Depression. If she chose to deliver this speech using a cause and effect arrangement, then her main points would look like this:

> Body
> I. Main point: Cause #1: Speculation
> II. Main point: Cause #2: Stock Market Crash
> III. Main point: Effects: Unemployment, Deflation

In this speech the first cause (speculation) leads to the second cause (stock market crash), and both ultimately have the effect of increased unemployment and deflation. This approach follows a time sequence, but that order is predicated only on causes and their subsequent effects.

## Problem-Solution Organizational Pattern

Another organizational pattern for informative speeches that also relates to the chronological sequencing of main points is problem-solution arrangement. *Problem-solution arrangement* orders points by first discussing a problem and then explaining how it was addressed. This organizational pattern is chronological, and when employed in an informative speech it discusses events of the past. If a speaker advocates for a solution to a current problem, then he veers dangerously close to changing the purpose of the speech from conveying information to changing an audience's perception about an issue. In an informative speech it is best to use this form of chronological ordering to explain events of the past or available solutions in the present, rather than discussing current issues that do not contain a resolution. It is also essential not to advocate or label a particular solution "the best way" to solve a problem. Later in the book we will discuss how this organizational pattern can be effectively employed in a persuasive speech, but for now our focus remains on its use in an informative presentation.

When using the problem-solution arrangement in an informative speech it is essential to present the problem as what happened and the solution as how it was corrected. For example, take Leslie, whose specific purpose for her informative

**cause and effect arrangement**
orders your points first by discussing the cause of something that occurred and then moving to an explanation of the impact of its occurrence

**problem-solution arrangement**
orders points by first discussing a problem and then how it was addressed; a subset of chronological order

speech is to tell the audience how to fix a reservation error that involves an online booking agent, like Priceline. Here the problem is simple—an error in a submitted online reservation—and she wants to teach her audience how to fix that error. Using the problem-solution arrangement for her main points, her speech would look like this:

> Body
> I.   Main point: Problem: Making an Error on an Online Reservation
> II.  Main point: Solution #1: Call the Agency
> III. Main point: Solution #2: Call the Airline

Here, Leslie effectively orders her points by laying out the problem and then describing the available solutions for fixing the problem. In this speech there is no space for advocating for a specific solution, merely an explanation of ways a person could solve the problem. Remember, her general purpose is to inform; what her audience does with that information is entirely up to them.

Map of the Battle of Gettysburg

## Spatial Organizational Pattern

Sometimes informative speeches do not need to be sequentially ordered, but rather the best way to achieve your specific purpose might be by organizing your main points according to space. *Spatial order* arranges points according to geography or logical movement through an area, so it is easy to see how certain topics could be covered in this manner. Spatial ordering of main points is typically applied to informative speeches about events and objects, as we will now demonstrate.

The spatial ordering of main points can be encouraged through a simple change in a specific purpose statement. For instance, Roland plans to deliver an informative speech with the specific purpose of informing his audience about the battlefield at the Battle of Gettysburg. This specific purpose is subtly different from a speech designed to inform an audience about the Battle of Gettysburg, but the simple adjustment encourages a spatial, rather than chronological, ordering of the main points. With Roland's specific purpose in mind, his speech would probably best be structured in the following manner:

**spatial order**
arranges points according to geography or logical movement through an area

> Body
> I.   Main point: Little Round Top
> II.  Main point: Big Round Top
> III. Main point: Cemetery Hill

Roland organizes his points so that he goes around the battlefield at Gettysburg to discuss the layout of each particular area where fighting took place. It is not organized according to chronology, but rather according to the landscape of the battlefield, thus making it a spatial ordering of main points and not a chronological arrangement.

Informative speeches about objects also can call for a spatial arrangement of main points. The specific purpose of Gwyneth's speech, for example, is to inform her audience about the chain of islands in the Caribbean called the Lesser Antilles. She might structure her speech by separating the islands into groups according to their location in the chain so it would look something like this:

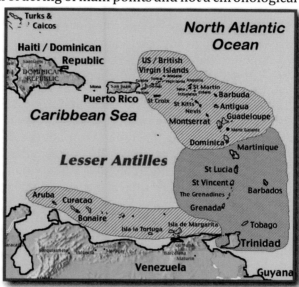

Map of the Lesser Antilles Islands

> Body
> I.   Main point: Northernmost Islands
> II.  Main point: Central Islands
> III. Main point: Southernmost Islands

This structure allows her to categorize the islands and move down the Lesser Antilles chain in the order of the islands' geographic location. This helps the audience make sense of where the islands are, and it allows Gwyneth to achieve her specific purpose in a logical manner.

## Topical Organizational Pattern

**topical arrangement**
the organization of main points by subpoints that do not naturally fit together in another way

If your informative speech does not fit one of the four organizational strategies discussed above, do not fear, there is one other option that remains open to you. The ***topical arrangement*** of main points works when your specific purpose encourages the division of main points into logical subpoints. These subpoints do not fit together in a chronological or spatial way and have certain characteristics that differentiate them from each other; however, they still share enough in common so as to logically relate to the topic of the speech. This organizational pattern could be applied to any of the four types of informative speeches except, typically, processes.

Informative speeches about concepts can be arranged in a topical fashion. Carlos wants to deliver a speech with the specific purpose of informing an audience about the four food groups, and so his speech topic does not invite any pattern we have discussed so far. Instead, he separates the concept of the four food groups into their distinctive categories and structures his speech accordingly:

> Body
> I.   Main point: Dairy
> II.  Main point: Vegetables
> III. Main point: Grains
> IV.  Main point: Meats

These main points are the categories of the four food groups, and thus, they provide four logically related areas to cover in the speech. Rather than a distinct chronology, spatial arrangement, or problem or cause, this speech is organized around logical subsets of information.

Crafting an informative speech about an event can also employ a topical arrangement of main points. Take, for example, a speech with the specific purpose of informing the audience about the Revolutionary War. This speech can cover the individual generals, the major battles, and the ramifications of the war. Those points are not chronologically or spatially related, and thus they provide an opportunity for using a topical organizational pattern like this:

> Body
> I.   Main point: Major Generals of the Revolutionary War
> II.  Main point: Battles of the Revolutionary War
> III. Main point: Results of the Revolutionary War

Here a topic that one might think would only be covered using a chronological pattern has been shifted to fit a topical pattern. It is a perfect example of how the organization of a speech can be adjusted simply by reformulating the specific purpose.

Finally, informative speeches about objects can be constructed using the topical arrangement pattern. Take the example of the islands we used a little while ago. Gwyneth could easily have chosen a topical organizational pattern by discussing aspects of the island chain instead of their location. For instance, she could have focused on their colonial history, weather differences, and tourist destinations. Again, these aspects of the islands are not related by time or space, but they are worthy of discussion, and so if Gwyneth wished she could have structured her speech in this way:

Body
I.   Main point: Colonial History of the Lesser Antilles Islands Chain
II.  Main point: Weather of the Lesser Antilles Islands
III. Main point: Tourist Destinations in the Lesser Antilles Islands

These main points can be structured to logically flow into each other. For example, colonial history introduces interesting aspects of the islands that might attract visitors, information on the weather suggests when to visit, and the tourist destinations segment provides information on popular attractions to visit.

Choosing the proper organizational pattern makes all the difference in a speech. It demonstrates logical thinking on behalf of the speaker and allows an audience to follow the main points of a speech, thus enabling speakers to achieve their specific purpose. Arranging the points in the body of the speech is only one part of the equation. The other half is seamlessly connecting them so the speech stays fluid and smooth by using connective statements (recall our discussion of the transition statements used at the end of an introduction). In the next section we will discuss several strategies for connecting main points and creating smooth movement between the points of an informative speech.

## Connective Statements within the Body

Determining your main points and how to arrange them is only half the task of developing a good body for your speech. The other half is connecting the points in a coherent fashion. There are several ways in which you can signal your speech is about to move to a new main point. In this part of the chapter we will discuss two methods, in addition to transitions which we mentioned earlier, that you can use to move from one point to another.

The first type of connective is an *internal preview*. Internal previews often work in conjunction with transitions by using two statements to segue between the two points:

> "Now that we have covered the scoring rules of baseball let's look at how those rules relate to other professional sports. First we will examine football, then we will discuss hockey, and finally we will conclude by showing the differences between baseball and soccer scoring."

**internal preview**
serves as an outline of what is to come next in a speech and is often combined with transition statements

The first sentence serves as the transition and the second provides a preview of what is to come.

*Internal summary,* the second type of connective we will discuss, is a statement that summarizes what you already covered and precedes transitions. Like internal previews, this summary serves as a roadmap for you and your audience and is most useful when you are covering several different main points in the body of your speech. For instance, consider this internal summary:

**internal summary**
a statement that summarizes what you already have covered and precedes transitions

"We have explored the early cultures of Latin America and what happened when the Spanish discovered South America. The history of South America, however, did not end with the arrival of the Spanish."

Notice how the summary of what has been covered occurs before the transition to a new main point. This is the inverse order of an internal preview, but it can have the same effect.

Once the body is complete you must still use one last connective to signal the conclusion. In the next section we will discuss that particular device as well as how to structure the conclusion for your informative speech. Before moving on, review the checklist for preparing the body of the speech provided in Figure 11.1.

**Figure 11.1**
**Checklist for Preparing the Speech Body**

| | |
|---|---|
| ✔ | Have a clearly worded specific purpose |
| ✔ | Ensure your thesis does what you want it to |
| ✔ | Choose the proper organizational design that fits your specific purpose |
| ✔ | Have transitions between each main point |
| ✔ | Use connectives for speech clarity |

## INFORMATIVE SPEECH CONCLUSIONS

Informative speeches conclude in a slightly different way than other speeches. It is important to remember, however, that even an informative speech can have a persuasive impact, especially if loaded words are used. Rhetorician Richard Weaver (see the nearby box) noted the use of "god terms" and "devil terms" that can affect the meaning of a speech. With that in mind, it is important to carefully consider word choices within conclusions so as not to change the purpose of the entire speech from providing information to calling an audience to action.

In this section we will explain the dimensions of an informative speech conclusion, beginning with the signal that the speech has entered its final phase. We then lay out how to construct a summary, and finally, how to conclude with a strong statement.

### Signposts

**signpost**

a connective that lets the audience know what is next; most effective form of connective for moving from the last main point to the conclusion

Once you completely cover all the main points you previewed in the introduction you need to let the audience know the presentation is about to wrap up. This is done with a statement called a *signpost*. These statements typically let the audience know you are moving from the body to the end of the speech, although they also can appear within the body of a speech. A signpost itself is a connective, but it is best suited for the move from the last main point to the conclusion.

## SPOTLIGHTING THEORISTS: RICHARD M. WEAVER

### Richard M. Weaver (1910–1963)

Richard Weaver was born in North Carolina. Five years later his father died and his mother moved the family to Lexington, Kentucky. Weaver worked his way through school at the University of Kentucky and graduated with a degree in English in 1932. Upon graduating, Weaver was unable to find work given the poor economic climate created by the Great Depression. The young graduate was bitter and joined the Socialist Party, but after a few years its ideas fell out of favor with him and he left the party.

He eventually received a scholarship to Vanderbilt University and studied under John Crowe Ransom, where he was introduced to southern agrarianism, an anti-progress movement. In 1942 Weaver achieved a Ph.D. at Louisiana State University and began a career teaching and writing about rhetorical theory and composition.[6]

Weaver was very interested in the nature of human beings and how language was used in expression. Weaver became known for describing such ways of knowing as argument by definition. He was enthralled with orator Edmund Burke and the Lincoln-Douglas debates of 1858. Weaver was also interested in understanding how orators could use loaded words to make a point. He labeled those "god terms" and "devil terms."

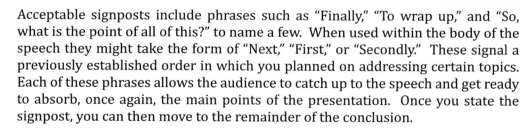

Weaver noted that god words, such as science, progress, freedom, and democracy, had positive cultural connotations, whereas devil words, such as communist and fascist, had negative connotations.[7] Weaver later declared that no words are value-free, because each contains a worldview.[8]

Weaver also wrote about culture and rhetoric's place in it. He felt that society in general was declining. Weaver noted that scientific progress was not all that should be considered when analyzing culture. He pointed to things such as scientism and cultural relativism as warning signs in the structure of societies.

Weaver died at age 53 in 1963.

Acceptable signposts include phrases such as "Finally," "To wrap up," and "So, what is the point of all of this?" to name a few. When used within the body of the speech they might take the form of "Next," "First," or "Secondly." These signal a previously established order in which you planned on addressing certain topics. Each of these phrases allows the audience to catch up to the speech and get ready to absorb, once again, the main points of the presentation. Once you state the signpost, you can then move to the remainder of the conclusion.

## Speech Summaries

Once you let the audience know that you are about to conclude your speech, you need to provide them with a summary of what you just told them. The *summary* is the central part of the conclusion, and it is where you reiterate the speech's

**summary**
the central part of the conclusion; it is where you reiterate the speech's thesis statement and recap the main points you addressed throughout the body

thesis statement and recap the main points you addressed throughout the body. There are a few key aspects of the summary that require discussion.

Whereas a speech preview in the introduction clearly states the thesis before the preview of the main points, many conclusions do the opposite—although that is not required. The restatement of the thesis needs to occur either before or after the summary of main points and it also must be phrased differently than the original thesis statement in the introduction. Do not simply "cut and paste" the thesis into the proper slot in the conclusion. The same goes for the summary statements of the main points.

Again, you have options with regard to the summary statements for the main points. You can either combine them into a single complex statement or address each one individually. Choose whichever method makes the most sense and is clearest to the audience. Look at the following example of two different ways to summarize a speech:

> **Option #1:** "Today we learned about the history of the city of New York (restatement of thesis). First, I explained how the Dutch bought part of what is now New York for a box of trinkets. Then, I detailed the controversial group of politicians that ran the city for years, Tammany Hall. Finally, I sketched an overview of the city in the years following the attacks of 9/11."

> **Option #2:** "Today we learned about the history of the city of New York (restatement of thesis). We covered the early days with the Dutch, the years under Tammany Hall, and finally the more recent state of affairs since 9/11."

Both of these options equally reiterate the central thesis and main points in a way the audience can understand. The main points also are addressed in the order in which they appear in the speech, again emphasizing a symmetry that is easy for listeners to follow.

A signpost and good summary are not, however, the only components of an effective conclusion.

## Clinchers

**clincher**
.........
the final statement of your speech

After reminding the audience of what they just heard it is time to issue the final statement of your speech, the *clincher*. Clinchers for informative speeches are very different than clinchers for persuasive or epideictic speeches as they do not really have an emotional dimension. There is no call to action as there might be in a persuasive speech conclusion and no recognition of the importance of the moment as there might be in an epideictic address. Rather, informative speeches end with a statement regarding the topic itself.

Clinchers for informative speeches might refer to a short story you used as your attention-getter. They may also be a quotation from another source, so long as you have not already used one as your attention-getter. These quotations also need to relate to your speech topic. So, if you informed your class about D-Day and World War II, you might quote Britain's Queen Elizabeth, who said:

> *"There are only a few occasions in history when the course of human destiny depended on the events of a single day. June 6, 1944, was one of those days."[9]*

Or perhaps you spoke about how to paint, in which case you might end with the following quotation from Leonardo da Vinci:

> *"Painting is poetry that is seen rather than felt."*

Clinchers also could simply be a statement regarding the knowledge you just provided the audience. Due to the nature of the speech, clinchers need to let the audience know what they learned and alert the audience that the speech has concluded.

One effective way of crafting a clincher is to end with a signpost in much the same way the conclusion itself began with one. Think of using phrases such as, "So, I will conclude by saying," "I wish to leave you with this," or "The last thing I wish to say." These phrases let the audience know the words you are about to utter are the final words of the speech.

## SUMMARY

In this chapter we explained how to use the information from the previous chapter to construct an informative speech. We discussed the elements of an informative speech introduction, the various ways it can be organized, and the components of an informative speech conclusion. These tools, along with a properly constructed speech outline, will help you create an effective and interesting informative speech.

## KEY TERMS

attention-getter   229

cause and effect arrangement   237

chronological order   235

clincher   244

famous quotation   230

initial credibility   232

internal preview   241

internal summary   241

problem-solution arrangement   237

rhetorical question   229

signpost   242

spatial order   238

summary   243

topical arrangement   239

transition   234

## REVIEW QUESTIONS

1. What are the three types of attention-getter devices discussed in this chapter?

2. What are five different ways you can organize the main points in an informative speech?

3. What are the four types of connectives you can use to smoothly move from one main point to the next?

4. What are the five important elements of a speech introduction?

5. What are the three important dimensions of a speech conclusion?

## THINK ABOUT IT

1. Is there such a thing as a purely informative speech?

2. Are there any other ways to order points in an informative speech without affecting the purpose of the speech?

3. Can you think of any ways to creatively and excitingly craft a clincher without calling an audience to action?

## ACTIVITIES FOR ACTION

1. Choose a topic which you know little about but would like to know more. Write out a series of questions about the topic you want answered, then place them in order according to one of the organizational patterns discussed for informative speeches. After you determine which pattern of organization you will use, figure out one or two additional ways of organizing the speech. After you have done that, determine the pros and cons for each organizational method.

2. Take all the objects from your bookbag and lay them on a table. Select an object and then write down all the major characteristics of the chosen item. Next, practice organizing an informative speech by developing the main points for an informative speech about the object you chose.

## ENDNOTES

1. General David Petraeus, "Opening Statement to the Joint House Committee on the Situation in Iraq," http://www.americanrhetoric.com/speeches/wariniraq/davidpetraeusoniraq.htm (accessed April 9, 2009).

2. Ibid.

3. Rupert Murdoch at Boyer Lecture, http://www.abc.net.au/rn/boyerlectures/stories/2008/2397940.htm#transcript (accessed June 25, 2011).

4. Ibid.

5.  Ibid.

6.  Karen Foss, Sonja Foss, and Ronald Trapp, *Contemporary Perspectives on Rhetoric* (2nd Ed.) (Prospect Heights, IL: Waverland Press, 1991).

7.  Richard Weaver, *The Ethics of Rhetoric.* (Davis, CA: Hermagoras Press, 1985). (Original publication was in 1953 by Regnery/Gateway, published by permission).

8.  Patricia Bizzell and Bruce Herzberg, *The Rhetorical Tradition: Readings from Classical Times to the Present* (Boston, MA: Bedford Books of St. Martin's Press, 1990).

9.  As quoted in a speech by Reverend Billy Graham entitled, "Leadership in the Third Millennium." For transcript see: David Edmison and Edward P. Badovinac (Eds.), *The Empire Club of Canada Speeches 1995-1996,* The Empire Club Foundation, Toronto, CA, 1996, 81.

THE SPEAKER:  The Tradition and Practice of Public Speaking

# Types of Persuasion

## CHAPTER OVERVIEW

- Explains stasis theory, a central component of persuasive speech
- Details the differences between forms of deliberative persuasive speech and forensic persuasive speech
- Covers the elements of the persuasive process

# Practically SPEAKING

On June 12, 1994, police discovered the bodies of Nicole Brown Simpson and Ronald Goldman in the courtyard of Nicole Brown Simpson's Brentwood, California, residence. Simpson and Goldman died from excessive stab wounds, and immediately suspicion fell upon Simpson's ex-husband, former NFL star turned actor, O. J. Simpson. On June 13th authorities informed Simpson of the murders while he was on a business trip in Chicago. Upon his return, police took him into custody for questioning and he retained Robert Shapiro as his legal counsel. Within a few weeks a grand jury and judge decided that there was sufficient evidence to prosecute O. J. Simpson for the murders of his ex-wife and Goldman. On July 22, 1994, before presiding judge Lance Ito, O. J. pled not guilty to the crimes, and one of the most famous trials in American history began.

The trial opened on January 24, 1995, after a brief holiday recess. During the trial the defense managed to get admissions of procedural errors from members of the police department regarding the collection of DNA and other evidence. Additionally, the aforementioned detective, Mark Fuhrman, came under fire for supposedly making racist comments during the investigation. Eventually, after various legal maneuverings by both the prosecution and defense, the trial began to wind down.

On September 26–27, 1995, over a year after the deaths of Nicole Brown Simpson and Ronald Goldman, the prosecution and defense delivered their closing arguments.[1] Deputy District Attorney Marcia Clark and Prosecutor Christopher Darden delivered their closing argument first, making specific mention of the perception that Detective Fuhrman was a racist: "It would be a tragedy if, with such overwhelming evidence, you find the defendant not guilty because of the racist attitudes of one officer." Immediately following their presentation, the defense, represented by Johnny Cochrane and Barry Scheck, made its case to the jury, with the former referring to Fuhrman as a "lying, perjuring, genocidal racist," and the latter referring to a "cancer" at the heart of the investigation into the murders.[2] Ultimately, the arguments made by the defense proved to be more persuasive than those offered by the prosecution, and on October 3, 1995, the jury acquitted O. J. Simpson on both counts of murder.

The speeches made by both the prosecution and the defense in the O. J. Simpson trial are examples of one type of persuasive speech. Aristotle divided persuasive speeches into two categories. Regardless of which category of persuasive speech is delivered, it is always focused upon one issue or concern. In this chapter we will begin by exploring the characteristics that create different issues of dispute in a persuasive speech. Then we will discuss the similarities and differences of Aristotle's two types of persuasive speeches. Finally, we will cover how the persuasive process works. Understanding the types of persuasive speeches and how they work is the first step in being able to discern a speaker's arguments.

# FORMS OF PERSUASIVE SPEECH

In this section of the chapter we will identify the different types of persuasive speeches using both classical and contemporary terms. At the heart of any persuasive attempt is what classical philosophers referred to as "the issue in dispute," or what contemporary scholars call "the question." Quintilian, the Roman philosopher and teacher, wrote extensively about the different types of issues that are disputed in a persuasive argument, so we will first discuss those four forms of disputes.

In more contemporary times instructors have reduced those four types of arguments into three, and so after examining Quintilian's work we will demonstrate the three forms of persuasive questions most people teach today. Ultimately, they get at the same thing: What is the focus of a speaker's persuasive appeal? We will then define the two types of persuasive speeches proposed by Aristotle and how they relate to the issues in dispute. Finally, we will discuss how to use persuasion to respond to arguments made by another person.

## Quintilian and Stasis Theory

One common element to any persuasive speech is the fact that it revolves around an issue that is in dispute. The speaker thus attempts to persuade his audience that they should agree with the speaker's interpretation of the issue in dispute. This central focus is called *stasis*, or the basic issue in dispute between one or more speaking parties. Stasis does not change in a persuasive situation, or put more succinctly, what the sides argue over does not change, even though their positions on it might do so due to persuasion. In his book, *Institutione Oratoria*, Quintilian provided the best explanation of the different types of stasis, or disputed issues, that may exist in a persuasive situation.[3] He proposed, in effect, four different forms of stasis, and in this section of the chapter we discuss each of them.

**stasis**
the basic issue in dispute between one or more speaking parties

The first form of stasis is what was at play during the O. J. Simpson trial discussed in the opening of the chapter. *Conjectural stasis* exists when the central issue of disagreement is whether something occurred or not. The issue at stake in the Simpson murder case was whether or not O. J. killed Nicole Brown Simpson and Ronald Goldman. All criminal court cases address issues of conjectural stasis.

**conjectural stasis**
when the issue in dispute is whether something occurred or not

**definitive stasis**
................
when the issue in dispute is the meaning of a term

A second form of stasis is *definitive stasis*, or a dispute over the meaning of a term. When two sides define a term in two different ways, then there is definitive stasis. One arena where this occurs is in politics, where terms and phrases are defined differently by each candidate or party. Take, for instance, the issue of marriage. Some define marriage as a contractual agreement between only a man and a woman. Others, however, interpret it as a contractual bond between any two consenting adults, regardless of gender. When two sides apply different definitions as to what marriage is, then their central issue of disagreement is an example of definitive stasis.

**qualitative stasis**
................
when the issue in dispute involves the morality, ethicality or value of an action

When the sides in an argument seek to persuade an audience about the moral or ethical nature of an action, then their central issue of discussion involves *qualitative stasis*. Debates about issues of qualitative stasis also include those that cover what is best in a given situation. In the O. J. Simpson case, the district attorney's office decided not to seek the death penalty. Arguments for whether or not to seek the death penalty exemplify an issue where the topic is a matter of qualitative stasis. Assuming his guilt, would it be right to kill O. J. as punishment for murdering his ex-wife and Ronald Goldman? At the heart of such a question is the morality of capital punishment, thus making the issue of disagreement one of qualitative stasis.

**translative stasis**
................
when the issue in dispute is the competency of the judge or arbiter

The final form of stasis proposed by Quintilian occurs when both sides debate the competency of the judge in their dispute; in effect, both sides make judgments about the judge. *Translative stasis* exists when both sides argue over whether a judge or arbiter is competent to make a decision. In 1989 when New York mafia leader John Gotti was on trial, news accounts reported the judge, John Reis Bartels, who was 91 and appointed by President Dwight D. Eisenhower in 1959, fell asleep during the proceedings. Both the judge and the lawyers in the case disputed those stories, arguing that the judge merely closed his eyes during long witness testimonies. The lawyers felt Bartels was competent to serve as judge in the case, while the newspaper reporters questioned his ability to oversee the trial.[4] The debate over the competency of the 91-year-old Bartels was an example of an issue of translative stasis.

Whenever speakers attempt to persuade an audience to change their beliefs or values, or even to act in a particular way, there is a central issue in dispute between the two sides. That issue of dispute can be over whether something actually occurred, how to define a specific term, determining if an action is right or wrong, or whether a judge is competent to make a decision. These different issues represent what Quintilian referred to as stasis, because the issue the two sides argue over never changes. It is important to you as a speaker and audience member to know what the disputed issue is because it allows you to maintain your focus and identify the key points to the argument, thereby enabling you to come to a reasoned conclusion. Today we commonly refer to stasis theory in a simpler way and categorize the central issue in dispute as a question.

## SPOTLIGHTING THEORISTS: QUINTILIAN

### Quintilian (35–99 B.C.)

Quintilian was the last of the great classical rhetoricians produced by Greece or Rome. He followed in the footsteps of Cicero and Isocrates and attempted to expand Cicero's work by proposing reforms to educational practices throughout the Empire. Quintilian began his career in much the same way as other famous Greeks and Romans—as a lawyer—but did not choose fame and fortune in the political arena.

Quintilian made his mark as a teacher, not a lawyer or politician. He received a grant from the Emperor Vespasian and worked at a school subsidized by Vespasian. Quintilian's resistance to corruption in politics and the prevailing standards of Roman education at the time were not overtly noticeable, but rather emerged through more subtle actions. Unlike other schools of his time, Quintilian frowned on physical punishment as a means of teaching his students, instead attempting to foster a family dynamic between himself and his charges.

Like Isocrates, Quintilian felt that students should be well-read on a variety of subjects in order to master both concepts and language.

His school, therefore, emphasized more reading than repetitive performance exercises. Quintilian famously stated that education should produce "the good man speaking well." This "good man" combined all the positive attributes of a Platonistic speaker who committed himself to seeking the truth, with the Ciceronian and Isocratean emphasis on developing public virtue and character in the service of society.

Quintilian's lone surviving work is the *Institutio Oratorio,* or the *Institutes of Oratory.* This massive project was divided into 12 books, each dealing with a different aspect of the speaking process and education in general. Book One lays out the ideal curriculum and talks about early childhood education; Books Two and Three discuss stasis theory at length; Books Four through Six develop Cicero's concept of invention; Book Seven addresses arrangement; Books Eight and Nine deal with Style; Book Ten identifies the "right" authors a speaker should emulate; Book Eleven covers memory, delivery, and decorum; and Book Twelve covers the character of the perfect orator, or "the good man speaking well."[5]

## Contemporary Persuasive Questions

What Quintilian and his Roman colleagues called stasis theory we now refer to as the issue in question. Today, we identify three different types of questions, but each has its roots in stasis theory. These questions, just like stasis, identify the focus for the persuasive appeal, allowing both the speaker and the audience to avoid going off on tangents. The key element of any successful ethical persuasive appeal is that it remains focused on advocating an answer to one of these three types of persuasive questions.

**question of fact**

when a speaker seeks to persuade people about how to interpret facts

When a speaker seeks to persuade people about how to interpret facts she is addressing a *question of fact*. Whenever the reliability, veracity or interpretation of something is in doubt, then a question of fact exists. A persuasive speech about a question of fact is different from a technical/informative speech because a speaker seeks to persuade people, not teach them. This type of persuasive speech is similar to what Quintilian termed conjectural stasis. To explain, let us look again at the O. J. Simpson example. The jury entertained serious doubts about whether O. J. committed the crime or not. Therefore, in the trial and in their closing arguments, the lawyers attempted to persuade the audience (the jury) that their answer to the question of fact (did O. J. kill his ex-wife and Ronald Goldman?) was correct.

**question of value**

a persuasive speech about the rightness or wrongness of an idea, action, or issue

The second type of question a persuasive speech addresses is similar to what Quintilian referred to as qualitative stasis. Today, these types of persuasive speeches are referred to as speeches regarding a *question of value*. When the focus of the speech involves whether something is right or wrong, it is considered to be a speech about valuing one thing over another. Questions about value are not limited to moral and ethical questions but also include disagreements over prioritizing certain items, as one does in a budget. When you prioritize something you are valuing certain items or ideas more than others. These speeches also might advocate that one thing is better than another, such as a speech where you attempt to persuade an audience that buying a hybrid car is better than buying a traditional vehicle.

**question of policy**

when a speaker takes a position on whether an action should or should not be taken

The third and final type of question deals with a *question of policy*, whereby speakers take a position on whether an action should or should not be taken. Like questions of value, questions of policy share some characteristics with qualitative stasis, but they also contain some qualities not thoroughly explained by Quintilian's definitions of issues in dispute. Questions of policy focus on action, and often disputes over answers to what action to take occur in deliberative bodies such as governments and organizational committees. A union might hold a meeting where members discuss whether or not to go on strike. Legislators may dispute whether or not to vote for a bill that raises taxes to pay for more teachers. When solving a problem requires a specific action, then there exists a question of policy.

Notice that Quintilian's stasis theory does not really address questions of policy directly, nor does the contemporary approach address definitive or translative stasis directly. Instead, under the contemporary structure, definitive and translative stasis are included in questions of fact, as the definition of a term or the competency of a judge can be considered questions of fact. In the case of Quintilian, he would most likely argue that questions of policy address issues of qualitative stasis, or whether taking such action is right or wrong. The important thing, however, is to see that how we talk about persuasion today developed from the classical understanding and approach to persuasion and argument. In the next part of this chapter we will explore the two different types of persuasive speech proposed by Aristotle and where they take place.

# 12

# ARISTOTLE ON PERSUASIVE SPEAKING

Stasis theory focuses on the issues and central ideas of a persuasive speech, but as we hope to illustrate in this chapter and this book, a speech is more than its subject; it also includes the situation and the purpose. So, in this section we discuss the difference between the two forms of persuasive speech proposed by Aristotle and where the issues in dispute can be found in each.

## Aristotle's Two Types of Persuasion

People sometimes try to persuade others to take action either regarding an issue currently at work or as a response to something that might occur in the future. These types of speeches occur most often in decision-making bodies such as the floor of Congress. Such persuasive speeches deliberate over problems and issues while proposing solutions to them. Legislative speech, or what Aristotle referred to as *deliberative speech*, therefore represents one category of persuasive speech. These speeches often attempt to answer questions of policy or questions of value as they try to prioritize problems and propose solutions to those dilemmas.

**deliberative speech**
one of two forms of persuasive speech proposed by Aristotle; it often takes place in legislative settings and focuses on discussing policies and actions to be taken

One example of deliberative persuasive speaking occurred during the 2008 financial crisis, when members of the House of Representatives and Senate and the Bush administration gave speeches regarding the fiscal emergency and how to properly approach solving it. Some advocated a large federal investment, while others felt the market should be left to correct itself. A third group even debated the size of the federal investment that should be made, proposing even more spending than other groups. The speeches in support of these various positions were emblematic of deliberative persuasive appeals. Deliberative persuasive speech, however, is only one form of persuasive speech.

Aristotle recognized that not all persuasive speech is deliberative, such as in the case of courtroom arguments. Arguments in a courtroom where speakers debate the facts of a case and attempt to answer questions of justice rather than policy are examples of what Aristotle called *forensic speech*. Unlike deliberative speeches where arguments take place over the most effective way to manage resources and debate action to be taken, forensic speeches contain a *kategoria*, or accusation, and an *apologia*, or defense. Forensic oratory focuses on defining the past rather than proposing a path for the future. In order to craft an effective forensic speech you should be familiar with what your audience values, as well as how to wield evidence in the construction of a reasoned argument or position regarding the issue on which you are speaking.

**forensic speech**
an argument where speakers debate the facts of a case and attempt to answer questions of justice

**kategoria**
a forensic speech that makes an accusation

**apologia**
a forensic speech that makes a defense against an accusation

Forensic speaking is most common in courtrooms, but that is not the only place it occurs. In actuality, any time we take a position or present an argument to interpret something in a specific way we are making a forensic argument. For instance, in 2006 actor and director Mel Gibson was arrested for drunk driving and subsequently went on a tirade where he made anti-Semitic remarks. A short time later he issued a public apology for those remarks

Actor
Mel Gibson

and offered an explanation for what he said and why he said it. That explanation was a forensic argument because he presented an interpretation of the events and his feelings afterward and asked for forgiveness. The apology was ultimately accepted by the Anti-Defamation League and Gibson has been able to move on from the incident.

Situation and purpose influence persuasive appeals as much as topics. Certain topics are limited to, or better suited for, certain situations. Both play a role in focusing persuasive speeches and are therefore important tools for both speakers and audiences. As a speaker you need to stay focused on the issue in dispute, while providing a reasoned rationale for your argument. As an audience member you need to remain tuned to the issue presented by the speaker so you can follow the argument. In the next section we will discuss one type of persuasive speech that does not necessarily address a question per se, but rather seeks to respond to an argument made by someone else.

## Refutation Speeches

As you know by now, where there is persuasion there is dispute, and where there is a dispute there is a response. In fact, even the Greeks and Romans recognized that often persuasion is not simply advocating for a position in a vacuum; rather, it involves responding to the argument of another individual in an attempt to prove them wrong. There are two types of persuasive speeches that respond to an argument presented by another person. In this section we will detail these two types of speeches.

**rebuttal speech**
a speech that involves overcoming the opposition's argument by introducing other evidence that reduces the appeal of the opposition's claims

The first type of response is a **rebuttal speech**, which involves overcoming the opposition's argument by introducing other evidence that reduces the appeal of the opposition's claims. In a rebuttal speech you use evidence not cited by the other person to illustrate how the argument is incomplete or misleading, thus casting doubt on the veracity of her points. This type of speech often takes place in academic and political debates in which the person who goes second seeks to minimize the strength of the arguments made by the person who went first. A rebuttal speech's purpose is always to persuade the audience that the opposition's argument is incomplete and not as strong as it appears. Essentially, a rebuttal speech does not claim the other person's argument is false, but rather that it is not as strong as the speaker originally made it out to be.

Let's look at an example of a rebuttal speech. Kane delivered a speech that argued the city of Las Vegas should use tax revenue to build a stadium that would attract a professional sports team to the city. He emphasized how much money it would bring the city in the long run, how many jobs it would create in the short term, and how a sports team would give the city its own image. Jacquelyn then responded with her rebuttal.

Jacquelyn made several points that did not disprove Kane's argument but rather made it seem less appealing. She said that yes, there would be short-term benefits in terms of jobs created to build the stadium, but to fund such an operation would mean a tax hike on current residents. Further, she said the long-range benefits would be seen only if a professional sports team actually came to the city. She then pointed out there was no guarantee that would happen, which might leave the city with a big expensive arena and no team to use it. Finally, she pointed out Las Vegas already has an image and that a sports team would not help or change it much. Each of the points in Jacquelyn's rebuttal minimized the effect of Kane's original argument, while not disproving them. Even still, her speech was persuasive as her specific purpose was to persuade the audience that Kane's argument was not as appealing as he had made it sound.

The second speech that responds to another person's argument is a *speech of refutation*. A speech of refutation is slightly different from a rebuttal speech in that it does seek to prove the opposition's argument is wrong, or false. When refuting an argument you might focus on the faulty reasoning or lack of support provided by the other speaker. The specific purpose, then, for a speech of refutation is to persuade the audience that the opposition's argument is wrong or false. Let's look at an example of a speech of refutation.

**speech of refutation**
a speech that seeks to prove the opposition's argument is wrong, or false

Caitlin presented an argument to her class that global warming needs to be addressed. She pointed out that temperatures are rising due to increased carbon emissions, resulting in the melting of the polar ice caps. She then pressed for increased fuel efficiency standards and called on people to take public transportation whenever possible. Corey then responded with a speech of refutation where he cited scientific studies that disprove the idea of global warming. He argued that the temperature changes referred to by Caitlin are actually cyclical patterns in the Earth's temperature and are not due to carbon emissions and global warming. Thus, he said people should not feel undue pressure to carpool, ride the bus, or change the way cars are built. In his speech, Corey refuted Caitlin's argument by claiming it was false, or erroneous.

Unlike the case of Jacquelyn and her rebuttal speech, Corey did not accept certain elements of his opponent's argument, but rather pointed out faulty data by presenting contradictory evidence. The primary difference between a rebuttal and a refutation speech is that a rebuttal takes issue with the conclusions, whereas refutation speeches dispute the entire argument and evidence presented by the opposition. For a summary of the characteristics of rebuttal and refutation speeches, see Table 12.1. Persuasion is a complex process, whether you are refuting, rebutting, or proposing a position. In the next section we will examine how that process works.

**Table 12.1**

| Rebuttals and Refutations | |
|---|---|
| **Rebuttal Speech Characteristics** | **Speech of Refutation Characteristics** |
| Introduces evidence that lessens the impact of the evidence presented by the other person | Seeks to prove the opponent's argument is wrong or false |
| Uses evidence not cited by the other person | Focuses on the opponent's reasoning |
| Shows that the evidence you are rebutting is incomplete | Points to a lack of supporting material |

# THE PERSUASIVE PROCESS

Persuasion does not take place simply because there is a topic on which two or more sides disagree. In fact, the persuasive process is much more involved. Additionally, persuasion almost always requires time to succeed, and its effectiveness often must be measured in degrees. In this section of the chapter we will discuss the four stages of the persuasive process, the development and importance of credibility in that process, and how to avoid unethical behavior in a persuasive speech.

## Stages of Persuasion

Persuasion is a highly psychological process. When you attempt to persuade someone you are asking for someone to make a decision based on a logical argument regarding an issue in dispute. Persuasion is different from other less ethical ways of gaining agreement from an audience. In this part of the chapter we will discuss the four elements of the persuasive process and then demonstrate why persuasion, when employed correctly, is the most appropriate and ethical means for gaining agreement from an audience.

**issue awareness**
the first step in the persuasive process whereby the speaker alerts the audience about the issue requiring its attention

The persuasion process has four stages, and each is equally important. The first step in the persuasive process is called *issue awareness*, and we have already begun to discuss it. Issue awareness occurs when you, as the speaker, alert the audience about the existence of an issue requiring their attention. This stage occurs immediately in the introduction of your speech because it is what you use to entice the audience to listen. The issue should be couched in a manner that conveys its importance to the lives of those in the audience so that they feel a personal connection with the topic, thus making them more likely to listen. For example, if you are talking to your college classmates about the importance of Social Security reform they may not see a reason to listen as they will not collect Social Security for many years. But, if you begin by alerting them to the fact Social Security may very well be bankrupt by the time they are eligible to receive it, you make the issue that much more salient in their eyes, thus increasing the likelihood they will listen to you.

**comprehension**
the second step in the persuasive process in which the speaker provides context for the issue in dispute so the audience understands what the speaker is talking about

Once you gather the audience's attention by making them aware of the important issue on which you will speak you move to the second stage in the persuasive process. The second stage is *comprehension*, where you provide a context for the issue in dispute so the audience understands what you are talking about, thus allowing them to appreciate your position on the topic. Continuing with the Social Security example, this part of the process might involve a discussion of how Social Security came to be, what it involves, and how the government calculates the benefits for retirees. The comprehension stage then continues by laying out your position on the issue and why you feel the audience should share your view. This part of the persuasive process allows you to lay out the foundation of your argument for the audience, before moving to the third stage in the persuasive process.

The third step, and the fourth which follows it, focuses less on the speaker and more on the audience. After establishing a context and making your case to the audience it is up to them whether or not they accept your position. *Acceptance* of your message is the third stage in the persuasive process. They may, after thinking about the facts, decide not to agree with you; on the other hand, they may very well leave your speech convinced you are right. Knowing whether or not the audience truly agrees with you after hearing you speak is difficult to know, but understanding your goals as a speaker will enable you to have some idea as to whether or not your appeal was successful. A little later we will return to this discussion of measuring the effectiveness of your appeal.

**acceptance**
the third step in the persuasive process where the audience decides whether or not to agree with the position for which the speaker advocated

If members of the audience ultimately accept your position on the issue in dispute then the persuasive process moves to its fourth and final stage. *Integration*, the fourth stage of persuasion, may occur long after the lights have dimmed and the audience has moved on to other activities. Integration is when, after accepting your position, the audience integrates that position into their daily lives. It becomes a part of their identity and their own personal philosophy. This is easiest to see when audiences leave a speech where a speaker has called for immediate action, because when audience members act in the way suggested by the speaker, then it is obvious that they have integrated the speaker's point of view into their own lives.

**integration**
the fourth stage in the persuasive process in which the audience makes the speaker's position a part of its own personal philosophy and worldview

So, let us summarize the persuasive process. When attempting to persuade an audience you need to make them aware of what you are speaking about. Then, you must ensure that they understand the issue. This is especially important when speaking about a complex topic. Third, the audience needs to decide whether or not they will accept your argument. Finally, if they do accept your ideas they need to integrate them into how they now see things. This process can take place very rapidly, or it may take hours, days, or even weeks or years to accomplish. For a summary of the four stages of persuasion, see Figure 12.1. In the next section of the chapter we will discuss how to determine your expectations for persuasive appeals as a speaker, and how to determine their success after you make them.

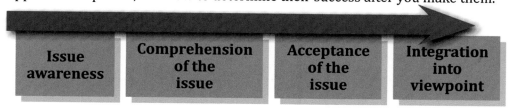

**Figure 12.1**
**Stages of the Persuasive Process**

| Issue awareness | Comprehension of the issue | Acceptance of the issue | Integration into viewpoint |

## Credibility and Persuasion

Whether or not we accept a person's argument often depends upon how credible he or she seems to us. Credibility represents a large part of what Aristotle called ethos, and it is an extremely important element of the persuasive process. As we mentioned in the previous chapter, speakers enter a speech with a certain level of credibility often as a result of their own background, perceived expertise on the topic on which they are speaking, appearance, and reputation. In this section we will revisit the concept of initial credibility which we covered in some depth in the last chapter and then explore how credibility can be increased or decreased during a speech, resulting in what the audience perceives as the speaker's credibility after the speech. We also will discuss several ways that your credibility can be damaged. To effectively persuade an audience you must first establish your credibility in the same way you might for an informative speech, but you also must build upon that credibility during the speech.

## Initial Credibility Revisited

We all bring a certain degree of credibility into any speaking situation, and this is our initial credibility. In persuasive speeches establishing credibility is just as important, if not more so, than for informative speeches because you are asking an audience not only to trust what you have to say, but to follow your advice and direction. You are asking them to believe in you and take a leap of faith. To this end we need to again talk about how to make sure you maximize your initial credibility in a persuasive situation.

**prior ethos**
credibility before the speech

Every time you speak you bring your reputation with you, and this is a major component of your *prior ethos*, or credibility before the speech. What you have done in the past, whether related to the topic of your speech or not, often creates an impression in the minds of the audience as to how credible and trustworthy you are as a source of information. Your experiences and prior knowledge can influence how receptive an audience will be to your persuasive appeal.

Prior ethos can also be influenced by your appearance. Think back to our discussion of speech delivery and consider how the way you dress, act, and look before the presentation may influence an audience. If you are speaking about a serious topic and want to identify with your audience, it is important to look the part. Let's look at the case of Sasha.

Sasha, a sales representative for Time Warner, was scheduled to deliver a pitch to Dannon Yogurt. She wanted Dannon to purchase advertising time on one of the network's television stations. She had heard that the company was predisposed to already make the purchase, so she thought it was a slam dunk and decided to go into the presentation wearing jeans and a Time Warner T-shirt. When she arrived everyone in the room was in business attire and she looked out of place. The host for the presentation, and everyone else in the room for that matter, did not feel that she took them or her job seriously and thus began the meeting with a negative perception of Sasha. This is simply an illustration of how prior ethos is affected by appearance. Now, let us turn to how we can manage ethos during a speech.

## Building Credibility During Your Speech

Credibility can be difficult for any public speaking student because your topics are often not something you have much experience with, and your audience has no knowledge of any previous speaking you may have done. This does not mean you cannot establish credibility in your introduction and increase it throughout your speech. There are several options for you, as a novice speaker, to establish and enhance your credibility in each speech. We call the credibility level you create during a speech *derived credibility* because it comes from what you say and how you present yourself in your presentation.

**derived credibility**
your level of credibility during a speech that comes from what you say and how you say it

Our suggestions for enhancing your credibility during your speech are not new. In fact they are simply contemporized versions of advice offered by Aristotle in Classical Greece. Aristotle actually laid out three ways to derive ethos, and contemporary scholars have given us a fourth way. The first was good character, the second sagacity, and the third good will, while social scientists have added dynamism to the list. Let us look at each of these and explain how they may operate within your speeches.

Aristotle defined character as a state of being virtuous, not as a feeling, a capacity, or even a tendency. According to Aristotle, having good character is not fleeting, or more simply, you cannot be a person of good character one moment and a person of bad character the next. A person of virtuous character is in a state of being where he has learned to have an appropriate emotional response to situations and avoid excessive displays that are inappropriate. For a practical example, think of the leaders to whom we gravitate. They are the ones who have a balanced response to situations and stay "calm under fire." For Aristotle this ability defines good character. In a speech this may manifest itself in a speaker who refrains from attacking another person, yelling, screaming, or attempting to inappropriately play upon negative emotions within the audience. It is, in short, behaving ethically.

Aristotle's second way of deriving ethos is through sagacity, or the demonstration of keen discernment and sound judgment. Discernment and judgment are demonstrated through the proper citation of relevant and important information and evidence. By verbally attributing sources you not only follow the ethical obligations of any speaker, but you also demonstrate you have read and researched the topic upon which you are speaking. Referencing experts and providing sufficient evidence for your argument illustrates your competence as a speaker and care for the audience. You also can show your audience keen judgment and discernment in how you approach the topic in question and examine alternative solutions. This will become clearer in the next few chapters as we discuss the different strategies for organizing persuasive speeches.

The third way Aristotle proposes that you can derive credibility during a speech is through demonstrating your goodwill toward the audience and the topic. Aristotle defined goodwill as an unselfish disposition that seeks the good for others regardless of what is good for us. This is a very difficult concept to grasp, but let's think about it. It is putting the good of the community, friends, and others above your own desires. This is, for all intents and purposes, a reminder for us as speakers that we should not have hidden agendas or try to deceive the audience for personal gain. When persuading an audience we derive more ethos by making our motives clear and honestly assessing the benefit of our appeal for the audience. Goodwill begins and ends with honesty toward the audience about evidence and motives.

Aristotle, however, was not the only one to provide us with ways to enhance our ethos during a speech. Social scientists today have added the concept of dynamism as a way to increase our credibility during a speech. *Dynamism* refers to a strong, confident delivery that creates the impression with the audience that the speaker has practiced and thus cares about what she is talking about. Confident delivery is another way you can increase your credibility in class. No doubt you will have more than one speech in your class, and even if that is not the case, you will give more than one presentation throughout your career. The more you speak, the more confident you will become, and that confidence will translate into a better performance, thus increasing your credibility. Speaking confidently comes from practice and experience, and audiences tend to see speakers who appear confident as being more credible.

## Terminal Credibility

By the end of the speech you will have a new level of credibility as a speaker on your topic. The credibility with which you leave the speech is called *terminal credibility* because you do not have any more opportunities in that presentation to affect the way the audience sees you. Where you end up, however, is largely influenced by how you established and built your credibility throughout your speech.

Your terminal credibility will affect your reputation and public perception of your character going forward, and thus it will contribute to your initial credibility the next time you speak. To this end, every time you speak you have an opportunity to enhance your credibility in that moment and for the next time you deliver a presentation. This is how we develop a reputation, and if we speak each time with a virtuous character, demonstrate sagacity, and exhibit goodwill, then we will develop a strong positive reputation. Unfortunately, there are ways we can take steps in the other direction, and so we also must examine the ways you might damage your credibility and your reputation.

## Ways to Lose Credibility

There are three unethical behaviors that can potentially irreparably damage your image and credibility with any audience. The first of these is lying to the audience. There are several different ways in which you can lie to an audience. The first occurs when you willfully present false evidence to an audience. Creating new facts out of thin air just to advance your argument is not persuasion, it is *lying by commission. Lying by omission,* on the other hand, occurs when you choose not to acknowledge facts about your case that might damage it. Instead of leaving facts out, you should acknowledge them in the rebuttal portion of your speech, as it lets the audience know you did your research and have a response to potential problems with your position. Such a tactic actually increases your credibility with the audience.

A second behavior that can cause significant harm to your credibility occurs when you take advantage of an audience. This involves *manipulation*, or the deliberate misrepresentation of facts and evidence to an audience so that they will see what you want them to see, rather than presenting them with a reasoned argument and trusting their ability to come to a careful decision. One such example of use of manipulation by a speaker involved former President Bill Clinton when he made statements regarding his relationship with an intern, Monica Lewinsky. President Clinton misrepresented the nature of his association with Lewinsky by stating that he did not have "sexual relations" with her, when, in point of fact, he had sexual contact with her. The term Clinton used misled the audience by inferring he had no sexual relationship with Lewinsky. In this example he did not lie to the American people in that he did not have intercourse with Lewinsky, but he did mislead them as to the nature of their association.

Former President
Bill Clinton

One final way in which you can damage your credibility through unethical behavior is by using force instead of reason to obtain agreement from your audience. *Coercion*, or the use of force or threats to make someone do something against their will, can manifest itself in both physical and psychological ways. The least likely is physical, in that no one expects you to put a proverbial gun to the head of your audience to make them agree with you. It is possible, though, that you could coerce your audience by threatening them with negative consequences if they do not agree with you. For instance, you might be coerced into taking an extra shift at work by a boss who threatens to fire you if you do not comply. Psychological coercion involves making audiences unduly afraid of what will happen if they do not agree with you. Using such tactics will damage your credibility by making you appear as a fearmonger, rather than someone who can construct a rational plan to which people might agree.

**coercion**

the use of force or threats to make someone do something against his or her will

Your credibility, or ethos, is an essential part of every speech you deliver. If the audience believes you will tell the truth, then they are more likely to follow your argument and give you a fair hearing. The trust your audience has in you as a speaker is something you should protect by trying not to lie, manipulate, or coerce audiences into agreeing with your position. If your position is right, and you present a well-thought-out argument, then they should come to the same conclusions you do about the issue in dispute. If they do not, then at least you allowed them to make the choice on their own while making the best case you could. True rhetorical persuasion is a free-will choice for the audience.

## DEVELOPING EMOTION IN PERSUASIVE APPEALS

Ethos and logos, otherwise called credibility and logic, you will remember as only two of the three dimensions of persuasion and speech identified by Aristotle. The third, pathos, also must be addressed because it complements both ethos and logos in the persuasive process. The thing to remember here is that employing pathos alone in a persuasive appeal distracts the audience from the issue at hand in an effort to have them make a decision based purely on emotion, rather than evidence or information. Such a speech design is unethical. So, let's take a moment and discuss the proper place for pathos in persuasive speech.

Pathos is concerned with the audience's emotions, sympathies, and imaginations; used effectively, it connects those things with the topic of the speech in a way that increases the likelihood of achieving your speech's purpose. Pathos can help make abstract concepts and statistical data more palpable and real for an

## SPEAKING of CIVIC ENGAGEMENT

### Keynote Address at the Restoring Honor to America Rally
### by Glenn Beck

Delivered August 28, 2010, at the Lincoln Memorial, Washington, D.C.

For the last several years there have been few figures in America who have been more controversial than Glenn Beck. He is unpopular with the political left, and with some on the right. He is known for some outrageous statements, for his openness about being a recovering addict, and for extolling his religious faith.

Beck chose to hold the "Restoring Honor to America Rally" and deliver his speech on the anniversary of Dr. Martin Luther King, Jr.'s "I Have A Dream," speech drawing criticism from Reverend Al Sharpton and others. In the speech Beck noted the setting and also pointed out great Americans, from Abraham Lincoln to Martin Luther King, Jr., and what he believed they stood for.

At several points in the speech he used these American icons, and other lesser known individuals, to enhance the emotional dimensions of his appeal for American renewal. In fact, his final words were a moving tribute to an American who suffered due to serving his country:

"To close tonight with a prayer, I want to introduce you to Dave Roever. He's a Vietnam veteran. He was on a mission and he pulled a phosphorous grenade. It went off in his hand. A phosphorous grenade is 5,000 degrees, half the temperature of the sun. His face was horribly scarred. He told me that he actually put his head in his pillow and he screamed, because he didn't want anybody to hear him in the hospital scream and he removed his face from the pillow and then he didn't care who heard him scream because his face was left in the pillow. He's a man that tried to kill himself because he thought, 'My wife will not want me. No one will.' What is left of this scarred man? I am happy to say he's turned his life over to God and his wife stood by his side and as he said, 'kissed him on the one good part of his face and looked him in his one good eye and together they have made their way.'"[6]

Notice how he vividly depicts Dave Roever and then connects that depiction with what Beck believes all Americans need to do. Such is the power of pathos.

audience. Ultimately, however, proper use of pathos depends upon knowledge of the audience to whom you are speaking.

Pathos is primarily accomplished in four different steps. The first step is to determine the emotion that you want to convey and engender in your audience. Do you want to make them angry? Excited? Do you want them to feel pity? Compassion? The emotion you want to create is the goal of the particular pathos appeal, and thus what you choose to use to achieve that goal must have the emotion at its core.

Once you determine the emotion you wish to convey and encourage in the audience, step two involves connecting it to an object. That object can be a person, place, or thing but it must be tangible and recognizable to the audience. It is the thing for which you want the audience to feel the emotion and to which you want them to connect. As a general rule, people connect better to singular specific objects and not large masses of things. Thus, people feel pity when ads for the American Society for the Prevention of Cruelty to Animals (ASPCA) depict one dog that has been injured or abandoned, but they may not feel so strongly about pictures of multiple dogs. The same principle applies for speeches: connect the emotion to a concrete singular object to which the audience can relate.

Step three is the use of language and/or images that evoke the specific emotion you wish to encourage the audience to feel. Pictures and strategic language choices help to accomplish this, and this stage is where you make the decisions about when and how to describe the object and the emotion. Different words can convey different emotions to the audience and can elicit different responses from them as well. For instance, when describing a policy you could choose to label it "moronic" or "ill-advised." What emotions does each trigger? How does that emotional reaction enhance or damage the perception the audience may have of you as the speaker? These are important considerations for you when crafting your speeches. You need to make sure your emotional language choices are not the primary driver for persuasion, but rather that they complement the evidence you use and reinforce your goodwill and virtuous character to the audience.

In today's mediated environment we also can use visual imagery to capitalize on pathos in our persuasive appeals. A moment ago we talked about ASPCA advertisements and how they use pictures of dogs to help give an audience an object with which they can connect. Visual images in this respect can be powerful vehicles for pathos appeals because they provide the audience with a specific object on which to focus their attention; meanwhile, the narrator provides the verbal message containing the emotional dimension sought by the use of the image.

The final step of incorporating pathos into your persuasive messages involves the story, or narrative, you provide about the object. The story uses the vivid language in stage three while also connecting the emotion to the overall logic of the persuasive appeal. In other words, the story needs to be connected in some way not just to the emotion, but to the overall speech topic. If you are seeking to help the ASPCA, for example, you might tell a vivid story about a golden retriever who was abandoned and found half-starved walking the street in front of your home sniffing around garbage bags for food. This quick anecdote uses vivid language in telling a story related to the purpose of your speech in a way that is designed to create a feeling of pity for the dog. That dog then becomes a synecdoche for all dogs helped by the ASPCA, thus helping to provide the audience with both a logical and an emotional reason for acting upon your message.

Pathos does not necessarily restrict itself to animals or simple subjects. In fact, we often use other people as a source for creating pathos in a speech. Look at a speech delivered by radio personality Glenn Beck at the "Restoring Honor to America Rally" in 2010 (see the nearby box). Beck believed Americans had lost their way and sought to reconnect them with feelings of patriotism. Throughout his keynote speech Beck used tangible objects, often monuments and people, to elicit feelings of patriotism and pride in his audience and emotionally connect them with his message. Beck's choice of venue, the Lincoln Memorial on the anniversary of Martin Luther King, Jr.'s "I Have A Dream" speech at that very same location, drew much criticism, but nevertheless his speech serves as an example of the use of pathos in persuasive appeals.

Pathos is a powerful persuasive tool when used appropriately. It can enhance your credibility as a speaker as well as augment the power of the logic behind your appeal. It involves four important steps, beginning with determining what type of emotion you want your audience to feel. Next, connect that emotion to a singular object and use vivid language to tell a story about that object in a way that connects it with the larger purpose of your speech.

## Summary

Persuasion takes place when there is an issue in dispute or, as Quintilian called it, an issue of stasis. Over the years stasis theory has developed into what we now call persuasive questions. These issues in dispute are part of larger categories of persuasive speeches, identified by Aristotle as deliberative or forensic in nature. Regardless of the issue in dispute, or the form of persuasive speech you undertake, persuasion always follows the same process: issue awareness, comprehension, acceptance, and integration. In order to successfully implement the persuasive process your audience must believe in your credibility as a speaker.

## KEY TERMS

## REVIEW QUESTIONS

1. What are the four types of stasis proposed by Quintilian?
2. What are the three forms of questions that a persuasive speech may address?
3. What are the two types of persuasive speeches proposed by Aristotle?
4. What are the three types of credibility a speaker has/can have?
5. What are the three ways you can irreparably harm your own credibility?
6. What has dynamism added to our understanding of credibility?

## THINK ABOUT IT

1. Are there any types of issues in dispute not covered by the four forms of stasis proposed by Quintilian?
2. Are there any other ways you can damage your credibility?  Enhance it?
3. If it is so unethical, why do people often manipulate data or lie to audiences to achieve their goals?
4. Could dynamism not be a factor in credibility?

## ACTIVITIES FOR ACTION

1. Look at the stages of the persuasive process in this chapter. Think about how you have had your mind changed in the past, and identify how that process unfolded for you. Then, if there are differences, devise an alternative method for explaining how the persuasive process worked in your example. Are there different stages?  Fewer?  More?
2. Imagine a politician who has been caught cheating on his spouse, has been arrested for drunk driving, and has a tax lien on his property. If you were his political consultant, what would you suggest he do to increase his credibility? What might he do to re-establish his credibility?

# ENDNOTES

1. The timeline of events can be found at: http://www.law.umkc.edu/faculty/projects/ftrials/Simpson/Simpsonchron.html (accessed October 16, 2008).

2. CNN, "OJ Simpson Trial: Marcia Clark, Johnny Cochrane Deliver Closings," http://www.cnn.com/2007/US/law/12/11/court.archive.simpson11/index.html (accessed October 16, 2008).

3. Patricia Bizzell and Bruce Herzberg, *The Rhetorical Tradition: Readings From Classical Times to the Present* (2nd Ed.) (Boston, MA: Bedford St. Martin's, 2001), 38-39.

4. Thomas Morgan, "Competency of Judge, 91, in Gotti Case Questioned," *The New York Times* (April 20, 1989). Available: http://query.nytimes.com/gst/fullpage.html?res=950DEFDC173CF933A15757C0A96F948260 (accessed October 17, 2008).

5. Bizzell and Herzberg, 38-39.

6. Glenn Beck, http://www.americanrhetoric.com/speeches/glennbeckrestoringhonorkeynote.htm (accessed June 9, 2011).

# Reasoning and Persuasion

# Practically SPEAKING

Harvard University was founded in Boston, Massachusetts, in 1636 and is the oldest institution of higher education in North America. Established by the Great and General Court of the Massachusetts Bay Colony, the school was named after John Harvard, who left his library and half of his estate to the college upon his death in 1638. At the time it had nine students and one teacher—a far cry from the 18,000+ students and approximately 2,000 faculty there today![1]

Seven presidents, including John Adams and John Kennedy, and 40 Nobel Laureates have graduated from Harvard. Our current president, Barack Obama, graduated from Harvard Law School. It is the most prestigious university in the United States, and its law school is one of its more well-known programs. Former Massachusetts Governor William Weld and Supreme Court Justice Stephen G. Breyer are just two notable contemporary graduates of the Harvard Law School who have in recent years made a name for themselves.[2] The Harvard Law School is also famous for things other than graduates.

For the last 50 years the Harvard Law School Forum has invited domestic and international celebrities to speak to the campus on a host of different issues. Included among the speakers who have come to the Forum in the past are Fidel Castro, Gerald Ford, and even sex therapist Dr. Ruth. No speaker in recent years, however, has caused more of a stir than former head of the National Rifle Association (NRA) and Oscar-winning actor, the late Charlton Heston.[3]

On February 16, 1999, Heston addressed a crowd of about 200 people, consisting of students, faculty, conservatives, and liberals. The speech, entitled "Winning the Cultural War," inspired much debate around the campus for about a month after he delivered it, and if it wasn't for one event it probably would have faded into obscurity. On March 15, 1999, almost a month to the day after he gave the speech, popular conservative talk show host Rush Limbaugh read Heston's speech word for word on the air. After his rendition, thousands of people sought copies of the speech transcript, flooding both the Harvard Law School Forum and Limbaugh's radio station with requests.[4] The now immensely popular speech had only one problem: its argument.

Within the speech itself Heston attempted to make a logical argument; however, he was not very successful, despite the fact people loved the speech. He employed many of the logical fallacies later explained in this chapter to make his case. The unfortunate outcome of this was the wide support for his point of view coming from an audience that did not critically examine the message itself. In this chapter we will discuss both the classical models for reasoning and the more recent Toulmin model for constructing an argument, neither of which Heston used. Finally, we will use examples from his "Winning the Cultural War" speech as well as other texts to illustrate the different types of logical fallacies employed by speakers. By the end of this chapter the differences between correct and proper logic and improper appeals will be stark and easy to identify.

# CLASSICAL MODEL OF REASONING

We construct ethical and effective arguments by providing clear evidence to support our claims. When we demonstrate the connection between the evidence and our claims we demonstrate reasoning skills. Aristotle proposed two different basic forms of reasoning, deductive and inductive, and in this section we will detail the elements of both. We also will explore several different forms of reasoning that can help you make an argument stronger.

## Syllogisms and Enthymemes

Building an argument is much like building a house. A house is not simply placed into existence; it is built, brick by brick, around a structure. The bricks in an argument are the evidence you present, but they are useless without placing them in and around a structure that makes sense. That basic structure for an argument is called a *syllogism*. A syllogism is a form of *deductive reasoning*, or an argument that reasons from known premises to an inevitable conclusion. That conclusion is inevitable because it is contained within the premises of the argument.

Syllogisms always contain three different parts. The first is called the *major premise*, which is a general statement about the subject of your argument. This statement is taken to be completely accurate, and not a statement about something that is probable or possible. The second part of a syllogism is called the *minor premise*, which is a statement about a specific case related to the general characteristics of the major premise. The final part of a syllogism is the conclusion drawn from the components of both the major and minor premises. Essentially, the conclusion is the claim made by the speaker, the minor premise is the evidence, and the major premise represents the reasoning that links them both.

The conclusion in a syllogism is true when the major and minor premises are true. The classic example of a syllogism told in classrooms for years looks like this:

| | |
|---|---|
| *Major premise:* | All men are mortal. |
| *Minor premise:* | Socrates is a man. |
| *Conclusion:* | Therefore, Socrates is mortal. |

**syllogism**
basic structure of a deductive argument that comes to an absolute conclusion

**deductive reasoning**
an argument that reasons from known premises to an inevitable conclusion

**major premise**
the first part of a syllogism, consisting of a general statement about the subject of your argument

**minor premise**
a statement about a specific case related to the general characteristics of the major premise

As you can see, the major premise is true, as all men are mortal. If, however, we find a man who is immortal then the major premise becomes false and the argument falls apart. The fact about the specific case in the minor premise is also true, as Socrates is a man. If, though, Socrates is a dog or a plant, then the minor premise becomes untenable. The conclusion also flows from the facts in both the major and minor premises, and since those facts are true then the conclusion is also true. It is important to remember, though, that despite the simplicity of this example there are a variety of different syllogisms.

We define syllogisms by their component parts. For example, in the first type of syllogism we will discuss, *categorical syllogism*, the argument is based on membership in a category. Within a categorical syllogism the major premise establishes the group in which the evidence should fit. Like all other syllogisms, a categorical syllogism's major premise states universal generalities. Here is an example:

**categorical syllogism**
a syllogism in which the argument is based on membership in a group

| | |
|---|---|
| *Major premise:* | All pitchers are baseball players. |
| *Minor premise:* | Alvin is a pitcher. |
| *Conclusion:* | Therefore, Alvin is a baseball player. |

Within categorical syllogisms such as the one involving Alvin, there are certain requirements. First, a categorical syllogism contains only three items that it uses to make the case. Secondly, each of the three terms must be used in the syllogism twice. Third, each term can be used only once in each premise. Next, items may appear in a conclusion only if they have originally appeared in either the major or minor premise. Finally, in terms of tone, one premise must be stated in a positive way, but if one premise is negative, then the conclusion also must be negative. Let's look at one more example:

| | |
|---|---|
| *Major premise:* | All students cannot pass if they do not deliver all their speeches. |
| *Minor premise:* | Shaquana is a student. |
| *Conclusion:* | Therefore, Shaquana will not pass if she does not deliver all her speeches. |

Notice the negative conclusion due to the negative major premise. Notice also that all the items in the syllogism appear twice.

**disjunctive syllogism**
a syllogism in which the major premise includes two or more mutually exclusive alternatives

A second form of syllogism, the *disjunctive syllogism*, contains two or more mutually exclusive alternatives. This means that only one of the alternatives may be true, not both. In order for this line of reasoning in an argument to work, the minor premise must either accept only one alternative or exclude all alternatives but one. Let's look at this example:

| | |
|---|---|
| *Major premise:* | Either COM 101 is in Room 234 or it is in Room 345. |
| *Minor premise:* | COM 101 is not in Room 234. |
| *Conclusion:* | Therefore, COM 101 is in Room 345. |

Because the minor premise rejected one of the two alternatives, then the other logically became true. Unfortunately, most disjunctive syllogisms are not this simple and involve more than two alternatives.

In life we often present and are presented with situations in which it appears as though there are only two alternatives when that is not the case. So, in order for a disjunctive syllogism to be sound, the major premise must consist of all the possible alternatives. Here is an example of a disjunctive syllogism with multiple alternatives:

> *Major premise:*     I must take Math, English, or an elective course this semester.
>
> *Minor premise:*     I will take an elective course this semester.
> *Conclusion:*        Therefore, I will not take English or Math this semester.

In this example, one item is selected from among the three different options, making the choice obvious. The two main requirements for a valid disjunctive syllogism are that the alternatives must be mutually exclusive and all the alternatives must be presented.

The third and final type of syllogism we will discuss is called a ***conditional syllogism***. Here, the major premise contains a hypothetical condition and its outcome. These are more commonly referred to as "if-then" statements. The "if" portion of the major premise is called the ***antecedent***, while the "then" statement is labeled the ***consequent*** because it is a direct result of the occurrence of the "if." Just like every other syllogism, this form also depends on the universality of the major premise. In other words, the "if-then" must be true in all cases. Look at this example of a conditional syllogism:

> *Major premise:*     If we increase revenue then we will not need to downsize the workforce.
>
> *Minor premise:*     We increased revenue.
> *Conclusion:*        Therefore, we do not need to downsize the workforce.

**conditional syllogism**
• • • • • • • • • • •
a syllogism in which the major premise contains a hypothetical condition and its outcome

**antecedent**
• • • • • • • • • • •
the hypothetical condition in the major premise of a conditional syllogism

**consequent**
• • • • • • • • • • •
the outcome of the hypothetical condition in the major premise of a conditional syllogism

Conditional syllogisms require that the antecedent and consequent are both accepted and explain only what you know. That would not have been the case had there been the following slight change to the minor premise and conclusion:

> *Major premise:*     If we increase revenue then we will not need to downsize the workforce.
>
> *Minor premise:*     We did not downsize the workforce.
> *Conclusion:*        Therefore, we increased revenue.

This argument is invalid because there could be other explanations for the conclusion than the one offered. In other words, something else could have contributed to not downsizing the workforce given the structure of the syllogism. An easy way to understand this is to see the statement as "if-then" and not "then-if."

**enthymeme**
. . . . . . . . . . . . . . .
a syllogism missing
one or two of its parts

Syllogisms provide a logical way to lay out a claim and its support in a way that allows you to see if your argument is valid and makes logical sense. When we speak, we rarely include the major premise, minor premise, and conclusion in our verbal explanation to an audience. Rather we delete one or two of the three elements of the syllogism and allow the audience to reason them out on their own. When a syllogism misses one or two of its parts it is called an *enthymeme*.

## SPEAKING of CIVIC ENGAGEMENT

### Women's Rights Are Human Rights
### by Hillary Clinton

Delivered September 5, 1995, at the United Nations 4th World Conference on Women in Beijing, China

First Lady Hillary Clinton advocated for the rights of both children and women during her husband's time in office. In 1995 she traveled to the 4th United Nations Conference on Women in China, a communist country where birth rates are tightly controlled by the government and human rights violations are often in the news. It is also a nation that allows little political dissent.

As First Lady she had significant prior ethos and initial credibility, and she derived more by noting her involvement on the issue of women's rights:

"Over the past 25 years, I have worked persistently on issues relating to women, children, and families. Over the past two-and-a half years, I've had the opportunity to learn more about the challenges facing women in my own country and around the world."[5]

Mrs. Clinton made her case often through the use of enthymemes, or syllogisms missing one or more parts. Take the following passage as an example: "What we are learning around the world is that if women are healthy and educated, their families will flourish. If women are free from violence, their families will flourish. If women have a chance to work and earn as full and equal partners in society, their families will flourish. And when families flourish, communities and nations do as well."[6]

Mrs. Clinton uses this parallel structure to enthymematically argue for better treatment of women around the world. It is an enthymeme because it is a syllogism missing a part. If it were a syllogism it would look more like this: Communities and nations wish for their members to flourish. Women are members of communities and nations. Therefore, communities and nations wish for women to flourish. The enthymematic argument sounded a lot easier on the ears than the syllogism and also got the point across more creatively and effectively.

Enthymemes are truncated syllogisms. Look at each of the three forms of syllogisms discussed above and eliminate the minor premise. Do they still make sense? Of course, because the supporting evidence offered by the minor premise is common knowledge that does not bear repeating to an audience. In the example of Socrates we could just as soon have said "Socrates is mortal" and you would have been able to internalize the major and minor premises.

The fact of the matter is we speak using enthymemes more often than syllogisms. This is because we can assume the audience does not need to hear certain parts of the syllogism to understand the message. When Hillary Clinton, then First Lady, took to the podium in Beijing during the United Nations 4th World Conference on Women in the mid-1990s and argued to shed light on women's issues she did not need to lay out her logic step by step. She could assume the audience could fill in certain elements for themselves. In essence, the speech serves as a great example of how people speak enthymematically, not syllogistically.

Whereas syllogisms are a form of deductive reasoning, enthymemes are not always deductive. In fact, often they employ ***inductive reasoning***, or an argument that comes to a probable instead of an absolute conclusion. Most arguments you will encounter and use in a speech employ inductive enthymemes because often we argue over things that we do not know are absolutely true, so we argue they are probably true. For example, Leon wants to persuade his audience to exercise because they are out of shape. He then makes a case about the simplest form of exercise. He states that exercise is usually a good way to lose weight and get in shape. He then argues running would probably be a good way for his audience to exercise. Leon says probably, because someone in the audience may have a heart condition or some other issue that would preclude him or her from running. In this example Leon makes an inductive argument using an enthymeme because it is a probable conclusion and the argument is missing a piece of the case (a statement indicating running is a form of exercise).

**inductive reasoning**

an argument that comes to a probable, instead of an absolute, conclusion

You can also construct visual enthymemes. Visual enthymemes make a case without using words. Rather, they show images that make an argument. Advertisements frequently do this. Take a video that begins with people looking unhappy on the couch. Then a product, let's say a soft drink, is introduced and everyone becomes happy. The syllogism inherent in these images is:

| | |
|---|---|
| *Major premise:* | People are happy when they have something to drink. |
| *Minor premise:* | Fizzy-Bubbler is a drink. |
| *Conclusion:* | People with Fizzy-Bubbler are happy. |

There are no words used to describe this argument, only images, but the case is effective. You can use visual aids to construct visual enthymemes to augment the case you make in your speech.

Syllogisms and enthymemes are the foundation of any argument within a persuasive attempt. They are used to connect evidence to your claims, and when used effectively, they strengthen your case. In the next section we expand our discussion of reasoning to include several different ways you can connect different types of evidence to support specific claims you make.

## Types of Reasoning

Syllogisms and enthymemes are the forms we use to make arguments, but different types of evidence dictate the types of reasoning we use to make our case. Good persuasive speeches wield several different types of evidence when presenting a reasoned argument to an audience. As Aristotle noted, reasoning can be either deductive or inductive, depending on whether it seeks to demonstrate a certainty or a probability. In this section of the chapter we will cover three different types of reasoning, each of which uses different forms of evidence.

**reasoning by example**

the process of inferring general conclusions and making general claims from specific cases

The most common form of reasoning involves taking specific cases and making general conclusions based upon their characteristics. The process of inferring general conclusions and making general claims from specific cases is called *reasoning by example*. On rare occasions only one case or example allows you to make a generalization, but more often than not you will need to use multiple cases to strengthen your ability to make a general claim. Additionally, there are several important elements you must pay attention to when choosing the examples that support your claim.

**Table 13.1**

| Tips for Reasoning by Example |
| --- |
| • Ensure the example is relevant |
| • Try to provide more than one example |
| • Make sure the examples are typical of the issue |
| • Make sure the example does not contradict the point you are making |

**reasoning by analogy**

when you compare two similar cases in order to argue that what is true in one case is also true in the other

First, the examples must be relevant to the case you make. The more closely you can tie the examples to the claim, the stronger your claim will be. You also must provide a reasonable number of examples to support your case. Relying on just one may make it appear that there is not enough evidence to support your argument. The examples you use must also be typical and represent that larger population of which they serve as a sample. Finally, you must be sure that the examples you choose do not contradict your argument. Table 13.1 provides some tips for reasoning by example.

**literal analogy**

when the two cases being compared are classified the same way

**figurative analogy**

when the two cases being compared are from completely different classifications

A second form of reasoning you may use in your speech involves making a comparison. *Reasoning by analogy* is when you compare two similar cases in order to argue that what is true in one case is also true in the other. Analogies can be constructed in two ways. A *literal analogy* occurs when the two cases being compared are classified the same way. For instance, if you argue that a certain crime prevention program will work in Los Angeles because it will work in Houston, you are making a literal analogy between two real cities. The other form of analogy, *figurative analogy*, occurs when the items are from completely different classifications. These analogies employ metaphors, such as this example: The art of compromise is a lot like modern art. Compromise and modern art are not in the same classification. However, the analogy allows you to take characteristics of one and ascribe them to the other.

When reasoning by analogy you must be aware of several things. First, the items you are comparing must have significant points of similarity, and those points must be crucial to the comparison you are making. You may need to explain those connections, but as long as you can do so in a cogent manner then you should be fine. You also need to recognize that all analogies have points of difference, but so long as these points of difference are not critical or important to your comparison then the analogy should work. Also, you must remember that, as effective as figurative analogies are, they cannot be used for making a logical proof for your argument; instead, they can be used in explanations. To make a logical proof, you must instead rely on literal analogies. Analogical reasoning is an effective way to make a point because it allows you to use more concrete language and make your point using items with which your audience may be more familiar. See Table 13.2 for some tips for reasoning by analogy.

**Table 13.2**

| Tips for Reasoning by Analogy |
| --- |
| • Points must be similar |
| • Points need to be crucial to the case |
| • Connections may need to be explained |
| • All analogies have differences |
| • Figurative analogies cannot be used for proof |
| • Figurative analogies can be used for explanation |

The third and final form of reasoning is called *reasoning by cause*, and it refers to arguments that claim one event or factor produces an effect. Almost all causal reasoning is based on probabilities. Here is an example of one such case: Obtaining a college education will allow students to get better paying jobs when they graduate. The cause is a college education and the effect is a better paying job; however, we all know that a college degree is not a guarantee that you will get a better paying job—it merely increases the probability that such an effect will come to pass. Causal reasoning can be very persuasive with an audience, but it must be carefully constructed.

**reasoning by cause**
arguments that claim one event or factor produces an effect

Much like the other forms of reasoning we have discussed so far, causal reasoning also must be conducted with several things in mind. First, the cause you discuss must be relevant to the effect you describe. For example, let's say you claim that chewing a new piece of gum during every inning of a baseball game causes your team to win. These two events are completely unrelated and the gum chewing almost assuredly does not have any bearing on the result of a baseball game. A second aspect of the relationship you must be aware of is whether the cause you discuss is the only possible cause for the effect in your argument. Almost always, more than one cause contributes to an effect, and recognizing this in your speech is important. Also at issue is whether the cause is actually capable of producing the effect you discuss. For instance, some people believed that John McCain's selection of Governor Sarah Palin as his running mate in the 2008 presidential election caused him to lose. Although it may sound reasonable on the surface, vice-presidential picks often have little to no bearing on the results of an election. See Table 13.3 for some tips for reasoning by cause.

**Table 13.3**

| Tips for Reasoning by Cause |
| --- |
| • Make sure the cause is relevant to the effect<br>• Consider if there are other possible causes<br>• Determine if the cause is really capable of producing the effect |

**necessary cause**
a condition that must be present for the effect to occur

**sufficient cause**
a condition that automatically produces the effect in question

Finally, and most importantly, you must determine if the cause you present is necessary and sufficient. A **necessary cause** is a condition that must be present for the effect to occur. A temperature less than 32 degrees Fahrenheit must be present for freezing to occur. A **sufficient cause** is a condition that automatically produces the effect in question. For example, a broken spine is a sufficient condition for paralysis. When sufficient conditions are known, they can be brought together to ensure an event's occurrence. See Figure 13.1 for additional examples.

**Figure 13.1**
**Examples of Necessary Cause and Sufficient Cause**

**Necessary Cause Examples**

- People need water to live
- Oxygen must be present for fire to burn
- Metal will expand when the temperature becomes hot enough

**Sufficient Cause Examples**

- A gunshot wound to the head is sufficient to cause death
- Stealing at work is a sufficient cause to be fired
- Lack of fertilizer is a sufficient cause for a plant to die

Enthymemes often employ each of these three forms of reasoning to make a case for a speaker. Knowing how to carefully craft arguments using each of these reasoning processes will help make your speech that much more effective. Everything we have discussed so far, however, represents the classical model of reasoning prescribed by Aristotle. This is not the only way to craft an argument in a speech. In the next part of this chapter we will discuss another option for constructing effective arguments, the Toulmin model.

# THE TOULMIN MODEL

Not everyone argues according to formal logic, and in the 1950s British philosopher Stephen Toulmin developed an alternative model to account for this difference. This is not to say he sought to replace classical forms of argument; rather, he believed they could be updated to better reflect how we argue every day. Most importantly, he felt people do not, nor should they, make all elements of the argument explicit. His model offers more flexibility than the syllogism but retains some structure in terms of the components he proposes as essential to an argument.

## SPOTLIGHTING THEORISTS: STEPHEN TOULMIN

### Stephen Toulmin (1922–2009)

Born in London, England, this British philosopher is responsible for one of the most influential contributions to argument in the 20th century. Initially not a rhetorician by trade, Toulmin earned his undergraduate degree in mathematics and physics from King's College. After World War II, Toulmin returned to school and earned his doctorate in Philosophy from Cambridge, and it was there that he met a person who became one of the largest influences on his professional career: Ludwig Wittgenstein.

Wittgenstein studied the uses and meanings of language, and Toulmin followed suit in his own academic pursuits. His dissertation examined the role reasoning played in ethical arguments and discussions. Toulmin saw shortcomings in using the classical formal methods of logic and reasoning, and this observation colored much of his future works.

In 1958, while working at the University of Leeds, Toulmin published an essay entitled, "The Uses of Argument." It was very well received by rhetoricians, although philosophers typically did not praise the work. This essay developed a more contemporary mode of argument, one which provided rhetoricians and scholars of argument a new way to examine and propose different arguments.

Over the years Toulmin taught at various prestigious institutions across the United States, including Columbia, Dartmouth, Northwestern, Stanford, and the University of Chicago. He was a Fellow in the American Academy of the Arts and Sciences; an Honorable Doctor of Technology in the Royal Institute of Technology in Stockholm, Sweden; the Thomas Jefferson Lecturer in 1997 for the National Endowment of the Humanities; and in 2005 he served as the Gifford Lecturer at the University of Edinburgh.

In 2007 Stephen Toulmin was named the Henry R. Luce Professor of Multiethnic and Transnational Studies at the University of Southern California. Toulmin died of heart failure on December 4, 2009, in Los Angeles.

## Elements of the Model

The first element of the Toulmin model is the idea that you are seeking to convey. This is your *claim*, and it is the most fundamental part of the argument. Without the claim there is no argument and ultimately, no persuasion. In a speech there are two forms of claims. The first claim is the *central claim*, called the thesis in informative speeches, and it represents the main point of which you seek to convince the audience. A *minor claim* is one that connects evidence within the speech to a particular point. If those connections are successfully made then the minor claims will support the central claim and thus make persuasion more likely.

The evidence that supports minor claims within the argument also has a place in the Toulmin model. In the Toulmin model, evidence is called the grounds.

**claim**
the idea that you are seeking to convey

**central claim**
the main point of which you seek to convince the audience

**minor claim**
connects evidence within the speech to a particular point

**grounds**
·········
evidence in the Toulmin model

The *grounds* are similar to the minor premise in a syllogism, but there can be more than one component of the grounds. In fact, the more grounds you have the better because they allow you to make a stronger connection. You cannot allow the audience to come to the same conclusion you do based on the evidence, so therefore the model does not stop with a supported claim.

**warrant**
·········
explains why the grounds support the claim and makes that connection clear to the audience

After you state your claim and provide evidence for that claim you need to provide a *warrant* for the grounds you laid out. The warrant explains why the grounds support the claim and makes that connection clear to the audience. Sometimes you do not need to explicitly state warrants, as they often are implied by the evidence and claims, but it is important to know that connection as the speaker in case you are challenged on the strength of your case.

**backing**
·········
the justification for a warrant

Just as the claims require grounds to support them, your warrants also need support, or a justification for accepting them. These justifications are called *backing*, and they can include anything from history, theory, or generally accepted values that cement the connection provided by the warrant. Backing is important because it allows you an opportunity to personalize the claims you make and further identify with the audience.

**qualifier**
·········
a statement that establishes the boundaries in which the argument is true

Even most of the arguments made with the Toulmin model do not express certainty, but instead they argue about probability. In some ways, the Toulmin model is better suited for making probabilistic arguments. For instance, the fifth component of the Toulmin model involves statements that indicate the strength of your claims. These statements, also called *qualifiers*, establish the boundaries in which the argument is true. Qualifiers include words such as "possibly," "usually," and "likely." Qualifiers let the audience know that you acknowledge there is the possibility your argument could be wrong or disputed.

**potential rebuttal**
·········
a statement that outlines the conditions which would make your central claim untrue

The sixth component of the Toulmin model addresses the potential for opposition to your argument. According to the model, speeches should include a statement that outlines the conditions which would make your central claim untrue. This statement is also called a *potential rebuttal*, and is similar to the rebuttal component of the speech arrangement proposed by the Greeks and Romans long ago. The difference is that the Greeks and Romans sought to diffuse potential opposing positions within the speech, whereas Toulmin advocates outlining when your specific claims would not be true. They essentially get at the same goal through slightly different methods.

**verifier**
·········
provides the credibility for the grounds and backing provided in the speech

The final element of the Toulmin model is called the verifier. A *verifier* essentially provides the credibility for the grounds and backing used in the speech. For instance, when you offer a quotation from a source, you provide verifiers that could include the organization for which that person works, or the titles of books and articles they have written on the subject. Verifiers also can include details about how research cited in a speech was conducted. You can explicitly state verifiers, or leave some for the audience to infer, but they help strengthen your claims and support speaker credibility. The chart in Table 13.4 provides an example of the Toulmin model used for arguing in favor of a new parking deck on a college campus.

| The Toulmin Model of Argument | | | Table 13.4 |
|---|---|---|---|

| Element of the Model | Element Function | Example |
|---|---|---|
| Claim | The idea that you are seeking to convey | The university should build a new parking deck. |
| Grounds | Evidence in the model | There are not enough parking spaces for student needs due to growth. |
| Warrant | Explains why the grounds support the claim | Parking decks are the primary places where students park their vehicles. |
| Backing | The justification for the warrant | In the past when parking spaces were needed the university built decks. |
| Potential rebuttal | A statement which outlines the conditions which would make your central claim untrue | A new parking deck may not be necessary if the university comes up with a plan for shuttles or such plans as ride share |
| Verifier | Provides the credibility for the grounds and backing in your speech | The university hired a parking consultant and she recommended building a new parking deck |

The Toulmin model presents a flexible alternative to the classical models of argumentation. It contains seven elements, some of which you do not need to explicitly state. At its core, the model says you develop an argument by presenting strong evidence that warrants support of a specific claim. This model of argumentation is a more holistic approach to speech-making and persuasion than the classical model as it is easier to apply to the structure of an entire speech. However, it is important to understand that both the classical model and the Toulmin model can be used to create an effective and successful persuasive appeal. As the Greeks, Romans, and Toulmin noted, creating a reasoned argument is not easy. In fact, the "easy road" to argument often involves using improper modes of argument known as logical, or reasoning, fallacies. In the next section we will discuss ways in which the reasoning process we have discussed so far can be damaged or perverted through the use of such fallacies.

# REASONING FALLACIES

Making a reasoned argument may seem like a simple task, and we all may believe that we use reason properly all the time, but in fact many times we use fallacious, or erroneous, reasoning. There are 10 common reasoning fallacies that distort the reasoning process by appearing to be logical when, in actuality, they are not. In this section we will discuss these 10 different reasoning fallacies and illustrate how they damage your ability to make an ethical and effective persuasive claim.

## Types of Fallacies

**begging-the-question fallacy**
when a speaker presumes certain things are facts when they have not yet been proven to be truthful

The first of the reasoning fallacies we will discuss is dangerous because it presumes truth without proof. The ***begging-the-question fallacy*** occurs when a speaker presumes certain things are facts when they have not yet been proven to be truthful. This fallacy is easy to identify as speakers using this fallacy make statements that begin with statements like, "Everyone knows that," and "It should go without saying." These phrases assume that the statement that follows is an absolute indisputable truth, even though that is almost always not the case. When seen as a truth, the information then becomes false grounds upon which the remainder of the argument rests.

At the beginning of the chapter we told the story of a speech given by Charlton Heston at Harvard in 1999. We mentioned that the speech included quite a few logical fallacies, and the begging-the-question fallacy was one of them. At one point Heston stated that:

> "Americans know something without a name is undermining the nation."[7]

This statement presumes that every American believes there is something wrong with the country, while he provides no evidence to back up this likely erroneous statement. Accepting the implicit argument in this statement, however, is the foundation of the speech and without analyzing it for what it is, the audience simply accepts it and moves closer to agreeing with Heston. Begging-the-question is faulty logic that depends upon audiences accepting broad assumptions with no support.

**non sequitur fallacy**
when you make an unwarranted move from one idea to the next

A second form of reasoning not based on logic is the non sequitur fallacy, from the Latin for "does not follow." A ***non sequitur fallacy*** occurs when you make an unwarranted move from one idea to the next. Often this happens because you do not provide evidence or you fail to clearly connect your evidence to your claim. In other words, the evidence does not relate to the claim you make. If the relationship between the evidence and your argument remains unclear and you still move to the next point, then you have committed a non sequitur.

Heston also included non sequiturs in his speech. Take this passage, for example:

> "As I have stood in the crosshairs of those who target Second Amendment freedoms, I've realized that firearms are not the only issue. No, it's much, much bigger than that. I've come

to understand that a cultural war is raging across our land, in which, with Orwellian fervor, certain acceptable thoughts and speech are mandated."[8]

The passage starts with a discussion of firearms and the Second Amendment but then suddenly moves to freedom of speech, which involves the First Amendment. He provides no evidence for the move from one issue to the next, except to say it involves a larger problem.

Non sequiturs can sometimes be confused with a third type of logical fallacy. The *slippery slope fallacy* is a logical fallacy that assumes once an action begins it will follow, undeterred, to an eventual and inevitable conclusion. Whereas the non sequitur makes leaps from claim to claim without evidence, the slippery slope assumes a predetermined path for events simply because the first stage has occurred. Again, Heston's speech at Harvard provides us with a perfect example:

> "What does all of this mean? It means that telling us what to think has evolved into telling us what to say, so telling us what to do can't be far behind."[9]

Here, Heston assumes that people are being told what to think and say. Additionally, since that is happening, people will inevitably be told what to do. There is no evidence for any of these stages; however, there is a presupposition they are true. More importantly, he assumes a direct causal connection between each stage that eliminates the possibility of other contributing factors or the occurrence of a change in the process he has outlined. In other words, he presents the appearance of an inevitable series of events, thus fitting the description of a slippery slope fallacy.

A fourth logical fallacy also involves erroneously assuming causal connection between two events. The *post hoc, ergo propter hoc fallacy* comes from the Latin for "after this, because of this" and assumes that because one event happened after another, then the preceding event caused the event that followed. Many superstitions have grown from this fallacy. For example, consider the superstitious belief that a black cat walking across your path brings bad luck. As if the color of a cat can cause bad things to happen to you! In persuasive arguments such as the one presented by Heston at Harvard, however, it is much more seductive.

In the final segment of his speech Heston attempted to demonstrate a point regarding the power of social activism. He described his attendance at a stockholder meeting for Time/Warner, which at the time produced an album by rapper Ice-T entitled "Cop-Killer." At the meeting he read the lyrics of two songs, one depicting acts of violence against police and another about sodomizing two 12-year-old nieces of Al and Tipper Gore. After these renditions, he claimed that:

> "Two months later Time/Warner terminated Ice-T's contract."[10]

This statement assumes that Heston's actions caused the termination of Ice-T's contract, yet that most likely is not the case. His speech may have contributed to

**slippery slope fallacy**

a logical fallacy that assumes once an action begins it will lead, undeterred, to an eventual and inevitable conclusion

example: slippery slope fallacy

**post hoc, ergo propter hoc fallacy**

from the Latin for "after this, because of this"; assumes that because one event happened after another, then the preceding event caused the event that followed

example: post hoc, ergo propter hoc fallacy

that outcome, but it is very doubtful, without specific statements corroborating the claim, that Heston's speech at the stockholder meeting caused the ensuing termination. He erroneously assumed that since Ice-T was fired after his speech, then his speech must have been the cause.

Another common logical fallacy involves options and ultimatums. Many times speakers present their audiences with only two alternatives, as if there were no other options. This type of argument is indicative of the ***either-or fallacy***, in which you present two options and declare that one of them must be correct while the other must be incorrect. Many candidates in elections operate with this faulty reasoning, declaring that, "you will vote Republican, or you will vote Democrat." Such reasoning presents a false image of the political landscape and the choices every voter has. There are multiple parties they can vote for, and they can also choose not to vote.

A sixth fallacy of reasoning attempts not to present an image of fewer alternatives than actually exist but rather to divert attention away from the issues and arguments at stake. The ***red herring fallacy*** exists when a speaker introduces an irrelevant issue or piece of evidence to divert attention from the subject of the speech. Red herrings begin with the topic under discussion, then introduce something else as though it is relevant to the original topic, and then ultimately disregard the initial topic altogether. Here is an example of a red herring at work:

example: red herring fallacy

> "I believe we need to increase enrollment requirements for undergraduate education. With fewer students, we can help solve the budget crisis we face today."

The budget crisis, although seemingly related to increased admission standards, is actually not related to the requirements for entry into college, and thus serves as a red herring. To avoid this fallacy it is important to make sure your evidence directly supports your claims.

The next reasoning fallacy we will discuss is also concerned with the evidence you provide for claims within your speech. Sometimes individuals feel that they should do something because everyone else does it, but as speakers we must avoid using this type of reasoning as a justification for agreeing with our argument. When we attempt to persuade people by arguing our position is reasonable because so many other people are doing it or agree with it, we are employing the bandwagon, or ***ad populum fallacy***. Many magazine advertisements, beer commercials, and speeches employ this fallacy by trying to convince you of the popularity of an item, event, or idea. Many speeches fall victim to this fallacy by relying on too much qualitative evidence and peer testimonials and not enough hard data to support claims and conclusions.

Appeals to the masses are not the only types of appeals that are illegitimate and invalid. Sometimes the reason speakers provide for their argument relies entirely on their ethos or the credibility or venerability of a tradition because it has significant authority. An appeal for persuasion based on higher authority or tradition is emblematic of the ***ad verecundium fallacy***. Again we return to the Charlton Heston speech at Harvard for an example of this fallacy at work.

One of the main claims advanced by Heston was a call for his audience to:

> "disobey social protocol that stifles and stigmatizes personal freedom."[11]  He explained that disobedience is justified and honorable because of the fact people like "Gandhi, Thoreau, and Jesus and every other great man who led those in the right against those with the might" did it before.  He went on to say that "disobedience is in our DNA."[12]

Such appeals justify disobedience based on the authority and tradition of the action, not for any other reason.  Other more common examples of the ad verecundium fallacy include when your parents tell you to do something "because I am your mother/father."  There is no logical connection between the action advocated and the reason provided for you to act.

When logic fails them, speakers sometimes revert to attacking their opponent in a debate instead of criticizing his/her ideas in a reasonable manner.  When speakers attack the person making the argument, and not the argument itself, it is representative of the *ad hominem fallacy*.  Ad hominem attacks often exist under the guise of attacks on a speaker's credibility, but in truth they are irrelevant to the argument and do not justify claims about the topic of debate.  For instance, when an attorney in a court case argues that a prostitute's testimony should not be admitted because prostitutes are not trustworthy or reliable sources it is an example of an ad hominem attack.  In this case, the credibility of the individual making the claim is not in question, nor is the content of the testimony; instead, the prosecutor makes him or her seem unreliable by attacking the profession through stereotypes.

**ad hominem fallacy**
when speakers attack the person making the argument and not the argument itself

We can look to references made by Heston for examples of the ad hominem fallacy as well.  In his speech he claimed that as a result of his support for the NRA the public attacked him.  At one point he said:

> "I ran for office, I was elected, and now I serve... I serve as a moving target for the media who have called me everything from 'ridiculous' and 'duped' to a 'brain-injured, senile, crazy old man.'"[13]

Now, Heston himself did not use an ad hominem, but he pointed out that others used that line of reasoning against him by attacking him and not his position on guns.

The tenth and final common reasoning fallacy we will discuss most often occurs in the rebuttal section of a speech.  The *straw man fallacy* occurs when a speaker ignores the actual position of an opponent and substitutes it with a distorted and exaggerated position.  The speaker then proceeds to attack the incorrect position because it is easier to defeat, although the process itself is illogical because it does not accurately respond to the original position.

**straw man fallacy**
when a speaker ignores the actual position of an opponent and substitutes it with a distorted and exaggerated position

Think about a political debate over funding the defense department, specifically the development of a missile defense shield in Europe.  Candidate X wants to cease funding the research behind this project, and Candidate Y responds by saying, "I cannot believe you do not support protecting the American people." First, the original position specifically called to question one program, not the entire goal of defense. Second, Candidate Y substituted that one program with a more exaggerated position that was easier to attack. Equating the development of a missile defense shield with not protecting the American people is illogical and erroneous based on Candidate X's original position; thus it is illustrative of the straw man fallacy.

The fact that there are 10 common logical fallacies should serve as a warning to you to be careful when you construct your speeches. Your claims must be well supported and the evidence you use must relate to those claims. These 10 fallacies are seductive in their simplicity, but destructive in their effects. They damage your credibility as a speaker and also potentially take advantage of your audience. Although it involves more effort and work, the payoff of taking the time to construct a proper speech that avoids these fallacies far outweighs the consequences of using them. See Table 13.5 for a summary and additional examples of these 10 fallacies.

**Table 13.5**

| Chart of Fallacies and Examples | | |
|---|---|---|
| Fallacy | The Error in Reasoning | Example |
| Begging-the-question | When a speaker presumes certain things are facts when they have not yet been proven to be truthful | "Oh, everyone knows that we are all Christians." |
| Non sequitur | When you make an unwarranted move from one idea to the next | "Well, look at the size of this administration building; it is obvious this university does not need more funding." |
| Slippery slope | Assumes that once an action begins it will follow, undeterred, to an eventual and inevitable conclusion | "If we let the government dictate where we can pray, soon the government will tell us we cannot pray." |
| Post hoc, ergo propter hoc | Assumes that because one event happened after another, then the preceding event caused the event that followed | "Every time Sheila goes to a game with us, our team loses. She is bad luck." |
| Either-or | Presents two options and declares that one of them must be correct while the other must be incorrect | "We either raise tuition or massively increase class size." |

| Red herring | When a speaker introduces an irrelevant issue or piece of evidence to divert attention from the subject of the speech | "Why do you question my private life issues, when we have social problems with which to deal?" |
|---|---|---|
| Ad populum | When we attempt to persuade people by arguing our position is reasonable because so many other people are doing it or agree with it | "Why shouldn't I cheat on this exam? Everyone else cheats." |
| Ad verecundium | An appeal to persuasion based on higher authority or tradition | "If the president of Harvard says it is a good idea, then we should follow suit." Or, "That is how we have always done it." |
| Ad hominem | When speakers attack the person making the argument and not the argument itself | "We can't believe anything he says; he is a convicted felon." |
| Straw man | When a speaker ignores the actual position of an opponent and substitutes it with a distorted and exaggerated position | "Oh, you think we should agree to a cut in our salaries. Why do you want to bleed us dry?" |

## SUMMARY

This chapter provided you with various ways to construct a well-reasoned, ethical, and effective argument. Whether you choose to employ the classical mode of argument or the more contemporary Toulmin model, you now have a blueprint for crafting a solid persuasive speech. It is also important to remember, any one speech can use different types of reasoning to accomplish its goals. The classical approach includes three different ways to reason involving different types of evidence. The Toulmin model may be, at times, more flexible but also emphasizes the importance of connecting evidence to your arguments. Whichever route you take, you must take care to avoid logical fallacies within your argument, no matter how tempting it may seem to use them.

## KEY TERMS

ad hominem fallacy   285

ad populum fallacy   284

ad verecundium fallacy   284

antecedent   273

backing   280

begging-the-question fallacy   282

categorical syllogism   272

central claim   279

claim   279

conditional syllogism   273

consequent   273

deductive reasoning   271

disjunctive syllogism   272

either-or fallacy   284

enthymeme   274

figurative analogy   276

grounds   280

inductive reasoning   275

literal analogy   276

major premise   271

minor claim   279

minor premise   271

necessary cause   278

non sequitur fallacy   282

post hoc, ergo propter hoc fallacy   283

potential rebuttal   280

qualifier   280

reasoning by analogy   276

reasoning by cause   277

reasoning by example   276

red herring fallacy   284

slippery slope fallacy   283

straw man fallacy   285

sufficient cause   278

syllogism   271

verifier   280

warrant   280

## REVIEW QUESTIONS

1.  What are the three types of syllogisms proposed by Aristotle?
2.  What is the difference between an enthymeme and a syllogism?
3.  What are the three different types of reasoning from evidence?
4.  What are the seven components of the Toulmin reasoning model?
5.  What are the 10 logical fallacies?

## THINK ABOUT IT

1.  Are there any circumstances under which ad hominem attacks are acceptable? When?
2.  What are some enthymemes you are exposed to every day through advertising?
3.  How ethical are the persuasive appeals in advertising and political campaigns today?  Do they employ logical fallacies?  If so, which ones?
4.  How can you be sure to avoid argument fallacies?
5.  As an audience member, do you have an obligation to voice concern about a speaker's fallacies?

## ACTIVITIES FOR ACTION

1. Find a copy of the text for the "Winning the Cultural War" speech by Charlton Heston mentioned in the opening of this chapter. Look through the text closely and see how many logical fallacies you can identify. Then, have a friend read the speech and see what his or her initial impression is. After they tell you, point out all the logical fallacies in the speech to them and see if they change their minds.

2. Identify a speech topic and use the Toulmin model to structure your speech. Then, examine it and devise a counter-argument to that speech using the Toulmin model as well.

3. One evening, while watching television, pay close attention to the commercials. As you watch, refer to the reasoning fallacies described in this chapter, and see how many you find. As you note them, think about whether the advertisements that used the fallacies were interesting or effective. Did the fallacies have anything to do with the success of the ad?

## ENDNOTES

1. Harvard University, "The Early History of Harvard University," http://www.hno.harvard.edu/guide/intro/index.html (accessed November 7, 2008).

2. Harvard Law School, "Alumni News and Publications," http://www.law.harvard.edu/alumni/news/index.html (accessed November 7, 2008).

3. "Winning the Cultural War" (February 16, 1999), http://isocracytx.net/hp-org/hestonlaw.html (accessed November 7, 2008).

4. Ibid.

5. http://www.americanrhetoric.com/speeches/hillaryclintonbeijingspeech.htm (last accessed: June 6, 2011).

6. Ibid.

7. "Winning the Cultural War," para. #6.

8. Ibid. para. #4.

9. Ibid. para. #11-12.

10. Ibid. para. #23-27.

11. Ibid. para. #19.

12. Ibid.

13. Ibid. para. #3.

# Crafting a Persuasive Speech

## CHAPTER OVERVIEW

14

- Discusses the Classical Greek and Roman approaches to structuring persuasive speeches
- Explains how to combine classical and contemporary approaches in developing introductions and conclusions for persuasive speeches
- Describes the various organizational patterns for persuasive speeches

# PracticallySPEAKING

In 1924 at a small YMCA in Santa Ana, California, a small group of people got together to help each other become better public speakers and have a little bit of fun in the process. Over the years, that small group expanded and became a group called Toastmasters International, a non-academic leader in helping people develop oral communication skills. This nonprofit organization now boasts nearly 235,000 members in over 11,700 clubs like the one in Santa Ana that started it all, in 92 different countries.[1]

Toastmasters begins by using a manual to help members develop certain speaking skills. It focuses on the use of humor, gestures, and eye contact. Once the initial manual is completed members then progress to more advanced manuals that narrow the skill's focus considerably. Thousands of corporations, companies, and civic organizations encourage their employees and affiliates to participate in Toastmasters because of the practical benefits gained from the group.

Toastmasters International also contributes much in the way of community service. It promotes youth programs designed around developing oral communication and leadership skills. It supports "Gavel Clubs" where it brings speech training inside prison walls. It works with community organizations and businesses to help them tell their story to the community in which they reside. Additionally, it offers short courses on crafting a speech.[2]

One of the central focuses of the Toastmasters International programs on crafting a speech is organization. In fact, it makes a point to tell people one of the ten most common errors in public speaking is lack of preparation and organization. When you do not organize your thoughts in a logical manner and then present them to an audience, it makes it at best difficult and at worst nearly impossible for your audience to follow what you are saying and ultimately get anything out of your presentation.

Persuasive speeches must be carefully arranged to ensure the speaker achieves his or her specific purpose. In fact, persuasive speeches were the foremost concern of the Greeks and Romans. In the first part of the chapter we will discuss the ways in which Classical Greeks and Romans taught students how to construct persuasive speeches. Then, we will discuss how you can incorporate aspects of the model for developing an informative speech (discussed in Chapter 11). Finally, we will offer several different organizational patterns you can use for the various types of persuasive speeches identified in the previous chapters.

# CLASSICAL SPEECH STRUCTURE

It should come as no surprise that the Greeks and Romans were among the first to break down a speech into its component parts. Today, we use different terminology, but the segments of the speech are essentially the same. It appears the most effective way to organize a persuasive speech has changed very little over the course of the last 2,500 years! As the saying goes, "if it ain't broke, don't fix it." In this part of the chapter we will discuss the three sections of a persuasive speech as identified by the Greeks and Romans: the exordium, the narrative, and the conclusion.

## The Speech Exordium

As we discussed in Chapter 10, the introduction is your best opportunity to establish a rapport with your audience, which is very important in persuasive speeches as your goal is to get them to listen and respond to your position. This importance was not lost on the Greeks and Romans either, so perhaps the best way to understand how to craft an effective introduction to a persuasive speech is to begin with an examination of classical speech structure. In this section we will discuss introductions using the terminology of the Greeks and Romans, who called it a speech exordium. We will explain why they saw it as important and then detail the elements of an exordium.

The Greeks and Romans referred to the start of a speech as the *exordium*, as they understood it as the place in the speech where you convince an audience to listen to your position. In fact, Quintilian stated that the purpose of the exordium is to prepare the audience to listen intently to the remainder of the presentation.[3] One of the ways you accomplish this task is by capturing the interest of the audience and the other is by establishing your credibility as a speaker.

**exordium**

the place in the speech where you convince an audience to listen to your position; Latin label for the introduction of a speech

A good exordium captures the interest of the audience almost immediately by connecting the topic to something the audience might be interested in. Aristotle argued that this process included an effort to make the audience hold a favorable impression of the speaker and the topic. After you gain their interest with your opening statement using one of the attention-getters identified in Chapter 10, you need to begin the case for why the audience should listen to what you have to say on the topic. You do this by demonstrating knowledge of the subject matter.

Although the exordium was considered one of the most important parts of a speech by the Greeks and Romans, they felt it should not be the first part of the speech you prepare, for two reasons. First, Cicero warned his students that it was impossible to effectively introduce arguments yet to be crafted. You may know what you want to say, but until you write it down you don't know how you will say it or the order in which you will present the points. Essentially, Cicero suggested writing the bulk of the speech before creating the exordium.

The second reason classical speakers felt the exordium should be composed last also illustrates a key difference between an introduction for an informative and a persuasive speech. Cicero stated that the quality of the case the speaker presents should determine the type of exordium created. He proposed two ways to begin a speech, although he also pointed out that there are rare situations when exordiums are not necessary; however, those rare instances do not exist for informative speeches. The first type of exordium Cicero discussed he called an introduction.

**introduction**
one form of exordium where speakers use plain language to lay out their case in an effort to get a confused and ill-informed audience to pay attention

**insinuation**
a form of exordium reserved for cases made about disputed topics to audiences with animosity toward the topic or the speaker

Cicero defined the ***introduction*** as an exordium that lays out the speaker's case in plain language so that the audience becomes receptive and attentive. They are often most useful when an audience is confused or ill-informed and when the topic is not controversial. Introductions today are often understood as the only way to start a speech, whereas for Cicero they were simply one way to do so. That is why this method of crafting an exordium seems familiar—it's similar to how we described starting an informative speech a few chapters ago.

Cicero reserved the other form of exordium, ***insinuation***, for cases made about disputed topics to audiences with animosity toward the topic or the speaker. A common insinuation exordium promises the audience you will be short and to the point when you know they are tired of hearing about the issue on which you are speaking. These work to reduce the reluctance of an audience to listen and allow speakers to make their case. Unlike introductions, insinuations do not need to unpack information for the audience to relieve confusion, because the audience is already informed—in fact, possibly overinformed!—about the subject matter.

Regardless of which type of Ciceronian exordium you might use to begin your persuasive speech, there are various ways to gain the attention of an audience while making them more receptive to your speech by enhancing your credibility. The first way involves stressing the importance of the topic of your speech and connecting it to the lives of the audience members. For example, if you deliver a speech arguing to update the technology of a factory in a town, you might also stress the importance of your topic to the community at large, telling them that the plant is outdated and may close if the technology isn't improved and thus the expensive update will actually save jobs for the community. Either way, you need to connect the audience to the topic in a personal way that increases the likelihood they will listen to what you have to say. This is something typically not necessary with informative speech introductions because the audience is there to learn something and thus wants to be there.

One final piece of advice offered by the Romans on exordiums is important to note. Cicero believed, as did his Roman counterpart Quintilian, that exordiums must be serious in nature, as this lends gravity and importance to the topic of the address. Cicero maintained that when a topic already has the support of the audience before the speech begins, then a rhetor might best eliminate the exordium because it could make the speaker seem condescending. In such situations speakers still previewed their speech, but they did away with the elements of the exordium that attempted to raise the interest of the audience. Quintilian additionally advised that if a speaker entertains doubts about the audience's knowledge of the issue under consideration then he or she should briefly review the situation in the exordium. Both of these suggestions underscore ways for you to lend gravity to your speech and increase your ethos within the exordium.

The Greeks and Romans understood that the exordium is the first impression a speaker makes on an audience but the last part of the speech to be composed. Its content is driven by the topic and the disposition of the audience toward the speaker, and its goals are to get the attention of the audience, establish a speaker's credibility, and ensure receptivity to the speaker's message. Once these goals are accomplished they taught students to move to the body, or what they called the narrative.

## The Speech Narrative

Aristotle argued that the introduction was one of only two elements of a speech, referring to the second component as the argument proper. The Romans taught that the body of the speech that followed the exordium contained three parts: the statement of facts, the argument, and the refutation. In this way they expanded Aristotle's approach to arranging a speech. In this section we will discuss the elements of the narrative of the speech, or what we now call the body, by addressing the three areas identified by the Romans.

When we use the term "narrative" today we think of a coherent story, or even fiction. Our understanding of the term differs from that of the Classical Greeks and Romans when applied to constructing a speech. For them the narrative of the speech consisted of several parts arranged in a coherent order. They did not provide an exact recipe for that order, acknowledging that each speaking situation called for a different response and thus a need for the speaker to arrange his or her points differently. The first of these parts they called the *statement of facts*, an explanation of what the audience needs to know in order to appreciate the main argument of the speech.

**statement of facts**
an explanation of what the audience needs to know in order to appreciate the main argument of the speech

The statement of facts helps speakers familiarize their audience with the relevant details about their topic. Cicero and Quintilian both recognized that this portion of the narrative might not be necessary all the time, while at other times it might be the only part of the narrative required of a speaker. If an audience is familiar with the case you present, then a brief statement of facts might be all that is needed. For instance, if you plan to convince the student body at your school that they need to build a new recreation center through an additional student fee, you may not need to explain why since the students might be well aware of the need.

When your goal is simply to inform an audience, then the statement of facts is the only element of the narrative you need to develop. Here, an audience is confused or ill-informed about your topic and your goal is to convey information to them. The facts of the case are all you need to present an informative speech, as you are neither making an argument nor countering any opposition to your point of view. In persuasion, however, arguments flow from the facts of the case—even when they are not explicitly outlined in the narrative by the speaker.

The Greeks and the Romans believed that the argument was the core of any speech, and this is certainly true when your purpose is persuasion. The *argument*, also called the *proof* or *confirmation*, is the portion of the speech that validates your position on the issue laid out in the statement of facts. It is, for all intents and purposes, the central idea of your speech laid bare for the audience. Whereas in an informative speech the thesis statement is a one-sentence sum of the goal of your speech, the Greeks and Romans taught that in a persuasive speech the argument portion of your speech details all of your evidence and claims regarding your topic.

**argument**
················
also called the *proof* or *confirmation*; the portion of the speech that validates your position on the issue laid out in the statement of facts

The argument portion of the speech often contains more than one claim, and choosing the way to organize these claims to maximize your ability to persuade your audience is tricky. The Greeks and Romans both taught their students not to start with their strongest, most persuasive claim; rather, they suggested that in many cases you should end with it. This allows your argument to end on its highest and best note, rather than a weaker, less persuasive point. Quintilian suggested spending more time developing the strongest point than the weaker arguments, which he proposed should be lumped together if at all possible. On the latter suggestion he famously wrote, "They may not have the overwhelming force of a thunderbolt, but they will have all the destructive force of hail."[4] After you organize your claims in the argument portion of your speech, you still must be aware of the opposition.

**refutation**
················
response to potential opposition to your argument

The third component of the narrative part of the speech according to the classical speech teachers is where you attempt to anticipate opposition to your argument. The *refutation*, or the response to opposition to your argument, is only relevant for persuasive speeches and, even then, situational factors largely determine where you place it. For example, if your audience prefers the position opposing yours, it might be best to lay out the refutation as reasons not to agree with the opposition before you even detail your argument. In this instance, moving the refutation to a position immediately following the exordium might be wise. However, when an audience is hostile toward either you or your argument, even Quintilian would encourage you to hold the refutation for as long as possible.

The Greeks and Romans believed the refutation is an important part of any speech for two reasons. First, it demonstrates that you have thought about and researched the issue on which you are speaking, thus enhancing your own credibility. Second, it makes you appear more objective, making it easier for people to listen to your point of view. In other words, if people don't view you as partisan about an issue, then they will be more likely to be persuaded by your arguments.

Determining the order of the statement of facts, argument, and refutation is the first of a two-step process. The second step in constructing the narrative involves connecting each to the other, in other words, providing the glue that enables your argument to make sense. You can accomplish this by using one of the several different connective statements we discussed in Chapter 11. Connective statements are common to both informative and persuasive speeches.

All told, for the Greeks and Romans, the narrative, or body, of a speech is the most time-consuming and difficult to develop. Placing the three elements of the narrative—the statement of facts, the argument, and the refutation—into the best possible order and making that arrangement seem natural and smooth takes time. Additionally, determining that order is significantly influenced by situational factors like audience disposition. Cicero, Quintilian, and others would argue that it is important to approach constructing the narrative not as an inflexible recipe for success, but rather as a guide for helping you determine the best way to arrange the main points of your speech. Later in this chapter we will discuss some tried and true organizational patterns that may further help you develop and arrange your persuasive speech, but for now we need to finish discussing the third part of a persuasive speech: the conclusion. As you are leaving the narrative, you should signal your audience that you are moving into the conclusion with a signpost, just as you would for an informative speech.

## The Speech Peroration

If the narrative, or body, is important because it contains the core point of the address, then the conclusion is important because it summarizes that idea for the audience. Aristotle and Cicero both contributed to our understanding of the content and goals of a conclusion, or as they called it, the ***peroration***. Conclusions represent the last opportunity for a speaker to present his or her case to the audience and leave the audience with something to remember.

**peroration**
speech conclusion

Think about the last speech that you heard. What do you remember? The evidence? A statistic, perhaps? More than likely, you remember how that speaker finished the speech, the last words spoken. This is illustrative of the ***principle of recency***, or the idea that the last message you heard is most likely to be the one you remember. For this reason it is important to finish a persuasive speech with a bang, and not a whimper. You want the audience to leave knowing what you want them to do or believe and why.

**principle of recency**
the idea that the last message you heard is most likely to be the one you remember

Aristotle taught that conclusions accomplish four things. First, they need to leave the audience with a positive impression of you as the speaker. Failing that, they need to at least leave the audience with a less than enthusiastic view of your opponent. Second, conclusions need to both augment the force and presence of your arguments while diminishing the power of those that may be offered by your opponent. Third, Aristotle argued conclusions must incite the proper emotions in an audience. Finally, he believed conclusions should restate the arguments and supporting facts central to the speech's goal.

Cicero followed up on Aristotle's approach by advocating three distinct things speakers could do in their conclusion. First, like Aristotle, he stated speakers should summarize their ideas. This summary should briefly review the statement of facts and take a moment to encapsulate each of the main points the speaker presented. Second, Cicero called for speakers to use the conclusion to cast anyone who disagreed with them in a bad light through emotional appeals. Finally, where Aristotle argued conclusions must incite the proper emotions, Cicero gave the emotion a name: sympathy. He also said that the audience's sympathy should be toward the speaker and the topic, not one or the other. In fact, in his book *De Inventione*, Cicero provided quite a number of specific ways to accomplish this (for a few examples, see Table 14.1).

**Table** 14.1

| Emotional Appeals | |
|---|---|
| **Goal** | **Emotional Appeal Example[5]** |
| Invoke authority | "As a 10-year cancer survivor I am proof of the benefits of this treatment." |
| Point out the effects of success or failure | "When we took this approach in a similar situation my plan worked, while my opponent's failed." |
| Show what will happen if the state of affairs remains unchanged | "Just look at what happened three years ago when we faced a similar challenge, and we did nothing. It is time to act decisively." |
| Demonstrate that the state of affairs violates community values | "The current crisis in our area goes against everything most of us believe in, against what our parents taught us, and against the ideals with which we grew up." |
| Ask the audience to identify with those injured or insulted | "My friends, think how you and your family would feel if you were treated in such a shabby manner. Put yourself in their place and ask yourself how you would feel." |

The classical construction of a speech in this manner, however, has not been lost to history. In fact, we can find many examples of speeches structured this way. One of the more famous classically structured speeches in modern times came from one of the most eloquent and inspiring leaders of the twentieth century: Winston Churchill. Shortly after taking the position of prime minister in May 1940, Churchill delivered his now famous "Blood, Toil, Tears and Sweat" speech to Parliament (see the nearby box). In it he provided a brief exordium, a statement of facts, and a peroration all worthy of praise from Cicero and Quintilian, thus demonstrating to students of speech that what was true about speech over 2,000 years ago is still true today.

Both Cicero and Aristotle noted the importance of conclusions in persuasive speeches. They knew that just as exordiums, or introductions, were the first opportunity to make a strong case to the audience, perorations, or conclusions, were the last best chance to win the audience over. In the next part of the chapter we will explain some ways in which the classical approach to crafting a persuasive speech can be incorporated by you when developing your persuasive presentations.

# CONTEMPORARY SPEECH INTRODUCTIONS AND CONCLUSIONS

Now that we have illustrated the importance of persuasive speeches to the Greeks and Romans and discussed how they understood the practice of persuasive speaking, we need to show you how these ideas translate to you and your efforts at creating persuasive appeals.  In this section we will provide you with some strategies for developing effective introductions and conclusions (or, as the Greeks and Romans called them, exordiums and perorations).  We will then spend the final portion of the chapter exploring several different organizational strategies for the body of a persuasive speech.

## Strategies for Persuasive Introductions

The Greeks and Romans noted the uniqueness of introductions in providing several different options for developing them, and these observations also illustrate the differences that exist between persuasive and informative introductions.  That said, there are similarities between the two types of speech introductions.  This section will note the similarities while also providing you with ways to effectively construct an introduction appropriate for a persuasive speech.

Cicero and Quintilian's recommendation that the introduction be the last part of the speech you write is true with persuasive as well as informative speeches.  You should not set up the introduction until you know what you are going to say and have an idea of the knowledge level and disposition of your audience.  This information is key to making sure you effectively preview your speech's main points, capture the audience's interest, establish credibility, and focus the audience's attention.

Those four goals of an introduction, you may well remember, are the same for informative as well as persuasive speeches.  You need to get an audience's attention, but as Cicero and Quintilian noted with regard to persuasive speeches, you must be sure to do so without offending the audience.  You must be attuned to the audience's feelings about the topic or the occasion and determine whether a traditional introduction or Ciceronian insinuation would benefit the speech most.  You also need to establish your credibility almost immediately by stating why an audience should listen to you on a particular subject.  Finally, you need to preview your speech's main points in much the same way you would do so for an informative speech.  See Table 14.2 for a summary of tips for an effective persuasive introduction.

One thing you should note from Cicero and Quintilian is their belief that introductions are serious.  Many people believe that today the best way to get an audience's attention is with a joke, but that is not something the Romans, or we, would recommend—especially for persuasive speeches.  Telling a joke is very risky, because if people do not laugh you start off on a poor note, and you might

## Blood, Toil, Tears and Sweat
## by newly elected Prime Minister Winston Churchill

Delivered May 13, 1940, to the British House of Commons

Prime Minister Winston Churchill delivered a terse, yet powerful call to action shortly after becoming prime minister of Great Britain in May 1940. As if the war was not a large enough complication for the new leader, outgoing Prime Minister Neville Chamberlain received a boisterous round of applause, while Churchill was greeted with a subdued reaction from members of the House of Commons, thus illustrating the fragile coalition supporting Churchill and his government.[6]

At the time of the address Adolf Hitler's Nazi war machine was crushing opposition everywhere it went. Britons were concerned that their country's safety, freedom, and sovereignty were at risk. Churchill rose to the task of inspiring confidence in both his leadership and the country itself with this brief (only 688 words) address to parliament.

In his statement of facts, Churchill noted he selected a five-person war cabinet that contained diverse political views. He pointed out that Britain was already fighting in Norway and Holland, that the Mediterranean was a concern, and that the air battle over the remainder of Europe was "continuous." He argued that these facts required that "many preparations have to be made here at home."

Churchill proclaimed the famous line: "I have nothing to offer but blood, toil, tears and sweat"[7] as part of his rebuttal, and aimed it at those who might criticize the swift creation of the cabinet without "ceremony." In fact, his phrase made it seem like he pled with them to accept it because he was essentially trying his best.

In his peroration the prime minister closed with a clarion call to action after admitting the country faced "many, many long months of struggle and suffering." These words, his declaration of a policy of victory, and his concluding statement of, "Come then, let us go forward together with our united strength"[8] all created emotional connections between the initially divided audience, himself, and his policies.

also unintentionally offend someone in the audience, thus damaging your ability to move the audience to action. Instead of a joke, make use of the attention-getters we discussed in Chapter 11.

Finally, students delivering a persuasive speech should be aware of what their instructors expect in an introduction. Some instructors may, for instance, also require students to state their name or the title of their speech. Be sure you know what is expected before you write your introduction.

| Tips for an Effective Persuasive Introduction | Table 14.2 |
|---|---|
| • Develop the introduction last | |
| • Capture the attention of the audience | |
| • Establish your credibility | |
| • Focus the audience's attention | |

## Strategies for Persuasive Conclusions

Just as with introductions, there are elements common to both informative and persuasive conclusions. After reading how the Greeks and Romans approached perorations we now realize there are differences between informative and persuasive speech conclusions. In this section of the chapter we will discuss the similarities and differences while also providing tips on how you can create a strong conclusion to your persuasive speech.

One of the aspects of conclusions shared by both informative and persuasive speeches is the need for a signpost at the start of the conclusion. Signposts serve the same function for persuasive speech conclusions that they do for informative speech conclusions: They let the audience know the speech is almost over.

Similarly, both informative and persuasive speech conclusions should summarize each of the main points in the speech and demonstrate how they connect to and support your argument. You should never introduce new evidence in a conclusion, but rather re-emphasize the fundamental points of your speech. This allows the audience to walk away from your presentation understanding your central point and how you got there. Rarely will an audience recall the specific evidence you lay out, but they will remember your main points. With regard to persuasive speeches this summary also enables you to build up your clincher, which can be a much more powerful statement than in an informative speech.

Although both informative and persuasive speeches have clinchers, in a persuasive speech there is much more room for creativity and direct calls to action. The reason for this is simple: The general purpose of a persuasive speech is to persuade, so the last thing the audience should hear should be a call to action.

The success of your persuasive speech conclusion often depends on your ability to channel and incite the proper ethos through this clincher. This is where Aristotle and Cicero's goal of creating audience sympathy toward the speaker or topic should be accomplished. The clincher should not take long to state, and there are a variety of ways to construct an effective clincher for a persuasive speech, as we discussed in Chapter 11. Most importantly, however, in persuasive speeches it is essential for you to find a way to issue a call to action that the audience can reasonably and realistically accomplish.

A common error novice speakers make in their persuasive speech conclusions is reserving their persuasive effort for the clincher. Do not wait until the last statement to persuade the audience. The clincher should be the last push and a logical next step based on the case you have made throughout the speech. In short, the conclusion should feed off of the body and accentuate your case and its significance for the audience.

One final note about conclusions bears mentioning. Conclusions should not be very long. In fact, they should take about as long as your introduction and thus typically account for no more than 20% of your speech. If your conclusion rambles on it loses its effectiveness and you lose your audience. If it is too short, your audience may never truly understand the point of your speech. Remember, your conclusion is the last chance you have to underscore your case and its importance for your audience. Table 14.3 provides a summary of tips for creating persuasive speech conclusion.

**Table 14.3**

| Tips for a Persuasive Speech Conclusion |
| --- |
| • Provide a signpost at the beginning of the conclusion |
| • Summarize the main points |
| • Do not present new evidence |
| • Emphasize the fundamental points |
| • Build up the clincher |
| • Do not wait until the conclusion to present persuasive appeals |
| • Accentuate the speech body and case |
| • Make it approximately the same length as the introduction |

Conclusions are essential elements of any good persuasive speech. They involve letting the audience know you are almost finished, restating your argument and main points, and clinching your appeal with a call to action. They share some similarities with conclusions for informative speeches, but there are key differences you must be aware of when putting together your speech. Developing strong introductions and conclusions is only two-thirds of the process of crafting a successful persuasive appeal. In the next section we will explore the various methods that you might use to properly organize the "meat" of your persuasive speech.

# ORGANIZATIONAL PATTERNS FOR PERSUASIVE SPEECHES

The general and specific purpose statements of a persuasive speech differ from those of an informative address, but they too help you determine how to arrange your points. A closing argument in a courtroom is a persuasive speech where the general purpose is "to persuade" and the specific purpose is tied to the facts of the case. For example, the lawyer for Kelly, who was accused of stealing money from a CVS pharmacy, gave a closing argument where the specific purpose was "to persuade the jury that Kelly did not steal the money because she had no motive or opportunity to commit the crime." This specific purpose statement encouraged the lawyer to use a particular organizational pattern to accomplish his speaking goals. In this section of the chapter we will detail some of the common organizational strategies you can effectively employ for persuasive speeches.

Although persuasive speeches have very different general and specific purposes than informative/technical speeches, the two types of speeches are similar in that the specific purpose often dictates what organizational pattern should be used. Persuasive speeches can be directed at a specific problem or the problem's fundamental cause. They also can be focused on arguing that one option is better than another. Finally, there are persuasive speeches that attempt to move people to immediate action. Depending on which of these purposes is your goal, you may choose any one of four potential organizational patterns.

## Problem-Solution Order

If you seek to convince an audience that a specific policy or action will solve an existing problem, the ***problem-solution order*** might be best. In this arrangement you first convince the audience that there is a problem and then make the case that the solution you propose will alleviate that problem. To effectively arrange this speech you must first establish a clear specific purpose that states exactly what you want your audience to do. Then you must consider several important questions to evaluate the merits of your case as you develop it and prepare to present it to your audience.

**problem-solution order**
......
a means of organizing a persuasive speech in which you discuss the problem first and follow with a discussion of your preferred solution

The first question deals with the definition and scope of the problem. You need to establish how you see the problem at hand and convince your audience to see it that way as well. If they disagree with your definition of the problem then you will never get the audience to buy into your solution; you will be stuck arguing over what Quintilian called definitive stasis. So, before even offering a solution you need to clearly establish the scope of the problem you plan to address. In explaining the scope of the predicament you may wish to inquire as to whether any party has been harmed by the problem and allow them to explain. This can help create an emotional connection between the audience and the issue, thus enabling you to add some pathos to your appeal.

Once the dilemma that faces the audience has been established you need to move on to the solution. The initial part of this portion of your speech should answer the question of evaluative criteria. In other words, establish by what criteria a potential solution to the problem should be judged. After constructing this list of criteria for evaluating a solution you should check your proposed solution against it to ensure that what you propose actually resolves the problem. If it does not, then your solution is unlikely to be adopted by the audience.

Finally, you need to explain to the audience how your solution can be put into effect. The "how" element is important because it is the prescription for action that you want the audience to follow. It should contain practical and specific steps for the audience to take that will actually enact the solution and solve the problem facing the community.

Let's look at the hypothetical case of Lionel to illustrate how a simple problem-solution speech might be approached. Lionel is tired of the potholes in the road in front of his house, so he attends the city council meeting and addresses the members. First he explains that the road in front of his house contains 10 potholes in a three-block span, and then he informs the council that these potholes have caused several thousand dollars in damage to the cars that drive that road in the last month alone. He then proposes that they use city funds to fill the potholes with macadam to avoid further damage.

In this speech, Lionel details the problem and proposes a solution once the problem has been made clear to everyone. Using the problem-solution order this speech roughly looks like the following:

> Body
>
> Main point: State of the road in front of the house *(problem)*
>
> Main point: Funding road repairs *(solution)*

This can be an effective way of convincing an audience to support your plan; however, it is not always the most compelling way to propose a solution. Sometimes, you need to do more.

## Problem-Cause-Solution Order

Problems, be they public or personal, always have a root cause and to effectively resolve the problem you need to address that root cause, otherwise the symptoms will recur. To this end you must look at the situation to determine the causes of the problem facing the audience and then decide whether or not the cause can actually be addressed. If it can, then the speech needs to recognize the problem faced by the community as well as add a discussion of why the problem exists—its cause. In short, you must convince the audience not only that a problem exists, but that the problem exists because of a root cause and that addressing that root cause is the most effective way to handle the situation. Let's return to Lionel and see how this works.

Does it not make even better sense to not just fix the potholes, but to make sure they don't happen again? This would involve changing the specific purpose and, as a result, the organization of the main points in the speech. Lionel's specific purpose would change to reflect his new goal, and it would be something like this: "To persuade the audience to redesign the street where potholes have damaged cars so that they will not occur again."

The goal for Lionel now is to address the problem (potholes) by providing a solution to it and its cause (poor design of the street).

> Body
>
> Main point: The state of the road in front of his house *(problem)*
>
> Main point: The poor street design *(cause)*
>
> Main point: Funding for proper road repairs *(solution)*

His speech arrangement now is *problem-cause-solution order*, where he first discusses the immediate problem, then explains what caused it, and finally provides a solution that addresses both the potholes and the poor street design.

**problem-cause-solution order**

a means of organizing a persuasive speech in which you discuss the problem first, then its root cause, and then your preferred solution that addresses both the problem and its inherent cause

## Comparative Advantages

More often than not, you will not be the only one offering solutions to a problem. In fact, having multiple ideas about how to fix something or address an issue is commonplace. The important thing to remember is to research and evaluate all the other potential solutions that might be offered to the problem. After doing so, if you believe yours is the best approach, then it might be helpful to recognize the fact you are aware of other potential solutions, but that they would not be the best option. This approach looks at the strengths and weaknesses of other solutions and compares them to your own. Such an approach can help increase your ethos with the audience and make your case even stronger.

Continuing with the example of Lionel and the dangerous potholes, perhaps he is not the only one who has brought this issue to the attention of the city council. In fact, the council already knows about and agrees there is a problem and its cause is poor street design. Let's say that the day before Lionel arrives to give his speech the council comes out in favor of a plan to fill the potholes but not redesign the street because it would be cost prohibitive to do so. Lionel, aware of this alternate plan, needs a different specific purpose and organizational pattern than in either of the two previous scenarios. Now his specific purpose is "to persuade his audience that paying the money to fix the street now is a better solution than simply fixing the potholes."

**comparative advantage**

an organizational pattern that uses each main point to explain why the speaker's solution is better than another proposed solution

He then structures the body of his speech by using a *comparative advantage* organizational pattern, in which every main point in the argument explains why redesigning the street is better than just fixing the potholes and not addressing their root cause.

> Body
>
> Main point: Fixing potholes is temporary; a proper repair job will be permanent
>
> Main point: Fixing the road will create a smoother surface
>
> Main point: Fixing the road correctly will be less expensive in the long run

The case of Lionel and his topic illustrates several different ways of organizing persuasive speeches. Each one helps to establish a strong case for taking a particular policy. There is, however, one more organizational pattern for persuasive speeches we need to discuss and it is particularly useful when seeking immediate action from an audience.

## Monroe's Motivated Sequence

**Monroe's Motivated Sequence**
............
a five-step organizational pattern that combines psychological elements with speech persuasion to move an audience to action

The fourth organizational pattern for your main points we will discuss provides a way to effectively arrange a speech designed to incite immediate action in your audience. Alan Monroe, a professor at Purdue University, developed what we call **Monroe's Motivated Sequence** in the 1930s. The five-step sequence combines psychological elements with speech persuasion in an effort to move an audience to action. First, Monroe advocated something the Greeks and Romans also called for: getting the attention of your audience. Then he argued a speaker should clearly lay out the need for change, something again advocated by the classical philosophers we discussed earlier. Once you clearly establish the problem you satisfy the need by providing a solution to that problem. Fourth, Monroe's sequence calls for you to intensify the audience's desire for your solution to the problem by visualizing its success. This involves the use of imagery and asks the audience to actually see themselves doing what you call for—at least to see it in their mind's eye. Finally, once you state your case and get your audience to visualize your solution's success, you can use emotionally stirring language to tell them how to act.[9]

As an example, suppose a student wants to persuade his audience to get involved in cleaning up a park on his college campus that is strewn with trash and debris. He then composes the following order for his points using Monroe's Motivated Sequence:

| | |
|---|---|
| Attention: | "Do you think we should have a pleasant outdoor place to enjoy nature, to hang out with friends? To take walks, play sports, have cookouts, and entertain?" |
| Need: | "We do not have that on our campus, and there is a nearby park we could use, but it is overrun with weeds and trash and is currently unacceptable." (Pictures would be a good visual aid at this juncture.) |
| Satisfaction: | "We could all pitch in, share the work, and it would not be that big of a burden on anyone." |
| Visualization: | "A place to hang out, play ball, walk, enjoy fresh air and nature, and have cookouts—and we would have made that possible." (Visuals of a beautiful outdoor setting would be effective at this point.) |

## SPOTLIGHTING THEORISTS: ALAN H. MONROE

### Alan H. Monroe

Alan H. Monroe served as a member of the faculty at Purdue University in Indiana beginning in 1924. He was initially hired as an instructor in English to teach basic courses in the English department. He quickly infused the English curriculum with classes such as Principles of Speech and Debating in English. Today, we recognize these topics as Communication rather than English courses. Through Monroe's efforts Purdue University established a strong Communication department known for teaching and research.[10]

In 1927 Monroe became the head of the Speech faculty in the English department at Purdue, but he was not formally recognized in that role until 1941. Along with other members of the then English department at Purdue, Monroe led efforts during the 1930s to expand the curriculum, specifically adding courses in oral interpretation, public address, and debate. In 1935 Monroe published the first edition of his book *Principles and Types of Speech*, which is now in its 16th edition, a testament to the ingenuity and importance of what Monroe accomplished while at Purdue.

In 1948 Purdue inaugurated its own Ph.D. program in Speech Communication, largely through Monroe's efforts. Monroe worked using relationships he had developed in the Purdue Department of Psychology to help push the Speech Communication department toward a Ph.D. program. He resigned as head of the department in 1963, after successfully creating an independent Communication department, separate from English, with its own robust undergraduate and graduate curriculum.

As a researcher, Monroe is best remembered for the development of the Monroe's Motivated Sequence model for persuasive speeches that seek immediate action. This model is still taught today, and if you look closely you can see it at play in things as varied as commercials and political speeches. Alan Monroe truly made a mark on the campus of Purdue University as well as the discipline of communication and public speaking education.

Action:  "Will you join me in making this dream come true? Again, the work will be shared, and we will have made an improvement for all to enjoy."

Let's take a moment and look at each one of these elements.

The first step, gaining the audience's attention, is nothing new; it simply employs a rhetorical question to raise the audience's awareness of the speech topic. Any form of attention-getter we covered earlier in the book would be acceptable for this stage of Monroe's Motivated Sequence. The second step of establishing need is a way of presenting a problem to the audience, but it differs slightly from the way we discussed it when we explained the problem-solution order.

Of course, the need for the audience may be to solve a problem. In fact, solving a problem is a terrific motivator when the audience recognizes there is a dilemma that affects them and that needs to be resolved. That said, for Monroe's Motivated Sequence establishing a need can also include constructing, or illuminating, a need of which the audience may not be aware. For instance, in the above example, students on the campus may not really notice the need for the clean park because they may just have adapted to using other facilities for enjoying nature and entertaining.

Also consider persuading an audience to purchase a particular product. The audience may not see a real need for making the purchase at the time, so the speaker needs to explain why the need does in fact exist. Not all problems that exist are obvious to an audience, and so sometimes speakers need to work extra hard to establish a need before persuading an audience to act. In short, Monroe's Motivated Sequence recognizes that a speaker needs to both raise awareness of a problem and create a need to address it.

Once the need has been established, you next must produce a way to satisfy the need. It would be tremendously awkward, if not unethical, to tell people there is a problem but not give them a way to solve it! Monroe labels this step "satisfaction" because it is the point in the speech where the solution is provided and couched in a way that firmly satisfies the need. This can be through the proposal of a solution to specific policy or through encouraging an audience to take a particular course of action. Here is where you must offer solid reasoning and evidence to illustrate how your proposed solution will satisfy the need and why it is an appropriate and effective remedy for the problem facing the community. We must be mindful, however, when doing this that we do not fall into the trap of using reasoning fallacies in an effort to achieve our goal. The means of satisfying the need, and the tools we use to tell the audience about those means, are just as important as the end goal of attaining audience support and action. So, let us look at how we might go about accomplishing the satisfaction step in Monroe's Motivated Sequence.

In the example regarding the dirty park on campus, satisfaction is achieved through a group effort to clean the park. In the case of seeking to convince an audience to purchase a product, the speaker needs to show how the product will fulfill a personal need or desire for the audience. For example, if you tell an audience that bad breath is both unhealthy and unattractive and thus they need to keep it from occurring, then you need to tell them that the path to satisfying that need to avoid bad breath can be fulfilled by purchasing and using Colgate toothpaste.

Monroe's Motivated Sequence does not stop at satisfaction, however, as the next step is getting the audience to visualize fulfilling the need. Visualization uses concrete language and calls upon the audience to actually see themselves as the instruments of satisfying the established need. It helps the speaker further connect the audience with the issue, its solution, and the speaker by getting them to picture a future where the need has been fulfilled. Such efforts employ both emotional and logical appeals to the audience. Ultimately, when the audience can see themselves taking part in an action that effectively satisfies a need for either themselves or the community, it becomes a simple task to call them to action—the final step of Monroe's Motivated Sequence.

All told, Monroe's Motivated Sequence represents a modernized pattern of organization for a balanced persuasive appeal to an audience. It's five steps are easy to follow as both a speaker and an audience and are most effective when immediate action is sought.

Whether you are debating policy positions, factual accuracies, the value of one solution over another, or calling an audience to act, there are a wide variety of organizational patterns you can use in a persuasive speech. Just like informative speeches, persuasive speech arrangement largely depends on the formulation of your specific purpose, but once that is crafted the speech can quickly take shape. Knowing the main parts of a speech and how to organize your main points can help you get ready to prepare your presentation. The most crucial step in speech creation remains organizing the product of your research in a cogent, coherent, and persuasive manner. For a summary of the organizational patterns for persuasive speeches covered in this chapter, see Table 14.4.

| Organizational Patterns for Persuasive Speeches |
| --- |
| • Problem-solution |
| • Problem-cause-solution |
| • Comparative advantage |
| • Monroe's Motivated Sequence |

**Table 14.4**

## SUMMARY

The Greeks and Romans separated persuasive speeches into a variety of different parts: the exordium, the narrative, and the peroration. They paid particular attention to the narrative and broke it down into several component parts, including the statement of facts, argument proper, and refutation. Today we use terms like introduction, body, and conclusion to describe the elements of a speech, but the ideas about what must be done in each part to achieve a persuasive purpose are the same. In this chapter we also identified some of the common elements between informative and persuasive speeches, while elaborating on their differences; most notably, those differences relate to the various ways you can organize a persuasive speech. Finally, we encourage you to refer to Chapter 9 on outlining for models that can help you develop your persuasive speech.

## KEY TERMS

## REVIEW QUESTIONS

1. What are the three components of persuasive speeches according to the Greeks and Romans?

2. What are the two types of exordiums proposed by Cicero?

3. What four things did Aristotle say a peroration should do?

4. What are the four ways you can organize the main points in a persuasive speech?

5. What are the five parts of Monroe's Motivated Sequence?

## THINK ABOUT IT

1. Would it ever be a good idea to present your strongest argument first?

2. How do you measure whether your credibility increases or decreases during a speech?

3. Is it ethical to induce emotions in a conclusion or in any part of the speech? Why or why not?

4. How could you use Monroe's Motivated Sequence in everyday language?

## ACTIVITIES FOR ACTION

1. Working in a group of three members, develop several different ways to get an audience's attention. Then, state several ways you could establish credibility. Finally, figure out a way that statements could both get the attention of the audience and establish credibility, thereby killing two birds with one stone.

2. In this chapter we discussed Monroe's Motivated Sequence. Divide into groups of three and assign each group a product on the market right now. Give each group 10 minutes to create a "commercial" where Monroe's Motivated Sequence is used to sell the assigned product. The catch is every person in each group must have a speaking role in the skit.

# ENDNOTES

1. Toastmasters International, "What Is Toastmasters?" http://www.toastmasters.org/MainMenuCategories/WhatisToastmasters.aspx (accessed September 19, 2008).

2. Toastmasters International, "Community Service," http://www.toastmasters.org/MainMenuCategories/WhatisToastmasters/CommunityService.aspx (accessed September 19, 2008).

3. Quintilian, *The Institutes of Oratory,* translated by H. E. Butler, Loeb Classical Library (Cambridge: Harvard University Press, 1980), IV, i, 5.

4. Ibid., V, xii, 5.

5. Sharon Crowley and Debra Hawhee, *Ancient Rhetorics for Contemporary Students*, 4th Ed. (New York: Pearson Education, 2008).

6. Winston Churchill, "Blood, Toil, Tears and Sweat," Speech to the British House of Commons, http://www.historyplace.com/speeches/churchill.htm (accessed June 13, 3011).

7. Ibid.

8. Ibid.

9. Raymie E. McKerrow, Bruce E. Gronbeck, Douglas Ehninger, and Alan H. Monroe, *Principles and Types of Speech Communication,* 15th Ed. (New York: Longman: 2003).

10. W. Charles Redding, "An Informal History of Communication at Purdue," http://www.cla.purdue.edu/communication/graduate/informalhistory.pdf.

THE SPEAKER:  The Tradition and Practice of Public Speaking

# Epideictic Address

# **Practically**SPEAKING

Every year hundreds of thousands of students graduate from universities and colleges just like yours. Graduation is the ultimate goal of any college student; it is why you go to class and study hard. When you complete the requisite classes and credit hours you are rewarded with a ceremony, a celebration of your success and accomplishments. But graduations honor more than your past exploits and achievements, they mark the commencement of another stage in your life. These commencement ceremonies involve several speakers, from the college president to the class valedictorian. Sometimes, universities arrange for a special guest to deliver remarks and advice for the graduating class. These special commencement speakers are often famous alumni, politicians, or even actors. As a way of paying tribute to these guests, they are sometimes rewarded with an honorary degree from the university. Many people from many different walks of life have delivered these addresses in the hopes of imparting some words of wisdom to a group of students about to head off and experience life in the professional world. Some examples: Former First Lady Barbara Bush at Wellesley College (1990), Oliver Stone at the University of California, Berkeley (1994), author Doris Kearns Goodwin at Dartmouth College (1998), and comedian Jon Stewart at William and Mary College (2004). Even comedian Will Ferrell has gotten into the act, addressing Harvard University in 2003.

Each of these individuals brought something unique with them to the lectern that they shared with their audiences. Some, like Ferrell at Harvard, may not seem like good matches, but nevertheless the campus invited them to share their thoughts on the importance of the occasion with the community. To each person graduation means something different, but the event itself provides significance and direction to the speech.

You do not need to be told that the speeches of Jon Stewart and Barbara Bush contained markedly different content delivered in vastly different tones. Still, though their perspectives differed, both shared the importance of the occasion and what it means to them with the people in attendance. They commemorated the moment.

In this chapter we will discuss epideictic, or commemorative, address and how it differs from informative and persuasive speaking. How is it that a comedian, a First Lady, an actor, and an author can all deliver speeches about the same event when they seemingly have little in common with each other? The answer is that speaking on special occasions is a unique brand of public speaking that depends not so much on the speaker, but on the scene around the speaker. That is not to say epideictic speech does not share some qualities with the other types of speaking discussed so far; however, by and large it has a different purpose.

We will first discuss both the common and different elements of epideictic address and informative speaking, followed by a discussion in which we compare and contrast commemorative speaking and persuasive messages. We will then discuss several different forms of epideictic speeches you may encounter throughout your lives. Finally, we will explore the purpose of this form of speaking and how it has changed over time.

# Epideictic Address: The Third Genre

Epideictic address commemorates an occasion and celebrates elements of scene. Even when the special occasion is a death, the speech (called a eulogy) is designed to celebrate the person's life. The two important components of these speeches are their emotional attachment to the scene, or moment, and their use of pathos. These are the cornerstones of an effective epideictic address, and they are what differentiates commemorative speaking from informative and persuasive speaking as a genre.

## Epideictic vs. Informative Speaking

Informative and commemorative speeches share two significant characteristics. The first is that when speakers seek to deliver a commemorative speech they also inform the audience about the event they are commemorating. Second, they also provide information to the audience about the criteria of importance for the event. Both of these elements involve providing information to an audience, but what makes the two forms of speech different is the purpose and language used in delivering that information.

Both an informative and a commemorative speech about an event pass information along to the audience to help them understand what is being commemorated. This information is essential for any commemorative event as it helps establish a close connection between speakers and their audiences. The language used to describe the event also is different from an informative speech as it will highlight special qualities in a way that evokes more emotion than when a person simply informs the audience about the event.

President Obama speaking at Fort Hood

315

Take the case of President Barack Obama memorializing the 13 people who died in the Soldier Readiness Center of Fort Hood when a gunman opened fire on November 5, 2009. Obama very well could have told the American people what happened, but instead he used more emotionally provocative language. Let's look at an excerpt from the speech he delivered during the memorial service at Fort Hood five days after the incident:

**Informative Language:**

> "Thirteen people died and another thirty were injured when a gunman opened fire at the Soldier Readiness Center of Fort Hood, the largest U.S. military base in the world. It was the first attack on U.S. servicemen by a U.S. serviceman since the Fort Bragg incident in 1995 when Sgt. William J. Kruetzer, Jr., killed one and wounded seventeen others."

**Obama's Commemorative Language:**

> "We come together filled with sorrow for the 13 Americans that we have lost; with gratitude for the lives that they led; and with a determination to honor them through the work we carry on. This is a time of war. Yet these Americans did not die on a foreign field of battle. They were killed here, on American soil, in the heart of this great state and the heart of this great American community. This is the fact that makes the tragedy even more painful, even more incomprehensible. For those families who have lost a loved one, no words can fill the void that's been left. We knew these men and women as soldiers and caregivers. You knew them as mothers and fathers; sons and daughters; sisters and brothers. But here is what you must also know: Your loved ones endure through the life of our nation. Their memory will be honored in the places they lived and by the people they touched."[1]

Obama did not simply establish the facts of the event, he spoke of it as a "tragedy" and referred to the 13 individuals as "mothers and fathers, sons and daughters, sisters and brothers." This phrasing creates a personal connection to the victims and evokes sadness in the face of what happened. Later, in his conclusion, Obama again used vivid emotional language to describe what happened:

**Informative Language:**

> "The thirteen people who died at Fort Hood did so not at war, but at home. People connected with the event will always remember their military service."

**Obama's Commemorative Language:**

> "Here, at Fort Hood, we pay tribute to 13 men and women who were not able to escape the horror of war, even in the comfort of home. Later today, at Fort Lewis, one community will gather to remember so many in one Stryker Brigade who have fallen in

Afghanistan. Long after they are laid to rest—when the fighting has finished, and our nation has endured; when today's servicemen and women are veterans, and their children have grown—it will be said that this generation believed under the most trying of tests; believed in perseverance—not just when it was easy, but when it was hard; that they paid the price and bore the burden to secure this nation, and stood up for the values that live in the hearts of all free peoples. So we say goodbye to those who now belong to eternity. We press ahead in pursuit of the peace that guided their service."[2]

Obama spoke of the fact these servicemen and women were "not able to escape the horror of war, even in the comfort of home" and poetically declared those who perished "now belong to eternity." The former statement employed antithesis in a very effective way to emphasize that the work done by those in military is not simply conducted at war in distant foreign lands, but is done at home. He also discussed both the victims and the event itself in relation to time, artistically referring to how the memory of the individuals involved will continue on for us, but that their souls will live on for "eternity." This commemoration for the 13 victims by President Obama is an excellent example of the difference in word usage between an informative and an epideictic address.

**Table 15.1**

| Informative vs. Epideictic Speech | |
|---|---|
| **Similarities** | **Differences** |
| • Use of information, providing details/data about the topic's importance to the audience | • Epideictic speech highlights special qualities that evoke more emotion |

Like informative speeches, epideictic address involves informing the public about the significance of an event and the characteristics that make it worthy of commemoration. The speeches differ in terms of their purpose and the language they use to convey meaning. These similarities and differences are summarized in Table 15.1. Next, we will look at how epideictic address is both similar and different from persuasive speaking to illustrate how they are truly their own genre of speech.

## Epideictic vs. Persuasive Speaking

Epideictic address shares several characteristics with persuasive speech; however, there are again significant differences. On some level persuasion takes place when commemorating an event—even though it often is simply reinforcing a belief and not calling someone to action. Just as in persuasive speaking, this effort requires evidence and justification to support the commemoration. Unlike persuasive speaking in which logic and emotion work hand in hand to validate a reasoned position, epideictic address involves much more emotionality than logic and stresses the importance of connecting the feelings of the speaker with those of the audience.

One of the central tasks of a commemorative speech is to convince or reinforce the audience of the importance of an event. There are reasons why people pay tribute to the day, person, or idea spoken about, and the rhetor must connect the audience with those reasons. Let's look at a commemorative speech that illustrates the commonalities between persuasive and epideictic address.

Former President George W. Bush at the annual Thanksgiving Turkey Pardon

The United States celebrates Thanksgiving on the last Thursday of every November. President Abraham Lincoln began this tradition in 1863 to commemorate the first successful harvest by the pilgrims of Plymouth. Americans celebrate by holding a feast, usually involving a cooked turkey and harvest vegetables. Presidents, in recent years, commemorate the event by delivering a speech while also pardoning a turkey. In 2007 President George W. Bush took part in the tradition and delivered comments that stressed the importance of the occasion rooted in a communal understanding of history:

> "The Thanksgiving Proclamation which I signed this morning is a Presidential tradition which began with George Washington. The days of Thanksgiving are an American tradition. We've observed this tradition since the Pilgrims. Americans have always been a grateful people: we're grateful for our freedom; we're grateful for our families; we're grateful for our beautiful country."[3]

Here Bush traced the history of the day's importance back to the nation's inception, mentioning George Washington and the Pilgrims by name. He also expounded on the values shared by all Americans who share that history, claiming they "always" shared them. This wording reinforces the importance of the day for Americans and their cultural history. The importance of the day lends *gravitas* to the speech and adds to the pathos within the phrases.

**gravitas**
importance

Both a persuasive speech about why an event, person, or idea should be commemorated and an epideictic speech extolling the event, person, or idea seek to convince the audience of the importance of the event. However, how they do it differs. Let's return to the Thanksgiving example. Had the president been seeking to persuade people of the need for a day of Thanksgiving, he would have needed to supply much more historical data and reasons for such an action. Since he was in fact commemorating the day, he needed only to revisit and reinforce why it needed to be celebrated, and he did so by reconstructing the history of the American people and Thanksgiving Day.

Bush tied Thanksgiving to both George Washington and the Pilgrims, essentially equating the two. Historically, however, Washington took office over 150 years after the Pilgrims had their first harvest at Plymouth, making the two distinctly different. Bush also stated Americans "have always been a grateful people," although the Pilgrims were not technically Americans. Bush employed the communicative strategy of **rhetorical history**, re-appropriating historical events and redefining them to suit his purposes. Bush did not mislead people regarding the connection between Washington and the Pilgrims and the importance of Thanksgiving, but the president did not use the logical structure necessary for a persuasive speech. This difference illustrates how epideictic address shares qualities with persuasive speaking while also maintaining characteristics that make it a unique genre of speech (see Table 15.2).

**rhetorical history**
the appropriation and redefinition of historical events to augment an argument

**Table 15.2**

| Persuasive vs. Epideictic Speeches | |
| --- | --- |
| Similarities | Differences |
| • Use of persuasive strategies<br>• Use of evidence and justification | • Epideictic speeches<br> ▪ Are less rigid<br> ▪ Are more emotional<br> ▪ Have some focus upon the event's importance |

Speeches that commemorate disasters, like Obama's Fort Hood address, or those that pay tribute to an important day, like Bush's Thanksgiving Day speech, are only two types of epideictic speeches. In the next part of this chapter we will discuss several other types of commemorative speeches, when they are used, and how to successfully craft them.

# DIFFERENT FORMS OF EPIDEICTIC ADDRESS

Epideictic address occurs more than people may realize. Every graduation ceremony, presidential appearance, retirement event, and wedding toast provides an opportunity for a commemorative address. In this part of the chapter we will discuss three types of commemorative speeches and the guidelines they all follow. First, we will discuss the saddest occasion, eulogies. Second, we will move toward more light-hearted special moments, exploring the dimensions of award ceremonies and the two types of speeches that take place in that setting: the award presentation and the award reception. Finally, we will cover toasts, which typically take place at weddings, retirement events, and dinners.

## Eulogies

Every religion maintains a different tradition when it comes to dealing with death. One common attribute involves a celebration of the life of the deceased. Many cultures allow for a **eulogy**, or a speech that pays tribute to the life of the deceased, by family members and close friends. These speeches are not intended to increase the sadness already felt in the audience, but rather to provide comfort through stories about the deceased that extol their virtues.

**eulogy**
a speech that pays tribute to the life of the deceased

## Eulogy of Coretta Scott King
## by Maya Angelou

Delivered February 7, 2006, in Atlanta, GA

Maya Angelou led a life that had followed many paths, from living in rural Arkansas during the Jim Crow era and experiencing racial bigotry directed at her, to mastering several languages. She is well known for her writing and for her work in the civil rights movement. She worked closely with Dr. Martin Luther King, Jr., and became the northern coordinator for the Southern Christian Leadership Conference. When King was assassinated, Angelou, like many in the civil rights movement, was devastated. In 2011, for her work on civil rights and her achievements in literature, President Barack Obama presented Ms. Angelou with the highest civilian honor an American can receive, the Presidential Medal of Freedom.[4]

Upon the death of King's widow, Coretta Scott King, Maya Angelou was asked to deliver a eulogy alongside civil rights icon, Joseph Lowery, and all four living presidents at the time: Jimmy Carter, George H. W. Bush, Bill Clinton, and George W. Bush.

Early in the eulogy Angelou noted that no matter what the situation, Coretta Scott King always remained "serene."[5] Still early in the speech, Ms. Angelou used repetition to tell the audience the beliefs of Ms. King: "She believed religiously in non-violent protest. She believed it could heal a nation mired in a history of slavery and all its excesses."[6]

Ms. Angelou tied herself to the King family past, noting that Dr. King had been assassinated on her birthday in 1968, and that she and Coretta Scott King spoke on the anniversary of that tragedy every year. She referred to the King family as part of her family, and recognized that while delivering the eulogy for Coretta Scott King she was representing many people.

In the conclusion of the eulogy Ms. Angelou used aspects of Coretta Scott King's life to comment on more important social values and human behavior, thus making the eulogy about more than just King: "I pledge to you, my sister, I will never cease. I mean to say I want to see a better world. I mean to say I want to see some peace somewhere. I mean to say I want to see some honesty, some fair play. I want to see kindness and justice. This is what I want to see and I want to see it through my eyes and through your eyes, Coretta Scott King."[7]

Eulogies can be impromptu, but typically a person delivering a eulogy has a few days to prepare. Most often, family members of the deceased approach those whom they wish to deliver eulogies in advance so the speaker can prepare. On rare occasions someone who may not have known the deceased very well is asked to present a eulogy. This is common in politics when presidents and politicians deliver eulogies for other leaders and social figures who have passed away. Take, for example, the death of Coretta Scott King in early 2006. Over three dozen speakers eulogized the civil rights activist and wife of Martin Luther King, Jr. Included in that group were four U.S. presidents, who knew of her but did not know her, and the famous author Maya Angelou who, in fact, did know Ms. King. Due to their ethos, the presidents were all able to deliver remarks appropriate to the occasion that were not reflective of a close personal relationship with Ms. King, while Angelou provided a more personal account.

A eulogy is a story about a person's life, but not necessarily a biography. Fewer rules constrain this narrative. For example, a traditional biography will include all points about a person's life, whether they were positive achievements or perhaps things of which a person might not be proud. Eulogies are intensely positive and do not dwell on the failings of the person's life, as such memories do not help the audience celebrate the person they have lost.

Eulogies, unlike biographies, are not complete narratives of a person's life. These commemorative speeches touch only on specific moments and do not typically remind the audience of the trek of the individual from birth to death. The selected moments within the speech also can, and should if possible, be personal recollections about the speaker's relationship to and encounters with the deceased. These personal stories help to both enhance the credibility of the speaker and create a vivid, positive, and energetic account of the deceased that helps people reflect on their own experiences with that person.

An example of infusing a eulogy with these personal reflections and sense of gratitude toward the deceased can be found in the eulogy for former President Ronald Reagan delivered by his former vice president and successor, George H. W. Bush in 2004. Here is an excerpt from that speech:

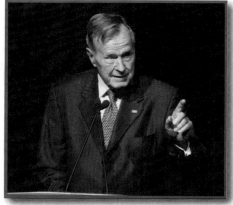

Former President George H. W. Bush

> As his vice president for eight years, I learned more from Ronald Reagan than from anyone I encountered in all my years of public life. I learned kindness; we all did. I also learned courage; the nation did...

> In leaving the White House, the very last day, he left in the yard outside the Oval Office door a little sign for the squirrels. He loved to feed those squirrels. And he left this sign that said, "Beware of the dog," and to no avail, because our dog Millie came in and beat the heck out of the squirrels.

> But anyway, he also left me a note, at the top of which said, "Don't let the turkeys get you down."[8]

Here, a person who worked closely with the deceased president reflected on an intimate encounter very few shared and of which the public was unaware. This stressed the humor of Reagan and allowed Bush to call the audience to remember similar such moments they had with the former president.

A last characteristic of eulogies is that they typically involve a level of humor. It is not only accepted, but often expected that there be some jesting and joking within a eulogy. This is not to say the jests are at the expense of the deceased, but rather the humor may be derived from stories about that person's life and actions that were funny. Humor is an effective way of both celebrating the humanity of the person who has passed while also raising the spirits of those they have left behind. The key characteristics of eulogies are summarized in Table 15.3.

**Table 15.3**

| Eulogies |
| --- |
| • Celebrate the deceased's life |
| • Tend to be prepared in advance |
| • Are given usually by someone who knew the deceased |
| • Share life stories about the deceased, rather than providing a biography |
| • Mention select memories |
| • Can contain some humor |

## Award Ceremonies

A more light-hearted special occasion where people deliver speeches is at an award ceremony. Award ceremonies range from degree conferrals to Oscar awards, all the way to business conferences where annual awards are doled out. These are much more jovial events than eulogies and typically involve two speeches, one by the presenter of the award and one by the recipient. The presentation and reception speeches vary in terms of content; however, both are typically short in duration.

Oscar host
Billy Crystal

Presenters often have time to prepare their speech, and as such they should take care to accomplish several tasks within their speech. First, they should describe the award itself and the criteria used to select the recipient, although they should be careful not to reveal the name of the winner until the very end of the speech to preserve a sense of excitement and anticipation. If possible, they also should acknowledge any connection between the event, scene, or award and the recipient. Is the place where the ceremony is being held of special note? Does it enhance the moment or the award? Presenters usually can take a few minutes, but not much longer, as they are not the person people came to see and hear.

Once the presenter has acknowledged the name of the award winner, the recipient usually gets a brief moment to address the audience. Depending on the ceremony and the nature of the award, these speeches can be limited to 30 seconds or in some cases the recipient may get several minutes to address the audience. An example of the shorter version of acceptance speeches can be found at the annual Oscar Awards Ceremony in Hollywood. There, award winners usually get only a handful of seconds to thank everyone involved in their success before being rushed offstage so the next award can be announced. Examples of occasions where longer acceptance speeches are more typical include Hall of Fame induction ceremonies for professional sports associations and candidate nomination or victory addresses during political campaigns.

**Table 15.4**

| Acceptance Speeches |
|---|
| • Offer thanks to the presenter |
| • Show humility |
| • When possible, group people to thank them |
| • Express appreciation for the moment |
| • Demonstrate knowledge of the event |

Acceptance speeches should do several things, and the more time the speaker has the easier they are to creatively and eloquently accomplish. Initially, the award recipient should thank the person presenting the award as well as the organization who crafted the award. The most important aspect of an acceptance speech is humility, as the speaker should always be grateful and not appear arrogant in his or her reception of the honor. These speeches also should contain moments of reflection about the road the person has traveled to reach that moment. Next, those who have played an instrumental role in one's achievement should be thanked. However, it is important not to try and thank everyone, and to group people in your recognition whenever possible. That is to say, thank your family rather than thanking each member specifically.

Award acceptance speeches also need to show an appreciation for the moment and use language that reflects the speaker's knowledge of the event's purpose. When the speech is used for a means to do something other than demonstrate gratitude and commemorate the event or individual, audiences do not receive the speaker well at all. In 2003 when Michael Moore won the Oscar for Best Documentary for his work on *Bowling for Columbine* he began his speech with a thank you reference to his colleagues on the project but then railed against the president for the war in Iraq. Such comments were inappropriate given the nature of the event and the award, and as a result, much of the audience booed Moore and the band played very quickly to usher him off stage. This is a perfect example of a person delivering the wrong type of speech at a moment designed to commemorate an achievement.

One other fundamental difference between an award acceptance speech and an award presentation speech relates to delivery style. As we mentioned earlier, presenters often have time to prepare, but the same is not often the case with an award recipient. Sometimes honorees are notified in advance and have time to prepare a speech, but more often than not they are only aware they are a nominee for the award. As such, they should prepare potential remarks in the event they win and are called upon to speak. In terms of delivery, then, award acceptance speeches are usually impromptu addresses whereas award presentation speeches are more extemporaneous. See Table 15.4 for a summary of the objectives of acceptance speeches.

## Toasts

Retirement dinners, weddings, and other less ceremonial moments often include toasts by one or more individuals. Toasts are typically short in duration and are considered long if they last longer than 2-3 minutes. Most toasts are actually planned and the speaker uses an extemporaneous style, but some speakers deliver toasts in an impromptu manner. In most instances, toasts, celebrate an individual, but sometimes they commemorate items, as in the christening of a new boat.

Toasts are celebratory in nature and employ far less formal language than other speeches. Often they are signified by a tapping of a glass to gain the attention of the audience. Speakers then explain their connection to the event and the person or event they plan to toast. These explanations are narratives, but they are much shorter than those narratives offered during a eulogy. Toasts also commonly take a humorous tone, with speakers telling jokes and making quips about themselves and the honoree throughout the speech. That said, the humor should be appropriate to the audience and the event. For example, do not tell a vulgar joke or anecdote to an audience at a wedding.

Wedding toasts are one of the most common toasts in American society. Depending on the wedding, the best man and maid of honor typically each deliver a toast to the bride and groom. In some ceremonies, parents, the bride, or the groom may even deliver an address to the wedding gathering. Each of these speeches is short and celebrates an aspect of the newly wed couple the person is familiar with. They also contain a wish of good luck for the couple's future together. For a summary of toasts and their objectives, see Table 15.5.

## SPOTLIGHTING THEORISTS: ISOCRATES

### Isocrates (436–338 B.C.)

One of the 10 greatest orators of ancient Greece, otherwise called the Attic Orators, Isocrates taught rhetoric to many Greeks and influenced the work of Cicero, Quintilian, and many other Roman rhetoricians. He was born into a wealthy family that provided him with an opportunity to receive a good education. Unfortunately, following the Peloponnesian War his family was stripped of its money, forcing Isocrates to find gainful employment.

Isocrates's early efforts to make a living involved work as a logographer, or courtroom speechwriter. Later, around 392 B.C., he opened his own school to teach rhetoric. Although he charged a much higher fee than most schools at the time, he still amassed many students and eventually reconstituted his family's fortune.

Isocrates focused on practical speaking in situations where finding absolute truth was not possible. He believed that the ideal orator was someone who not only possessed talent in delivery but was also well learned in a variety of different areas. Additionally, he felt a speaker needed to be virtuous in intent, value freedom—or at least the Greek notion of it—and practice self-control. A good Isocratean speaker, therefore, could knowledgeably speak on a variety of different topics, in a variety of different situations, and do so in an ethically sound manner.

One of the most influential concepts in rhetoric most linked to Isocrates is that of kairos. Kairos is the notion of timing, so it was said, "Kairos is all," or as we now say it, "Timing is everything." Kairos is the speaker's ability to adapt to any occasion and deliver a speech fit for that moment. This is relevant to all speaking situations, including those for which epideictic address is necessary.

A good ceremonial speaker can adapt to the audience, the moment, and the topic to deliver a knowledgeable, ethical, and practical speech that balances the importance of the moment with the emotion of the audience. Proper attention to kairos enables someone to speak well at any event. Kairos is all.

| Toasts | Table 15.5 |
| --- | --- |

- Are typically short in duration
- Tend to be planned in advance
- Are delivered extemporaneously
- Use informal language
- Include an explanation of one's connection to the person or event
- Use humor, if possible

# GOALS AND STRATEGIES FOR EPIDEICTIC ADDRESS

Commemorative addresses seek to achieve a variety of goals and there are some strategies to help you achieve those ends. Regardless of the form of the speech, or the forum in which the speech takes place, all epideictic speeches share similar goals.

## Epideictic Goals

Generally speaking, all epideictic addresses seek to achieve four goals. First and foremost, they attempt to commemorate an occasion, person, idea, or object. Secondly, they establish a connection between the object being honored, the people gathered to pay tribute, and the event that has brought them together. Next, these speeches construct a narrative about the commemorated thing that presents it in a positive light. Finally, an epideictic address conveys the importance of the act of paying tribute to the object(s).

The most important purpose of an epideictic address is to commemorate something. Commemorations can be both happy and sad events. For instance, President Obama's Fort Hood address we discussed earlier commemorated a sad event, while commencement addresses pay tribute to happy occasions. The speeches at both events help to augment the special nature of the moment, thus making it worthy of commemoration. To enhance the special nature of the moment, the speaker tries to connect the honoree to the people in attendance and the event that has brought them all together. Epideictic speeches enhance the intimate special quality of the occasion by successfully establishing a strong relationship between the three. For example, a person being honored at a retirement event thanks the people there by referencing how much the audience's presence means to them and expressing gratitude that they have taken time out of their lives to celebrate this moment with them.

The third goal of commemorative addresses involves creating a narrative about the person or object to which people are paying tribute. This narrative selects characteristics of the honoree and perhaps an event from the past and tells a story about why the person deserves to be commemorated. The goal of the story is not only tied to the moment itself, but tied to the memory of the moment in years to come. In this way an epideictic address provides people with something worthy of remembering in the years that follow.

One final goal of epideictic address is to convey the importance of the event to the audience. When there is a commemorative address a speaker honors something, and as such the importance of the honor and the event needs to be established. Without providing gravitas to the event, it loses meaning. Think of this as another example of the heightened importance of the connection between scene, act, and agency in public speaking. For a summary of the goals for an epideictic speech, see Table 15.6.

| Goals for an Epideictic Speech | Table 15.6 |
|---|---|

- Attempt to commemorate an occasion, person, idea, or object
- Establish a connection between the object being honored, the people gathered to pay tribute, and the event that has brought them together
- Construct a narrative about the commemorated object that presents it in a positive light
- Convey the importance of the act of paying tribute to the object(s)

## Epideictic Strategies

There are several rhetorical strategies available to a person delivering an epideictic address. These help enhance the speaker's ability to achieve the goals just discussed.

The first rhetorical tactic available to a speaker commemorating an event relates to emotional language. As we have emphasized throughout the chapter, epideictic address involves a substantial amount of pathos. So, as a speaker commemorating something, you should strive to use specific terms and phrases that evoke the emotion you seek to engender in your audience.

"Love," for instance, comes from a family of language terms that evoke that same emotion. "Adore," "worship," "find affectionate," and "deeply care for" are just a few phrases synonymous with "love" that could be used in its place to achieve the same results. It is important to know what you want your audience to feel while listening to you, and then to find the proper terms to create that feeling for them while you speak.

A second strategy involves the focus of the speech. Commemorative events focus on something other than you as the speaker. Therefore, it is of little importance to go into great detail regarding your qualifications to speak at the event. Instead, the focus should be on the topic, whether it be an award, an idea, a person, or an event. Focus the speech on the topic, what has brought everyone together, by using language terms that evoke the emotion that you want the audience to feel.

Another strategy for crafting a successful commemorative speech involves making connections between the event and the topic as quickly as possible. Establishing the relationship between the event and the topic allows the speech to progress without the speaker as the focus and endows the event that has brought people together with a greater significance than the speaker. These connections are also not as simple as saying, "Thank you all for being here." They involve greater description about the event and the honoree and they repeatedly stress the connection between the two.

Finally, and perhaps most importantly, speakers need to recognize that commemorative speeches are typically short. Therefore, brevity is valued. Be succinct in your wording and allow people to take in the surroundings rather than spend too much time listening to you. This characteristic is essential in award presentation speeches, where the presenter is not the focus and should allow the recipient more time to speak on the special occasion. The essential nature of brevity in commemorative addresses makes it even more important for speakers to determine how much time they have to speak before developing and delivering their presentation.

## SUMMARY

Epideictic address, or commemorative speaking, is an important and common genre of speech. It shares similarities with both informative and persuasive speaking, but its emphasis on pathos, construction of history, and strong connection to scene justify it as a different genre. From eulogies to graduation speeches, to toasts and award presentations, commemorative addresses occur at several moments during our lives. Key strategies for successfully commemorating an idea, person, or event almost always rely on emotional language that constructs a story about the person or object being honored.

## KEY TERMS

eulogy   319

gravitas   318

rhetorical history   319

## REVIEW QUESTIONS

1. In what ways are commemorative speeches different from informative speeches?
2. In what ways are commemorative speeches different from persuasive speeches?
3. What are three general types of epideictic addresses?
4. What are the goals of a commemorative speech?
5. Describe a language strategy for evoking pathos in a commemorative address.

## THINK ABOUT IT

1. Is there a fourth genre of speech, other than informative, persuasive, and epideictic?
2. How does language evoke emotion in an audience?
3. Are there certain occasions where negative language would be called for in an epideictic address?
4. Do different types of epideictic address have different challenges?

1.  Brainstorm on a piece of paper all the "special occasions" where you have heard an epideictic speech. Then, next to each, briefly explain why they were not informative or persuasive speeches.

2.  Take a few minutes and try to come up with actual examples of each type of epideictic speech identified in this chapter. What are their common themes? Characteristics? What is different about each?

## ENDNOTES

1.  Barack H. Obama, "Remarks by the President at Memorial Service at Fort Hood," http://www.whitehouse.gov/the-press-office/remarks-president-memorial-service-fort-hood (accessed November 24, 2009).

2.  Ibid.

3.  George W. Bush, "National Thanksgiving Turkey Spared," http://www.whitehouse.gov/news/releases/2002/11/20021126-4.html (accessed July 8, 2008).

4.  Maya Angelou Biography, http://www.achievement.org/autodoc/page/ang0bio-1 (accessed June 14, 2011).

5.  http://www.americanrhetoric.com/speeches/mayaangeloueulogyforcorettaking.htm (accessed June 14, 2011).

6.  Ibid.

7.  Ibid.

8.  George H. W. Bush, "Eulogy for Ronald Reagan," http://www.americanrhetoric.com/speeches/georgehbushreaganeulogy.htm (accessed July 9, 2008).

THE SPEAKER:  The Tradition and Practice of Public Speaking

# Constructing an Epideictic Address

## 16

### CHAPTER OVERVIEW

- Discusses how to construct an introduction to an epideictic address
- Describes the primary method for organizing the body of an epideictic address
- Explains ways to conclude an epideictic address

# Practically SPEAKING

As we mentioned in the previous chapter, one occasion that calls for an epideictic speech is a death. This practice was as common in Classical Greece as it is today, perhaps even more so. In fact, after wars prominent statesmen and public figures were chosen to give speeches to the public in honor of the dead. One such figure who gave at least two funeral orations after wars was Pericles of Athens, considered by many historians to be one of the greatest city leaders during that period.

Although we do not have the actual texts of his speeches verbatim, we have transcriptions from the Athenian historian, Thucydides, who attempted to capture the essence of Pericles's speeches in his notes. In what we now refer to as Pericles's *Funeral Oration*, the Athenian leader not only honored the dead from a recent war, but used the occasion to articulate what he understood as the appropriate relationship between the individual and the state. In short, he used the speech to connect the people to their government through the meaning he ascribed to the occasion.

When Pericles spoke to the public, rather than referring to the dead as individuals, he chose to provide their deaths with a larger meaning. He recognized the immense sadness and possible reduction of faith in the state that can come from so much loss of life, so he used his *Funeral Oration* to remind the audience that the nation was worthy of such sacrifice. In effect, he praised both the fallen of the city and the city itself.[1]

The *Funeral Oration* itself is organized into four distinct parts, with an introduction and conclusion accounting for two of them. The body is topically separated between honoring the dead and honoring the city. The speech was, obviously, a speech of praise and Pericles's organization allowed him to do just that.

We may not think that these types of public eulogies occur in today's society, but they are, in fact, more common than we might think. Lincoln's speech at Gettysburg was a public eulogy, for instance. Also, when former presidents pass away there is broadcast coverage of their funerals where state officials, and often the current president, give eulogies. An even more recent example came when President Barack Obama eulogized those who lost their lives when a gunman opened fire at an event sponsored by Congresswoman Gabrielle Giffords at a Tucson, Arizona, supermarket on January 8, 2011.

In his speech, Obama did much the same thing as Pericles in terms of using the moment to honor the deceased and praise the country. So, as you can see, public eulogies are just as common and just as potent as they were in ancient Greece and they serve the same purposes.

Eulogies are just one type of epideictic address, as we noted in the last chapter, but the organizational structure and style of each form of epideictic speech is relatively similar. In this chapter we will discuss those common attributes in terms of how to construct an introduction, body, and conclusion for an epideictic speech.

# Epideictic Speech Introductions

From their very beginning, epideictic addresses are very different from informative and persuasive forms of speech. We mentioned in the last chapter what some of those differences were, as well as a few similarities. In this section we will elaborate on those differences by explaining how to craft an effective introduction for an epideictic address. First, we will discuss the formulation of the specific purpose statement for an epideictic address. Then we will explain the elements of an introduction, as it requires different things than introductions for informative and persuasive speeches.

## Formulating the Specific Purpose

In his discussion of epideictic speeches, Aristotle described them as speeches designed to "praise or blame" something or someone. Although a bit simple, this is a rather accurate account of what these types of speeches do and how they differ from informative and persuasive speeches. That said, it is important for us to understand the complex nature of these speeches in a bit more detail. In this part of the chapter we will discuss how to articulate the complex nature of an epideictic address from the very start.

First, let's take a look at determining the general purpose. This is a relatively simple task for informative and persuasive speeches as the general purpose flows from their labels. That is to say, the general purpose for an informative speech is "to inform," and the general purpose for a persuasive speech is "to persuade." This, however, is not the case with epideictic speech. It makes no sense to have a general purpose stated as "to epideictic." Instead, the general purpose is a bit more varied depending on the occasion. It could be, for instance, "to celebrate," "to praise," or "to commemorate," just to name a few. Understanding the general purpose of an epideictic speech is essential for developing the speech in an effective manner, but then so is knowing what the specific purpose is as well.

The specific purpose for an epideictic speech is always tied to the moment or the occasion on which you give the speech. It also needs to articulate the value or idea that the occasion represents, because with epideictic speech the event or person is not the most important element of the speech; rather, celebrating the value or idea that person or thing represents is the core purpose of an epideictic speech. For instance, Candy's general purpose is to commemorate, and her specific purpose is to commemorate the new Gordon P. Goodspeed Library on her campus. The building was named after a person who graduated from the college, went on to write 15 national best-selling novels, and then donated the funds to build the library. If that is the context, then her specific purpose statement might be: "To commemorate the opening of the Gordon P. Goodspeed Library in honor of a distinguished graduate who valued education." This specific purpose ties the event to a value and captures the essential points in Candy's speech by providing an explanation of the person and event, as well as the importance of education represented by this building.

In short, the specific purpose of epideictic address is to discuss the larger meaning inherent in an event, person, or thing. This is quite different from an informative speech in which the specific purpose is to describe, define, or teach an audience about something. When starting to write an epideictic address, it is important that you identify the larger value represented by the topic of your speech in your specific purpose (see Table 16.1). Think back to the example of Pericles in the opening of the chapter. He used the funeral for soldiers to talk not about what happened to them but about the ideas they represented and for which they fought and died. After developing a clear specific purpose for your epideictic address, you can then move on to crafting the speech itself, and that begins with the introduction.

**Table 16.1**

| Specific Purpose Examples for Epideictic Speeches | |
|---|---|
| Eulogy | "To present to the audience the major achievements and characteristics of the deceased" |
| Acceptance speech | "To thank all those who made my winning the award possible" |
| Toast | "To inform the audience of my intent to honor the person at the event" |

## Strategies for Epideictic Introductions

As you might guess, epideictic speeches have quite different introductions than informative and persuasive speeches. First, the types of attention-getters they use are different, simply because of the nature of the speech. In terms of establishing a thesis or an argument, there again is a difference between the three speeches. Finally, in an epideictic speech, previews are either not used at all or they are very subtle. It may be that the only real common element between the three different speeches and their introductions is the need for a clear and appropriate transition to the body.

### Attention-Getters

Attention-getters serve an important function for both informative and persuasive speeches, and they are central to an epideictic address as well, although not in the same way. Audiences for epideictic addresses typically want to be there to hear the speech, and as such you do not need to fight to get their attention immediately. Instead, you should use the attention-getter to reinforce for the audience why they (and you) are in attendance. As a means of illustrating, let's return to the speech being given by Candy. Everyone at the dedication of the new library has chosen to attend and expects to hear a speech, so getting their attention is not the main purpose of the attention-getter in her speech; rather, her attention-getter is designed to remind them of the importance of that choice to attend. So, beginning her speech with a statement to that effect helps achieve those ends: "Thank you for coming here today to dedicate our new library, a building that will serve as the foundation for future student education here at the university." This statement captures the audience not by startling them or telling them something they did not know. Instead, it reminds them of what the library represents to the university (education), thus reinforcing the importance of the event and by extension their attendance.

## Reinforcement Statements

You might recall that in other speeches, once you have delivered your opening line you need to quickly move to your thesis or argument. Although you need to establish your central idea in the introduction of an epideictic speech, it is not entirely a thesis in the informative speech sense, nor is it an argument as described for persuasive speeches. Epideictic speeches use what we will call a **reinforcement statement**, or an expression of the connection between the event and the social value it represents. We call it reinforcement because members of the audience typically share the value and so, as a speaker, you simply reinforce the importance and power of that social value. This relationship between the speech, the event, and the social value it represents is illustrated in Figure 16.1.

**reinforcement statement**
an expression of the connection between the event and the social value it represents

The main point of an epideictic speech varies depending on the type of speech it is, but it always includes two elements. The first is an emotional dimension. For instance, if you are accepting an award, your reinforcement statement should express humility and/or gratitude. If, however, you are introducing someone for an award, it should contain a level of pride and happiness. In terms of eulogies, grief should be there but it should be tempered with hope.

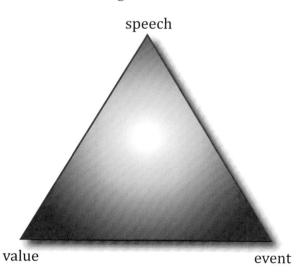

**Figure 16.1**
**Epideictic Elements**

Providing the emotional dimension for understanding the event/person/thing that the speech is about is a central component of the reinforcement statement in the introduction of an epideictic address.

The second component of a reinforcement statement is the connection between the value and the event itself. Not only must the statement evoke an emotional appreciation for the moment, it also must articulate the value the moment represents. In short, it must create an image of the event as a symbol for something larger. What is the meaning behind the occasion that has brought everyone together to hear your speech? For instance, Coach Parsons is about to announce the winner of the "Most Improved Player" for the high school basketball team. His reinforcement statement is as follows: "This guy worked harder than any player I have ever coached, always asking for extra practice time and always pushing himself in the weight room." Here the topic is clear (the winner of the award) and the value the individual and the award represents is also clear: hard work.

The purpose of a reinforcement statement in an epideictic speech is the same as the purpose of a thesis statement in an informative speech and an argument in a persuasive speech. All three share some qualities but they are different in two primary respects. First, a reinforcement statement contains a strong degree of emotionality. Second, a reinforcement statement connects the occasion to some higher shared social value. Once you have developed an introduction and a reinforcement statement, it is time to finish the introduction of your epideictic address.

### Remainder of Introduction

As we have discussed in previous chapters, informative and persuasive speeches contain a clear and deliberate preview in their introductions immediately following the thesis statement or argument. Epideictic speeches contain no such previews. In fact, if an epideictic speech contains a preview it is very subtle. We will not discuss how to construct such previews, but rather emphasize the need to move from the reinforcement statement to the body of the speech in a smooth fashion that does not take away from the heightened expectations and meaning established in your reinforcement statement.

Rather than previewing the stories that support the value inherent in the moment, the introduction needs to move directly to those stories. You do this by using a carefully crafted transition; often, this same transition serves as both the notice that the brief introduction is over and the introduction of the next topic. For example, in Pericles's *Funeral Oration,* he begins the first main point of his speech by stating, "I shall begin by speaking about our ancestors, since it is only right and proper on such an occasion to pay them the honor of recalling what they did."[3] In this transitional statement, Pericles moves from his opening discussion about what values and principles the deceased stood for to a discussion that connects the past to the present moment. It thus serves as a marker for the audience that something new is coming next.

Do not be fooled into thinking that because the introduction to an epideictic address is shorter it is therefore easier. In many ways it is harder because it needs to establish an emotional connection between the occasion, the speaker, the audience, and a shared social value in short order. This requires the more elaborate language we discussed in the previous chapter, as well as a clear understanding of the audience and the scene. Different occasions, however, call for different epideictic addresses, and in the next part of the chapter we will discuss how to organize and develop a body for various epideictic addresses.

# EPIDEICTIC SPEECH BODY

The body of an epideictic speech, regardless of the occasion, is also quite different from the bodies of informative and persuasive speeches. One primary difference is in the form of evidence. Epideictic speeches are a series of stories that serve as examples of the connection between the topic of the speech, the occasion, and the shared social value represented by the event. These stories are narratives and often do not include much in the way of startling statistics or testimony. What is essential when telling these stories is that the connection between the story and the shared social value is clear to the audience.

These stories are typically organized in one of two different ways. The first is chronological, like in the case of Pericles. Following this pattern you would be telling stories of the past in sequential order, but always connecting the purpose of the story to the shared social value that belies the speech. The other organizational pattern is topical, which works if there are multiple stories that illustrate different parts of the shared social value. Each part then becomes a topic, and the topics, not the chronology, dictate in which order the stories are presented. In this part of the chapter we will provide suggestions for the types of stories that might be used in the bodies of some common forms of epideictic speeches.

## Eulogies

Eulogies are often believed to be sad speeches, but they need not be. A good eulogy takes time and focus to develop because you need to determine the emotion you wish to convey to the audience, as well as identify the value the departed's life represented for everyone in attendance. Start the process of figuring this out by looking inward and seeing what the person meant to you. In terms of emotions, sadness is a natural part of a eulogy, but hope and happiness can also be part of the emotions of the day. After all, it is important to see a eulogy as a chance to celebrate the person's life and what they meant to those who were close to them.

The stories within the body of a eulogy should be examples of the shared value and feeling the person represented. You should not treat the stories as a simple chronology of their life, because then you reduce the meaning of the person to what they did, rather than what they represented. For example, Kassandra was asked to deliver a eulogy of her grandfather and in it she wanted to express the

## Remarks at the Tucson Memorial Service by President Barack Obama

Delivered January 12, 2011

On January 8, 2011, a deranged gunman, Jared Loughner, opened fire into a crowd seeking to meet U.S. Representative Gabrielle (Gabby) Giffords. Six people died, among them a federal judge and a nine-year-old girl, and many more were wounded. Representative Giffords suffered head wounds from the shooting and it was feared that this popular politician would also die (as of this writing, Representative Giffords is making a recovery that can only be labeled miraculous).[3]

This tragedy was shocking to the nation, but much more so to the community in which it occurred. It was only fitting that the President of the United States address the large crowd at the memorial service.

President Obama began his speech with these poignant words:

"To the families of those we've lost; to all who called them friends; to the students of this university, the public servants gathered tonight, and the people of Tucson and Arizona: I have come here tonight as an American who, like all Americans, kneels to pray with you today, and will stand by you tomorrow."[4]

He assured the audience that the nation stood with them, and he quoted comforting scripture.

He then gave a brief biography of each person who was killed, noting some had given their lives to save others. One of the most emotional segments was dedicated to the young girl who perished:

"And then there is nine-year-old Christina Taylor Green. Christina was an A student, a dancer, a gymnast, and a swimmer. She often proclaimed that she wanted to be the first woman to play in the major leagues, and as the only girl on her Little League team, no one put it past her. She showed an appreciation for life uncommon for a girl her age, and would remind her mother, 'We are so blessed. We have the best life.' And she'd pay those blessings back by participating in a charity that helped children who were less fortunate."[5]

The loss of anyone is a tragedy, but even more so when the unnecessary death is one who is so young. President Obama's story about Christina celebrated the energy of youth, and reinforced the idea that Americans of any age value and appreciate life. Later in this speech he said that heroes are found in everyday life and noted that the acts of the heroes in this tragedy were a challenge to everyone else to use the tragedy to make themselves become better. The speech celebrated lives in a personal way but did so while showing how those lives represented values larger than themselves—values every member of the community shared and celebrated.

**SPEAKING of CIVIC ENGAGEMENT**

idea that he represented the importance of generosity. With that as her goal, she told three stories that showed her grandfather giving his time, donating his money, and offering to help a friend in need. These stories were organized topically, not chronologically, but each allowed for a celebration of the individual and a reinforcement of the shared value of generosity.

The need for a story that provides some value or feeling shared with the person or group being eulogized is also apparent in public eulogies, like the one President Obama delivered in Tucson in 2011. Although he did not know any of the deceased victims, Obama crafted an artful story extolling the virtues of American society through the individuals who lost their lives in that horrific attack. He did this topically rather than chronologically because he did not know those who were killed and also did not want to spend time on what happened; rather he wanted to use what happened to help the community celebrate the lives of the individuals and turn them into a synecdoche for values cherished by Americans everywhere. In this speech, there is a clear connection between the eulogized, the stories told about them, and the values they represented; as such, it is good example of an epideictic address.

Eulogies do not always need to contain three main points; in fact, often they contain more. What is more important than the number of stories contained in the eulogy is that they are all related to the shared value you wish to express in the speech. Next, we will turn our attention to a happier form of epideictic address: wedding toasts.

## Wedding Toasts

Wedding toasts share some similarities with eulogies, but there are also some obvious differences. Both are epideictic in that their purpose is to express emotionality and a shared social value through the discussion of an event or moment. Both often include a celebration of love. One key difference, however, is in the brevity of wedding toasts compared to the sometimes extensive nature of eulogies. That brevity makes it even more important to have a tight focus and concise summary of the stories you tell in the body of the speech.

The best organizational pattern for a good wedding toast is topical. People in the audience already know the bride and groom (presumably) so you do not need to recount their lives to the audience. What you need to do is identify the shared social value you believe their partnership exemplifies. Often, people choose love or kindness, but other values could also work, like perseverance and a sense of community. Ask yourself, when you think of the couple, what value comes to mind? What does a marriage represent to you?

Your stories should then be illustrations of how the couple individually and/or together exemplifies that value. The stories should be short and you should use vivid language whenever possible. For example, if you wish to tell the story of when you first saw the couple together, which of the following versions do you think works best?

*Example A:* "I met Sandy and Charles together at a bar downtown."

*Example B:* "I first saw Sandy and Charles together at a swanky bar in downtown Seattle where we went to see a Coldplay concert."

Obviously, Example B has much greater detail and is more vivid for the audience. It also allows you to make a swift move to connecting that moment to the value represented by the two individuals.

As we mentioned in the last chapter, brevity is important with wedding toasts, so however many short stories you tell, make sure they are not so lengthy that they cause the speech to drone on and lose its meaning. In a perfect scenario, you can begin with a story about each of the individuals, followed by a story in which they are a couple, because that topical progression illustrates the event: two separate people joining as one in marriage. Next, we will discuss how to organize speeches delivered at award ceremonies.

## Award Ceremonies

Much like wedding toasts, award ceremony speeches are often expected to be short. There are some exceptions, such as when an entire event is in honor of one individual, but more often than not these speeches are only a few minutes at best. So, like wedding toasts, it is important to know what shared social value you wish to get across and select brief stories that will help demonstrate that value to the audience. This process is quite different when presenting and when accepting an award. In this part of the chapter we will discuss both.

Academy award winner
Sandra Bullock

When presenting an award, the focus should be on the value that the award itself represents, not on yourself or the individual receiving the honor. Again, the organization of the body should be topical or, in some circumstances, chronological. If you are to present one of many different awards (like the Oscars or Emmys), focus on values by sharing one or two brief stories. For instance, you might choose to recall the previous winner of the award and link their story to what the award represents. You also might focus on the namesake of the award and link their activities to the shared social value you believe the award demonstrates.

If, however, you are presenting an award to the sole honoree of the event (i.e., Person of the Year) then you have more time to build up the award winner and the moment. In this speech you might wish to focus on telling a chronology of stories from different stages of the honoree's life and tie each story to the shared social value. You also might use the tried and true topical method of picking certain aspects of the person's character that illustrate the shared social value, but do not necessarily come in sequence. Either way, these speeches must connect the moment, the honoree, and the value for the audience. When receiving an award, however, your body is slightly different.

There are two types of award acceptance speeches you might deliver. First, if you are the only honoree of the evening, or if you are the main honoree of a ceremony, then you will potentially deliver a long address. The other type of award acceptance speech occurs when you are one of many people receiving an award. In this instance you will give a very brief address. In each case it is important to know how much time you have to speak because that will determine the number of stories you will be able to place in the body of your speech.

In the event you are lucky enough to be the honoree at an event where you get to give a long speech, there are certain things you should consider when crafting your acceptance speech. First, what is the core value of the award or the group who is bestowing the award on you? Second, what stories can you tell that connect you to that mission or shared value? Let's look at an example.

Lionel Fox was being honored by United Cerebral Palsy, a nonprofit group that advocates for people with disabilities, for his hard work helping people with cerebral palsy in his neighborhood. In fact, the organization held a fundraiser around the event where Lionel was to be honored, and he was expected to deliver a speech accepting the award. He was told he would have about 10 minutes, and so he decided on four stories he wanted to tell, each about individuals with cerebral palsy with whom he worked. Each story reinforced the central mission of United Cerebral Palsy and exemplified the value of service to one's community. Because he had the time, Lionel was able to relay his stories in a very effective manner, but time is not something everyone has when they give an acceptance speech.

Award acceptance speeches are more often than not very short. Think about the amount of time people have to speak when accepting Oscars, Emmys, or Tonys. Usually they have a minute or less at those award ceremonies to deliver their speech, and in most instances you will have only a few minutes. This means you need to maximize the time you spend connecting the occasion to the shared value you wish to express. And as we have repeatedly mentioned, that value should be related to what the award represents.

The trick with a short acceptance speech is to find one or two examples that convey what you want to convey. Simply listing "thank yous" is an awful way to spend your time in the speech, but making the thank you part of a story that helps augment the meaning of the moment is a good way to structure the body of the speech. Acceptance speeches are very hard to deliver because of how short they are, which means even more care must go into creating them.

In the next part of this chapter we will discuss how to properly construct a conclusion to an epideictic address.

## EPIDEICTIC SPEECH CONCLUSIONS

Much like conclusions for informative and persuasive speeches, there needs to be a clear transition to the conclusion of an epideictic speech. One thing that is different, however, is that there is no definitive summary in an epideictic speech like there is in an informative or persuasive speech. Finally, the clincher of an epideictic speech is unique in that, in many cases, it does not refer to the topic but to the shared social value the topic represents. In this part of the chapter we will discuss what should be done instead of a summary and how to construct a good clincher for an epideictic speech.

## Summary

As we have mentioned, epideictic speeches do not contain summaries in the sense that informative and persuasive speeches do. Much like the preview in the introduction of an epideictic speech, the summary should be subtle and not defined. In short, do not say "First, we spoke about...then we discussed." This type of approach destroys the emotional dimension of the speech and does little to reinforce the shared social values you have spent the rest of the speech discussing. So, in lieu of a traditional summary, in an epideictic speech conclusion you should concentrate on the shared social value. Let's look at some examples in common epideictic speeches.

Eulogies do not conclude by simply restating the stories you relayed about the deceased. Instead, they conclude by stressing what those stories represented. For instance, if you tell a story about how the person always made you laugh when you were around them, then in the summary you might summarize that by stating how you learned to love life from the way they lived theirs. The focus, then, is not on the individual or their death, but rather on the meaning of their life.

As you might guess, wedding toasts do not lend themselves to the traditional summary either. These speeches typically end by connecting the shared social values the wedding represents to an expression of hope and luck for the future. For example, if you are concluding a toast to newlyweds, you might summarize a story you told in the body about how they met by saying something to the effect of, "May the spark you felt when you first met become the fire that fuels your relationship every day." Here passion and love become what is summarized, instead of what actually happened in the story.

Award speeches also do not allow for typical summaries in their conclusions. In presenting an award you need to use the conclusion to build toward the announcement of the award winner, and simply recapping the main points of the speech does not allow you to do this. In accepting an award, you also do not want to recall all the stories you just told the audience. In both instances, the summary should help the audience reconnect the shared social value being celebrated with the award and then, by extension, the award winner.

Summaries for epideictic addresses are much more subtle than in informative and persuasive speeches. Clinchers are also different in epideictic speeches, as we will discuss next.

## SPOTLIGHTING THEORISTS: KATHLEEN HALL JAMIESON AND KARLYN KOHRS CAMPBELL

Epideictic speeches are the most common type of speech we encounter. As you discovered in this chapter, they come in the form of wedding toasts, award speeches, and eulogies. All of those are speeches any individual might give or hear, but two scholars, Kathleen Hall Jamieson and Karlyn Kohrs Campbell, have focused some of their research on epideictic speeches delivered by presidents. In fact, their book on the genre of presidential rhetoric, *Deeds Done in Words*, contains several chapters on different forms of epideictic address delivered by various presidents of the United States. They point out that presidential inaugural addresses in particular help define the principles that guide our government and call on our commonalities in the wake of divisive elections. These important tasks are only accomplished through the use of epideictic address.

### Dr. Kathleen Hall Jamieson (1946– )

A noted rhetorical and political scholar, Hall Jamieson is the Elizabeth Ware Packard Professor of Communication at the Annenberg School for Communication and Walter and Leonore Annenberg Director of the Annenberg Public Policy Center on the campus of the prestigious University of Pennsylvania.[6] As director, she also supervises FactCheck, a nonprofit organization housed at Annenberg that looks into the factual accuracy of U.S. political advertisements.

Among many other awards and honors, she was awarded the Speech Communication Association's (now the National Communication Association) Golden Anniversary Book Award for *Packaging the Presidency* (Oxford, 1984) and *Eloquence in an Electronic Age* (Oxford, 1988).

Jamieson has often been interviewed on political issues on both public television and public radio and has been interviewed by Bill Moyers on PBS's NOW program.[7] She has researched and written on numerous political and rhetorical topics, focusing primarily on presidential discourse. She is known as one of the country's foremost experts on political advertising and campaigns.

### Dr. Karlyn Kohrs Campbell (1937– )

A professor in the Department of Communication Studies at the University of Minnesota, Campbell specializes in studying feminist and political discourse.

Since earning her Ph.D. from the University of Minnesota in 1968, Campbell has won many awards, chief among them the National Communication Association's Scholarship Award and an Honorary Doctorate of Humanities from Michigan State University.[8]

In addition to her current and previous work at Minnesota, she has also served in several different capacities elsewhere. She was a fellow with the Joan Shorenstein Center on the Press, Politics, and Public Policy at Harvard University's Kennedy School of Government in 1992. She was also the director of the Women's Center at the University of Kansas.

Jamieson and Campbell have been highly instrumental in our understanding of the uses of epideictic oratory, particularly as it pertains to presidential discourse.

# Clinchers

Clinchers serve different purposes in different epideictic speeches. In eulogies, they recall the meaning of the deceased's life for everyone in attendance. In wedding toasts, they express well wishes for the new bride and groom. Clinchers for award presentation speeches announce the winner, while those for award reception speeches thank the audience by expressing again how much the award means. In this part of the chapter we will briefly discuss the characteristics of an effective clincher in each of those types of commemorative speeches.

When you deliver a eulogy you spend quite a bit of time using stories to connect the audience with the meaning inherent in the life of the deceased. The clincher represents your last opportunity to stress that connection to the audience. It should strike a somber, yet hopeful, tone and concentrate more on the undying quality of the shared social value you connected the person to, rather than on the person himself.

Wedding toasts must strike a happy and hopeful tone, something quite different from a eulogy. As is typical with these occasions, the shared social value usually is love or passion, and that should be stressed again in the clincher while also wishing the newlyweds luck in their future together. Unlike some conventional approaches, it is inadvisable to have a humorous clincher for a wedding toast, as it should be a serious expression of happiness and hope.

Award introduction speeches represent unique epideictic speeches and as such their clinchers are also unique. The clincher for an award introduction speech is almost always the same, in that it is the time when you name the award recipient for the first time. Just naming the recipient, however, is not enough because you have spent a great deal of time in your speech establishing a connection between the individual, the award, and a shared social value they both represent. It is important to creatively introduce the individual so the audience carries the connection of the three elements (award, recipient, shared social value) into the person's appearance and subsequent acceptance speech. The key point to remember with these speeches is that the name of the person is what the audience has waited to hear.

When accepting a speech, clinchers must again carefully continue to connect the shared social value with the award. This is done through using the clincher to express a deep appreciation for the meaning of the award and your subsequent reception of it. Thanking the audience is not enough in a clincher for an award acceptance speech, you must also express your understanding of what the award means to you and to those in attendance.

# A Final Note on Epideictic Speeches

Although we have focused on three primary forms of epideictic addresses in our discussion of introductions, bodies, and conclusions, there are a variety of other types of commemorative speeches, and many of these speeches are not only known to you, but are subjects of significant critical analysis. For instance, many scholars have paid a lot of attention to presidential inaugural speeches. In fact,

Kathleen Hall Jamieson and Karlyn Kohrs Campbell have examined inaugurals and developed five characteristics that every inaugural shares (see the nearby box). The point is, epideictic speech is more common than you might first believe and an important part of our lives. It is much more than speech for special occasions; it is the speech that makes mundane occasions special.

## SUMMARY

In this chapter we extended our conversation about epideictic address by providing you with more concrete ways to develop an effective commemorative speech. We began by exploring the elements of a good epideictic introduction, specifically by showing how it does not contain a traditional preview. We then explained that most, if not all, epideictic addresses are topically organized around stories that exemplify the shared social value that underlies the speech's purpose. Finally, we discussed the different elements of epideictic conclusions and showed that, among other things, they do not contain traditional summaries.

## KEY TERMS

reinforcement statement    335

## REVIEW QUESTIONS

1. What is the thesis statement or argument called in an epideictic speech?

2. What component(s) of an introduction is not in an epideictic speech but is in informative and persuasive speeches?

3. What is the primary way of organizing the main points in an epideictic speech?

4. What are the three elements that need to be connected in an epideictic speech?

5. What component(s) of a conclusion is not in an epideictic speech but is in informative and persuasive speeches?

## THINK ABOUT IT

1. What other forms of epideictic speeches are common in society?

2. Can you imagine an epideictic address not tied to a shared social value?

3. How do you determine the stories you use as main points in an epideictic address?

4. Which type of epideictic address would be most difficult for you to perform? Why?

## ACTIVITIES FOR ACTION

1. Think about your best friend, and then prepare and deliver a wedding toast as the maid of honor or best man at his or her wedding.

2. Imagine you are nearing the end of your life at some point in the future. Think about all those things you had hoped to accomplish in your life and the things for which you would like to be remembered. Now, write an obituary that would appear in a local paper following your untimely death. Then, write a eulogy that you would like someone to deliver for you at your own funeral. Finally, look at both the obituary and the eulogy and identify the similarities and differences between the two.

## ENDNOTES

1. Richard A. Katula, "Seven Greek and Roman Speeches," in *A Synoptic History of Classical Rhetoric* (2nd Ed.), edited by James J. Murphy and Richard A. Katula with Forbes I. Hill, Donovan J. Ochs, and Prentice A. Meador (Davis, CA: Hermagoras Press, 1995), 221-223.

2. Katula, 221.

3. "In Attack's Wake, Political Repercussions," http://www.nytimes.com/2011/01/09/us/politics/09giffords.html (accessed June 14, 2011).

4. Text of President Obama's Memorial Speech, http://www.nytimes.com/2011/01/09/us/politics/09giffords.html (accessed June 14, 2011).

5. Ibid.

6. http://www.asc.upenn.edu/ascfaculty/FacultyBio.aspx?id=129 (accessed April 28, 2009).

7. http://www.pbs.org/now/politics/jamieson.html (accessed April 28, 2009).

8. http://www.comm.umn.edu/faculty/profile.php?UID=campb003 (accessed April 28, 2009).

# Appendix

# SPEECH EXAMPLES

## Persuasive Speech: "Finish Your Degree"

I ran into a high school friend of mine the other day, a person who finished in the top 10 percent of our class but decided to drop out of college in the middle of sophomore year. She is now working as a manager at a local department store—the same store she worked at in high school. This person makes about $12 an hour and has some benefits as a full-time employee—but no more room for growth at the company. I don't tell this story to get you to pity her, but rather to illustrate the difference between finishing a college degree and not doing so. As a college student with dreams of my own that involve more than managing a department store, I decided to research some more concrete information on why we should all finish our degree programs. Even though there is nothing you can do to guarantee success in life, I want to encourage you to get that degree, and today I am going to tell you why. First, I will share the economic benefits of finishing college. Then I am going to explain the other benefits you can earn in the job market with a college degree. Finally, I am going to detail the health and wellness incentives for finishing your degrees. So, let's get started so that we can finish our degrees.

Our professors think a degree makes us a more rounded person, but let's be honest, we want the degree for financial reasons. The United States Census Bureau shows that an associate's degree recipient will make approximately $1.2 million

This short story serves to capture the audience's attention by making the topic of the speech real for them.

This statement establishes the speaker's credibility by citing his/her position as a student and explaining that the speaker did research the topic.

These sentences preview how the speaker plans on making his/her case to the audience.

Here is the speaker's argument, clearly stated for the audience.

This is an effective, if simple, transition to the main body of the speech.

Here is proper verbal attribution of the source of the evidence the speaker used to support his/her claim.

more than a person with just a high school degree throughout his/her working career, and it gets even better for those who complete their BA. Listen to this: A person with a bachelor's degree will earn around $2.1 million more in his/her career than a worker with just a high school degree.[1] My friends, does that sound significant to you? It does to me.

The economics don't just stop with total earnings. In 2007–2008 the U. S. economy went into recession and we all heard the gloomy forecasts about investments, and most especially the high unemployment numbers. Fox News reported in December 2008 that those without a college degree had a jobless rate of 7.2%, but those with a degree had a jobless rate of 3.7%.[2] That report quoted Lawrence Mishel, president of the Economic Policy Institute in Washington, D.C., as saying: "College grads have a privileged position in the labor market.'"[3] One of the reasons is that a person with a degree earns more and has a more secure job, but it is also much easier for a person with a college degree to take a demotion.[4] Essentially, a college degree gives you more security. Now that I have provided you with evidence that the college degree is worth the effort economically, let's look at some other benefits to getting that degree.

With a college degree you get more money, and with that you also get better benefits. A report by Collegeboard.com in 2007 noted that college graduates are more likely to have a job that provides health insurance and retirement benefits. College grads also are noted as having better overall health, probably because of their health insurance.[5] Degreeadvantage. com noted that studies show that a college graduate's children had a better life, were able to save more money, made wiser decisions on purchases, and had improved time off work. It also noted that research found that college grads are more rational thinkers, more willing to accept other opinions, more consistent in their application of logic and ethics, and better managers."[6] Additionally, grads "pass on" those positive things to future descendants.[7]

Here is proper verbal attribution of the source of the evidence the speaker used to support his/her claim.

Here is a rhetorical question embedded within the speech. The audience is not expected to answer it, but it serves the purpose of transitioning to the next point and underscoring the power of the previous evidence.

Not convinced to stick with your degree program? Well here is more evidence. The collegeboard.com report I mentioned earlier noted that college grads are less likely to smoke, pay more in taxes to society, and are less likely to need government assistance. Additionally, college grads are more likely to be involved in civic activities, volunteer, vote, donate their own blood, and be tolerant of the opinions of others.[8] All in all, in addition to the doors of financial opportunity a college degree opens, what those college professors tell you about becoming a well-rounded citizen through your college education is also true. There really is a reason why getting a college degree is so coveted by our parents, families, and society.

Here is a useful example of a metaphor in that opportunity is not actually a door.

Here is a signpost for the conclusion.

In summary, there are significant financial advantages to getting a college degree. With a college degree you will earn an average of over $2 million more than if you dropped out, and you are much more likely to have a job in a down economy like the one we face today. Then there are the quality of life issues for both you and your family. You will be more likely to have health insurance; you will live a happier life; you will be more open-minded; and, you will be more likely to get involved in the community. Yeah, it may take awhile, but we are all here anyway so let's finish that degree to improve our lives. As Nike has said for years: "Just do it."

Here is a summary of the main points offered within the speech.

This employs a famous quotation from an ad campaign as the clincher.

## ENDNOTES

1. Jennifer Cheeseman Day and Eric C. Newburger, "The Big Payoff: Educational Attainment and Synthetic Estimates of Work-Life Earnings," *Current Population Reports, Special Studies*, 23-210, Washington, D.C.: Commerce Dept., Economics and Statistics Administration, Census Bureau. [Online], 2002, http://www.census.gov/prod/2002pubs/p23-210.pdf (accessed December 3, 2009).
2. Christopher Leonard, "College Grads Avoid Brunt of Layoffs," *Foxnews.com*, January 10, 2009, http://www.foxnews.com/wires/2009Jan10/0,4670,MeltdownCollegeGraduates,00.html (accessed December 3, 2009).
3. Ibid.

4. Ibid.

5. Sandy Baum and Jennifer Ma, "Education Pays: The Benefits of Higher Education for Individuals and Society," *College Board* (2007), http://www.collegeboard.com/prod_downloads/about/news_info/trends/ed_pays_2007.pdf (accessed December 3, 2009).

6. Larry L. Rowley and Sylvia Hurtado, "The Non-Monetary Benefits of an Undergraduate Education," University of Michigan: Center for the Study of Higher and Postsecondary Education, 2002.

7. Ibid.

8. Baum and Ma, "Education Pays."

# Informative Speech: "Black Friday"

This is a solid attention-getter because it uses material an audience can relate to in order to draw them in to listen.

To all of us, Thanksgiving means time with family, watching football, eating good food, and sleeping off turkey-coma. To companies, it also means that Black Friday is right around the corner. We have all heard of Black Friday, the day that follows Thanksgiving, but have you ever wondered where its nickname comes from and what it actually means? That is, what it means beyond lots of shopping! Well, as a general manager of a major retail store here in town who depends on Black Friday, I want to help explain both how Black Friday earned its dark moniker and why it is important to you and me. First, I will discuss what the term "black" means in relation to this specific date. Then, I will discuss why the day is so popular for retailers and stores around the country. Finally, I will discuss what Black Friday typically means for the holiday season to you, me, and the country. That meaning, however, begins with understanding the date's dark designation.

This is the speaker's credibility statement that tells the audience why s/he is qualified to speak about the topic.

Here is a clear preview of the main points of the speech and the order in which they will appear. It also indicates the main points will be conveyed in a topical order.

Here is the speaker's thesis statement that clearly lays out the goal of the speech.

"The date's dark designation" is a good example of alliterative language in that three words in a row start with the same consonant sound.

Here is a solid transition from the introduction to the body of the speech.

The term "black" has either a racial meaning or a negative association in most uses; however, it has an altogether different meaning when it comes to Black Friday. "Black" is often crudely used to denote someone who is African American in descent; however, Black Friday is not an ethnic holiday or celebration. "Black" also can mean dark, or evil, as in "black magic" or "black stain," but Black Friday is neither evil nor dark . . . unless of course you get up at 3 a.m. to wait in line for Best Buy to open! "Black" as it is used in Black Friday actually has its origins in accounting. When companies are in debt they are said to be "in the red," but when they are making money then they are "in the black." Black Friday is called "black" because it is the day that signals the largest sales period for companies around the country. Essentially, it is the day they start to move from the red on the balance sheet to the black. But why is the Friday following Thanksgiving the day that is most important to retailers for sales? The answer is simple, really.

This is an example of a rhetorical question, where even though the speaker is asking something, s/he is not waiting for the audience to answer. Rather, the speaker answers the question for the audience.

The largest retail shopping period of the year occurs before the Christmas holiday in December, and the Friday after Thanksgiving is the kick-off to the holiday shopping season. For many workers, the day after Thanksgiving is the last holiday they have before Christmas, so they take advantage of it by getting most of their holiday shopping out of the way early. People purchase toys, clothes, books, music, and electronics to give away to family and friends as holiday gifts. Heck, we even buy ourselves holiday gifts on Black Friday. In fact, according to the National Retail Federation, from 1999–2008 holiday retail sales during this period accounted for between 18.49% and 20.51% of the entire retail sales for the year.[1] That's roughly 9% of the year accounting for 20% of the sales for the year. Black Friday, as the first official day of the holiday season, is often seen as a barometer for how well retailers will do in the days leading up to Christmas. Now that I have illustrated where Black Friday gets its name and why it is deserved, I will next explain why this date is an important one for all of us.

> Here the speaker provides evidence that supports the main point about Black Friday as the beginning of the largest shopping period of the year.

> The word barometer in this context is actually an example of a metaphor. A barometer measures atmospheric pressure, but here it is used to mean something different.

> This is a topic sentence indicating the main point of this section of the speech.

> This is an example of an internal summary because it lays out what has already been covered in the speech.

As many of us know, our governments are funded by taxes, and one type of tax that generates revenue for our cities, towns, counties, and states is a sales tax. Sales taxes are used to fund things like education, road repairs, health services, and other such essential social programs, and thus they are very important for all of us as we all use them at one time or another. Sales taxes are generated when we purchase most products, with the exception of things like food and prescription medicine. The more retailers sell, the more taxes the government generates, the better the services it can provide for the community. So given the high percentage of sales in late November and December, having a strong holiday shopping season indicated by a strong showing on Black Friday is essential for the year-round operations of government. Black Friday, then, is an important day to watch for all of us, and not just because of the great sales and deals that appear in stores everywhere!

This is a signpost that is used by the speaker to indicate the beginning of the conclusion.

Here is the summary of the main points provided within the body of the speech.

Finally, it is important to understand that Black Friday is more than just a day at the mall. It is the day that begins the period where retail stores return to making a profit thanks to large numbers of holiday shoppers and their purchases. It also gives an indication of how much in sales taxes our government will collect, thereby helping us see what social services they will be able to provide. Black Friday is perhaps the most important shopping day of the year for all of us. So, once you wake up from your turkey-coma, remember all those big sales you saw in the paper while eating gobs of pumpkin pie were not dreams, but vital attempts to drum up business.

This is a simple restatement of the thesis for the entire speech, just to remind the audience again what they were supposed to learn from the speech.

Here is an example of a simple, yet effective, clincher for an informative speech. It relates back to the attention-getter at the start of the speech through the reference to turkey-coma, providing nice closure for the entire speech.

## ENDNOTES

1. National Retail Federation, "2009 Holiday Survival Guide," http://www.nrf.com/modules.php?name=Pages&sp_id=1142 (accessed December 2, 2009).

THE SPEAKER:  The Tradition and Practice of Public Speaking

# Key Terms

## A

**abstract 162**
words are not concrete or tangible items; they are only representations

**accent 83**
nonverbal behaviors that augment a verbal message

**acceptance 259**
the third step in the persuasive process where the audience decides whether or not to agree with the position advocated by the speaker

**accuracy 54**
the truthfulness or correctness of a source

**achievers 146**
people who are motivated by success, politically conservative, and work-oriented; they value the familiar

**acoustics 117**
the way sound travels in a room

**active listening 38**
listening to understand a message by processing, storing, and potentially evaluating a message; it also involves reactions by the listener in some form

**ad hominem fallacy 285**
when speakers attack the person making the argument and not the argument itself

**ad populum fallacy 284**
when we attempt to persuade people by arguing our position is reasonable because so many other people are doing it or agree with it

**ad verecundium fallacy 284**
an appeal for persuasion based on higher authority or tradition

**alliteration 169**
repeating the same consonant or vowel sound at the beginning of subsequent words

**ambiguous 162**
language that does not have precise, concrete meanings

**ambushing 40**
selective listening where the audience ignores the strengths of a message and hears only the weaknesses

**American Psychological Association (APA)  63**
preferred reference manual for social scientific communication scholars

**antecedent  273**
the hypothetical condition in the major premise of a conditional syllogism

**antithesis  169**
two ideas that sharply contrast with each other and are juxtaposed in a parallel grammatical structure

**anxiety disorder  30**
abnormal mental outlook where individuals experience high levels of apprehension that keep them from living life

**apologia  255**
a forensic speech that makes a defense against an accusation

**arbitrary  161**
symbols used to represent things that are not intrinsically connected to those things

**argument  296**
also called the proof or confirmation; the portion of the speech that validates your position on the issue laid out in the statement of facts

**arguments from the past  167**
appropriating historical events, facts, or people to justify present or future actions or explain events in the here-and-now

**arrangement  13**
the second canon of rhetoric where you determine the most effective way to organize your case for the topic and the audience

**articulation  76**
physically producing the sound needed to convey the word

**artistic proof  11**
constructed by the speaker for the occasion; concerns ethos, pathos, and logos

**asymmetrical balance  105**
emphasizes imbalance, thus creating an impression of stress, energy, and excitement

**attention-getter  229**
a device that immediately attracts the audience's interest to the subject that the speaker plans to discuss

**axial balance  105**
formal balance that strives for equal distribution of the elements of a visual so they do not appear tilted on one side of the image

# B

**background information  57**
material that provides context for a topic

**backing  280**
the justification for a warrant

**balance  105**
the positioning of elements within the image

**begging-the-question fallacy  282**
when a speaker presumes certain things are facts when they have not yet been proven to be truthful

**believers  146**
people motivated by ideals, but who do not have a significant amount of resources

**bias  54**
presenting information in a way that unfairly influences someone's perception of something

**bookend approach  116**
a version of the moderator approach whereby the first speaker in a group presentation is also the last speaker, providing both the introduction and conclusion for the group

# C

**categorical syllogism  272**
a syllogism in which the argument is based on membership in a group

**cause and effect arrangement  237**
orders your points first by discussing the cause of something that occurred and then moving to an explanation of the impact of its occurrence

**central claim  279**
the main point of which you seek to convince the audience

**channel  17**
the mode through which the message is conveyed to another party

**chart  95**
a visual device that helps you summarize and/or list blocks of information

**Chicago Manual of Style (CMS)  63**
preferred reference manual for rhetorical studies

**chronological order  235**
arranging points in the order in which they occur, or occurred, from start to finish

**civic engagement  21**
acting upon a sharp awareness of one's own sense of responsibility to his or her community

**claim  279**
the idea that you are seeking to convey

**clarity  11**
the ability of speakers to clearly articulate what they wish to say

**classroom response systems  154**
devices that allow students to answer questions posed during a lecture and provide tabulated results of the poll for everyone in the room in a timely manner

**clincher  244**
the final statement of your speech

**coercion  263**
the use of force or threats to make someone do something against his or her will

**color pattern  103**
collection of hues in your presentation aids

**communication apprehension  30**
the fear or anxiety associated with real or anticipated communication with another or others

**Communication/Mass Media Complete  59**
an electronic database for academic journals and popular sources related to communication and journalism

**comparative advantage  305**
an organizational pattern that uses each main point to explain why the speaker's solution is better than another proposed solution

**complement  83**
when the action demonstrates the message contained in the verbal content

**comprehension  258**
the second step in the persuasive process in which the speaker provides context for the issue in dispute so the audience understands what the speaker is talking about

**condensation symbol  126**
an element that evokes emotions by condensing them into one symbolic event

**conditional syllogism  273**
a syllogism in which the major premise contains a hypothetical condition and its outcome

**conference call  119**
use of the telephone to connect more than two parties on the same phone call

**conflict  83**
nonverbal cues that convey a message that contradicts the verbal statements of the speaker

**conjectural stasis  251**
when the issue in dispute is whether something occurred or not

**consequent  273**
the outcome of the hypothetical condition in the major premise of a conditional syllogism

**context  219**
the conditions surrounding the event

**contrast  106**
how objects and letters stick out from the background

**coordination  182**
all information on the same level has the same significance

**correctness  11**
the accuracy of information presented and the honest representation of the speaker

**crescendo  153**
an organizational pattern where the strongest point is placed at the end and is built up to by smaller main points

**critical thinking  223**
the ability for students to evaluate on their own the material they learn

# D

**dais** 122
the area a speaker speaks from

**decoding** 17
the process of taking a message that has been sent and using one's own experiences and knowledge to give it meaning

**deductive reasoning** 271
an argument that reasons from known premises to an inevitable conclusion

**definitive stasis** 252
when the issue in dispute is the meaning of a term

**dehumanization** 171
making people seem less than human in order to more easily motivate action against them

**deliberative speech** 255
one of two forms of persuasive speech proposed by Aristotle; it often takes place in legislative settings and focuses on discussing policies and actions to be taken

**delivery** 13
the fourth canon of rhetoric; the manner in which you physically and vocally present the speech

**demagoguery** 43
speech that attempts to win over an audience through appealing to their prejudices and emotions, particularly those of fear, anger, and frustration

**demographic data** 139
information on selected population characteristics used by the government, market researchers, and speech writers

**depth** 104
the graphic nature of an item; involves both level of detail and the amount of background provided for the image

**derived credibility** 261
your level of credibility during a speech that comes from what you say and how you say it

**Dewey Decimal Classification System** 59
the coding system for books, magazines, and journals used in libraries

**dialect** 76
aspects of articulation, grammar, vocabulary, and pronunciation that differ from Standard English

**disjunctive syllogism** 272
a syllogism in which the major premise includes two or more mutually exclusive alternatives

**division** 182
in order to divide a point you need to end up with two or more items

**dynamism** 262
a social science term for strong delivery that creates the impression with the audience that the speaker has practiced and thus cares about what he/she is talking about

# E

**efficacy  140**
the ability to produce a desired result

**either-or fallacy  284**
an argument in which you present two options and declare that one of them must be correct while the other must be incorrect

**encoding  16**
the process of attaching symbols to ideas and feelings so that others may understand them

**enkyklios paideia  48**
rounded education spread under the reign of Alexander the Great

**enthymeme  274**
a syllogism missing one or two of its parts

**episteme  8**
universal knowledge, or understanding about the common characteristics of like materials

**ethos  10**
the credibility of the speaker

**eulogy  319**
a speech that pays tribute to the life of the deceased

**evidentiary information  57**
information that supports main points within a speech and is directly related to the topic

**exigence  126**
a decisive point where a response is invited or required

**exit poll  139**
questions asked following an election that measure election results in terms of demographic categories

**exordium  293**
the place in the speech where you convince an audience to listen to your position; Latin label for the introduction of a speech

**experiencers  147**
people motivated by image who have the capability to express and improve it

**extemporaneous speech  86**
a speech delivered with notes but not the entire speech in front of the speaker

# F

**famous quotation  230**
actual statements closely related to the topic of the speech made by individuals the audience will easily recognize

**feedback  19**
the responses and reactions to the messages transmitted by the sender; is itself a new message sent back to the original sender

**figurative analogy  276**
when the two cases being compared are from completely different classifications

**fixed-response questions  148**
items on a survey that allow only for prescribed answers

**forensic speech  255**
an argument where speakers debate the facts of a case and attempt to answer questions of justice

**form  104**
how an item appears in terms of its representation, size, and texture

**formal survey  60**
time-consuming way of gathering data on a population that employs randomized sampling to ensure reliability and validity

**frame of reference  103**
our own singular perspective of the world around us

# G

**general purpose statement  183**
a brief statement representing what you aim to do with the speech; there are three types

**gesture  81**
a physical movement used to convey a message

**ghostwriting  56**
to write for and in the name of another person

**glazing over  40**
daydreaming instead of hearing the message

**global plagiarism  56**
taking an entire speech from a single source and pawning it off as your own

**graph  93**
a presentation device that indicates relationships found in numerical data

**gravitas  318**
importance

**grounds  280**
evidence in the Toulmin model

# H

**harmony  105**
when all parts and aspects of the presentation aid complement one another within the aid's framework

**hate speech  170**
rude and crude speech that attacks or demeans a particular social or ethnic group, many times with the intent of inciting action against that group

**hearing  36**
the physiological process of processing sounds, conducted by one's ears and brain

**heckler 130**
a self-aggrandizing member of the audience who tries to distract from the speech by confronting the speaker in the middle of a presentation

**hierarchical 163**
language that is structured according to more or less, higher or lower

# I

**ideograph 166**
an ill-defined, politically powerful term or phrase that can push people to action

**impromptu speech 87**
a presentation done with little or no preparation

**inartistic proof 11**
all the evidence, data, and documents that exist outside of the speaker and the audience, but nevertheless can aid in persuasion

**incremental plagiarism 55**
failure to give proper credit for parts of a speech that are borrowed from others

**inductive reasoning 275**
an argument that comes to a probable, instead of an absolute, conclusion

**informal survey 60**
polling a few people based on convenience

**information literacy 53**
the ability to figure out the type of information you need, find that information, evaluate it, and properly use it

**informative speech 209**
provides information in as neutral an environment as possible, where the speaker and the audience typically seek to teach and learn

**initial credibility 232**
the level of believability a speaker has before beginning his or her speech

**innovators 146**
people involved in change, who have high self-esteem and plenty of personal resources

**insinuation 294**
a form of exordium reserved for cases made about disputed topics to audiences with animosity toward the topic or the speaker

**integration 259**
the fourth stage in the persuasive process in which the audience makes the speaker's position a part of its own personal philosophy and worldview

**intermediate knowledge 8**
knowing what does not reflect an excess or a defect but instead what is intuitively correct to the persona

**internal preview 241**
serves as an outline of what is to come next in a speech and is often combined with transition statements

**internal summary 241**
a statement that summarizes what you already have covered and precedes transitions

**interviewing** 60
a direct method of gathering information from a human source that allows for questions to adapt to responses

**introduction** 294
one form of exordium where speakers use plain language to lay out their case in an effort to get a confused and ill-informed audience to pay attention

**invention** 12
the first canon of rhetoric where you choose the best possible arguments for your case

**issue awareness** 258
the first step in the persuasive process whereby the speaker alerts the audience about the issue requiring its attention

# J

**jargon** 217
terminology that relates to a specific activity

**JSTOR** 59
an electronic database for political journals

# K

**kairos** 6
Greek term meaning timing and recognition of the needs of the occasion

**kategoria** 255
a forensic speech that makes an accusation

**kinesics** 80
nonverbal behaviors related to movement

# L

**lectern** 122
a reading desk affixed to a stand

**Lexis-Nexis** 59
an electronic database for newspapers and magazines

**Likert scale** 145
a way of measuring how strong a person's beliefs, attitudes, and values are; they usually consist of 3–7 possible answers

**linear model of communication** 17
communication process that involves a sender who encodes a message and sends it through a channel where it competes with distracting forces called noise while on its way to a receiver who then decodes the message

**listening** 36
the psychological process of making sense out of sounds

**listening for appreciation** 37
listening for enjoyment; not high in cognitive commitment

**listening to comprehend  37**
listening to understand a concept or message

**listening to criticize  37**
listening to make a judgment about a message; involves a high level of cognitive commitment on the part of the audience

**literal analogy  276**
when the two cases being compared are classified the same way

**logos  10**
the logical dimension of the appeal

**lying by commission  262**
when a speaker willfully makes untrue statements to an audience

**lying by omission  262**
when a speaker willfully chooses not to acknowledge facts about his or her argument that might damage its effectiveness

# M

**major premise  271**
the first part of a syllogism, consisting of a general statement about the subject of your argument

**makers  147**
a low resource group that values self-sufficiency and the familiar

**manipulation  262**
the deliberate misrepresentation of facts and evidence to an audience

**manuscript speech  85**
when a speaker has an entire speech written out word-for-word in front of him/her as s/he speaks

**medium  146**
the channel through which the message travels (note: medium is singular for the plural term"media)"

**memorized speech  84**
when a speaker commits an entire speech to memory and delivers with no notes in front of him/her

**memory  13**
the fifth canon of rhetoric; refers to one's ability to recall names and important information in the middle of a speech as well as to deliver a cogent speech without notes

**message  16**
the actual content you send to an audience, both intentional and unintentional

**metaphor  164**
comparisons that show how two things are alike in an important way, despite being quite different in most ways

**minor claim  279**
connects evidence within the speech to a particular point

**minor premise  271**
a statement about a specific case related to the general characteristics of the major premise

**model  93**
a to-scale device that depicts an actual object

**moderator approach  116**
a way of delivering a group presentation whereby one person acts as the coordinator of the discussion flow and ensures a civil, organized, and complete delivery of information to the audience

**Modern Language Association (MLA)  63**
a citation style used in disciplines within the liberal arts and humanities

**Monroe's Motivated Sequence  306**
a five-step organizational pattern that combines psychological elements with speech persuasion to move an audience to action

**movement  104**
appearance of or actual activity depicted with an image

**multimedia presentation  101**
a presentation aid that combines and integrates video, audio, pictures, and notes into one medium

**myth  167**
a rhetorical construction that tries to explain natural events or cultural phenomena and is used to identify with a group and justify actions or beliefs

# N

**narrative coherence  168**
the degree to which a story makes sense in the world in which we live

**narrative fidelity  168**
the degree to which a story matches our own beliefs and experiences

**narrative paradigm  167**
humans are storytelling beings by nature

**necessary cause  278**
a condition that must be present for the effect to occur

**noise  17**
anything that interferes with the encoding, transmission, and reception of a message

**nonlistening  40**
providing the appearance of listening without actually paying complete attention to the message

**non sequitur fallacy  282**
when you make an unwarranted move from one idea to the next

# O

**object  96**
a tangible item used in conjunction with a speech

**Occam's Razor  107**
one should not increase, beyond what is necessary, the number of entities required to explain anything

**open-ended questions 148**
items on a survey that allow room for the person taking the survey to answer in his/her own words

# P

**parallelism 169**
similarly structuring related words, phrases, or clauses

**passive listening 38**
listening without reacting

**patchwork plagiarism 56**
stealing ideas from two or three sources without referencing them

**pathos 10**
the emotional dimensions of the appeal that can influence an audience's disposition toward the topic, speaker, or occasion

**peroration 297**
speech conclusion

**plagiarism 55**
to present another person's work or ideas as your own

**podium 122**
a platform used to raise the speaker higher

**post hoc, ergo propter hoc fallacy 283**
from the Latin for "after this, because of this"; assumes that because one event happened after another, then the preceding event caused the event that followed

**posture 81**
the position of your body

**potential rebuttal 280**
a statement that outlines the conditions which would make your central claim untrue

**practicality 107**
the proper places within the speech (the where, when, and how) you can and should make use of presentation aids

**prejudging 41**
entering into a presentation with a judgment already formed about the message being delivered

**preparation outlines 183**
detailed outlines that use full sentences next to symbols in an effort to help you organize the speech

**presentation aids 93**
visual devices used to assist a speaker in communicating ideas to the audience

**principle of recency 297**
the idea that the last message you heard is most likely to be the one you remember

**prior ethos 260**
credibility before the speech

**problem-cause-solution order  305**
a means of organizing a persuasive speech in which you discuss the problem first, then its root cause,  and then your preferred solution that addresses both the problem and its inherent cause

**problem-solution arrangement  237**
orders points by first discussing a problem and then how it was addressed; a subset of chronological order

**problem-solution order  303**
a means of organizing a persuasive speech in which you discuss the problem first and follow with a discussion of your preferred solution

**profanity  170**
coarse and irreverent language

**pronunciation  75**
the accepted standard of how a word sounds when spoken

**propriety  11**
good behavior and faithfulness to what one considers moral and just

**pseudolistening  40**
when someone attempts to hide their inattention to the speaker's message

**psychographics  144**
data that measures attitudes, beliefs, behaviors, and motivations

# Q

**quadrivium  48**
arithmetic, geometry, music, and astronomy

**qualifier  280**
a statement that establishes the boundaries in which the argument is true

**qualitative stasis  252**
when the issue in dispute involves the morality, ethicality, or value of an action

**question of fact  254**
when a speaker seeks to persuade people about how to interpret facts

**question of policy  254**
when a speaker takes a position on whether an action should or should not be taken

**question of value  254**
a persuasive speech about the rightness or wrongness of an idea, action, or issue

# R

**reasoning by analogy  276**
when you compare two similar cases in order to argue that what is true in one case is also true in the other

**reasoning by cause  277**
arguments that claim one event or factor produces an effect

**reasoning by example  276**
the process of inferring general conclusions and making general claims from specific cases

**rebuttal speech 256**
a speech that involves overcoming the opposition's argument by introducing other evidence that reduces the appeal of the opposition's claims

**receiver 17**
the person or persons who receive the encoded message sent by the sender

**red herring fallacy 284**
when a speaker introduces an irrelevant issue or piece of evidence to divert attention from the subject of the speech

**referential symbol 126**
an element in objects or events that refers to a specific message or aspect of a message

**refutation 296**
response to potential opposition to your argument

**regulate 83**
nonverbal actions that help govern the course of a speech or interaction

**reinforcement statement 335**
an expression of the connection between the event and the social value it represents

**repeat 83**
when physical actions restate verbal messages

**repetition 169**
repeating either the same phrasing pattern for main points, or a phrase you just stated, in order to maximize the audience's ability to receive the information

**research question 50**
the question about your topic you seek to answer

**rhetorical history 319**
the appropriation and redefinition of historical events to augment an argument

**rhetorical question 229**
asking the audience a question related to the subject that does not require an answer from them

**rhetorical situation 126**
moments that call for a rhetorical response

**rhetors 11**
speakers

**rostrum 122**
the area a speaker speaks from

# S

**self-fulfilling prophecy 32**
believing that something will happen before it actually does, and then when it does come true reinforcing the original expectation

**sender 16**
the person who desires to deliver a message to another person or group of people

**shorthand 197**
the process of shortening words or eliminating word clutter in the transcription process

**signpost 242**
a connective that lets the audience know what is next; most effective form of connective for moving from the last main point to the conclusion

**simile 165**
a comparison between two objects that allows each object in the comparison to retain its unique differences

**single-word approach 164**
meaning is derived from individual words used in a strategic way

**slang 77**
words derived from dialects that most people understand but do not use in professional writing or speaking

**slippery slope fallacy 283**
a logical fallacy that assumes once an action begins it will lead, undeterred, to an eventual and inevitable conclusion

**sociophobia 29**
the fear of social situations and/or people

**Socratic questioning 36**
the process of asking questions of a speaker focused on the responses to previous questions; its ultimate goal is to uncover the truth

**Sophists 4**
itinerant teachers who traveled from city-state to city-state in Classical Greece, training people in public speaking

**spare brain time 38**
the time available for your mind to wander due to your ability to process messages faster than the time it takes to construct them

**spatial order 238**
arranges points according to geography or logical movement through an area

**speaking outline 193**
a truncated form of your full-sentence preparation outline that does not include complete sentences

**specific purpose statement 184**
a narrower version of the general purpose statement that identifies what you will talk about, what you will say about it, and what you hope the audience will take away from the speech

**spectacle 126**
a symbolic event where the details send a deeper meaning

**speech of refutation 257**
a speech that seeks to prove the opposition's argument is wrong or false

**speech of self-presentation 210**
a speech where the speaker's topic is introducing himself or herself to the audience

**spotlight syndrome 31**
the belief encouraged by the room setup that all eyes are focused on you as the speaker

**stasis 251**
the basic issue in dispute between one or more speaking parties

**statement of facts 295**
an explanation of what the audience needs to know in order to appreciate the main argument of the speech

**straw man fallacy 285**
when a speaker ignores the actual position of an opponent and substitutes it with a distorted and exaggerated position

**strivers 146**
people who are low in resources, but motivated by achievement

**style 13**
the third canon of rhetoric; involves word choice, phrasing, and the level of formality in the language you use to present your case to the audience

**subordination 182**
the organization of a hierarchy of ideas where the most general appear first, followed by subsequently more specific ideas

**substitute 83**
physical actions that take the place of verbal messages

**sufficient cause 278**
a condition that automatically produces the effect in question

**summary 243**
the central part of the conclusion; it is where you reiterate the speech's thesis statement and recap the main points you addressed throughout the body

**survivors 147**
the lowest income bracket and the oldest median age of any VALS category

**syllogism 271**
basic structure of a deductive argument that comes to an absolute conclusion

# T

**tangential information 57**
evidence used to provide color and capture an audience's interest

**techne 8**
experiential knowledge; knowledge of particular events in the world around us; the least reliable form of knowledge

**terminal credibility 262**
the credibility with which you end the speech

**thesis statement 186**
the verbalized foundation of your entire speech in a single sentence which presents your topic, main points, and goal to the audience in an explicit and understandable way

**thinkers 146**
mature, responsible, well-educated professionals who are motivated by ideals

**tone  79**
the syllabic emphasis on a sound that expresses emotion or meaning

**topical arrangement  239**
the organization of main points by subpoints that do not naturally fit together in another way

**traditional aids  93**
aids that do not apply electronic means to communicate ideas to the audience

**transactional model of communication  18**
recognizes that we simultaneously send and receive messages; a cyclical model of the communication process

**transition  234**
a connective statement that signals you are finished with one point and moving on to another

**transitions  188**
connective statements  that signal you are finished with one point and moving on to another

**translative stasis  252**
when the issue in dispute is the competency of the judge or arbiter

**transparencies  96**
clear sheets containing information illuminated by a projector

**travel spectacle  127**
when the act of going somewhere sends a message

**trivium  48**
grammar, rhetoric, and logic

# U

**undercover interviewing  60**
when the interviewer disguises either himself or his purpose in an effort to trick someone into sharing more information than they may have if the interviewee knew to whom he or she was speaking

# V

**Values, Attitudes and Lifestyles (VALS) framework  145**
a tool used for categorizing individuals and groups according to their psychographic traits

**verifier  280**
provides the credibility for the grounds and backing provided in the speech

**video conferencing  120**
live transmission of the video and audio of a presenter who is in one place to an audience in another place

**vocalic  79**
anything that contributes to the creation or maintenance of sound in a person's voice

**vocalized pauses  80**
utterances that are not words and have no place in a speech, but are done instead of pausing the delivery of the speech

# W

**warrant  280**
explains why the grounds support the claim and makes that connection clear to the audience

**word-cluster approach  166**
meaning is conveyed through more complex structures such as stories

# KEY PEOPLE

# INDEX

necessary cause   278
Nichols, Marie Hochmuth  19, 20
noise   17
non sequitur fallacy   282
nonlistening   40

# O

Obama, Barack  52, 270, 315-320, 326, 332, 338-339
Obama, Michelle  22-23
object   96
Occam's Razor   107
Olivier, Sir Laurence  28, 32
open-ended questions   148

# P

Palin, Sarah  277
parallelism   169
passive listening   38
patchwork plagiarism   56
pathos   10
Pausch, Randy  49-50
Pericles  22, 332, 334, 336-337
peroration   297
Petraeus, David  228, 234
Philip of Macedon  2, 7, 9, 85
plagiarism   55
Plato  2, 5-12, 15-16, 20, 35
podium   122
post hoc, ergo propter hoc fallacy   283
posture   81
potential rebuttal   280
practicality   107
prejudging   41
preparation outline   183
presentation aids   93
principle of recency   297
prior ethos   260
problem-cause-solution order   305
problem-solution arrangement   237
problem-solution order   303
profanity   170
pronunciation   75
propriety   11
Protagoras  4-6, 10
pseudolistening   40
psychographics   144
Ptolemy I (Soter)   48
Ptolemy II (Philadelphus)   48

# Q

quadrivium   48
qualifier   280
qualitative stasis   252
question of fact   254
question of policy   254
question of value   254
Quintilian   2, 12, 14, 16, 41, 43, 85, 152-153, 251-
253, 254, 293, 295-299, 303, 325

# R

Reagan, Ronald  180, 321-322
reasoning by analogy   276
reasoning by cause   277
reasoning by example   276
rebuttal speech   256
receiver   17
red herring fallacy   284
referential symbol   126
refutation   296
regulate   83
reinforcement statement   335
repeat   83
repetition   169
research question   50
rhetorical history   319
rhetorical question   229
rhetorical situation   126
rhetors   11
Romney, Mitt  138, 143
Roosevelt, Eleanor  42
rostrum   122

# S

self-fulfilling prophecy   32
sender   16
Shapiro, Robert   250
shorthand   197
signpost   242
simile   165
Simpson, O. J.  250-254
single-word approach   164
slang   77
slippery slope fallacy   283
sociophobia   29
Socrates  6, 12, 35-36, 85, 271-272, 275
Socratic questioning   36
Sophists   4
spare brain time   38

THE SPEAKER: The Tradition and Practice of Public Speaking